The Complete

AIR FRYER

COOKBOOK

FOR BEGINNERS AND ADVANCED USERS

Amelia Mason

ISBN: 9798559999807

ASIN: B08N2XPVZ5

INTRODUCTION

Hello! Welcome to my book of recipes for the Air Fryer.

My recipes are simply too delicious to keep to myself. And it's the only cookbook you'll need to make the most delicious Air Fryer recipes you've ever tasted!

If there's one kitchen appliance I can't live without, it's my Air Fryer. This gadget has changed my life completely in the kitchen! Gone are the days when I spent hours each week, prepping and then cooking Recipes. And so many times those meals were tasteless, with leftovers that no one wanted to eat.

Then along came my Air Fryer… and now I make delectable Recipes every day. Quick cooking, tasty recipes - and I have leftovers my family fights and squabbles over! Like the juiciest pork shoulders and spicy rice dishes.

In my book, you'll find a collection of mouthwatering and flavorsome recipes from every cuisine.

One of the biggest appealing features of the Air Fryer is that it makes fresh and fast homey Recipes in no time.

Whether you're vegetarian or love your meat and chicken, my book has the best recipes for making amazing, healthy Recipes. And make sure you make an extravagant cheat recipe on those days when you're not counting calories and fat! Those are the best recipes of all. In this book,

I share my favorite recipes with you, and I'll help you get familiar with the Air Fryer, so you know exactly how to use one. Breakfasts, appetizers, Sunday dinners, and delightfully sweet desserts! I have just the recipe for you.

So now, let's learn all about the Air fryer so you can start cooking!

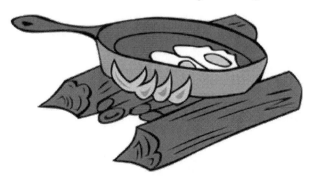

BASICS

Here's everything you need to know about air fryer...

How does it work?

With deep fryers, a heating element heats up oil, but with an air fryer, it's the hot air that does all the work. This technology is known as Rapid Air Technology, and it's the most important feature on most air fryers.

The heating element generates heat from the top of the unit, while an exhaust fan pushes the hot air down and keeps it moving.

This allows an even spread of superheated air which cooks the food up to two times faster than an oven.
Most units now include an adjustable thermostat, so you can control the temperature more precisely and cook a wider variety of food.

To prevent the air fryer from overheating, all units have a cooling system. It's built above the motor and protects the electronic parts. The exhaust system is similar to the cooling system, but it actually filters the air and reduces pressure.
It also helps reduce cooking smells. Air fryers work using a heating element that superheats the air.
This hot air cooks the food in a contained cooking chamber, reducing the need for more than 1 tablespoon of oil.

Other parts

1 Handle
2 Air Inlet
3 Heating Indicator
4 Power On Indicator
5 Temperature Control Slider
6 Timer Control Knob
7 Frying Basket
8 Crumb Basket
9 Crumb Basket Handle
10 Basket Release Button
11 Air Outlet (located at the back of the air fryer)

The cooking chamber –
 Bowl-shaped, the cooking chambers holds the food you want to cook. It has tiny holes in the bottom that allow the hot air to circulate up from the bottom. You can usually remove the

cooking chamber for cleaning by pulling it out by a handle, similar to how a coffee pot comes out from the coffee machine.

The food separator –

This slot-shaped divider fits into the cooking chamber and lets you cook two different types of food at one time, so they aren't overlapping.
The timer –

In addition to an adjustable thermostat, most air fryers also include a timer. These work like standard oven or microwave timers; there's nothing fancy or unusual about them.

Since Philips released the first air fryer, a variety of models have gone to market both from Philips and other companies. **Now, there are three main types: the basket, the paddle, and the convection oven.**

BASKET-

Pull-Out Drawer   Flip-Top

type air fryers have a removable basket inside the cooking chamber where you place the food. These are the most affordable air fryers, and depending on what you're cooking, you do have to shake the basket a few times while the food cooks. They are especially good at making battered foods like onion rings and have a pretty simple design.

PADDLE-

type fryers stir themselves with a paddle, so they are convenient for people who don't want to stir food themselves. Unlike basket fryers, they can also cook more liquid-based dishes like curries and risotto. They do require a little more oil to get started and tend to be more expensive.

THE CONVECTION OVEN-

while technically not a dedicated air fryer, should be included because it does use hot air to create crispy food. These are the priciest option, and can perform a variety of cooking tasks like toasting and roasting. They're similar to toaster ovens that way.

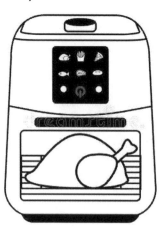

Contents

Air Fryer Lunch Recipes   39

Air Fryer Side Dish Recipes 57

Air Fryer Snack and Appetizer Recipes　　75

Air Fryer Fish and Seafood Recipes　　92

Air Fryer Poultry Recipes 114

Air Fryer Meat Recipes   136

Air Fryer Vegetable Recipes   155

Air Fryer Dessert Recipes   172

Measurement Conversion Chart

The charts below will help you to convert between different units of volume in US customary units.

Please note that US volume is not the same as in the UK and other countries, and many of the measurements are different depending on which country you are in.

It is very easy to get confused when dealing with US and UK units! The only good thing is that the metric units never change!

Every effort has been made to ensure that the Measurement Charts on this page are accurate.

Volume Equivalents (Liquid)

US Standard	US Standard (ounces)	Metric (approximate)
2 tablespoons	1 fl. oz.	30 mL
¼ cup	2 fl. oz.	60 mL
½ cup	4 fl. oz.	120 mL
1 cup	8 fl. oz.	240 mL
1½ cups	12 fl. oz.	355 mL
2 cups or 1 pint	16 fl. oz.	475 mL
4 cups or 1 quart	32 fl. oz.	1 L
1 gallon	128 fl. oz.	4 L

Volume Equivalents (Dry)

US Standard	Metric (approximate)
⅛ teaspoon	0.5 mL
¼ teaspoon	1 mL
½ teaspoon	2 mL
¾ teaspoon	4 mL
1 teaspoon	5 mL
1 tablespoon	15 mL
¼ cup	59 mL
⅓ cup	79 mL
½ cup	118 mL
⅔ cup	156 mL
¾ cup	177 mL
1 cup	235 mL

2 cups or 1 pint	475 mL
3 cups	700 mL
4 cups or 1 quart	1 L

Oven Temperatures

Fahrenheit (F)	Celsius (C) (approximate)
250°F	120°C
300°F	150°C
325°F	165°C
350°F	180°C
375°F	190°C
400°F	200°C
425°F	220°C
450°F	230°C

Weight Equivalents

US Standard	Metric (approximate)
½ ounce	15 g
1 ounce	30 g
2 ounces	60 g
4 ounces	115 g
8 ounces	225 g
12 ounces	340 g
16 ounces or 1 pound	455 g

Delicious Breakfast Potatoes

Preparation time: 10 minutes Cooking time: 35 minutes Servings: 4

INGREDIENTS:

- ✓ 2 tablespoons olive oil
- ✓ 3 potatoes, cubed
- ✓ 1 yellow onion, chopped
- ✓ 1 red bell pepper, chopped
- ✓ Salt and black pepper to the taste
- ✓ 1 teaspoon garlic powder
- ✓ 1 teaspoon sweet paprika
- ✓ 1 teaspoon onion powder

DIRECTIONS:

- Grease your air fryer's basket with olive oil, add potatoes, toss and season with salt and pepper.
- Add onion, bell pepper, garlic powder, paprika and onion powder, toss well, cover and cook at 370 degrees F for 30 minutes.
- Divide potatoes mix on plates and serve for breakfast.
- Enjoy!

Nutrition: calories 214, fat 6, fiber 8, carbs 15, protein 4

Tasty Cinnamon Toast

Preparation time: 10 minutes Cooking time: 5 minutes Servings: 6

INGREDIENTS:

- ✓ 1 stick butter, soft
- ✓ 12 bread slices
- ✓ ½ cup sugar
- ✓ 1 and ½ teaspoon vanilla extract
- ✓ 1 and ½ teaspoon cinnamon powder

DIRECTIONS:

- In a bowl, mix soft butter with sugar, vanilla and cinnamon and whisk well.
- Spread this on bread slices, place them in your air fryer and cook at 400 degrees F for 5 minutes,
- Divide among plates and serve for breakfast.
- Enjoy!

Nutrition: calories 221, fat 4, fiber 7, carbs 12, protein 8

Delicious Potato Hash

Preparation time: 10 minutes Cooking time: 25 minutes Servings: 4

INGREDIENTS:

- ✓ 1 and ½ potatoes, cubed
- ✓ 1 yellow onion, chopped
- ✓ 2 teaspoons olive oil
- ✓ 1 green bell pepper, chopped
- ✓ Salt and black pepper to the taste
- ✓ ½ teaspoon thyme, dried
- ✓ 2 eggs

DIRECTIONS:

- Heat up your air fryer at 350 degrees F, add oil, heat it up, add onion, bell pepper, salt and pepper, stir and cook for 5 minutes.
- Add potatoes, thyme and eggs, stir, cover and cook at 360 degrees F for 20 minutes.
- Divide among plates and serve for breakfast.
- Enjoy!

Nutrition: calories 241, fat 4, fiber 7, carbs 12, protein 7

Sweet Breakfast Casserole

Preparation time: 10 minutes Cooking time: 30 minutes Servings: 4

INGREDIENTS:

- ✓ 3 tablespoons brown sugar
- ✓ 4 tablespoons butter
- ✓ 2 tablespoons white sugar
- ✓ ½ teaspoon cinnamon powder
- ✓ ½ cup flour

For the casserole:

- ✓ 2 eggs
- ✓ 2 tablespoons white sugar
- ✓ 2 and ½ cups white flour
- ✓ 1 teaspoon baking soda
- ✓ 1 teaspoon baking powder
- ✓ 2 eggs
- ✓ ½ cup milk
- ✓ 2 cups buttermilk
- ✓ 4 tablespoons butter
- ✓ Zest from 1 lemon, grated
- ✓ 1 and 2/3 cup blueberries

DIRECTIONS:

- In a bowl, mix eggs with 2 tablespoons white sugar, 2 and ½ cups white flour, baking powder, baking soda, 2 eggs, milk, buttermilk, 4 tablespoons butter, lemon zest and blueberries, stir and pour into a pan that fits your air fryer.
- In another bowls, mix 3 tablespoons brown sugar with 2 tablespoons white sugar, 4 tablespoons butter, ½ cup flour and cinnamon, stir until you obtain a crumble and spread over blueberries mix.
- Place in preheated air fryer and bake at 300 degrees F for 30 minutes.
- Divide among plates and serve for breakfast.
- Enjoy!

Nutrition: calories 214, fat 5, fiber 8, carbs 12, protein 5

Eggs Casserole

Preparation time: 10 minutes Cooking time: 25 minutes Servings: 6

INGREDIENTS:

- ✓ 1 pound turkey, ground
- ✓ 1 tablespoon olive oil
- ✓ ½ teaspoon chili powder
- ✓ 12 eggs
- ✓ 1 sweet potato, cubed
- ✓ 1 cup baby spinach
- ✓ Salt and black pepper to the taste
- ✓ 2 tomatoes, chopped for serving

DIRECTIONS:

- In a bowl, mix eggs with salt, pepper, chili powder, potato, spinach, turkey and sweet potato and whisk well.
- Heat up your air fryer at 350 degrees F, add oil and heat it up.
- Add eggs mix, spread into your air fryer, cover and cook for 25 minutes.
- Divide among plates and serve for breakfast.
- Enjoy!

Nutrition: calories 300, fat 5, fiber 8, carbs 13, protein 6

Sausage, Eggs and Cheese Mix

Preparation time: 10 minutes Cooking time: 20 minutes Servings: 4

INGREDIENTS:

- ✓ 10 ounces sausages, cooked and crumbled
- ✓ 1 cup cheddar cheese, shredded
- ✓ 1 cup mozzarella cheese, shredded
- ✓ 8 eggs, whisked

- ✓ 1 cup milk
- ✓ Salt and black pepper to the taste
- ✓ Cooking spray

DIRECTIONS:

- In a bowl, mix sausages with cheese, mozzarella, eggs, milk, salt and pepper and whisk well.
- Heat up your air fryer at 380 degrees F, spray cooking oil, add eggs and sausage mix and cook for 20 minutes.
- Divide among plates and serve.
- Enjoy!

Nutrition: calories 320, fat 6, fiber 8, carbs 12, protein 5

Cheese Air Fried Bake

Preparation time: 10 minutes Cooking time: 20 minutes Servings: 4

INGREDIENTS:

- ✓ 4 bacon slices, cooked and crumbled
- ✓ 2 cups milk
- ✓ 2 and ½ cups cheddar cheese, shredded
- ✓ 1 pound breakfast sausage, casings removed and chopped
- ✓ 2 eggs
- ✓ ½ teaspoon onion powder
- ✓ Salt and black pepper to the taste
- ✓ 3 tablespoons parsley, chopped
- ✓ Cooking spray

DIRECTIONS:

- In a bowl, mix eggs with milk, cheese, onion powder, salt, pepper and parsley and whisk well.
- Grease your air fryer with cooking spray, heat it up at 320 degrees F and add bacon and sausage.
- Add eggs mix, spread and cook for 20 minutes.
- Divide among plates and serve.
- Enjoy!

Nutrition: calories 214, fat 5, fiber 8, carbs 12, protein 12

Biscuits Casserole

Preparation time: 10 minutes Cooking time: 15 minutes Servings: 8

INGREDIENTS:

- ✓ 12 ounces biscuits, quartered
- ✓ 3 tablespoons flour
- ✓ ½ pound sausage, chopped

18

- ✓ A pinch of salt and black pepper
- ✓ 2 and ½ cups milk
- ✓ Cooking spray

DIRECTIONS:

- Grease your air fryer with cooking spray and heat it over 350 degrees F.
- Add biscuits on the bottom and mix with sausage.
- Add flour, milk, salt and pepper, toss a bit and cook for 15 minutes.
- Divide among plates and serve for breakfast.
- Enjoy!

Nutrition: calories 321, fat 4, fiber 7, carbs 12, protein 5

Turkey Burrito

Preparation time: 10 minutes Cooking time: 10 minutes Servings: 2

INGREDIENTS:

- ✓ 4 slices turkey breast already cooked
- ✓ ½ red bell pepper, sliced
- ✓ 2 eggs
- ✓ 1 small avocado, peeled, pitted and sliced
- ✓ 2 tablespoons salsa
- ✓ Salt and black pepper to the taste
- ✓ 1/8 cup mozzarella cheese, grated
- ✓ Tortillas for serving

DIRECTIONS:

- In a bowl, whisk eggs with salt and pepper to the taste, pour them in a pan and place it in the air fryer's basket.
- Cook at 400 degrees F for 5 minutes, take pan out of the fryer and transfer eggs to a plate.
- Arrange tortillas on a working surface, divide eggs on them, also divide turkey meat, bell pepper, cheese, salsa and avocado.
- Roll your burritos and place them in your air fryer after you've lined it with some tin foil.
- Heat up the burritos at 300 degrees F for 3 minutes, divide them on plates and serve.
- Enjoy!

Nutrition: calories 349, fat 23, fiber 11, carbs 20, protein 21

Tofu Scramble

Preparation time: 5 minutes Cooking time: 30 minutes Servings: 4

INGREDIENTS:

- ✓ 2 tablespoons soy sauce

- ✓ 1 tofu block, cubed
- ✓ 1 teaspoon turmeric, ground
- ✓ 2 tablespoons extra virgin olive oil
- ✓ 4 cups broccoli florets
- ✓ ½ teaspoon onion powder
- ✓ ½ teaspoon garlic powder
- ✓ 2 and ½ cup red potatoes, cubed
- ✓ ½ cup yellow onion, chopped
- ✓ Salt and black pepper to the taste

DIRECTIONS:

- Mix tofu with 1 tablespoon oil, salt, pepper, soy sauce, garlic powder, onion powder, turmeric and onion in a bowl, stir and leave aside.
- In a separate bowl, combine potatoes with the rest of the oil, a pinch of salt and pepper and toss to coat.
- Put potatoes in your air fryer at 350 degrees F and bake for 15 minutes, shaking once.
- Add tofu and its marinade to your air fryer and bake for 15 minutes.
- Add broccoli to the fryer and cook everything for 5 minutes more.
- Serve right away.
- Enjoy!

Nutrition: calories 140, fat 4, fiber 3, carbs 10, protein 14

Oatmeal Casserole

Preparation time: 10 minutes Cooking time: 20 minutes Servings: 8

INGREDIENTS:

- ✓ 2 cups rolled oats
- ✓ 1 teaspoon baking powder
- ✓ 1/3 cup brown sugar
- ✓ 1 teaspoon cinnamon powder
- ✓ ½ cup chocolate chips
- ✓ 2/3 cup blueberries
- ✓ 1 banana, peeled and mashed
- ✓ 2 cups milk
- ✓ 1 eggs
- ✓ 2 tablespoons butter
- ✓ 1 teaspoon vanilla extract
- ✓ Cooking spray

DIRECTIONS:

- In a bowl, mix sugar with baking powder, cinnamon, chocolate chips, blueberries and banana and stir.
- In a separate bowl, mix eggs with vanilla extract and butter and stir.
- Heat up your air fryer at 320 degrees F, grease with cooking spray and add oats on the bottom.
- Add cinnamon mix and eggs mix, toss and cook for 20 minutes.
- Stir one more time, divide into bowls and serve for breakfast.
- Enjoy!

Nutrition: calories 300, fat 4, fiber 7, carbs 12, protein 10

Ham Breakfast

Preparation time: 10 minutes Cooking time: 15 minutes Servings: 6

INGREDIENTS:

- ✓ 6 cups French bread, cubed
- ✓ 4 ounces green chilies, chopped
- ✓ 10 ounces ham, cubed
- ✓ 4 ounces cheddar cheese, shredded
- ✓ 2 cups milk
- ✓ 5 eggs
- ✓ 1 tablespoon mustard
- ✓ Salt and black pepper to the taste
- ✓ Cooking spray

DIRECTIONS:

- Heat up your air fryer at 350 degrees F and grease it with cooking spray.
- In a bowl, mix eggs with milk, cheese, mustard, salt and pepper and stir.
- Add bread cubes in your air fryer and mix with chilies and ham.
- Add eggs mix, spread and cook for 15 minutes.
- Divide among plates and serve.
- Enjoy!

Nutrition: calories 200, fat 5, fiber 6, carbs 12, protein 14

Tomato and Bacon Breakfast

Preparation time: 10 minutes Cooking time: 30 minutes Servings: 6

INGREDIENTS:

- ✓ 1 pound white bread, cubed
- ✓ 1 pound smoked bacon, cooked and chopped ¼ cup olive oil

- ✓ 1 yellow onion, chopped
- ✓ 28 ounces canned tomatoes, chopped
- ✓ ½ teaspoon red pepper, crushed
- ✓ ½ pound cheddar, shredded
- ✓ 2 tablespoons chives, chopped
- ✓ ½ pound Monterey jack, shredded
- ✓ 2 tablespoons stock
- ✓ Salt and black pepper to the taste
- ✓ 8 eggs, whisked

DIRECTIONS:

- Add the oil to your air fryer and heat it up at 350 degrees F.
- Add bread, bacon, onion, tomatoes, red pepper and stock and stir.
- Add eggs, cheddar and Monterey jack and cook everything for 20 minutes.
- Divide among plates, sprinkle chives and serve.
- Enjoy!

Nutrition: calories 231, fat 5, fiber 7, carbs 12, protein 4

Tasty Hash

Preparation time: 10 minutes Cooking time: 15 minutes Servings: 6

INGREDIENTS:

- ✓ 16 ounces hash browns
- ✓ ¼ cup olive oil
- ✓ ½ teaspoon paprika
- ✓ ½ teaspoon garlic powder
- ✓ Salt and black pepper to the taste
- ✓ 1 egg, whisked
- ✓ 2 tablespoon chives, chopped
- ✓ 1 cup cheddar, shredded

DIRECTIONS:

- Add oil to your air fryer, heat it up at 350 degrees F and add hash browns.
- Also add paprika, garlic powder, salt, pepper and egg, toss and cook for 15 minutes.
- Add cheddar and chives, toss, divide among plates and serve.
- Enjoy!

Nutrition: calories 213, fat 7, fiber 8, carbs 12, protein 4

Tasty Baked Eggs

Preparation time: 10 minutes Cooking time: 20 minutes Servings: 4

INGREDIENTS:

- ✓ **4 eggs**
- ✓ **1 pound baby spinach, torn**
- ✓ **7 ounces ham, chopped**
- ✓ **4 tablespoons milk**
- ✓ **1 tablespoon olive oil**
- ✓ **Cooking spray**
- ✓ **Salt and black pepper to the taste**

DIRECTIONS:

- Heat up a pan with the oil over medium heat, add baby spinach, stir cook for a couple of minutes and take off heat.
- Grease 4 ramekins with cooking spray and divide baby spinach and ham in each.
- Crack an egg in each ramekin, also divide milk, season with salt and pepper, place ramekins in preheated air fryer at 350 degrees F and bake for 20 minutes.
- Serve baked eggs for breakfast.
- Enjoy!

Nutrition: calories 321, fat 6, fiber 8, carbs 15, protein 12

Breakfast Egg Bowls

Preparation time: 10 minutes Cooking time: 20 minutes Servings: 4

INGREDIENTS:

- ✓ **4 dinner rolls, tops cut off and insides scooped out**
- ✓ **4 tablespoons heavy cream**
- ✓ **4 eggs**
- ✓ **4 tablespoons mixed chives and parsley**
- ✓ **Salt and black pepper to the taste**
- ✓ **4 tablespoons parmesan, grated**

DIRECTIONS:

- Arrange dinner rolls on a baking sheet and crack an egg in each.
- Divide heavy cream, mixed herbs in each roll and season with salt and pepper.
- Sprinkle parmesan on top of your rolls, place them in your air fryer and cook at 350 degrees F for 20 minutes.
- Divide your bread bowls on plates and serve for breakfast.

- Enjoy!

Nutrition: calories 238, fat 4, fiber 7, carbs 14, protein 7

Delicious Breakfast Soufflé

Preparation time: 10 minutes Cooking time: 8 minutes Servings: 4

INGREDIENTS:

- ✓ **4 eggs, whisked**
- ✓ **4 tablespoons heavy cream**
- ✓ **A pinch of red chili pepper, crushed**
- ✓ **2 tablespoons parsley, chopped**
- ✓ **2 tablespoons chives, chopped**
- ✓ **Salt and black pepper to the taste**

DIRECTIONS:

- In a bowl, mix eggs with salt, pepper, heavy cream, red chili pepper, parsley and chives, stir well and divide into 4 soufflé dishes.
- Arrange dishes in your air fryer and cook soufflés at 350 degrees F for 8 minutes.
- Serve them hot.
- Enjoy!

Nutrition: calories 300, fat 7, fiber 9, carbs 15, protein 6

Air Fried Sandwich

Preparation time: 10 minutes Cooking time: 6 minutes Servings: 2

INGREDIENTS:

- ✓ **2 English muffins, halved**
- ✓ **2 eggs**
- ✓ **2 bacon strips**
- ✓ **Salt and black pepper to the taste**

DIRECTIONS:

- Crack eggs in your air fryer, add bacon on top, cover and cook at 392 degrees F for 6 minutes.
- Heat up your English muffin halves in your microwave for a few seconds, divide eggs on 2 halves, add bacon on top, season with salt and pepper, cover with the other 2 English muffins and serve for breakfast.
- Enjoy!

Nutrition: calories 261, fat 5, fiber 8, carbs 12, protein 4

Rustic Breakfast

Preparation time: 10 minutes Cooking time: 13 minutes Servings: 4

INGREDIENTS:

- ✓ **1 egg**
- ✓ **2 tablespoons olive oil**
- ✓ **3 tablespoons milk**
- ✓ **3.5 ounces white flour**
- ✓ **1 tablespoon baking powder**
- ✓ **2 ounces parmesan, grated**
- ✓ **A splash of Worcestershire sauce**

DIRECTIONS:

- Grease a cooking pan with the oil and add tomatoes, garlic and mushrooms.
- Add bacon and chipolatas, also add spinach and crack eggs at the end.
- Season with salt and pepper, place pan in the cooking basket of your air fryer and cook for 13 minutes at 350 degrees F.
- Divide among plates and serve for breakfast.
- Enjoy!

Nutrition: calories 312, fat 6, fiber 8, carbs 15, protein 5

Egg Muffins

Preparation time: 10 minutes Cooking time: 15 minutes Servings: 4

INGREDIENTS:

- ✓ **1 egg**
- ✓ **2 tablespoons olive oil**
- ✓ **3 tablespoons milk**
- ✓ **3.5 ounces white flour**
- ✓ **1 tablespoon baking powder**
- ✓ **2 ounces parmesan, grated**
- ✓ **A splash of Worcestershire sauce**

DIRECTIONS:

- In a bowl, mix egg with flour, oil, baking powder, milk, Worcestershire and parmesan, whisk well and divide into 4 silicon muffin cups.
- Arrange cups in your air fryer's cooking basket, cover and cook at 392, degrees F for 15 minutes.
- Serve warm for breakfast.
- Enjoy!

Nutrition: calories 251, fat 6, fiber 8, carbs 9, protein 3

Polenta Bites

Preparation time: 10 minutes Cooking time: 20 minutes Servings: 4

INGREDIENTS:

For the polenta:

- ✓ **1 tablespoon butter**
- ✓ **1 cup cornmeal**
- ✓ **3 cups water**
- ✓ **Salt and black pepper to the taste**

For the polenta bites:

- ✓ **2 tablespoons powdered sugar**
- ✓ **Cooking spray**

DIRECTIONS:

- In a pan, mix water with cornmeal, butter, salt and pepper, stir, bring to a boil over medium heat, cook for 10 minutes, take off heat, whisk one more time and keep in the fridge until it's cold.
- Scoop 1 tablespoon of polenta, shape a ball and place on a working surface.
- Repeat with the rest of the polenta, arrange all the balls in the cooking basket of your air fryer, spray them with cooking spray, cover and cook at 380 degrees F for 8 minutes.
- Arrange polenta bites on plates, sprinkle sugar all over and serve for breakfast.
- Enjoy!

Nutrition: calories 231, fat 7, fiber 8, carbs 12, protein 4

Creamy Hash Browns

Preparation time: 10 minutes Cooking time: 20 minutes Servings: 6

INGREDIENTS:

- ✓ **2 pounds hash browns**
- ✓ **1 cup whole milk**
- ✓ **8 bacon slices, chopped**
- ✓ **9 ounces cream cheese**
- ✓ **1 yellow onion, chopped**
- ✓ **1 cup cheddar cheese, shredded**
- ✓ **6 green onions, chopped**
- ✓ **Salt and black pepper to the taste**
- ✓ **6 eggs**
- ✓ **Cooking spray**

DIRECTIONS:

- Heat up your air fryer at 350 degrees F and grease it with cooking spray.
- In a bowl, mix eggs with milk, cream cheese, cheddar cheese, bacon, onion, salt and pepper and whisk well.

- Add hash browns to your air fryer, add eggs mix over them and cook for 20 minutes.
- Divide among plates and serve.
- Enjoy!

Nutrition: calories 261, fat 6, fiber 9, carbs 8, protein 12

Easy AirFried Scrambled Egg

Preparation: 2 minutes Cooking time: 20 minutes Servings: 2

INGREDIENTS:

- ✓ 2 eggs
- ✓ ¾ tablespoon unsalted butter Pepper and salt to taste
- ✓ Tomatoes, mushroom or cheese (optional)

DIRECTIONS:

- Whisk eggs into a bowl. Preheat Air Fryer at 140°F for about 5 minutes.
- Melt the butter in the preheated Air Fryer, tilting pan to spread out evenly.
- Now, pour the egg into the Air Fryer at 140°F for 10 minutes. Add your other Ingredients
- such as tomatoes, mushroom and cheese, if using.
- Whisk continuously every few minutes until fluffy and yellow.
- Serve egg, topped on toast and enjoyed with milk.

Extra Crunchy Breakfast Casserole

Preparation: 2 minutes Cooking time: 30 minutes Servings: 3-4

INGREDIENTS:

- ✓ 4 eggs
- ✓ 6 ounces of raw sweet sausage, remove from the casings
- ✓ ½ cup bread crumbs
- ✓ 1 cup shredded cheddar cheese Pinch salt and pepper

DIRECTIONS:

- Preheat the Air Fryer to 350°F. Cook the raw sausage for 10 minutes on medium-to-high heat, breaking it up with a wooden spoon to prevent clumping. Remove and set aside.
- Beat the eggs in a mixing bowl, until light and fluffy. Stir in half of the bread crumbs, half of the cheese, the cooked sausage meat, salt and pepper. Pour into a baking dish and sprinkle the remaining bread crumbs and shredded cheese on top.
- Place the baking dish in the Air Fryer basket, set the timer for 20 minutes. Remove, serve and enjoy!

Parmesan & Pesto Twists

Preparation: 10 minutes Cooking time: 25 minutes Servings: 4

INGREDIENTS:

- ✓ 12 ounces of packed butter puff pastry
- ✓ 1.8 ounces of cream cheese
- ✓ 3 teaspoons of flour
- ✓ ¼ cup of basil pesto
- ✓ 1 egg, whisked
- ✓ 1.8 ounces of grated Parmesan cheese

DIRECTIONS:

- Preheat your Air Fryer to 460°F.
- Spread flour on a surface lightly and roll the butter puff pastry into a rectangular shape.
- Divide into 2 from the middle and spread the pesto and cream cheese on one half and place the other half on top.
- Cut the sandwich into 2 from the middle, then cut each rectangular piece into 0.4" thick strips.
- Twist the strips, pull slightly to make longer. Using a pastry brush, coat the twists with the egg and sprinkle with parmesan cheese.
- Put into Air Fryer until it is risen and golden for about 25 minutes.

Air Fried French Toast

Preparation: 4 minutes Cooking time: 6 minutes Servings: 4

INGREDIENTS:

- ✓ 2 slices of sourdough bread
- ✓ 3 eggs
- ✓ 1 tablespoon of butter
- ✓ 1 teaspoon of liquid vanilla
- ✓ 3 teaspoons of honey
- ✓ 2 tablespoons of Greek yogurt Berries

DIRECTIONS:

- Preheat the air fryer to 356°F.
- Pour the vanilla in the eggs and whisk to mix. Spread the butter on all sides of the bread and soak in the eggs to absorb.
- Put the bread into the Air Fryer basket and cook for 3 minutes Turn the bread over and cook for another 3 minutes.
- Transfer to a place, top with yogurt and berries with a sprinkle of honey.

Wheat &Seed Bread

Preparation: 70 minutes Cooking time: 18 minutes Servings: 4

INGREDIENTS:

- ✓ 3½ ounces of flour
- ✓ 1 teaspoon of yeast
- ✓ 1 teaspoon of salt
- ✓ 3½ ounces of wheat flour
- ✓ ¼ cup of pumpkin seeds

DIRECTIONS:

- ⏱ Mix the wheat flour, yeast, salt, seeds and the plain flour together in a large bowl. Stir in ¾ cup of lukewarm water, and keep stirring until dough becomes soft.
- ⏱ Knead for another 5 minutes until the dough becomes elastic and smooth. Mold into a ball and cover with a plastic bag. Set aside for 30 minutes for it to rise.
- ⏱ Heat your Air Fryer to 392°F.
- ⏱ Transfer the dough into a small pizza pan and place in the Air Fryer. Bake for 18 minutes until golden. Remove and place on a wire rack to cool.

Croissant With Ham, Mushroom And Egg

Preparation: 5 minutes Cooking time: 8 minutes Servings: 1

INGREDIENTS

- ✓ 1 store-bought Croissant
- ✓ 3 slices honey shaved ham
- ✓ 4 honey cherry tomato, halved
- ✓ 4 small button mushroom, quartered
- ✓ 1 Egg
- ✓ 1.8 oz shredded cheddar cheese Handful salad greens
- ✓ 1/2 Rosemary Sprig, roughly chopped (optional)

DIRECTIONS:

- ⏱ Grease a baking dish lightly with butter.
- ⏱ Arrange the Ingredients in two layers, placing the cheese in the middle and top layer. Create a space in the centre of the ham mixture, break egg in it.
- ⏱ Sprinkle some black pepper, salt and rosemary over the mixture and place on the Air Fryer basket along with the croissant.

- ⏱ Baked in preheated 325°F temperature for 8 minutes. (Take out the croissant from the Air Fryer basket after 4 minutes).
- ⏱ Serve croissant and cheesy baked egg on plate along with some salad greens.

Oatmeal Muffins

Preparation: 5minutes Cooking time: 15 minutes Servings: 2-4

INGREDIENTS

- ✓ 2 Eggs
- ✓ 3½ ounce oats
- ✓ 3 ounce butter, melted
- ✓ 1/2 cup flour
- ✓ 1/4 teaspoon vanilla essence
- ✓ 1/2 cup icing sugar Pinch baking powder
- ✓ 1 tablespoon raisins Cooking spray

DIRECTIONS

- ⏱ Combine sugar and butter until soft. Whisk together the eggs and vanilla essence. Add it to the sugar/butter mix until soft peaks forms.
- ⏱ Combine flour, raisins, baking powder and oats in a separate bowl. Add it to the mixed Ingredients Grease the muffin molds lightly with cooking spray and fill with the batter mixture. Preheat the Air Fryer at 350°F.
- ⏱ Place the muffin molds into the Air Fryer tray. Let it cook for 12 minutes. Cool, serve and enjoy!

French Toast Delight

Preparation: minutes Cooking time: minutes Servings: 2

INGREDIENTS

- ✓ 4 bread slices
- ✓ 2 tablespoons butter
- ✓ 1/2 teaspoon cinnamon
- ✓ 2 Eggs
- ✓ Pinch salt
- ✓ Pinch ground cloves Pinch Nutmeg Icing sugar and maple syrup, to serve

DIRECTIONS

- ⏱ Preheat Air Fryer to350°F.Whisk together eggs, cloves, cinnamon, nutmeg, cloves and salt in a bowl. Butter sides of each bread slice and cut into strips.

- Soak the buttered bread strips in the egg mixture one after the other, and arrange in the tray. (Cook in two batches, if necessary).
- Cook 2 minutes and then remove the strips. Lightly coat bread strips with cooking spray on both sides. Place back the tray into the Air Fryer and cook another 4 minutes, checking to ensure they are cooking evenly.
- Remove bread from Air Fryer once it's golden brown. Sprinkle with icing sugar and drizzle with maple syrup.

Milky Semolina Cutlets

Preparation: 45 minutes Cooking time: 15 minutes Servings: 2

INGREDIENTS:

- ✓ 3 tablespoons of vegetable oil
- ✓ 1 cup of semolina
- ✓ 12 ounces of mixed vegetables (any of your choice), chopped
- ✓ 2½ pounds of milk
- ✓ ½ teaspoon salt
- ✓ ½ teaspoon black pepper, ground

DIRECTIONS:

- Pour the milk into a sauce pan and heat. Add the mixed vegetables and allow it to cook until they are soft for about 3 minutes.
- Add the pepper and salt and then the semolina. Cook until the mixture thicken; this will take about 10 minutes.
- Grease a flat plate with oil; spread the semolina mixture on it. Refrigerate for about 4 hours until it is firm.
- Heat the Air Fryer to 350°F.
- Remove from the refrigerator and cut into flat round shapes. Brush the cutlets with oil and place them into the Air Fryer.
- Cook for 10 minutes. Serve while hot with any sauce of your choice.

Rarebit Air-Fried Egg

Preparation: 5 minutes Cooking time: 5 minutes Servings: 2-4

INGREDIENTS:

- ✓ 4 Slices Sourdough
- ✓ 4 Eggs
- ✓ 1/3 cup ale
- ✓ 1½ cups cheddar, grated
- ✓ 1 teaspoon mustard powder
- ✓ 1/2 teaspoon paprika Black Pepper to taste
- ✓ 2 teaspoon Worcestershire Sauce

DIRECTIONS:

- Fry eggs, sunny side up and set to one side. Preheat Air Fryer to 350°F.
- In a bowl, add together the cheddar, ale, paprika, mustard powder, and Worcestershire sauce.
- Spread just one side of each slice of sourdough with the cheddar mixture. Place the bread slices into the Air Fryer tray. Cook for about 3 minutes until slightly browned.
- Top the rarebits with fried eggs and season with pepper to taste.

Blackberry French Toast

Preparation time: 10 minutes Cooking time: 20 minutes Servings: 6

INGREDIENTS:

- ✓ 1 cup blackberry jam, warm
- ✓ 12 ounces bread loaf, cubed
- ✓ 8 ounces cream cheese, cubed
- ✓ 4 eggs
- ✓ 1 teaspoon cinnamon powder
- ✓ 2 cups half and half
- ✓ ½ cup brown sugar
- ✓ 1 teaspoon vanilla extract
- ✓ Cooking spray

DIRECTIONS:

- Grease your air fryer with cooking spray and heat it up at 300 degrees F.
- Add blueberry jam on the bottom, layer half of the bread cubes, then add cream cheese and top with the rest of the bread.
- In a bowl, mix eggs with half and half, cinnamon, sugar and vanilla, whisk well and add over bread mix.
- Cook for 20 minutes, divide among plates and serve for breakfast. Enjoy!

Nutrition: calories 215, fat 6, fiber 9, carbs 16, protein 6

Smoked Sausage Breakfast Mix

Preparation time: 10 minutes Cooking time: 30 minutes Servings: 4

INGREDIENTS:

- ✓ 1 and ½ pounds smoked sausage, chopped and browned A pinch of salt and black pepper
- ✓ 1 and ½ cups grits
- ✓ 4 and ½ cups water
- ✓ 16 ounces cheddar cheese, shredded
- ✓ 1 cup milk
- ✓ ¼ teaspoon garlic powder
- ✓ 1 and ½ teaspoons thyme, chopped
- ✓ Cooking spray
- ✓ 4 eggs, whisked

DIRECTIONS:

Put the water in a pot, bring to a boil over medium heat, add grits, stir, cover, cook for 5 minutes and take off heat. Add cheese, stir until it melts and mix with milk, thyme, salt, pepper, garlic powder and eggs and whisk really well.

Heat up your air fryer at 300 degrees F, grease with cooking spray and add browned sausage.

Add grits mix, spread and cook for 25 minutes.

Divide among plates and serve for breakfast.

Enjoy!

Nutrition: calories 321, fat 6, fiber 7, carbs 17, protein 4

Delicious Potato Frittata

Preparation time: 10 minutes Cooking time: 20 minutes Servings: 6

INGREDIENTS:

- ✓ 6 ounces jarred roasted red bell peppers, chopped
- ✓ 12 eggs, whisked
- ✓ ½ cup parmesan, grated
- ✓ 3 garlic cloves, minced
- ✓ 2 tablespoons parsley, chopped

- ✓ Salt and black pepper to the taste
- ✓ 2 tablespoons chives, chopped
- ✓ 16 potato wedges
- ✓ 6 tablespoons ricotta cheese
- ✓ Cooking spray

DIRECTIONS:

- ◷ In a bowl, mix eggs with red peppers, garlic, parsley, salt, pepper and ricotta and whisk well.
- ◷ Heat up your air fryer at 300 degrees F and grease it with cooking spray.
- ◷ Add half of the potato wedges on the bottom and sprinkle half of the parmesan all over.
- ◷ Add half of the egg mix, add the rest of the potatoes and the rest of the parmesan.
- ◷ Add the rest of the eggs mix, sprinkle chives and cook for 20 minutes.
- ◷ Divide among plates and serve for breakfast.
- ◷ Enjoy!

Nutrition: calories 312, fat 6, fiber 9, carbs 16, protein 5

Asparagus Frittata

Preparation time: 10 minutes Cooking time: 5 minutes Servings: 2

INGREDIENTS:

- ✓ 4 eggs, whisked
- ✓ 2 tablespoons parmesan, grated
- ✓ 4 tablespoons milk
- ✓ Salt and black pepper to the taste
- ✓ 10 asparagus tips, steamed
- ✓ Cooking spray

DIRECTIONS:

- ◷ In a bowl, mix eggs with parmesan, milk, salt and pepper and whisk well.
- ◷ Heat up your air fryer at 400 degrees F and grease with cooking spray.
- ◷ Add asparagus, add eggs mix, toss a bit and cook for 5 minutes.
- ◷ Divide frittata on plates and serve for breakfast.
- ◷ Enjoy!

Nutrition: calories 312, fat 5, fiber 8, carbs 14, protein 2

Special Corn Flakes Breakfast

Casserole

Preparation time: 10 minutes Cooking time: 8 minutes Servings: 5

INGREDIENTS:

- ✓ 1/3 cup milk
- ✓ 3 teaspoons sugar
- ✓ 2 eggs, whisked
- ✓ ¼ teaspoon nutmeg, ground
- ✓ ¼ cup blueberries
- ✓ 4 tablespoons cream cheese, whipped
- ✓ 1 and ½ cups corn flakes, crumbled
- ✓ 5 bread slices

DIRECTIONS:

- In a bowl, mix eggs with sugar, nutmeg and milk and whisk well.
- In another bowl, mix cream cheese with blueberries and whisk well.
- Put corn flakes in a third bowl.
- Spread blueberry mix on each bread slice, then dip in eggs mix and dredge in corn flakes at the end.
- Place bread in your air fryer's basket, heat up at 400 degrees F and bake for 8 minutes.

Divide among plates and serve for breakfast.

Enjoy!

Nutrition: calories 300, fat 5, fiber 7, carbs 16, protein 4

Ham Breakfast Pie

Preparation time: 10 minutes
Cooking time: 25 minutes **Servings:** 6

INGREDIENTS:

- ✓ 16 ounces crescent rolls dough
- ✓ 2 eggs, whisked
- ✓ 2 cups cheddar cheese, grated
- ✓ 1 tablespoon parmesan, grated
- ✓ 2 cups ham, cooked and chopped
- ✓ Salt and black pepper to the taste
- ✓ Cooking spray

DIRECTIONS:

- Grease your air fryer's pan with cooking spray and press half of the crescent rolls dough on the bottom.
- In a bowl, mix eggs with cheddar cheese, parmesan, salt and pepper, whisk well and add over dough.
- Spread ham, cut the rest of the crescent rolls dough in strips, arrange them over ham and cook at 300 degrees F for 25 minutes.

- Slice pie and serve for breakfast.
- Enjoy!

Nutrition: calories 400, fat 27, fiber 7, carbs 22, protein 16

Breakfast Veggie Mix

Preparation time: 10 minutes Cooking time: 25 minutes Servings: 6

INGREDIENTS:

- ✓ 1 yellow onion, sliced
- ✓ 1 red bell pepper, chopped
- ✓ 1 gold potato, chopped
- ✓ 2 tablespoons olive oil
- ✓ 8 ounces brie, trimmed and cubed
- ✓ 12 ounces sourdough bread, cubed
- ✓ 4 ounces parmesan, grated
- ✓ 8 eggs
- ✓ 2 tablespoons mustard
- ✓ 3 cups milk
- ✓ Salt and black pepper to the taste

DIRECTIONS:

- Heat up your air fryer at 350 degrees F, add oil, onion, potato and bell pepper and cook for 5 minutes.
- In a bowl, mix eggs with milk, salt, pepper and mustard and whisk well.
- Add bread and brie to your air fryer, add half of the eggs mix and add half of the parmesan as well.
- Add the rest of the bread and parmesan, toss just a little bit and cook for 20 minutes.
- Divide among plates and serve for breakfast.
- Enjoy!

Nutrition: calories 231, fat 5, fiber 10, carbs 20, protein 12

Scrambled Eggs

Preparation time: 10 minutes Cooking time: 10 minutes Servings: 2

INGREDIENTS:

- ✓ 2 eggs
- ✓ 2 tablespoons butter
- ✓ Salt and black pepper to the taste
- ✓ 1 red bell pepper, chopped
- ✓ A pinch of sweet paprika

DIRECTIONS:

- In a bowl, mix eggs with salt, pepper, paprika and red bell pepper and whisk well.
- Heat up your air fryer at 140 degrees F, add butter and melt it.
- Add eggs mix, stir and cook for 10 minutes.
- Divide scrambled eggs on plates and serve for breakfast.
- Enjoy!

Nutrition: calories 200, fat 4, fiber 7, carbs 10, protein 3

Fast Eggs and Tomatoes

Preparation time: 5 minutes Cooking time: 10 minutes Servings: 4

INGREDIENTS:

- ✓ 4 eggs
- ✓ 2 ounces milk
- ✓ 2 tablespoons parmesan, grated
- ✓ Salt and black pepper to the taste
- ✓ 8 cherry tomatoes, halved
- ✓ Cooking spray

DIRECTIONS:

- Grease your air fryer with cooking spray and heat it up at 200 degrees F.
- In a bowl, mix eggs with cheese, milk, salt and pepper and whisk.
- Add this mix to your air fryer and cook for 6 minutes.
- Add tomatoes, cook your scrambled eggs for 3 minutes, divide among plates and serve.
- Enjoy!

Nutrition: calories 200, fat 4, fiber 7, carbs 12, protein 3

Air Fried Tomato Breakfast Quiche

Preparation time: 10 minutes Cooking time: 30 minutes Servings: 1

INGREDIENTS:

- ✓ 2 tablespoons yellow onion, chopped
- ✓ 2 eggs
- ✓ ¼ cup milk
- ✓ ½ cup gouda cheese, shredded
- ✓ ¼ cup tomatoes, chopped
- ✓ Salt and black pepper to the taste
- ✓ Cooking spray

DIRECTIONS:

- Grease a ramekin with cooking spray.
- Crack eggs, add onion, milk, cheese, tomatoes, salt and pepper and stir.

- Add this in your air fryer's pan and cook at 340 degrees F for 30 minutes.
- Serve hot.
- Enjoy!

Nutrition: calories 241, fat 6, fiber 8, carbs 14, protein 6

Breakfast Mushroom Quiche

Preparation time: 10 minutes Cooking time: 10 minutes Servings: 4

INGREDIENTS:

- ✓ 1 tablespoon flour
- ✓ 1 tablespoon butter, soft
- ✓ 9 inch pie dough
- ✓ 2 button mushrooms, chopped
- ✓ 2 tablespoons ham, chopped
- ✓ 3 eggs
- ✓ 1 small yellow onion, chopped
- ✓ 1/3 cup heavy cream
- ✓ A pinch of nutmeg, ground
- ✓ Salt and black pepper to the taste
- ✓ ½ teaspoon thyme, dried
- ✓ ¼ cup Swiss cheese, grated

DIRECTIONS:

- Dust a working surface with the flour and roll the pie dough.
- Press in on the bottom of the pie pan your air fryer has.
- In a bowl, mix butter with mushrooms, ham, onion, eggs, heavy cream, salt, pepper, thyme and nutmeg and whisk well.
- Add this over pie crust, spread, sprinkle Swiss cheese all over and place pie pan in your air fryer.
- Cook your quiche at 400 degrees F for 10 minutes.
- Slice and serve for breakfast.
- Enjoy!

Nutrition: calories 212, fat 4, fiber 6, carbs 7, protein 7

Smoked Air Fried Tofu Breakfast

Preparation time: 10 minutes Cooking time: 12 minutes Servings: 2

INGREDIENTS:

- ✓ 1 tofu block, pressed and cubed
- ✓ Salt and black pepper to the taste
- ✓ 1 tablespoon smoked paprika

- ✓ ¼ cup cornstarch
- ✓ Cooking spray

DIRECTIONS:

- ◷ Grease your air fryer's basket with cooking spray and heat the fryer at 370 degrees F.
- ◷ In a bowl, mix tofu with salt, pepper, smoked paprika and cornstarch and toss well.
- ◷ Add tofu to you air fryer's basket and cook for 12 minutes shaking the fryer every 4 minutes.
- ◷ Divide into bowls and serve for breakfast.
- ◷ Enjoy!

Nutrition: calories 172, fat 4, fiber 7, carbs 12, protein 4

Delicious Tofu and Mushrooms

Preparation time: 10 minutes Cooking time: 10 minutes Servings: 2

INGREDIENTS:

- ✓ 1 tofu block, pressed and cut into medium pieces
- ✓ 1 cup panko bread crumbs
- ✓ Salt and black pepper to the taste
- ✓ ½ tablespoons flour
- ✓ 1 egg
- ✓ 1 tablespoon mushrooms, minced

DIRECTIONS:

- ◷ In a bowl, mix egg with mushrooms, flour, salt and pepper and whisk well.
- ◷ Dip tofu pieces in egg mix, then dredge them in panko bread crumbs, place them in your air fryer and cook at 350 degrees F for 10 minutes.
- ◷ Serve them for breakfast right away.
- ◷ Enjoy!

Nutrition: calories 142, fat 4, fiber 6, carbs 8, protein 3

Breakfast Broccoli Quiche

Preparation time: 10 minutes Cooking time: 20 minutes Servings: 2

INGREDIENTS:

- ✓ 1 broccoli head, florets separated and steamed
- ✓ 1 tomato, chopped
- ✓ 3 carrots, chopped and steamed
- ✓ 2 ounces cheddar cheese, grated
- ✓ 2 eggs
- ✓ 2 ounces milk

- ✓ 1 teaspoon parsley, chopped
- ✓ 1 teaspoon thyme, chopped
- ✓ Salt and black pepper to the taste

DIRECTIONS:

- ◷ In a bowl, mix eggs with milk, parsley, thyme, salt and pepper and whisk well.
- ◷ Put broccoli, carrots and tomato in your air fryer.
- ◷ Add eggs mix on top, spread cheddar cheese, cover and cook at 350 degrees F for 20 minutes.
- ◷ Divide among plates and serve for breakfast.
- ◷ Enjoy!

Nutrition: calories 214, fat 4, fiber 7, carbs 12, protein 3

Creamy Eggs

Preparation time: 10 minutes Cooking time: 12 minutes Servings: 4

INGREDIENTS:

- ✓ 2 teaspoons butter, soft
- ✓ 2 ham slices
- ✓ 4 eggs
- ✓ 2 tablespoons heavy cream
- ✓ Salt and black pepper to the taste
- ✓ 3 tablespoons parmesan, grated
- ✓ 2 teaspoons chives, chopped
- ✓ A pinch of smoked paprika

DIRECTIONS:

- ◷ Grease your air fryer's pan with the butter, line it with the ham and add it to your air fryer's basket.
- ◷ In a bowl, mix 1 egg with heavy cream, salt and pepper, whisk well and add over ham.
- ◷ Crack the rest of the eggs in the pan, sprinkle parmesan and cook your mix for 12 minutes at 320 degrees F.
- ◷ Sprinkle paprika and chives all over, divide among plates and serve for breakfast.
- ◷ Enjoy!

Nutrition: calories 263, fat 5, fiber 8, carbs 12, protein 5

Cheesy Breakfast Bread

Preparation time: 10 minutes Cooking time: 8 minutes Servings: 3

INGREDIENTS:

- ✓ 6 bread slices
- ✓ 5 tablespoons butter, melted
- ✓ 3 garlic cloves, minced

- ✓ **6 teaspoons sun dried tomato pesto**
- ✓ **1 cup mozzarella cheese, grated**

DIRECTIONS:

- Arrange bread slices on a working surface.
- Spread butter all over, divide tomato paste, garlic and top with grated cheese.
- Add bread slices to your heated air fryer and cook them at 350 degrees F for 8 minutes.
- Divide among plates and serve for breakfast.
- Enjoy!

Nutrition: calories 187, fat 5, fiber 6, carbs 8, protein 3

Breakfast Bread Pudding

Preparation time: 10 minutes Cooking time: 22 minutes Servings: 4

INGREDIENTS:

- ✓ **½ pound white bread, cubed**
- ✓ **¾ cup milk**
- ✓ **¾ cup water**
- ✓ **2 teaspoons cornstarch**
- ✓ **½ cup apple, peeled, cored and roughly chopped 5 tablespoons honey**
- ✓ **1 teaspoon vanilla extract**
- ✓ **2 teaspoons cinnamon powder**
- ✓ **1 and 1/3 cup flour**
- ✓ **3/5 cup brown sugar**
- ✓ **3 ounces soft butter**

DIRECTIONS:

- In a bowl, mix bread with apple, milk with water, honey, cinnamon, vanilla and cornstarch and whisk well.
- In a separate bowl, mix flour with sugar and butter and stir until you obtain a crumbled mixture.
- Press half of the crumble mix on the bottom of your air fryer, add bread and apple mix, add the rest of the crumble and cook everything at 350 degrees F for 22 minutes.
- Divide bread pudding on plates and serve.
- Enjoy!

Nutrition: calories 261, fat 7, fiber 7, carbs 8, protein 5

Buttermilk Breakfast Biscuits

Preparation time: 10 minutes Cooking time: 8 minutes Servings: 4

INGREDIENTS:

- ✓ **1 and ¼ cup white flour**
- ✓ **½ cup self-rising flour**
- ✓ **¼ teaspoon baking soda**
- ✓ **½ teaspoon baking powder**
- ✓ **1 teaspoon sugar**
- ✓ **4 tablespoons butter, cold and cubed+ 1 tablespoon melted butter**
- ✓ **¾ cup buttermilk**
- ✓ **Maple syrup for serving**

DIRECTIONS:

- In a bowl, mix white flour with self-rising flour, baking soda, baking powder and sugar and stir.
- Add cold butter and stir using your hands.
- Add buttermilk, stir until you obtain a dough and transfer to a floured working surface.
- Roll your dough and cut 10 pieces using a round cutter.
- Arrange biscuits in your air fryer's cake pan, brush them with melted butter and cook at 400 degrees F for 8 minutes.
- Serve them for breakfast with some maple syrup on top.
- Enjoy!

Nutrition: calories 192, fat 6, fiber 9, carbs 12, protein 3

Breakfast Bread Rolls

Preparation time: 10 minutes Cooking time: 12 minutes Servings: 4

INGREDIENTS:

- ✓ **5 potatoes, boiled, peeled and mashed**
- ✓ **8 bread slices, white parts only**
- ✓ **1 coriander bunch, chopped**
- ✓ **2 green chilies, chopped**
- ✓ **2 small yellow onions, chopped**
- ✓ **½ teaspoon turmeric powder**
- ✓ **2 curry leaf springs**
- ✓ **½ teaspoon mustard seeds**

- ✓ **2 tablespoons olive oil**
- ✓ **Salt and black pepper to the taste**

DIRECTIONS:

- ① Heat up a pan with 1 teaspoon oil, add mustard seeds, onions, curry leaves and turmeric, stir and cook for a few seconds.
- ① Add mashed potatoes, salt, pepper, coriander and chilies, stir well, take off heat and cool it down.
- ① Divide potatoes mix into 8 parts and shape ovals using your wet hands.
- ① Wet bread slices with water, press in order to drain excess water and keep one slice in your palm.
- ① Add a potato oval over bread slice and wrap it around it.
- ① Repeat with the rest of the potato mix and bread.
- ① Heat up your air fryer at 400 degrees F, add the rest of the oil, add bread rolls, cook them for 12 minutes.
- ① Divide bread rolls on plates and serve for breakfast.
- ① Enjoy!

Nutrition: calories 261, fat 6, fiber 9, carbs 12, protein 7

Spanish Omelet

Preparation time: 10 minutes Cooking time: 10 minutes Servings: 4

INGREDIENTS:

- ✓ **3 eggs**
- ✓ **½ chorizo, chopped**
- ✓ **1 potato, peeled and cubed**
- ✓ **½ cup corn**
- ✓ **1 tablespoon olive oil**
- ✓ **1 tablespoon parsley, chopped**
- ✓ **1 tablespoon feta cheese, crumbled**
- ✓ **Salt and black pepper to the taste**

DIRECTIONS:

- ① Heat up your air fryer at 350 degrees F and add oil.
- ① Add chorizo and potatoes, stir and brown them for a few seconds.
- ① In a bowl, mix eggs with corn, parsley, cheese, salt and pepper and whisk.
- ① Pour this over chorizo and potatoes, spread and cook for 5 minutes.
- ① Divide omelet on plates and serve for breakfast.
- ① Enjoy!

Nutrition: calories 300, fat 6, fiber 9, carbs 12, protein 6

Egg White Omelet

Preparation time: 10 minutes Cooking time: 15 minutes Servings: 4

INGREDIENTS:

- ✓ **1 cup egg whites**
- ✓ **¼ cup tomato, chopped**
- ✓ **2 tablespoons skim milk**
- ✓ **¼ cup mushrooms, chopped**
- ✓ **2 tablespoons chives, chopped**
- ✓ **Salt and black pepper to the taste**

DIRECTIONS:

- ① In a bowl, mix egg whites with tomato, milk, mushrooms, chives, salt and pepper, whisk well and pour into your air fryer's pan.
- ① Cook at 320 degrees F for 15 minutes, cool omelet down, slice, divide among plates and serve.
- ① Enjoy!

Nutrition: calories 100, fat 3, fiber 6, carbs 7, carbs 4

Artichoke Frittata

Preparation time: 10 minutes Cooking time: 15 minutes Servings: 6

INGREDIENTS:

- ✓ **3 canned artichokes hearts, drained and chopped**
- ✓ **2 tablespoons olive oil**
- ✓ **½ teaspoon oregano, dried**
- ✓ **Salt and black pepper to the taste**
- ✓ **6 eggs, whisked**

DIRECTIONS:

- ① In a bowl, mix artichokes with oregano, salt, pepper and eggs and whisk well.
- ① Add the oil to your air fryer's pan, add eggs mix and cook at 320 degrees F for 15 minutes.
- ① Divide frittata on plates and serve for breakfast.
- ① Enjoy!

Nutrition: calories 136, fat 6, fiber 6, carbs 9, protein 4

Amazing Breakfast Burger

Preparation time: 10 minutes Cooking time: 45 minutes Servings: 4

INGREDIENTS:

- ✓ **1 pound beef, ground**
- ✓ **1 yellow onion, chopped**
- ✓ **1 teaspoon tomato puree**
- ✓ **1 teaspoon garlic, minced**
- ✓ **1 teaspoon mustard**
- ✓ **1 teaspoon basil, dried**

- ✓ 1 teaspoon parsley, chopped
- ✓ 1 tablespoon cheddar cheese, grated
- ✓ Salt and black pepper to the taste
- ✓ 4 bread buns, for serving

DIRECTIONS:

- ◷ In a bowl, mix beef with onion, tomato puree, garlic, mustard, basil, parsley, cheese, salt and pepper, stir well and shape 4 burgers out of this mix.
- ◷ Heat up your air fryer at 400 degrees F, add burgers and cook them for 25 minutes.
- ◷ Reduce temperature to 350 degrees F and bake burgers for 20 minutes more.
- ◷ Arrange them on bread buns and serve for a quick breakfast.
- ◷ Enjoy!

Nutrition: calories 234, fat 5, fiber 8, carbs 12, protein 4

Onion Frittata

Preparation time: 10 minutes Cooking time: 20 minutes Servings: 6

INGREDIENTS:

- ✓ 10 eggs, whisked
- ✓ 1 tablespoon olive oil
- ✓ 1 pound small potatoes, chopped
- ✓ 2 yellow onions, chopped
- ✓ Salt and black pepper to the taste
- ✓ 1 ounce cheddar cheese, grated
- ✓ ½ cup sour cream

DIRECTIONS:

- ◷ In a large bowl, mix eggs with potatoes, onions, salt, pepper, cheese and sour cream and whisk well.
- ◷ Grease your air fryer's pan with the oil, add eggs mix, place in air fryer and cook for 20 minutes at 320 degrees F.
- ◷ Slice frittata, divide among plates and serve for breakfast.
- ◷ Enjoy!

Nutrition: calories 231, fat 5, fiber 7, carbs 8, protein 4

Bell Peppers Frittata

Preparation time: 10 minutes Cooking time: 20 minutes Servings: 4

INGREDIENTS:

- ✓ 2 tablespoons olive oil
- ✓ ½ pounds chicken sausage, casings removed and chopped 1 sweet onion, chopped

- ✓ 1 red bell pepper, chopped
- ✓ 1 orange bell pepper, chopped
- ✓ 1 green bell pepper, chopped
- ✓ Salt and black pepper to the taste
- ✓ 8 eggs, whisked
- ✓ ½ cup mozzarella cheese, shredded
- ✓ 2 teaspoons oregano, chopped

DIRECTIONS:

- ◷ Add 1 tablespoon oil to your air fryer, add sausage, heat up at 320 degrees F and brown for 1 minute.
- ◷ Add the rest of the oil, onion, red bell pepper, orange and green one, stir and cook for 2 minutes more.
- ◷ Add oregano, salt, pepper and eggs, stir and cook for 15 minutes.
- ◷ Add mozzarella, leave frittata aside for a few minutes, divide among plates and serve.
- ◷ Enjoy!

Nutrition: calories 212, fat 4, fiber 6, carbs 8, protein 12

Cheese Sandwich

Preparation time: 10 minutes Cooking time: 8 minutes Servings: 1

INGREDIENTS:

- ✓ 2 bread slices
- ✓ 2 teaspoons butter
- ✓ 2 cheddar cheese slices
- ✓ A pinch of sweet paprika

DIRECTIONS:

- ◷ Spread butter on bread slices, add cheddar cheese on one, sprinkle paprika, top with the other bread slices, cut into 2 halves, arrange them in your air fryer and cook at 370 degrees F for 8 minutes, flipping them once, arrange on a plate and serve.
- ◷ Enjoy!

Nutrition: calories 130, fat 3, fiber 5, carbs 9, protein 3

Long Beans Omelet

Preparation time: 10 minutes Cooking time: 10 minutes Servings: 3

INGREDIENTS:

- ✓ ½ teaspoon soy sauce
- ✓ 1 tablespoon olive oil
- ✓ 3 eggs, whisked
- ✓ A pinch of salt and black pepper

- ✓ **4 garlic cloves, minced**
- ✓ **4 long beans, trimmed and sliced**

DIRECTIONS:

- ⏱ In a bowl, mix eggs with a pinch of salt, black pepper and soy sauce and whisk well.
- ⏱ Heat up your air fryer at 320 degrees F, add oil and garlic, stir and brown for 1 minute.
- ⏱ Add long beans and eggs mix, spread and cook for 10 minutes.
- ⏱ Divide omelet on plates and serve for breakfast.
- ⏱ Enjoy!

Nutrition: calories 200, fat 3, fiber 7, carbs 9, protein 3

French Beans and Egg Breakfast Mix

Preparation time: 10 minutes Cooking time: 10 minutes Servings: 3

INGREDIENTS:

- ✓ **2 eggs, whisked**
- ✓ **½ teaspoon soy sauce**
- ✓ **1 tablespoon olive oil**
- ✓ **4 garlic cloves, minced**
- ✓ **3 ounces French beans, trimmed and sliced**
  diagonally Salt and white pepper to the taste

DIRECTIONS:

- ⏱ In a bowl, mix eggs with soy sauce, salt and pepper and whisk well.
- ⏱ Heat up your air fryer at 320 degrees F, add oil and heat it up as well.
- ⏱ Add garlic and brown for 1 minute.
- ⏱ Add French beans and egg mix, toss and cook for 10 minutes.
- ⏱ Divide among plates and serve for breakfast.
- ⏱ Enjoy!

Nutrition: calories 182, fat 3, fiber 6, carbs 8, protein 3

Breakfast Doughnuts

Preparation time: 10 minutes Cooking time: 18 minutes Servings: 6

INGREDIENTS:

- ✓ **4 tablespoons butter, soft**
- ✓ **1 and ½ teaspoon baking powder**
- ✓ **2 an ¼ cups white flour**
- ✓ **½ cup sugar**
- ✓ **1/3 cup caster sugar**
- ✓ **1 teaspoon cinnamon powder**

- ✓ **2 egg yolks**
- ✓ **½ cup sour cream**

DIRECTIONS:

- ⏱ In a bowl, mix 2 tablespoons butter with simple sugar and egg yolks and whisk well.
- ⏱ Add half of the sour cream and stir.
- ⏱ In another bowls, mix flour with baking powder, stir and also add to eggs mix.
- ⏱ Stir well until you obtain a dough, transfer it to a floured working surface, roll it out and cut big circles with smaller ones in the middle.
- ⏱ Brush doughnuts with the rest of the butter, heat up your air fryer at 360 degrees F, place doughnuts inside and cook them for 8 minutes.
- ⏱ In a bowl, mix cinnamon with caster sugar and stir.
- ⏱ Arrange doughnuts on plates and dip them in cinnamon and sugar before serving.
- ⏱ Enjoy!

Nutrition: calories 182, fat 3, fiber 7, carbs 8, protein 3

Creamy Breakfast Tofu

Preparation time: 15 minutes Cooking time: 20 minutes Servings: 4

INGREDIENTS:

- ✓ **1 block firm tofu, pressed and cubed**
- ✓ **1 teaspoon rice vinegar**
- ✓ **2 tablespoons soy sauce**
- ✓ **2 teaspoons sesame oil**
- ✓ **1 tablespoon potato starch**
- ✓ **1 cup Greek yogurt**

DIRECTIONS:

- ⏱ In a bowl, mix tofu cubes with vinegar, soy sauce and oil, toss, and leave aside for 15 minutes.
- ⏱ Dip tofu cubes in potato starch, toss, transfer to your air fryer, heat up at 370 degrees F and cook for 20 minutes shaking halfway.
- ⏱ Divide into bowls and serve for breakfast with some Greek yogurt on the
- ⏱ side.
- ⏱ Enjoy!

Nutrition: calories 110, fat 4, fiber 5, carbs 8, protein 4

Veggie Burritos

Preparation time: 10 minutes Cooking time: 10 minutes Servings: 4

INGREDIENTS:

- ✓ **2 tablespoons cashew butter**
- ✓ **2 tablespoons tamari**

- ✓ 2 tablespoons water
- ✓ 2 tablespoons liquid smoke
- ✓ 4 rice papers
- ✓ ½ cup sweet potatoes, steamed and cubed
- ✓ ½ small broccoli head, florets separated and steamed 7 asparagus stalks
- ✓ 8 roasted red peppers, chopped
- ✓ A handful kale, chopped

DIRECTIONS:

- In a bowl, mix cashew butter with water, tamari and liquid smoke and whisk well.
- Wet rice papers and arrange them on a working surface.
- Divide sweet potatoes, broccoli, asparagus, red peppers and kale, wrap burritos and dip each in cashew mix.
- Arrange burritos in your air fryer and cook them at 350 degrees F for 10 minutes.
- Divide veggie burritos on plates d serve.
- Enjoy !

Nutrition: calories 172, fat 4, fiber 7, carbs 8, protein 3

Breakfast Fish Tacos

Preparation time: 10 minutes Cooking time: 13 minutes Servings: 4

INGREDIENTS:

- ✓ 4 big tortillas
- ✓ 1 red bell pepper, chopped
- ✓ 1 yellow onion, chopped
- ✓ 1 cup corn
- ✓ 4 white fish fillets, skinless and boneless ½ cup salsa
- ✓ A handful mixed romaine lettuce, spinach and radicchio 4 tablespoon parmesan, grated

DIRECTIONS:

- Put fish fillets in your air fryer and cook at 350 degrees F for 6 minutes.
- Meanwhile, heat up a pan over medium high heat, add bell pepper, onion and corn, stir and cook for 1-2 minutes.
- Arrange tortillas on a working surface, divide fish fillets, spread salsa over them, divide mixed veggies and mixed greens and spread parmesan on each at the end.
- Roll your tacos, place them in preheated air fryer and cook at 350 degrees F for 6 minutes more.
- Divide fish tacos on plates and serve for breakfast.

- Enjoy!

Nutrition: calories 200, fat 3, fiber 7, carbs 9, protein 5

Garlic Potatoes with Bacon

Preparation time: 10 minutes Cooking time: 20 minutes Servings: 4

INGREDIENTS:

- ✓ 4 potatoes, peeled and cut into medium cubes
- ✓ 6 garlic cloves, minced
- ✓ 4 bacon slices, chopped
- ✓ 2 rosemary springs, chopped
- ✓ 1 tablespoon olive oil
- ✓ Salt and black pepper to the taste
- ✓ 2 eggs, whisked

DIRECTIONS:

- In your air fryer's pan, mix oil with potatoes, garlic, bacon, rosemary, salt, pepper and eggs and whisk.
- Cook potatoes at 400 degrees F for 20 minutes, divide everything on plates and serve for breakfast.
- Enjoy!

Nutrition: calories 211, fat 3, fiber 5, carbs 8, protein 5

Spinach Breakfast Parcels

Preparation time: 10 minutes Cooking time: 4 minutes Servings: 2

INGREDIENTS:

- ✓ 4 sheets filo pastry
- ✓ 1 pound baby spinach leaves, roughly chopped ½ pound ricotta cheese
- ✓ 2 tablespoons pine nuts
- ✓ 1 eggs, whisked
- ✓ Zest from 1 lemon, grated
- ✓ Greek yogurt for serving
- ✓ Salt and black pepper to the taste

DIRECTIONS:

- In a bowl, mix spinach with cheese, egg, lemon zest, salt, pepper and pine nuts and stir.
- Arrange filo sheets on a working surface, divide spinach mix, fold diagonally to shape your parcels and place them in your preheated air fryer at 400 degrees F.
- Bake parcels for 4 minutes, divide them on plates and serve them with Greek yogurt on the side.
- Enjoy!

Nutrition: calories 182, fat 4, fiber 8, carbs 9, protein 5

Ham Rolls

Preparation time: 10 minutes Cooking time: 10 minutes Servings: 4

INGREDIENTS:

- ✓ **1 sheet puff pastry**
- ✓ **4 handful gruyere cheese, grated**
- ✓ **4 teaspoons mustard**
- ✓ **8 ham slices, chopped**

DIRECTIONS:

- ① Roll out puff pastry on a working surface, divide cheese, ham and mustard, roll tight and cut into medium rounds.
- ① Place all rolls in air fryer and cook for 10 minutes at 370 degrees F.
- ① Divide rolls on plates and serve for breakfast.
- ① Enjoy!

Nutrition: calories 182, fat 4, fiber 7, carbs 9, protein 8

Shrimp Frittata

Preparation time: 10 minutes Cooking time: 15 minutes Servings: 4

INGREDIENTS:

- ✓ **4 eggs**
- ✓ **½ teaspoon basil, dried**
- ✓ **Cooking spray**
- ✓ **Salt and black pepper to the taste**
- ✓ **½ cup rice, cooked**
- ✓ **½ cup shrimp, cooked, peeled, deveined and chopped ½ cup baby spinach, chopped**
- ✓ **½ cup Monterey jack cheese, grated**

DIRECTIONS:

- ① In a bowl, mix eggs with salt, pepper and basil and whisk.
- ① Grease your air fryer's pan with cooking spray and add rice, shrimp and spinach.
- ① Add eggs mix, sprinkle cheese all over and cook in your air fryer at 350 degrees F for 10 minutes.
- ① Divide among plates and serve for breakfast.
- ① Enjoy!

Nutrition: calories 162, fat 6, fiber 5, carbs 8, protein 4

Tuna Sandwiches

Preparation time: 10 minutes Cooking time: 5 minutes Servings: 4

INGREDIENTS:

- ✓ **16 ounces canned tuna, drained**
- ✓ **¼ cup mayonnaise**
- ✓ **2 tablespoons mustard**
- ✓ **1 tablespoons lemon juice**
- ✓ **2 green onions, chopped**
- ✓ **3 English muffins, halved**
- ✓ **3 tablespoons butter**
- ✓ **6 provolone cheese**

DIRECTIONS:

- ① In a bowl, mix tuna with mayo, lemon juice, mustard and green onions and stir.
- ① Grease muffin halves with the butter, place them in preheated air fryer and bake them at 350 degrees F for 4 minutes.
- ① Spread tuna mix on muffin halves, top each with provolone cheese, return sandwiches to air fryer and cook them for 4 minutes, divide among plates and serve for breakfast right away.
- ① Enjoy!

Nutrition: calories 182, fat 4, fiber 7, carbs 8, protein 6

Shrimp Sandwiches

Preparation time: 10 minutes Cooking time: 5 minutes Servings: 4

INGREDIENTS:

- ✓ **1 and ¼ cups cheddar, shredded**
- ✓ **6 ounces canned tiny shrimp, drained**
- ✓ **3 tablespoons mayonnaise**
- ✓ **2 tablespoons green onions, chopped**
- ✓ **4 whole wheat bread slices**
- ✓ **2 tablespoons butter, soft**

DIRECTIONS:

- ① In a bowl, mix shrimp with cheese, green onion and mayo and stir well.
- ① Spread this on half of the bread slices, top with the other bread slices, cut into halves diagonally and spread butter on top.
- ① Place sandwiches in your air fryer and cook at 350 degrees F for 5 minutes.
- ① Divide shrimp sandwiches on plates and serve them for breakfast. Enjoy!

Nutrition: calories 162, fat 3, fiber 7, carbs 12, protein 4

Breakfast Pea Tortilla

Preparation time: 10 minutes Cooking time: 7 minutes Servings: 8

INGREDIENTS:

- ✓ ½ pound baby peas
- ✓ 4 tablespoons butter
- ✓ 1 and ½ cup yogurt
- ✓ 8 eggs
- ✓ ½ cup mint, chopped
- ✓ Salt and black pepper to the taste

DIRECTIONS:

- Heat up a pan that fits your air fryer with the butter over medium heat, add peas, stir and cook for a couple of minutes.
- Meanwhile, in a bowl, mix half of the yogurt with salt, pepper, eggs and mint and whisk well.
- Pour this over the peas, toss, introduce in your air fryer and cook at 350 degrees F for 7 minutes.
- Spread the rest of the yogurt over your tortilla, slice and serve.
- Enjoy!

Nutrition: calories 192, fat 5, fiber 4, carbs 8, protein 7

Raspberry Rolls

Preparation time: 30 minutes Cooking time: 20 minutes Servings: 6

INGREDIENTS:

- ✓ 1 cup milk
- ✓ 4 tablespoons butter
- ✓ 3 and ¼ cups flour
- ✓ 2 teaspoons yeast
- ✓ ¼ cup sugar
- ✓ 1 egg

For the filling:

- ✓ 8 ounces cream cheese, soft
- ✓ 12 ounces raspberries
- ✓ 1 teaspoons vanilla extract
- ✓ 5 tablespoons sugar
- ✓ 1 tablespoon cornstarch
- ✓ Zest from 1 lemon, grated

DIRECTIONS:

- In a bowl, mix flour with sugar and yeast and stir.
- Add milk and egg, stir until you obtain a dough, leave it aside to rise for 30 minutes, transfer dough to a working surface and roll well.

- In a bowl, mix cream cheese with sugar, vanilla and lemon zest, stir well and spread over dough.
- In another bowl, mix raspberries with cornstarch, stir and spread over cream cheese mix.
- Roll your dough, cut into medium pieces, place them in your air fryer, spray them with cooking spray and cook them at 350 degrees F for 30 minutes.
- Serve your rolls for breakfast.
- Enjoy!

Nutrition: calories 261, fat 5, fiber 8, carbs 9, protein 6

Potato and Leek Frittata

Preparation time: 10 minutes Cooking time: 18 minutes Servings: 4

INGREDIENTS:

- ✓ 2 gold potatoes, boiled, peeled and chopped
- ✓ 2 tablespoons butter
- ✓ 2 leeks, sliced
- ✓ Salt and black pepper to the taste
- ✓ ¼ cup whole milk
- ✓ 10 eggs, whisked
- ✓ 5 ounces fromage blanc, crumbled

DIRECTIONS:

- Heat up a pan that fits your air fryer with the butter over medium heat, add leeks, stir and cook for 4 minutes.
- Add potatoes, salt, pepper, eggs, cheese and milk, whisk well, cook for 1 minute more, introduce in your air fryer and cook at 350 degrees F for 13 minutes.
- Slice frittata, divide among plates and serve.
- Enjoy!

Nutrition: calories 271, fat 6, fiber 8, carbs 12, protein 6

Espresso Oatmeal

Preparation time: 10 minutes Cooking time: 17 minutes Servings: 4

INGREDIENTS:

- ✓ 1 cup milk
- ✓ 1 cup steel cut oats
- ✓ 2 and ½ cups water
- ✓ 2 tablespoons sugar
- ✓ 1 teaspoon espresso powder
- ✓ 2 teaspoons vanilla extract

DIRECTIONS:

- In a pan that fits your air fryer, mix oats with water, sugar, milk and espresso powder, stir, introduce in your air fryer and cook at 360 degrees F for 17 minutes.
- Add vanilla extract, stir, leave everything aside for 5 minutes, divide into bowls and serve for breakfast.
- Enjoy!

Nutrition: calories 261, fat 7, fiber 6, carbs 39, protein 6

Mushroom Oatmeal

Preparation time: 10 minutes Cooking time: 20 minutes Servings: 4

INGREDIENTS:

- ✓ **1 small yellow onion, chopped**
- ✓ **1 cup steel cut oats**
- ✓ **2 garlic cloves, minced**
- ✓ **2 tablespoons butter**
- ✓ **½ cup water**
- ✓ **14 ounces canned chicken stock**
- ✓ **3 thyme springs, chopped**
- ✓ **2 tablespoons extra virgin olive oil**
- ✓ **½ cup gouda cheese, grated**
- ✓ **8 ounces mushroom, sliced**
- ✓ **Salt and black pepper to the taste**

DIRECTIONS:

- Heat up a pan that fits your air fryer with the butter over medium heat, add onions and garlic, stir and cook for 4 minutes.
- Add oats, water, salt, pepper, stock and thyme, stir, introduce in your air fryer and cook at 360 degrees F for 16 minutes.
- Meanwhile, heat up a pan with the olive oil over medium heat, add mushrooms, cook them for 3 minutes, add to oatmeal and cheese, stir, divide into bowls and serve for breakfast.
- Enjoy!

Nutrition: calories 284, fat 8, fiber 8, carbs 20, protein 17

Walnuts and Pear Oatmeal

Preparation time: 5 minutes Cooking time: 12 minutes Servings: 4

INGREDIENTS:

- ✓ **1 cup water**
- ✓ **1 tablespoon butter, soft**
- ✓ **¼ cups brown sugar**
- ✓ **½ teaspoon cinnamon powder**

- ✓ **1 cup rolled oats**
- ✓ **½ cup walnuts, chopped**
- ✓ **2 cups pear, peeled and chopped**
- ✓ **½ cup raisins**

DIRECTIONS:

- In a heat proof dish that fits your air fryer, mix milk with sugar, butter, oats, cinnamon, raisins, pears and walnuts, stir, introduce in your fryer and cook at 360 degrees F for 12 minutes.
- Divide into bowls and serve.
- Enjoy!

Nutrition: calories 230, fat 6, fiber 11, carbs 20, protein 5

Cinnamon and Cream Cheese Oats

Preparation time: 10 minutes Cooking time: 25 minutes Servings: 4

INGREDIENTS:

- ✓ **1 cup steel oats**
- ✓ **3 cups milk**
- ✓ **1 tablespoon butter**
- ✓ **¾ cup raisins**
- ✓ **1 teaspoon cinnamon powder**
- ✓ **¼ cup brown sugar**
- ✓ **2 tablespoons white sugar**
- ✓ **2 ounces cream cheese, soft**

DIRECTIONS:

- Heat up a pan that fits your air fryer with the butter over medium heat, add oats, stir and toast them for 3 minutes.
- Add milk and raisins, stir, introduce in your air fryer and cook at 350 degrees F for 20 minutes.
- Meanwhile, in a bowl, mix cinnamon with brown sugar and stir.
- In a second bowl, mix white sugar with cream cheese and whisk.
- Divide oats into bowls and top each with cinnamon and cream cheese. Enjoy!

Nutrition: calories 152, fat 6, fiber 6, carbs 25, protein 7

Cherries Risotto

Preparation time: 10 minutes Cooking time: 12 minutes Servings: 4

INGREDIENTS:

- ✓ **1 and ½ cups Arborio rice**
- ✓ **1 and ½ teaspoons cinnamon powder**

- ✓ 1/3 cup brown sugar
- ✓ A pinch of salt
- ✓ 2 tablespoons butter
- ✓ 2 apples, cored and sliced
- ✓ 1 cup apple juice
- ✓ 3 cups milk
- ✓ ½ cup cherries, dried

DIRECTIONS:

- ⊙ Heat up a pan that fist your air fryer with the butter over medium heat, add rice, stir and cook for 4-5 minutes.
- ⊙ Add sugar, apples, apple juice, milk, cinnamon and cherries, stir, introduce in your air fryer and cook at 350 degrees F for 8 minutes.
- ⊙ Divide into bowls and serve for breakfast.
- ⊙ Enjoy!

Nutrition: calories 162, fat 12, fiber 6, carbs 23, protein 8

Rice , Almonds and Raisins Pudding

Preparation time: 5 minutes Cooking time: 8 minutes Servings: 4

INGREDIENTS:

- ✓ 1 cup brown rice
- ✓ ½ cup coconut chips
- ✓ 1 cup milk
- ✓ 2 cups water
- ✓ ½ cup maple syrup
- ✓ ¼ cup raisins
- ✓ ¼ cup almonds
- ✓ A pinch of cinnamon powder

DIRECTIONS:

- ⊙ Put the rice in a pan that fits your air fryer, add the water, heat up on the stove over medium high heat, cook until rice is soft and drain.
- ⊙ Add milk, coconut chips, almonds, raisins, cinnamon and maple syrup, stir well, introduce in your air fryer and cook at 360 degrees F for 8 minutes.
- ⊙ Divide rice pudding in bowls and serve.
- ⊙ Enjoy!

Nutrition: calories 251, fat 6, fiber 8, carbs 39, protein 12

Dates and Millet Pudding

Preparation time: 10 minutes Cooking time: 15 minutes Servings: 4

INGREDIENTS:

- ✓ 14 ounces milk
- ✓ 7 ounces water
- ✓ 2/3 cup millet
- ✓ 4 dates, pitted
- ✓ Honey for serving

DIRECTIONS:

- ⊙ Put the millet in a pan that fits your air fryer, add dates, milk and water, stir, introduce in your air fryer and cook at 360 degrees F for 15 minutes.
- ⊙ Divide among plates, drizzle honey on top and serve for breakfast. Enjoy!

Nutrition: calories 231, fat 6, fiber 6, carbs 18, protein 6

Air Fryer Lunch Recipes

Fresh Chicken Mix

Preparation time: 10 minutes Cooking time: 22 minutes Servings: 4

INGREDIENTS:

- ✓ **2 chicken breasts, skinless, boneless and cubed**
- ✓ **8 button mushrooms, sliced**
- ✓ **1 red bell pepper, chopped**
- ✓ **1 tablespoon olive oil**
- ✓ **½ teaspoon thyme, dried**
- ✓ **10 ounces alfredo sauce**
- ✓ **6 bread slices**
- ✓ **2 tablespoons butter, soft**

DIRECTIONS:

- ⏱ In your air fryer, mix chicken with mushrooms, bell pepper and oil, toss to coat well and cook at 350 degrees F for 15 minutes.
- ⏱ Transfer chicken mix to a bowl, add thyme and alfredo sauce, toss, return to air fryer and cook at 350 degrees F for 4 minutes more.
- ⏱ Spread butter on bread slices, add it to the fryer, butter side up and cook for 4 minutes more.
- ⏱ Arrange toasted bread slices on a platter, top each with chicken mix and serve for lunch.
- ⏱ Enjoy!

Nutrition: calories 172, fat 4, fiber 9, carbs 12, protein 4

Hot Bacon Sandwiches

Preparation time: 10 minutes Cooking time: 7 minutes Servings: 4

INGREDIENTS:

- ✓ **1/3 cup bbq sauce**
- ✓ **2 tablespoons honey**
- ✓ **8 bacon slices, cooked and cut into thirds**
- ✓ **1 red bell pepper, sliced**
- ✓ **1 yellow bell pepper, sliced**
- ✓ **3 pita pockets, halved**
- ✓ **1 and ¼ cup butter lettuce leaves, torn**
- ✓ **2 tomatoes, sliced**

DIRECTIONS:

- ⏱ In a bowl, mix bbq sauce with honey and whisk well.
- ⏱ Brush bacon and all bell peppers with some of this mix, place them in your air fryer and cook at 350 degrees F for 4 minutes.
- ⏱ Shake fryer and cook them for 2 minutes more.
- ⏱ Stuff pita pockets with bacon mix, also stuff with tomatoes and lettuce, spread the rest of the bbq sauce and serve for lunch.
- ⏱ Enjoy!

Nutrition: calories 186, fat 6, fiber 9, carbs 14, protein 4

Buttermilk Chicken

Preparation time: 10 minutes Cooking time: 18 minutes Servings: 4

INGREDIENTS:

- ✓ **1 and ½ pounds chicken thighs**
- ✓ **2 cups buttermilk**
- ✓ **Salt and black pepper to the taste**
- ✓ **A pinch of cayenne pepper**
- ✓ **2 cups white flour**
- ✓ **1 tablespoon baking powder**
- ✓ **1 tablespoon sweet paprika**
- ✓ **1 tablespoon garlic powder**

DIRECTIONS:

- ⏱ In a bowl, mix chicken thighs with buttermilk, salt, pepper and cayenne, toss and leave aside for 6 hours.
- ⏱ In a separate bowl, mix flour with paprika, baking powder and garlic powder and stir,
- ⏱ Drain chicken thighs, dredge them in flour mix, arrange them in your air fryer and cook at 360 degrees F for 8 minutes.
- ⏱ Flip chicken pieces, cook them for 10 minutes more, arrange on a platter and serve for lunch.
- ⏱ Enjoy!

Nutrition: calories 200, fat 3, fiber 9, carbs 14, protein 4

Chicken Pie

Preparation time: 10 minutes Cooking time: 16 minutes Servings: 4

INGREDIENTS:

- ✓ **2 chicken thighs, boneless, skinless and cubed**
- ✓ **1 carrot, chopped**

- ✓ 1 yellow onion, chopped
- ✓ 2 potatoes, chopped
- ✓ 2 mushrooms, chopped
- ✓ 1 teaspoon soy sauce
- ✓ Salt and black pepper to the taste
- ✓ 1 teaspoon Italian seasoning
- ✓ ½ teaspoon garlic powder
- ✓ 1 teaspoon Worcestershire sauce
- ✓ 1 tablespoon flour
- ✓ 1 tablespoon milk
- ✓ 2 puff pastry sheets
- ✓ 1 tablespoon butter, melted

DIRECTIONS:

- Heat up a pan over medium high heat, add potatoes, carrots and onion, stir and cook for 2 minutes.
- Add chicken and mushrooms, salt, soy sauce, pepper, Italian seasoning, garlic powder, Worcestershire sauce, flour and milk, stir really well and take off heat.
- Place 1 puff pastry sheet on the bottom of your air fryer's pan and trim edge excess.
- Add chicken mix, top with the other puff pastry sheet, trim excess as well and brush pie with butter.
- Place in your air fryer and cook at 360 degrees F for 6 minutes.
- Leave pie to cool down, slice and serve for breakfast.
- Enjoy!

Nutrition: calories 300, fat 5, fiber 7, carbs 14, protein 7

Macaroni and Cheese

Preparation time: 10 minutes Cooking time: 30 minutes Servings: 3

INGREDIENTS:

- ✓ 1 and ½ cups favorite macaroni
- ✓ Cooking spray
- ✓ ½ cup heavy cream
- ✓ 1 cup chicken stock
- ✓ ¾ cup cheddar cheese, shredded
- ✓ ½ cup mozzarella cheese, shredded
- ✓ ¼ cup parmesan, shredded
- ✓ Salt and black pepper to the taste

DIRECTIONS:

- Spray a pan with cooking spray, add macaroni, heavy cream, stock, cheddar cheese, mozzarella and parmesan but also salt and pepper, toss well, place pan in your air fryer's basket and cook for 30 minutes.
- Divide among plates and serve for lunch.
- Enjoy!

Nutrition: calories 341, fat 7, fiber 8, carbs 18, protein 4

Lunch Fajitas

Preparation time: 10 minutes Cooking time: 10 minutes Servings: 4

INGREDIENTS:

- ✓ 1 teaspoon garlic powder
- ✓ ¼ teaspoon cumin, ground
- ✓ ½ teaspoon chili powder
- ✓ Salt and black pepper to the taste
- ✓ ¼ teaspoon coriander, ground
- ✓ 1 pound chicken breasts, cut into strips
- ✓ 1 red bell pepper, sliced
- ✓ 1 green bell pepper, sliced
- ✓ 1 yellow onion, chopped
- ✓ 1 tablespoon lime juice
- ✓ Cooking spray
- ✓ 4 tortillas, warmed up
- ✓ Salsa for serving
- ✓ Sour cream for serving
- ✓ 1 cup lettuce leaves, torn for serving

DIRECTIONS:

- In a bowl, mix chicken with garlic powder, cumin, chili, salt, pepper, coriander, lime juice, red bell pepper, green bell pepper and onion, toss, leave aside for 10 minutes, transfer to your air fryer and drizzle some cooking spray all over.
- Toss and cook at 400 degrees F for 10 minutes.
- Arrange tortillas on a working surface, divide chicken mix, also add salsa,
- sour cream and lettuce, wrap and serve for lunch.
- Enjoy!

Nutrition: calories 317, fat 6, fiber 8, carbs 14, protein 4

Lunch Chicken Salad

Preparation time: 10 minutes Cooking time: 20 minutes Servings: 4

INGREDIENTS:

- ✓ 2 ears of corn, hulled
- ✓ 1 pound chicken tenders, boneless
- ✓ Olive oil as needed
- ✓ Salt and black pepper to the taste
- ✓ 1 teaspoon sweet paprika
- ✓ 1 tablespoon brown sugar
- ✓ ½ teaspoon garlic powder
- ✓ ½ iceberg lettuce head, cut into medium strips
- ✓ ½ romaine lettuce head, cut into medium strips
- ✓ 1 cup canned black beans, drained
- ✓ 1 cup cheddar cheese, shredded
- ✓ 3 tablespoons cilantro, chopped
- ✓ 4 green onions, chopped
- ✓ 12 cherry tomatoes, sliced
- ✓ ¼ cup ranch dressing
- ✓ 3 tablespoons BBQ sauce

DIRECTIONS:

- Put corn in your air fryer, drizzle some oil, toss, cook at 400 degrees F for 10 minutes, transfer to a plate and leave aside for now.
- Put chicken in your air fryer's basket, add salt, pepper, brown sugar, paprika and garlic powder, toss, drizzle some more oil, cook at 400 degrees F for 10 minutes, flipping them halfway, transfer tenders to a cutting board and chop them.
- Cur kernels off the cob, transfer corn to a bowl, add chicken, iceberg lettuce, romaine lettuce, black beans, cheese, cilantro, tomatoes, onions, bbq sauce and ranch dressing, toss well and serve for lunch.
- Enjoy!

Nutrition: calories 372, fat 6, fiber 9, carbs 17, protein 6

Fish And Chips

Preparation time: 10 minutes Cooking time: 12 minutes Servings: 2

INGREDIENTS:

- ✓ 2 medium cod fillets, skinless and boneless
- ✓ Salt and black pepper to the taste
- ✓ ¼ cup buttermilk
- ✓ 3 cups kettle chips, cooked

DIRECTIONS:

- In a bowl, mix fish with salt, pepper and buttermilk, toss and leave aside for 5 minutes.

- Put chips in your food processor, crush them and spread them on a plate.
- Add fish and press well on all sides.
- Transfer fish to your air fryer's basket and cook at 400 degrees F for 12 minutes.
- Serve hot for lunch.
- Enjoy!

Nutrition: calories 271, fat 7, fiber 9, carbs 14, protein 4

Hash Brown Toasts

Preparation time: 10 minutes Cooking time: 7 minutes Servings: 4

INGREDIENTS:

- ✓ 4 hash brown patties, frozen
- ✓ 1 tablespoon olive oil
- ✓ ¼ cup cherry tomatoes, chopped
- ✓ 3 tablespoons mozzarella, shredded
- ✓ 2 tablespoons parmesan, grated
- ✓ 1 tablespoon balsamic vinegar
- ✓ 1 tablespoon basil, chopped

DIRECTIONS:

- Put hash brown patties in your air fryer, drizzle the oil over them and cook them at 400 degrees F for 7 minutes.
- In a bowl, mix tomatoes with mozzarella, parmesan, vinegar and basil and stir well.
- Divide hash brown patties on plates, top each with tomatoes mix and serve for lunch.
- Enjoy!

Nutrition: calories 199, fat 3, fiber 8, carbs 12, protein 4

Delicious Beef Cubes

Preparation time: 10 minutes Cooking time: 12 minutes Servings: 4

INGREDIENTS:

- ✓ 1 pound sirloin, cubed
- ✓ 16 ounces jarred pasta sauce
- ✓ 1 and ½ cups bread crumbs
- ✓ 2 tablespoons olive oil
- ✓ ½ teaspoon marjoram, dried
- ✓ White rice, already cooked for serving

DIRECTIONS:

- In a bowl, mix beef cubes with pasta sauce and toss well.

- ⏱ In another bowl, mix bread crumbs with marjoram and oil and stir well.
- ⏱ Dip beef cubes in this mix, place them in your air fryer and cook at 360 degrees F for 12 minutes.
- ⏱ Divide among plates and serve with white rice on the side.
- ⏱ Enjoy!

Nutrition: calories 271, fat 6, fiber 9, carbs 18, protein 12

Pasta Salad

Preparation time: 10 minutes Cooking time: 12 minutes Servings: 6

INGREDIENTS:

- ✓ **1 zucchini, sliced in half and roughly chopped**
- ✓ **1 orange bell pepper, roughly chopped**
- ✓ **1 green bell pepper, roughly chopped**
- ✓ **1 red onion, roughly chopped**
- ✓ **4 ounces brown mushrooms, halved**
- ✓ **Salt and black pepper to the taste**
- ✓ **1 teaspoon Italian seasoning**
- ✓ **1 pound penne rigate, already cooked**
- ✓ **1 cup cherry tomatoes, halved**
- ✓ **½ cup kalamata olive, pitted and halved**
- ✓ **¼ cup olive oil**
- ✓ **3 tablespoons balsamic vinegar**
- ✓ **2 tablespoons basil, chopped**

DIRECTIONS:

- ⏱ In a bowl, mix zucchini with mushrooms, orange bell pepper, green bell pepper, red onion, salt, pepper, Italian seasoning and oil, toss well, transfer to preheated air fryer at 380 degrees F and cook them for 12 minutes.
- ⏱ In a large salad bowl, mix pasta with cooked veggies, cherry tomatoes, olives, vinegar and basil, toss and serve for lunch.
- ⏱ Enjoy!

Nutrition: calories 200, fat 5, fiber 8, carbs 10, protein 6

Philadelphia Chicken Lunch

Preparation time: 10 minutes Cooking time: 30 minutes Servings: 4

INGREDIENTS:

- ✓ **1 teaspoon olive oil**
- ✓ **1 yellow onion, sliced**

- ✓ **2 chicken breasts, skinless, boneless and sliced Salt and black pepper to the taste**
- ✓ **1 tablespoon Worcestershire sauce**
- ✓ **14 ounces pizza dough**
- ✓ **1 and ½ cups cheddar cheese, grated**
- ✓ **½ cup jarred cheese sauce**

DIRECTIONS:

- ⏱ Preheat your air fryer at 400 degrees F, add half of the oil and onions and fry them for 8 minutes, stirring once.
- ⏱ Add chicken pieces, Worcestershire sauce, salt and pepper, toss, air fry for 8 minutes more, stirring once and transfer everything to a bowl.
- ⏱ Roll pizza dough on a working surface and shape a rectangle.
- ⏱ Spread half of the cheese all over, add chicken and onion mix and top with cheese sauce.
- ⏱ Roll your dough and shape into a U.
- ⏱ Place your roll in your air fryer's basket, brush with the rest of the oil and cook at 370 degrees for 12 minutes, flipping the roll halfway.
- ⏱ Slice your roll when it's warm and serve for lunch.
- ⏱ Enjoy!

Nutrition: calories 300, fat 8, fiber 17, carbs 20, protein 6

Tasty Cheeseburgers

Preparation time: 10 minutes Cooking time: 20 minutes Servings: 2

INGREDIENTS:

- ✓ **12 ounces lean beef, ground**
- ✓ **4 teaspoons ketchup**
- ✓ **3 tablespoons yellow onion, chopped**
- ✓ **2 teaspoons mustard**
- ✓ **Salt and black pepper to the taste**
- ✓ **4 cheddar cheese slices**
- ✓ **2 burger buns, halved**

DIRECTIONS:

- ⏱ In a bowl, mix beef with onion, ketchup, mustard, salt and pepper, stir well and shape 4 patties out of this mix.
- ⏱ Divide cheese on 2 patties and top with the other 2 patties.
- ⏱ Place them in preheated air fryer at 370 degrees F and fry them for 20 minutes.
- ⏱ Divide cheeseburger on 2 bun halves, top with the other 2 and serve for lunch.
- ⏱ Enjoy!

Turkish Koftas

Preparation time: 10 minutes Cooking time: 15 minutes Servings: 2

INGREDIENTS:

- ✓ **1 leek, chopped**
- ✓ **2 tablespoons feta cheese, crumbled**
- ✓ **½ pound lean beef, minced**
- ✓ **1 tablespoon cumin, ground**
- ✓ **1 tablespoon mint, chopped**
- ✓ **1 tablespoon parsley, chopped**
- ✓ **1 teaspoon garlic, minced**
- ✓ **Salt and black pepper to the taste**

DIRECTIONS:

- In a bowl, mix beef with leek, cheese, cumin, mint, parsley, garlic, salt and pepper, stir well, shape your koftas and place them on sticks.
- Add koftas to your preheated air fryer at 360 degrees F and cook them for 15 minutes.
- Serve them with a side salad for lunch.
- Enjoy!

Nutrition: calories 281, fat 7, fiber 8, carbs 17, protein 6

Chicken Kabobs

Preparation time: 10 minutes Cooking time: 20 minutes Servings: 2

INGREDIENTS:

- ✓ **3 orange bell peppers, cut into squares**
- ✓ **¼ cup honey**
- ✓ **1/3 cup soy sauce**
- ✓ **Salt and black pepper to the taste**
- ✓ **Cooking spray**
- ✓ **6 mushrooms, halved**
- ✓ **2 chicken breasts, skinless, boneless and roughly cubed**

DIRECTIONS:

- In a bowl, mix chicken with salt, pepper, honey, say sauce and some cooking spray and toss well.
- Thread chicken, bell peppers and mushrooms on skewers, place them in your air fryer and cook at 338 degrees F for 20 minutes.
- Divide among plates and serve for lunch.
- Enjoy!

Chinese Pork Lunch Mix

Preparation time: 10 minutes Cooking time: 12 minutes Servings: 4

INGREDIENTS:

- ✓ **2 eggs**
- ✓ **2 pounds pork, cut into medium cubes**
- ✓ **1 cup cornstarch**
- ✓ **1 teaspoon sesame oil**
- ✓ **Salt and black pepper to the taste**
- ✓ **A pinch of Chinese five spice**
- ✓ **3 tablespoons canola oil**
- ✓ **Sweet tomato sauce for serving**

DIRECTIONS:

- In a bowl, mix five spice with salt, pepper and cornstarch and stir.
- In another bowl, mix eggs with sesame oil and whisk well.
- Dredge pork cubes in cornstarch mix, then dip in eggs mix and place them in your air fryer which you've greased with the canola oil.
- Cook at 340 degrees F for 12 minutes, shaking the fryer once.
- Serve pork for lunch with the sweet tomato sauce on the side.
- Enjoy!

Nutrition: calories 320, fat 8, fiber 12, carbs 20, protein 5

Lunch Egg Rolls

Preparation time: 10 minutes Cooking time: 15 minutes Servings: 4

INGREDIENTS:

- ✓ **½ cup mushrooms, chopped**
- ✓ **½ cup carrots, grated**
- ✓ **½ cup zucchini, grated**
- ✓ **2 green onions, chopped**
- ✓ **2 tablespoons soy sauce**
- ✓ **8 egg roll wrappers**
- ✓ **1 eggs, whisked**
- ✓ **1 tablespoon cornstarch**

DIRECTIONS:

- In a bowl, mix carrots with mushrooms, zucchini, green onions and soy sauce and stir well.

- Arrange egg roll wrappers on a working surface, divide veggie mix on each and roll well.
- In a bowl, mix cornstarch with egg, whisk well and brush eggs rolls with this mix.
- Seal edges, place all rolls in your preheated air fryer and cook them at 370 degrees F for 15 minutes.
- Arrange them on a platter and serve them for lunch.
- Enjoy!

Nutrition: calories 172, fat 6, fiber 6, carbs 8, protein 7

Veggie Toast

Preparation time: 10 minutes Cooking time: 15 minutes Servings: 4

INGREDIENTS:

- ✓ **1 red bell pepper, cut into thin strips**
- ✓ **1 cup cremini mushrooms, sliced**
- ✓ **1 yellow squash, chopped**
- ✓ **2 green onions, sliced**
- ✓ **1 tablespoon olive oil**
- ✓ **4 bread slices**
- ✓ **2 tablespoons butter, soft**
- ✓ **½ cup goat cheese, crumbled**

DIRECTIONS:

- In a bowl, mix red bell pepper with mushrooms, squash, green onions and oil, toss, transfer to your air fryer, cook them at 350 degrees F for 10 minutes, shaking the fryer once and transfer them to a bowl.
- Spread butter on bread slices, place them in air fryer and cook them at 350 degrees F for 5 minutes.
- Divide veggie mix on each bread slice, top with crumbled cheese and serve for lunch.
- Enjoy!

Nutrition: calories 152, fat 3, fiber 4, carbs 7, protein 2

Stuffed Mushrooms

Preparation time: 10 minutes Cooking time: 20 minutes Servings: 4

INGREDIENTS:

- ✓ **4 big Portobello mushroom caps**
- ✓ **1 tablespoon olive oil**
- ✓ **¼ cup ricotta cheese**
- ✓ **5 tablespoons parmesan, grated**
- ✓ **1 cup spinach, torn**
- ✓ **1/3 cup bread crumbs**
- ✓ **¼ teaspoon rosemary, chopped**

DIRECTIONS:

- Rub mushrooms caps with the oil, place them in your air fryer's basket and cook them at 350 degrees F for 2 minutes.
- Meanwhile, in a bowl, mix half of the parmesan with ricotta, spinach, rosemary and bread crumbs and stir well.
- Stuff mushrooms with this mix, sprinkle the rest of the parmesan on top, place them in your air fryer's basket again and cook at 350 degrees F for 10 minutes.
- Divide them on plates and serve with a side salad for lunch.
- Enjoy!

Nutrition: calories 152, fat 4, fiber 7, carbs 9, protein 5

Quick Lunch Pizzas

Preparation time: 10 minutes Cooking time: 7 minutes Servings: 4

INGREDIENTS:

- ✓ **4 pitas**
- ✓ **1 tablespoon olive oil**
- ✓ **¾ cup pizza sauce**
- ✓ **4 ounces jarred mushrooms, sliced**
- ✓ **½ teaspoon basil, dried**
- ✓ **2 green onions, chopped**
- ✓ **2 cup mozzarella, grated**
- ✓ **1 cup grape tomatoes, sliced**

DIRECTIONS:

- Spread pizza sauce on each pita bread, sprinkle green onions and basil, divide mushrooms and top with cheese.
- Arrange pita pizzas in your air fryer and cook them at 400 degrees F for 7 minutes.
- Top each pizza with tomato slices, divide among plates and serve. Enjoy!

Nutrition: calories 200, fat 4, fiber 6, carbs 7, protein 3

Lunch Gnocchi

Preparation time: 10 minutes Cooking time: 17 minutes Servings: 4

INGREDIENTS:

- ✓ **1 yellow onion, chopped**
- ✓ **1 tablespoon olive oil**
- ✓ **3 garlic cloves, minced**
- ✓ **16 ounces gnocchi**

- ✓ ¼ cup parmesan, grated
- ✓ 8 ounces spinach pesto

DIRECTIONS:

- Grease your air fryer's pan with olive oil, add gnocchi, onion and garlic, toss, put pan in your air fryer and cook at 400 degrees F for 10 minutes.
- Add pesto, toss and cook for 7 minutes more at 350 degrees F.
- Divide among plates and serve for lunch.
- Enjoy!

Nutrition: calories 200, fat 4, fiber 4, carbs 12, protein 4

Tuna and Zucchini Tortillas

Preparation time: 10 minutes Cooking time: 10 minutes Servings: 4

INGREDIENTS:

- ✓ 4 corn tortillas
- ✓ 4 tablespoons butter, soft
- ✓ 6 ounces canned tuna, drained
- ✓ 1 cup zucchini, shredded
- ✓ 1/3 cup mayonnaise
- ✓ 2 tablespoons mustard
- ✓ 1 cup cheddar cheese, grated

DIRECTIONS:

- Spread butter on tortillas, place them in your air fryer's basket and cook them at 400 degrees F for 3 minutes.
- Meanwhile, in a bowl, mix tuna with zucchini, mayo and mustard and stir.
- Divide this mix on each tortilla, top with cheese, roll tortillas, place them in your air fryer's basket again and cook them at 400 degrees F for 4 minutes more.
- Serve for lunch.
- Enjoy!

Nutrition: calories 162, fat 4, fiber 8, carbs 9, protein 4

Squash Fritters

Preparation time: 10 minutes Cooking time: 7 minutes Servings: 4

INGREDIENTS:

- ✓ 3 ounces cream cheese
- ✓ 1 egg, whisked
- ✓ ½ teaspoon oregano, dried
- ✓ A pinch of salt and black pepper
- ✓ 1 yellow summer squash, grated

- ✓ 1/3 cup carrot, grated
- ✓ 2/3 cup bread crumbs
- ✓ 2 tablespoons olive oil

DIRECTIONS:

- In a bowl, mix cream cheese with salt, pepper, oregano, egg, breadcrumbs, carrot and squash and stir well.
- Shape medium patties out of this mix and brush them with the oil.
- Place squash patties in your air fryer and cook them at 400 degrees F for 7 minutes.
- Serve them for lunch.
- Enjoy!

Nutrition: calories 200, fat 4, fiber 7, carbs 8, protein 6

Lunch Shrimp Croquettes

Preparation time: 10 minutes Cooking time: 8 minutes Servings: 4

INGREDIENTS:

- ✓ 2/3 pound shrimp, cooked, peeled, deveined and chopped
- ✓ 1 and ½ cups bread crumbs
- ✓ 1 egg, whisked
- ✓ 2 tablespoons lemon juice
- ✓ 3 green onions, chopped
- ✓ ½ teaspoon basil, dried
- ✓ Salt and black pepper to the taste
- ✓ 2 tablespoons olive oil

DIRECTIONS:

- In a bowl, mix half of the bread crumbs with egg and lemon juice and stir well.
- Add green onions, basil, salt, pepper and shrimp and stir really well.
- In a separate bowl, mix the rest of the bread crumbs with the oil and toss well.
- Shape round balls out of shrimp mix, dredge them in bread crumbs, place them in preheated air fryer and cook the for 8 minutes at 400 degrees F.
- Serve them with a dip for lunch.
- Enjoy!

Nutrition: calories 142, fat 4, fiber 6, carbs 9, protein 4

Lunch Special Pancake

Preparation time: 10 minutes Cooking time: 10 minutes Servings: 2

INGREDIENTS:

- ✓ **1 tablespoon butter**
- ✓ **3 eggs, whisked**
- ✓ **½ cup flour**
- ✓ **½ cup milk**
- ✓ **1 cup salsa**
- ✓ **1 cup small shrimp, peeled and deveined**

DIRECTIONS:

- Preheat your air fryer at 400 degrees F, add fryer's pan, add 1 tablespoon butter and melt it.
- In a bowl, mix eggs with flour and milk, whisk well and pour into air fryer's pan, spread, cook at 350 degrees for 12 minutes and transfer to a plate.
- In a bowl, mix shrimp with salsa, stir and serve your pancake with this on the side.
- Enjoy!

Nutrition: calories 200, fat 6, fiber 8, carbs 12, protein 4

Scallops and Dill

Preparation time: 10 minutes Cooking time: 5 minutes Servings: 4

INGREDIENTS:

- ✓ **1 pound sea scallops, debearded**
- ✓ **1 tablespoon lemon juice**
- ✓ **1 teaspoon dill, chopped**
- ✓ **2 teaspoons olive oil**
- ✓ **Salt and black pepper to the taste**

DIRECTIONS:

- In your air fryer, mix scallops with dill, oil, salt, pepper and lemon juice, cover and cook at 360 degrees F for 5 minutes.
- Discard unopened ones, divide scallops and dill sauce on plates and serve for lunch.
- Enjoy!

Nutrition: calories 152, fat 4, fiber 7, carbs 19, protein 4

Chicken Sandwiches

Preparation time: 10 minutes Cooking time: 10 minutes Servings: 4

INGREDIENTS:

- ✓ **2 chicken breasts, skinless, boneless and cubed**
- ✓ **1 red onion, chopped**
- ✓ **1 red bell pepper, sliced**
- ✓ **½ cup Italian seasoning**

- ✓ **½ teaspoon thyme, dried**
- ✓ **2 cups butter lettuce, torn**
- ✓ **4 pita pockets**
- ✓ **1 cup cherry tomatoes, halved**
- ✓ **1 tablespoon olive oil**

DIRECTIONS:

- In your air fryer, mix chicken with onion, bell pepper, Italian seasoning and oil, toss and cook at 380 degrees F for 10 minutes.
- Transfer chicken mix to a bowl, add thyme, butter lettuce and cherry tomatoes, toss well, stuff pita pockets with this mix and serve for lunch.
- Enjoy!

Nutrition: calories 126, fat 4, fiber 8, carbs 14, protein 4

Beef Lunch Meatballs

Preparation time: 10 minutes Cooking time: 15 minutes Servings: 4

INGREDIENTS:

- ✓ **½ pound beef, ground**
- ✓ **½ pound Italian sausage, chopped**
- ✓ **½ teaspoon garlic powder**
- ✓ **½ teaspoon onion powder**
- ✓ **Salt and black pepper to the taste**
- ✓ **½ cup cheddar cheese, grated**
- ✓ **Mashed potatoes for serving**

DIRECTIONS:

- In a bowl, mix beef with sausage, garlic powder, onion powder, salt, pepper and cheese, stir well and shape 16 meatballs out of this mix.
- Place meatballs in your air fryer and cook them at 370 degrees F for 15 minutes.
- Serve your meatballs with some mashed potatoes on the side.
- Enjoy!

Nutrition: calories 333, fat 23, fiber 1, carbs 8, protein 20

Delicious Chicken Wings

Preparation time: 10 minutes Cooking time: 45 minutes Servings: 4

INGREDIENTS:

- ✓ **3 pounds chicken wings**
- ✓ **½ cup butter**

- ✓ 1 tablespoon old bay seasoning
- ✓ ¾ cup potato starch
- ✓ 1 teaspoon lemon juice
- ✓ Lemon wedges for serving

DIRECTIONS:

- In a bowl, mix starch with old bay seasoning and chicken wings and toss well.
- Place chicken wings in your air fryer's basket and cook them at 360 degrees F for 35 minutes shaking the fryer from time to time.
- Increase temperature to 400 degrees F, cook chicken wings for 10 minutes more and divide them on plates.
- Heat up a pan over medium heat, add butter and melt it.
- Add lemon juice, stir well, take off heat and drizzle over chicken wings.
- Serve them for lunch with lemon wedges on the side.
- Enjoy!

Nutrition: calories 271, fat 6, fiber 8, carbs 18, protein 18

Easy Hot Dogs

Preparation time: 10 minutes Cooking time: 7 minutes Servings: 2

INGREDIENTS:

- ✓ 2 hot dog buns
- ✓ 2 hot dogs
- ✓ 1 tablespoon Dijon mustard
- ✓ 2 tablespoons cheddar cheese, grated

DIRECTIONS:

- Put hot dogs in preheated air fryer and cook them at 390 degrees F for 5 minutes.
- Divide hot dogs into hot dog buns, spread mustard and cheese, return everything to your air fryer and cook for 2 minutes more at 390 degrees F.
- Serve for lunch.
- Enjoy!

Nutrition: calories 211, fat 3, fiber 8, carbs 12, protein 4

Japanese Chicken Mix

Preparation time: 10 minutes Cooking time: 8 minutes Servings: 2

INGREDIENTS:

- ✓ 2 chicken thighs, skinless and boneless
- ✓ 2 ginger slices, chopped
- ✓ 3 garlic cloves, minced
- ✓ ¼ cup soy sauce
- ✓ ¼ cup mirin
- ✓ 1/8 cup sake
- ✓ ½ teaspoon sesame oil
- ✓ 1/8 cup water
- ✓ 2 tablespoons sugar
- ✓ 1 tablespoon cornstarch mixed with
- ✓ 2 tablespoons water Sesame seeds for serving

DIRECTIONS:

- In a bowl, mix chicken thighs with ginger, garlic, soy sauce, mirin, sake, oil, water, sugar and cornstarch, toss well, transfer to preheated air fryer and cook at 360 degrees F for 8 minutes.
- Divide among plates, sprinkle sesame seeds on top and serve with a side salad for lunch.
- Enjoy!

Nutrition: calories 300, fat 7, fiber 9, carbs 17, protein 10

Prosciutto Sandwich

Preparation time: 10 minutes Cooking time: 5 minutes Servings: 1

INGREDIENTS:

- ✓ 2 bread slices
- ✓ 2 mozzarella slices
- ✓ 2 tomato slices
- ✓ 2 prosciutto slices
- ✓ 2 basil leaves
- ✓ 1 teaspoon olive oil
- ✓ A pinch of salt and black pepper

DIRECTIONS:

- Arrange mozzarella and prosciutto on a bread slice.
- Season with salt and pepper, place in your air fryer and cook at 400 degrees F for 5 minutes.
- Drizzle oil over prosciutto, add tomato and basil, cover with the other
- bread slice, cut sandwich in half and serve.
- Enjoy!

Nutrition: calories 172, fat 3, fiber 7, carbs 9, protein 5

Lentils Fritters

Preparation time: 10 minutes Cooking time: 10 minutes Servings: 2

INGREDIENTS:

- ✓ 1 cup yellow lentils, soaked in water for 1 hour and drained
- ✓ 1 hot chili pepper, chopped
- ✓ 1 inch ginger piece, grated
- ✓ ½ teaspoon turmeric powder
- ✓ 1 teaspoon garam masala
- ✓ 1 teaspoon baking powder
- ✓ Salt and black pepper to the taste
- ✓ 2 teaspoons olive oil
- ✓ 1/3 cup water
- ✓ ½ cup cilantro, chopped
- ✓ 1 and ½ cup spinach, chopped
- ✓ 4 garlic cloves, minced
- ✓ ¾ cup red onion, chopped
- ✓ Mint chutney for serving

DIRECTIONS:

- In your blender, mix lentils with chili pepper, ginger, turmeric, garam masala, baking powder, salt, pepper, olive oil, water, cilantro, spinach, onion and garlic, blend well and shape medium balls out of this mix.
- Place them all in your preheated air fryer at 400 degrees F and cook for 10 minutes.
- Serve your veggie fritters with a side salad for lunch.
- Enjoy!

Nutrition: calories 142, fat 2, fiber 8, carbs 12, protein 4

Lunch Potato Salad

Preparation time: 10 minutes Cooking time: 25 minutes Servings: 4

INGREDIENTS:

- ✓ 2 pound red potatoes, halved
- ✓ 2 tablespoons olive oil
- ✓ Salt and black pepper to the taste
- ✓ 2 green onions, chopped
- ✓ 1 red bell pepper, chopped
- ✓ 1/3 cup lemon juice
- ✓ 3 tablespoons mustard

DIRECTIONS:

- On your air fryer's basket, mix potatoes with half of the olive oil, salt and pepper and cook at 350 degrees F for 25 minutes shaking the fryer once.

- In a bowl, mix onions with bell pepper and roasted potatoes and toss.
- In a small bowl, mix lemon juice with the rest of the oil and mustard and whisk really well.
- Add this to potato salad, toss well and serve for lunch.
- Enjoy!

Nutrition: calories 211, fat 6, fiber 8, carbs 12, protein 4

Corn Casserole

Preparation time: 10 minutes Cooking time: 15 minutes Servings: 4

INGREDIENTS:

- ✓ 2 cups corn
- ✓ 3 tablespoons flour
- ✓ 1 egg
- ✓ ¼ cup milk
- ✓ ½ cup light cream
- ✓ ½ cup Swiss cheese, grated
- ✓ 2 tablespoons butter
- ✓ Salt and black pepper to the taste
- ✓ Cooking spray

DIRECTIONS:

- In a bowl, mix corn with flour, egg, milk, light cream, cheese, salt, pepper and butter and stir well.
- Grease your air fryer's pan with cooking spray, pour cream mix, spread and cook at 320 degrees F for 15 minutes.
- Serve warm for lunch.
- Enjoy!

Nutrition: calories 281, fat 7, fiber 8, carbs 9, protein 6

Bacon and Garlic Pizzas

Preparation time: 10 minutes Cooking time: 10 minutes Servings: 4

INGREDIENTS:

- ✓ 4 dinner rolls, frozen
- ✓ 4 garlic cloves minced
- ✓ ½ teaspoon oregano dried
- ✓ ½ teaspoon garlic powder
- ✓ 1 cup tomato sauce
- ✓ 8 bacon slices, cooked and chopped
- ✓ 1 and ¼ cups cheddar cheese, grated
- ✓ Cooking spray

DIRECTIONS:

- Place dinner rolls on a working surface and press them to obtain 4 ovals.
- Spray each oval with cooking spray, transfer them to your air fryer and cook them at 370 degrees F for 2 minutes.
- Spread tomato sauce on each oval, divide garlic, sprinkle oregano and garlic powder and top with bacon and cheese.
- Return pizzas to your heated air fryer and cook them at 370 degrees F for 8 minutes more.
- Serve them warm for lunch.
- Enjoy!

Nutrition: calories 217, fat 5, fiber 8, carbs 12, protein 4

Sweet and Sour Sausage Mix

Preparation time: 10 minutes Cooking time: 10 minutes Servings: 4

INGREDIENTS:

- ✓ **1 pound sausages, sliced**
- ✓ **1 red bell pepper, cut into strips**
- ✓ **½ cup yellow onion, chopped**
- ✓ **3 tablespoons brown sugar**
- ✓ **1/3 cup ketchup**
- ✓ **2 tablespoons mustard**
- ✓ **2 tablespoons apple cider vinegar**
- ✓ **½ cup chicken stock**

DIRECTIONS:

- In a bowl, mix sugar with ketchup, mustard, stock and vinegar and whisk well.
- In your air fryer's pan, mix sausage slices with bell pepper, onion and sweet and sour mix, toss and cook at 350 degrees F for 10 minutes.
- Divide into bowls and serve for lunch.
- Enjoy!

Nutrition: calories 162, fat 6, fiber 9, carbs 12, protein 6

Meatballs and Tomato Sauce

Preparation time: 10 minutes Cooking time: 15 minutes Servings: 4

INGREDIENTS:

- ✓ **1 pound lean beef, ground**
- ✓ **3 green onions, chopped**
- ✓ **2 garlic cloves, minced**
- ✓ **1 egg yolk**
- ✓ **¼ cup bread crumbs**

- ✓ **Salt and black pepper to the taste**
- ✓ **1 tablespoon olive oil**
- ✓ **16 ounces tomato sauce**
- ✓ **2 tablespoons mustard**

DIRECTIONS:

- In a bowl, mix beef with onion, garlic, egg yolk, bread crumbs, salt and pepper, stir well and shape medium meatballs out of this mix.
- Grease meatballs with the oil, place them in your air fryer and cook them at 400 degrees F for 10 minutes.
- In a bowl, mix tomato sauce with mustard, whisk, add over meatballs, toss them and cook at 400 degrees F for 5 minutes more.
- Divide meatballs and sauce on plates and serve for lunch.
- Enjoy!

Nutrition: calories 300, fat 8, fiber 9, carbs 16, protein 5

Stuffed Meatballs

Preparation time: 10 minutes Cooking time: 10 minutes Servings: 4

INGREDIENTS:

- ✓ **1/3 cup bread crumbs**
- ✓ **3 tablespoons milk**
- ✓ **1 tablespoon ketchup**
- ✓ **1 egg**
- ✓ **½ teaspoon marjoram, dried**
- ✓ **Salt and black pepper to the taste**
- ✓ **1 pound lean beef, ground**
- ✓ **20 cheddar cheese cubes**
- ✓ **1 tablespoon olive oil**

DIRECTIONS:

- In a bowl, mix bread crumbs with ketchup, milk, marjoram, salt, pepper and egg and whisk well.
- Add beef, stir and shape 20 meatballs out of this mix.
- Shape each meatball around a cheese cube, drizzle the oil over them and rub.
- Place all meatballs in your preheated air fryer and cook at 390 degrees F for 10 minutes.
- Serve them for lunch with a side salad.
- Enjoy!

Nutrition: calories 200, fat 5, fiber 8, carbs 12, protein 5

Steaks and Cabbage

Preparation time: 10 minutes Cooking time: 10 minutes Servings: 4

INGREDIENTS:

- ✓ ½ pound sirloin steak, cut into strips
- ✓ 2 teaspoons cornstarch
- ✓ 1 tablespoon peanut oil
- ✓ 2 cups green cabbage, chopped
- ✓ 1 yellow bell pepper, chopped
- ✓ 2 green onions, chopped
- ✓ 2 garlic cloves, minced
- ✓ Salt and black pepper to the taste

DIRECTIONS:

- ⏱ In a bowl, mix cabbage with salt, pepper and peanut oil, toss, transfer to air fryer's basket, cook at 370 degrees F for 4 minutes and transfer to a bowl.
- ⏱ Add steak strips to your air fryer, also add green onions, bell pepper, garlic, salt and pepper, toss and cook for 5 minutes.
- ⏱ Add over cabbage, toss, divide among plates and serve for lunch. Enjoy!

Nutrition: calories 282, fat 6, fiber 8, carbs 14, protein 6

Succulent Lunch Turkey Breast

Preparation time: 10 minutes Cooking time: 47 minutes Servings: 4

INGREDIENTS:

- ✓ 1 big turkey breast
- ✓ 2 teaspoons olive oil
- ✓ ½ teaspoon smoked paprika
- ✓ 1 teaspoon thyme, dried
- ✓ ½ teaspoon sage, dried
- ✓ Salt and black pepper to the taste
- ✓ 2 tablespoons mustard
- ✓ ¼ cup maple syrup
- ✓ 1 tablespoon butter, soft

DIRECTIONS:

- ⏱ Brush turkey breast with the olive oil, season with salt, pepper, thyme, paprika and sage, rub, place in your air fryer's basket and fry at 350 degrees F for 25 minutes.
- ⏱ Flip turkey, cook for 10 minutes more, flip one more time and cook for another 10 minutes.
- ⏱ Meanwhile, heat up a pan with the butter over medium heat, add mustard and maple syrup, stir well, cook for a couple of minutes and take off heat.

- ⏱ Slice turkey breast, divide among plates and serve with the maple glaze drizzled on top.
- ⏱ Enjoy!

Nutrition: calories 280, fat 2, fiber 7, carbs 16, protein 14

Italian Eggplant Sandwich

Preparation time: 10 minutes Cooking time: 16 minutes Servings: 2

INGREDIENTS:

- ✓ 1 eggplant, sliced
- ✓ 2 teaspoons parsley, dried
- ✓ Salt and black pepper to the taste
- ✓ ½ cup breadcrumbs
- ✓ ½ teaspoon Italian seasoning
- ✓ ½ teaspoon garlic powder
- ✓ ½ teaspoon onion powder
- ✓ 2 tablespoons milk
- ✓ 4 bread slices
- ✓ Cooking spray
- ✓ ½ cup mayonnaise
- ✓ ¾ cup tomato sauce
- ✓ 2 cups mozzarella cheese, grated

DIRECTIONS:

- ⏱ Season eggplant slices with salt and pepper, leave aside for 10 minutes and then pat dry them well.
- ⏱ In a bowl, mix parsley with breadcrumbs, Italian seasoning, onion and garlic powder, salt and black pepper and stir.
- ⏱ In another bowl, mix milk with mayo and whisk well.
- ⏱ Brush eggplant slices with mayo mix, dip them in breadcrumbs, place them in your air fryer's basket, spray with cooking oil and cook them at 400 degrees F for 15 minutes, flipping them after 8 minutes.
- ⏱ Brush each bread slice with olive oil and arrange 2 on a working surface.
- ⏱ Add mozzarella and parmesan on each, add baked eggplant slices, spread tomato sauce and basil and top with the other bread slices, greased side down.
- ⏱ Divide sandwiches on plates, cut them in halves and serve for lunch.
- ⏱ Enjoy!

Nutrition: calories 324, fat 16, fiber 4, carbs 39, protein 12

Creamy Chicken Stew

Preparation time: 10 minutes Cooking time: 25 minutes Servings: 4

INGREDIENTS:

- ✓ 1 and ½ cups canned cream of celery soup
- ✓ 6 chicken tenders
- ✓ Salt and black pepper to the taste
- ✓ 2 potatoes, chopped
- ✓ 1 bay leaf
- ✓ 1 thyme spring, chopped
- ✓ 1 tablespoon milk
- ✓ 1 egg yolk
- ✓ ½ cup heavy cream

DIRECTIONS:

- ⏱ In a bowl, mix chicken with cream of celery, potatoes, heavy cream, bay leaf, thyme, salt and pepper, toss, pour into your air fryer's pan and cook at 320 degrees F for 25 minutes.
- ⏱ Leave your stew to cool down a bit, discard bay leaf, divide among plates and serve right away.
- ⏱ Enjoy!

Nutrition: calories 300, fat 11, fiber 2, carbs 23, protein 14

Lunch Pork and Potatoes

Preparation time: 10 minutes Cooking time: 25 minutes Servings: 2

INGREDIENTS:

- ✓ 2 pounds pork loin
- ✓ Salt and black pepper to the taste
- ✓ 2 red potatoes, cut into medium wedges
- ✓ ½ teaspoon garlic powder
- ✓ ½ teaspoon red pepper flakes
- ✓ 1 teaspoon parsley, dried
- ✓ A drizzle of balsamic vinegar

DIRECTIONS:

- ⏱ In your air fryer's pan, mix pork with potatoes, salt, pepper, garlic powder, pepper flakes, parsley and vinegar, toss and cook at 390 degrees F for 25 minutes.
- ⏱ Slice pork, divide it and potatoes on plates and serve for lunch.
- ⏱ Enjoy!

Nutrition: calories 400, fat 15, fiber 7, carbs 27, protein 20

Turkey Cakes

Preparation time: 10 minutes Cooking time: 10 minutes Servings: 4

INGREDIENTS:

- ✓ 6 mushrooms, chopped
- ✓ 1 teaspoon garlic powder
- ✓ 1 teaspoon onion powder
- ✓ Salt and black pepper to the taste
- ✓ 1 and ¼ pounds turkey meat, ground
- ✓ Cooking spray
- ✓ Tomato sauce for serving

DIRECTIONS:

- ⏱ In your blender, mix mushrooms with salt and pepper, pulse well and transfer to a bowl.
- ⏱ Add turkey, onion powder, garlic powder, salt and pepper, stir and shape cakes out of this mix.
- ⏱ Spray them with cooking spray, transfer them to your air fryer and cook at 320 degrees F for 10 minutes.
- ⏱ Serve them with tomato sauce on the side and a tasty side salad.
- ⏱ Enjoy!

Nutrition: calories 202, fat 6, fiber 3, carbs 17, protein 10

Cheese Ravioli and Marinara Sauce

Preparation time: 10 minutes Cooking time: 8 minutes Servings: 6

INGREDIENTS:

- ✓ 20 ounces cheese ravioli
- ✓ 10 ounces marinara sauce
- ✓ 1 tablespoon olive oil
- ✓ 1 cup buttermilk
- ✓ 2 cups bread crumbs
- ✓ ¼ cup parmesan, grated

DIRECTIONS:

- ⏱ Put buttermilk in a bowl and breadcrumbs in another bowl.
- ⏱ Dip ravioli in buttermilk, then in breadcrumbs and place them in your air fryer on a baking sheet.
- ⏱ Drizzle olive oil over them, cook at 400 degrees F for 5 minutes, divide them on plates, sprinkle parmesan on top and serve for lunch
- ⏱ Enjoy!

Nutrition: calories 270, fat 12, fiber 6, carbs 30, protein 15

Beef Stew

Preparation time: 10 minutes Cooking time: 20 minutes Servings: 4

INGREDIENTS:

- ✓ **2 pounds beef meat, cut into medium chunks**
- ✓ **2 carrots, chopped**
- ✓ **4 potatoes, chopped**
- ✓ **Salt and black pepper to the taste**
- ✓ **1 quart veggie stock**
- ✓ **½ teaspoon smoked paprika**
- ✓ **A handful thyme, chopped**

DIRECTIONS:

- In a dish that fits your air fryer, mix beef with carrots, potatoes, stock, salt, pepper, paprika and thyme, stir, place in air fryer's basket and cook at 375 degrees F for 20 minutes.
- Divide into bowls and serve right away for lunch.
- Enjoy!

Nutrition: calories 260, fat 5, fiber 8, carbs 20, protein 22

Meatballs Sandwich

Preparation time: 10 minutes Cooking time: 22 minutes Servings: 4

INGREDIENTS:

- ✓ **3 baguettes, sliced more than halfway through**
- ✓ **14 ounces beef, ground**
- ✓ **7 ounces tomato sauce**
- ✓ **1 small onion, chopped**
- ✓ **1 egg, whisked**
- ✓ **1 tablespoon bread crumbs**
- ✓ **2 tablespoons cheddar cheese, grated**
- ✓ **1 tablespoon oregano, chopped**
- ✓ **1 tablespoon olive oil**
- ✓ **Salt and black pepper to the taste**
- ✓ **1 teaspoon thyme, dried**
- ✓ **1 teaspoon basil, dried**

DIRECTIONS:

- In a bowl, combine meat with salt, pepper, onion, breadcrumbs, egg, cheese, oregano, thyme and basil, stir, shape medium meatballs and add them to your air fryer after you've greased it with the oil.
- Cook them at 375 degrees F for 12 minutes, flipping them halfway.
- Add tomato sauce, cook meatballs for 10 minutes more and arrange them on sliced baguettes.

- Serve them right away.
- Enjoy!

Nutrition: calories 380, fat 5, fiber 6, carbs 34, protein 20

Bacon Pudding

Preparation time: 10 minutes Cooking time: 30 minutes Servings: 6

INGREDIENTS:

- ✓ **4 bacon strips, cooked and chopped**
- ✓ **1 tablespoon butter, soft**
- ✓ **2 cups corn**
- ✓ **1 yellow onion, chopped**
- ✓ **¼ cup celery, chopped**
- ✓ **½ cup red bell pepper, chopped**
- ✓ **1 teaspoon thyme, chopped**
- ✓ **2 teaspoons garlic, minced**
- ✓ **Salt and black pepper to the taste**
- ✓ **½ cup heavy cream**
- ✓ **1 and ½ cups milk**
- ✓ **3 eggs, whisked**
- ✓ **3 cups bread, cubed**
- ✓ **4 tablespoons parmesan, grated**
- ✓ **Cooking spray**

DIRECTIONS:

- Grease your air fryer's pan with coking spray.
- In a bowl, mix bacon with butter, corn, onion, bell pepper, celery, thyme, garlic, salt, pepper, milk, heavy cream, eggs and bread cubes, toss, pour into greased pan and sprinkle cheese all over
- Add this to your preheated air fryer at 320 degrees and cook for 30 minutes.
- Divide among plates and serve warm for a quick lunch.
- Enjoy!

Nutrition: calories 276, fat 10, fiber 2, carbs 20, protein 10

Special Lunch Seafood Stew

Preparation time: 10 minutes Cooking time: 20 minutes Servings: 4

INGREDIENTS:

- ✓ **5 ounces white rice**
- ✓ **2 ounces peas**
- ✓ **1 red bell pepper, chopped**

- ✓ 14 ounces white wine
- ✓ 3 ounces water
- ✓ 2 ounces squid pieces
- ✓ 7 ounces mussels
- ✓ 3 ounces sea bass fillet, skinless, boneless and chopped
- ✓ 6 scallops
- ✓ 3.5 ounces clams
- ✓ 4 shrimp
- ✓ 4 crayfish
- ✓ Salt and black pepper to the taste
- ✓ 1 tablespoon olive oil

DIRECTIONS:

- In your air fryer's pan, mix sea bass with shrimp, mussels, scallops, crayfish, clams and squid.
- Add the oil, salt and pepper and toss to coat.
- In a bowl, mix peas salt, pepper, bell pepper and rice and stir.
- Add this over seafood, also add whine and water, place pan in your air fryer and cook at 400 degrees F for 20 minutes, stirring halfway.
- Divide into bowls and serve for lunch.
- Enjoy!

Nutrition: calories 300, fat 12, fiber 2, carbs 23, protein 25

Air Fried Thai Salad

Preparation time: 10 minutes Cooking time: 5 minutes Servings: 4

INGREDIENTS:

- ✓ 1 cup carrots, grated
- ✓ 1 cup red cabbage, shredded
- ✓ A pinch of salt and black pepper
- ✓ A handful cilantro, chopped
- ✓ 1 small cucumber, chopped
- ✓ Juice from 1 lime
- ✓ 2 teaspoons red curry paste
- ✓ 12 big shrimp, cooked, peeled and deveined

DIRECTIONS:

- In a pan that fits your, mix cabbage with carrots, cucumber and shrimp, toss, introduce in your air fryer and cook at 360 degrees F for 5 minutes.
- Add salt, pepper, cilantro, lime juice and red curry paste, toss again,

- divide among plates and serve right away.
- Enjoy!

Nutrition: calories 172, fat 5, fiber 7, carbs 8, protein 5

Sweet Potato Lunch Casserole

Preparation time: 10 minutes Cooking time: 50 minutes Servings: 6

INGREDIENTS:

- ✓ 3 big sweet potatoes, pricked with a fork
- ✓ 1 cup chicken stock
- ✓ Salt and black pepper to the taste
- ✓ A pinch of cayenne pepper
- ✓ ¼ teaspoon nutmeg, ground
- ✓ 1/3 cup coconut cream

DIRECTIONS:

- Place sweet potatoes in your air fryer, cook them at 350 degrees F for 40 minutes, cool them down, peel, roughly chop and transfer to a pan that fits your air fryer.
- Add stock, salt, pepper, cayenne and coconut cream, toss, introduce in your air fryer and cook at 360 degrees F for 10 minutes more.
- Divide casserole into bowls and serve.
- Enjoy!

Nutrition: calories 245, fat 4, fiber 5, carbs 10, protein 6

Zucchini Casserole

Preparation time: 10 minutes Cooking time: 16 minutes Servings: 8

INGREDIENTS:

- ✓ 1 cup veggie stock
- ✓ 2 tablespoons olive oil
- ✓ 2 sweet potatoes, peeled and cut into medium wedges
- ✓ 8 zucchinis, cut into medium wedges
- ✓ 2 yellow onions, chopped
- ✓ 1 cup coconut milk
- ✓ Salt and black pepper to the taste
- ✓ 1 tablespoon soy sauce
- ✓ ¼ teaspoon thyme, dried
- ✓ ¼ teaspoon rosemary, dried
- ✓ 4 tablespoons dill, chopped
- ✓ ½ teaspoon basil, chopped

DIRECTIONS:

- Heat up a pan that fits your air fryer with the oil over medium heat, add onion, stir and cook for 2 minutes.
- Add zucchinis, thyme, rosemary, basil, potato, salt, pepper, stock, milk, soy sauce and dill, stir, introduce in your air fryer, cook at 360 degrees F for 14 minutes, divide among plates and serve right away.
- Enjoy!

Nutrition: calories 133, fat 3, fiber 4, carbs 10, protein 5

Coconut and Chicken Casserole

Preparation time: 10 minutes Cooking time: 25 minutes Servings: 4

INGREDIENTS:

- 4 lime leaves, torn
- 1 cup veggie stock
- 1 lemongrass stalk, chopped
- 1 inch piece, grated
- 1 pound chicken breast, skinless, boneless and cut into thin strips
- 8 ounces mushrooms, chopped
- 4 Thai chilies, chopped
- 4 tablespoons fish sauce
- 6 ounces coconut milk
- ¼ cup lime juice
- ¼ cup cilantro, chopped
- Salt and black pepper to the taste

DIRECTIONS:

- Put stock into a pan that fits your air fryer, bring to a simmer over medium heat, add lemongrass, ginger and lime leaves, stir and cook for 10 minutes.
- Strain soup, return to pan, add chicken, mushrooms, milk, chilies, fish sauce, lime juice, cilantro, salt and pepper, stir, introduce in your air fryer and cook at 360 degrees F for 15 minutes.
- Divide into bowls and serve.
- Enjoy!

Nutrition: calories 150, fat 4, fiber 4, carbs 6, protein 7

Turkey Burgers

Preparation time: 10 minutes Cooking time: 8 minutes Servings: 4

INGREDIENTS:

- 1 pound turkey meat, ground
- 1 shallot, minced

- ✓ A drizzle of olive oil
- ✓ 1 small jalapeno pepper, minced
- ✓ 2 teaspoons lime juice
- ✓ Zest from 1 lime, grated
- ✓ Salt and black pepper to the taste
- ✓ 1 teaspoon cumin, ground
- ✓ 1 teaspoon sweet paprika
- ✓ Guacamole for serving

DIRECTIONS:

- In a bowl, mix turkey meat with salt, pepper, cumin, paprika, shallot, jalapeno, lime juice and zest, stir well, shape burgers from this mix, drizzle the oil over them, introduce in preheated air fryer and cook them at 370 degrees F for 8 minutes on each side.
- Divide among plates and serve with guacamole on top.
- Enjoy!

Nutrition: calories 200, fat 12, fiber 0, carbs 0, protein 12

Salmon and Asparagus

Preparation time: 10 minutes Cooking time: 23 minutes Servings: 4

INGREDIENTS:

- ✓ 1 pound asparagus, trimmed
- ✓ 1 tablespoon olive oil
- ✓ A pinch of sweet paprika
- ✓ Salt and black pepper to the taste
- ✓ A pinch of garlic powder
- ✓ A pinch of cayenne pepper
- ✓ 1 red bell pepper, cut into halves
- ✓ 4 ounces smoked salmon

DIRECTIONS:

- Put asparagus spears and bell pepper on a lined baking sheet that fits your air fryer, add salt, pepper, garlic powder, paprika, olive oil, cayenne pepper, toss to coat, introduce in the fryer, cook at 390 degrees F for 8 minutes, flip and cook for 8 minutes more.
- Add salmon, cook for 5 minutes, more, divide everything on plates and serve.
- Enjoy!

Nutrition: calories 90, fat 1, fiber 1, carbs 1.2, protein 4

Easy Chicken Lunch

Preparation time: 10 minutes Cooking time: 20 minutes Servings: 6

INGREDIENTS:

- ✓ 1 bunch kale, chopped
- ✓ Salt and black pepper to the taste
- ✓ ¼ cup chicken stock
- ✓ 1 cup chicken, shredded
- ✓ 3 carrots, chopped
- ✓ 1 cup shiitake mushrooms, roughly sliced

DIRECTIONS:

- ⏱ In a blender, mix stock with kale, pulse a few times and pour into a pan that fits your air fryer.
- ⏱ Add chicken, mushrooms, carrots, salt and pepper to the taste, toss, introduce in your air fryer and cook at 350 degrees F for 18 minutes.
- ⏱ Enjoy!

Nutrition: calories 180, fat 7, fiber 2, carbs 10, protein 5

Chicken and Corn Casserole

Preparation time: 10 minutes Cooking time: 30 minutes Servings: 6

INGREDIENTS:

- ✓ 1 cup clean chicken stock
- ✓ 2 teaspoons garlic powder
- ✓ Salt and black pepper to the taste
- ✓ 6 ounces canned coconut milk
- ✓ 1 and ½ cups green lentils
- ✓ 2 pounds chicken breasts, skinless, boneless and cubed 1/3 cup cilantro, chopped
- ✓ 3 cups corn
- ✓ 3 handfuls spinach
- ✓ 3 green onions, chopped

DIRECTIONS:

- ⏱ In a pan that fits your air fryer, mix stock with coconut milk, salt, pepper, garlic powder, chicken and lentils.
- ⏱ Add corn, green onions, cilantro and spinach, stir well, introduce in your air fryer and cook at 350 degrees F for 30 minutes.
- ⏱ Enjoy!

Nutrition: calories 345, fat 12, fiber 10, carbs 20, protein 44

Chicken and Zucchini Lunch Mix

Preparation time: 10 minutes Cooking time: 20 minutes Servings: 4

INGREDIENTS:

- ✓ 4 zucchinis, cut with a spiralizer
- ✓ 1 pound chicken breasts, skinless, boneless and cubed
- ✓ 2 garlic cloves, minced
- ✓ 1 teaspoon olive oil
- ✓ Salt and black pepper to the taste
- ✓ 2 cups cherry tomatoes, halved
- ✓ ½ cup almonds, chopped

For the pesto:

- ✓ 2 cups basil
- ✓ 2 cups kale, chopped
- ✓ 1 tablespoon lemon juice
- ✓ 1 garlic clove
- ✓ ¾ cup pine nuts
- ✓ ½ cup olive oil
- ✓ A pinch of salt

DIRECTIONS:

- ⏱ In your food processor, mix basil with kale, lemon juice, garlic, pine nuts, oil and a pinch of salt, pulse really well and leave aside.
- ⏱ Heat up a pan that fits your air fryer with the oil over medium heat, add garlic, stir and cook for 1 minute.
- ⏱ Add chicken, salt, pepper, stir, almonds, zucchini noodles, garlic, cherry tomatoes and the pesto you've made at the beginning, stir gently, introduce in preheated air fryer and cook at 360 degrees F for 17 minutes.
- ⏱ Divide among plates and serve for lunch.
- ⏱ Enjoy!

Nutrition: calories 344, fat 8, fiber 7, carbs 12, protein 16

Chicken, Beans, Corn and Quinoa Casserole

Preparation time: 10 minutes Cooking time: 30 minutes Servings: 8

INGREDIENTS:

- ✓ 1 cup quinoa, already cooked
- ✓ 3 cups chicken breast, cooked and shredded

- 14 ounces canned black beans
- 12 ounces corn
- ½ cup cilantro, chopped
- 6 kale leaves, chopped
- ½ cup green onions, chopped
- 1 cup clean tomato sauce
- 1 cup clean salsa
- 2 teaspoons chili powder
- 2 teaspoons cumin, ground
- 3 cups mozzarella cheese, shredded
- 1 tablespoon garlic powder
- Cooking spray
- 2 jalapeno peppers, chopped

DIRECTIONS:

- Spray a baking dish that fits your air fryer with cooking spray, add quinoa, chicken, black beans, corn, cilantro, kale, green onions, tomato sauce, salsa, chili powder, cumin, garlic powder, jalapenos and mozzarella, toss, introduce in your fryer and cook at 350 degrees F for 17 minutes.
- Slice and serve warm for lunch.
- Enjoy!

Nutrition: calories 365, fat 12, fiber 6, carbs 22, protein 26

Air Fryer Side Dish Recipes

Garlic Potatoes

Preparation time: 10 minutes Cooking time: 20 minutes Servings: 6

INGREDIENTS:

- ✓ **2 tablespoons parsley, chopped**
- ✓ **5 garlic cloves, minced**
- ✓ **½ teaspoon basil, dried**
- ✓ **½ teaspoon oregano, dried**
- ✓ **3 pounds red potatoes, halved**
- ✓ **1 teaspoon thyme, dried**
- ✓ **2 tablespoons olive oil**
- ✓ **Salt and black pepper to the taste**
- ✓ **2 tablespoons butter**
- ✓ **1/3 cup parmesan, grated**

DIRECTIONS:

- In a bowl, mix potato halves with parsley, garlic, basil, oregano, thyme, salt, pepper, oil and butter, toss really well and transfer to your air fryer's basket.
- Cover and cook at 400 degrees F for 20 minutes, flipping them once.
- Sprinkle parmesan on top, divide potatoes on plates and serve as a side dish.
- Enjoy!

Nutrition: calories 162, fat 5, fiber 5, carbs 7, protein 5

Eggplant Side Dish

Preparation time: 10 minutes Cooking time: 10 minutes Servings: 4

INGREDIENTS:

- ✓ **8 baby eggplants, scooped in the center and pulp reserved Salt and black pepper to the taste A pinch of oregano, dried**
- ✓ **1 green bell pepper, chopped**
- ✓ **1 tablespoon tomato paste**
- ✓ **1 bunch coriander, chopped**
- ✓ **½ teaspoon garlic powder**
- ✓ **1 tablespoon olive oil**
- ✓ **1 yellow onion, chopped**
- ✓ **1 tomato chopped**

DIRECTIONS:

- Heat up a pan with the oil over medium heat, add onion, stir and cook for 1 minute.
- Add salt, pepper, eggplant pulp, oregano, green bell pepper, tomato paste, garlic power, coriander and tomato, stir, cook for 1-2 minutes more, take off heat and cool down.
- Stuff eggplants with this mix, place them in your air fryer's basket and cook at 360 degrees F for 8 minutes.
- Divide eggplants on plates and serve them as a side dish.
- Enjoy!

Nutrition: calories 200, fat 3, fiber 7, carbs 12, protein 4

Mushrooms and Sour Cream

Preparation time: 10 minutes Cooking time: 10 minutes Servings: 6

INGREDIENTS:

- ✓ **2 bacon strips, chopped**
- ✓ **1 yellow onion, chopped**
- ✓ **1 green bell pepper, chopped**
- ✓ **24 mushrooms, stems removed**
- ✓ **1 carrot, grated**
- ✓ **½ cup sour cream**
- ✓ **1 cup cheddar cheese, grated**
- ✓ **Salt and black pepper to the taste**

DIRECTIONS:

- Heat up a pan over medium high heat, add bacon, onion, bell pepper and carrot, stir and cook for 1 minute.
- Add salt, pepper and sour cream, stir cook for 1 minute more, take off heat and cool down.
- Stuff mushrooms with this mix, sprinkle cheese on top and cook at 360 degrees F for 8 minutes.
- Divide among plates and serve as a side dish.

Enjoy!

Nutrition: calories 211, fat 4, fiber 7, carbs 8, protein 3

Eggplant Fries

Preparation time: 10 minutes Cooking time: 5 minutes Servings: 4

INGREDIENTS:

- ✓ **Cooking spray**
- ✓ **1 eggplant, peeled and cut into medium fries**
- ✓ **2 tablespoons milk**
- ✓ **1 egg, whisked**

- ✓ 2 cups panko bread crumbs
- ✓ ½ cup Italian cheese, shredded
- ✓ A pinch of salt and black pepper to the taste

DIRECTIONS:

- In a bowl, mix egg with milk, salt and pepper and whisk well.
- In another bowl, mix panko with cheese and stir.
- Dip eggplant fries in egg mix, then coat in panko mix, place them in your air fryer greased with cooking spray and cook at 400 degrees F for 5 minutes.
- Divide among plates and serve as a side dish.
- Enjoy!

Nutrition: calories 162, fat 5, fiber 5, carbs 7, protein 6

Fried Tomatoes

Preparation time: 10 minutes Cooking time: 5 minutes Servings: 4

INGREDIENTS:

- ✓ 2 green tomatoes, sliced
- ✓ Salt and black pepper to the taste
- ✓ ½ cup flour
- ✓ 1 cup buttermilk
- ✓ 1 cup panko bread crumbs
- ✓ ½ tablespoon Creole seasoning
- ✓ Cooking spray

DIRECTIONS:

- Season tomato slices with salt and pepper.
- Put flour in a bowl, buttermilk in another and panko crumbs and Creole seasoning in a third one.
- Dredge tomato slices in flour, then in buttermilk and panko bread crumbs, place them in your air fryer's basket greased with cooking spray and cook them at 400 degrees F for 5 minutes.
- Divide among plates and serve as a side dish.
- Enjoy!

Nutrition: calories 124, fat 5, fiber 7, carbs 9, protein 4

Cauliflower Cakes

Preparation time: 10 minutes Cooking time: 10 minutes Servings: 6

INGREDIENTS:

- ✓ 3 and ½ cups cauliflower rice
- ✓ 2 eggs

- ✓ ¼ cup white flour
- ✓ ½ cup parmesan, grated
- ✓ Salt and black pepper to the taste
- ✓ Cooking spray

DIRECTIONS:

- In a bowl, mix cauliflower rice with salt and pepper, stir and squeeze excess water.
- Transfer cauliflower to another bowl, add eggs, salt, pepper, flour and parmesan, stir really well and shape your cakes.
- Grease your air fryer with cooking spray, heat it up at 400 degrees, add cauliflower cakes and cook them for 10 minutes flipping them halfway.
- Divide cakes on plates and serve as a side dish.

Enjoy!

Nutrition: calories 125, fat 2, fiber 6, carbs 8, protein 3

Creamy Brussels Sprouts

Preparation time: 10 minutes Cooking time: 25 minutes Servings: 8

INGREDIENTS:

- ✓ 3 pounds Brussels sprouts, halved
- ✓ A drizzle of olive oil
- ✓ 1 pound bacon, chopped
- ✓ Salt and black pepper to the taste
- ✓ 4 tablespoons butter
- ✓ 3 shallots, chopped
- ✓ 1 cup milk
- ✓ 2 cups heavy cream
- ✓ ¼ teaspoon nutmeg, ground
- ✓ 3 tablespoons prepared horseradish

DIRECTIONS:

- Preheated you air fryer at 370 degrees F, add oil, bacon, salt and pepper and Brussels sprouts and toss.
- Add butter, shallots, heavy cream, milk, nutmeg and horseradish, toss again and cook for 25 minutes.
- Divide among plates and serve as a side dish.
- Enjoy!

Nutrition: calories 214, fat 5, fiber 8, carbs 12, protein 5

Cheddar Biscuits

Preparation time: 10 minutes Cooking time: 20 minutes Servings: 8

INGREDIENTS:

- ✓ 2 and 1/3 cup self-rising flour

- ✓ ½ cup butter+ 1 tablespoon, melted
- ✓ 2 tablespoons sugar
- ✓ ½ cup cheddar cheese, grated
- ✓ 1 and 1/3 cup buttermilk
- ✓ 1 cup flour

DIRECTIONS:

- In a bowl, mix self-rising flour with ½ cup butter, sugar, cheddar cheese and buttermilk and stir until you obtain a dough.
- Spread 1 cup flour on a working surface, roll dough, flatten it, cut 8 circles with a cookie cutter and coat them with flour.
- Line your air fryer's basket with tin foil, add biscuits, brush them with melted butter and cook them at 380 degrees F for 20 minutes.
- Divide among plates and serve as a side.
- Enjoy!

Nutrition: calories 221, fat 3, fiber 8, carbs 12, protein 4

Zucchini Fries

Preparation time: 10 minutes Cooking time: 12 minutes Servings: 4

INGREDIENTS:

- ✓ 1 zucchini, cut into medium sticks
- ✓ A drizzle of olive oil
- ✓ Salt and black pepper to the taste
- ✓ 2 eggs, whisked
- ✓ 1 cup bread crumbs
- ✓ ½ cup flour

DIRECTIONS:

- Put flour in a bowl and mix with salt and pepper and stir.
- Put breadcrumbs in another bowl.
- In a third bowl mix eggs with a pinch of salt and pepper.
- Dredge zucchini fries in flour, then in eggs and in bread crumbs at the end.
- Grease your air fryer with some olive oil, heat up at 400 degrees F, add zucchini fries and cook them for 12 minutes.
- Serve them as a side dish.
- Enjoy!

Nutrition: calories 172, fat 3, fiber 3, carbs 7, protein 3

Herbed Tomatoes

Preparation time: 10 minutes Cooking time: 15 minutes Servings: 4

INGREDIENTS:

- ✓ 4 big tomatoes, halved and insides scooped out Salt and black pepper to the taste
- ✓ 1 tablespoon olive oil
- ✓ 2 garlic cloves, minced
- ✓ ½ teaspoon thyme, chopped

DIRECTIONS:

- In your air fryer, mix tomatoes with salt, pepper, oil, garlic and thyme, toss and cook at 390 degrees F for 15 minutes.
- Divide among plates and serve them as a side dish.
- Enjoy!

Nutrition: calories 112, fat 1, fiber 3, carbs 4, protein 4

Roasted Peppers

Preparation time: 10 minutes Cooking time: 20 minutes Servings: 4

INGREDIENTS:

- ✓ 1 tablespoon sweet paprika
- ✓ 1 tablespoon olive oil
- ✓ 4 red bell peppers, cut into medium strips
- ✓ 4 green bell peppers, cut into medium strips
- ✓ 4 yellow bell peppers, cut into medium strips
- ✓ 1 yellow onion, chopped
- ✓ Salt and black pepper to the taste

DIRECTIONS:

- In your air fryer, mix red bell peppers with green and yellow ones.
- Add paprika, oil, onion, salt and pepper, toss and cook at 350 degrees F for 20 minutes.
- Divide among plates and serve as a side dish.
- Enjoy!

Nutrition: calories 142, fat 4, fiber 4, carbs 7, protein 4

Creamy Endives

Preparation time: 10 minutes Cooking time: 10 minutes Servings: 6

INGREDIENTS:

- ✓ 6 endives, trimmed and halved

- ✓ **1 teaspoon garlic powder**
- ✓ **½ cup Greek yogurt**
- ✓ **½ teaspoon curry powder**
- ✓ **Salt and black pepper to the taste**
- ✓ **3 tablespoons lemon juice**

DIRECTIONS:

- ⏱ In a bowl, mix endives with garlic powder, yogurt, curry powder, salt, pepper and lemon juice, toss, leave aside for 10 minutes and transfer to your preheated air fryer at 350 degrees F.
- ⏱ Cook endives for 10 minutes, divide them on plates and serve as a side dish.
- ⏱ Enjoy!

Nutrition: calories 100, fat 2, fiber 2, carbs 7, protein 4

Delicious Roasted Carrots

Preparation time: 10 minutes Cooking time: 20 minutes Servings: 4

INGREDIENTS:

- ✓ **1 pound baby carrots**
- ✓ **2 teaspoons olive oil**
- ✓ **1 teaspoon herbs de Provence**
- ✓ **4 tablespoons orange juice**

DIRECTIONS:

- ⏱ In your air fryer's basket, mix carrots with herbs de Provence, oil and orange juice, toss and cook at 320 degrees F for 20 minutes.
- ⏱ Divide among plates and serve as a side dish.
- ⏱ Enjoy!

Nutrition: calories 112, fat 2, fiber 3, carbs 4, protein 3

Potato Wedges

Preparation time: 10 minutes Cooking time: 25 minutes Servings: 4

INGREDIENTS:

- ✓ **2 potatoes, cut into wedges**
- ✓ **1 tablespoon olive oil**
- ✓ **Salt and black pepper to the taste**
- ✓ **3 tablespoons sour cream**
- ✓ **2 tablespoons sweet chili sauce**

DIRECTIONS:

- ⏱ In a bowl, mix potato wedges with oil, salt and pepper, toss well, add to air fryer's basket and cook at 360 degrees F for 25 minutes, flipping them once.

- ⏱ Divide potato wedges on plates, drizzle sour cream and chili sauce all over and serve them as a side dish.
- ⏱ Enjoy!

Nutrition: calories 171, fat 8, fiber 9, carbs 18, protein 7

Mushroom Side Dish

Preparation time: 10 minutes Cooking time: 8 minutes Servings: 4

INGREDIENTS:

- ✓ **10 button mushrooms, stems removed**
- ✓ **1 tablespoon Italian seasoning**
- ✓ **Salt and black pepper to the taste**
- ✓ **2 tablespoons cheddar cheese, grated**
- ✓ **1 tablespoon olive oil**
- ✓ **2 tablespoons mozzarella, grated**
- ✓ **1 tablespoon dill, chopped**

DIRECTIONS:

- ⏱ In a bowl, mix mushrooms with Italian seasoning, salt, pepper, oil and dill and rub well.
- ⏱ Arrange mushrooms in your air fryer's basket, sprinkle mozzarella and cheddar in each and cook them at 360 degrees F for 8 minutes.
- ⏱ Divide them on plates and serve them as a side dish.
- ⏱ Enjoy!

Nutrition: calories 241, fat 7, fiber 8, carbs 14, protein 6

Sweet Potato Fries

Preparation time: 10 minutes Cooking time: 20 minutes Servings: 2

INGREDIENTS:

- ✓ **2 sweet potatoes, peeled and cut into medium fries**
  Salt and black pepper to the taste
- ✓ **2 tablespoons olive oil**
- ✓ **½ teaspoon curry powder**
- ✓ **¼ teaspoon coriander, ground**
- ✓ **¼ cup ketchup**
- ✓ **2 tablespoons mayonnaise**
- ✓ **½ teaspoon cumin, ground**
- ✓ **A pinch of ginger powder**
- ✓ **A pinch of cinnamon powder**

DIRECTIONS:

- ⏱ In your air fryer's basket, mix sweet potato fries with salt, pepper, coriander, curry powder and oil, toss

well and cook at 370 degrees F for 20 minutes, flipping them once.
- ⏲ Meanwhile, in a bowl, mix ketchup with mayo, cumin, ginger and cinnamon and whisk well.
- ⏲ Divide fries on plates, drizzle ketchup mix over them and serve as a side dish.
- ⏲ Enjoy!

Nutrition: calories 200, fat 5, fiber 8, carbs 9, protein 7

Toasted Seasoned Nuts

Preparation: 5 minutes Cooking time: 50 minutes Servings: 3

INGREDIENTS:

- ✓ ¼ teaspoon garlic cloves, ground
- ✓ ½ pound of cashews
- ✓ 4 tablespoons of sugar
- ✓ 8 ounces of pecan halves
- ✓ 1 egg white, whisked
- ✓ 1 teaspoon of salt
- ✓ ½ teaspoon of cinnamon
- ✓ ¼ teaspoon of mixed spice
- ✓ ¼ teaspoon of cayenne pepper
- ✓ 1 cup of almonds

DIRECTIONS:

- ⏲ Mix the sugar, garlic, mixed spice, pepper, salt, cinnamon and egg together in a bowl.
- ⏲ Heat your Air Fryer to 300°F.
- ⏲ Put the cashews, almonds and pecan, into the egg mixture and toss.
- ⏲ Coat the fryer basket with oil using a brush and pour half the nut mixture on it. Toast for 25 minutes until crunchy, stirring the nuts at intervals. Do same with the second batch of nuts.
- ⏲ Store in a sealed jar if not eaten immediately.

Nacho Coated Prawns

Preparation: 30 minutes Cooking time: 8 minutes Servings: 3-4

INGREDIENTS:

- ✓ 9 ounces of nacho chips
- ✓ 1 egg, whisked
- ✓ 18 medium sized prawns

DIRECTIONS:

- ⏲ Remove the shell and veins from the prawns, wash thoroughly and wipe dry.

- ⏲ Grind the chips in a bowl until pieces are as that of breadcrumbs.
- ⏲ Dip each prawn into the egg and then coat with the chip crumbs.
- ⏲ Heat the air fryer to 356°F.
- ⏲ Put the prawns into the air fryer and cook for 8 minutes. Serve with salsa or sour cream.

Cheesy Mustard And Ham Rounds

Preparation: 35 minutes Cooking time: 10 minutes Servings: 6

INGREDIENTS:

- ✓ 2 cups of Gruyere cheese, grated
- ✓ 6 slices of ham
- ✓ 1 tablespoon of mustard
- ✓ 1 sheet of pre-rolled puff pastry

DIRECTIONS:

- ⏲ Cover your work bench with flour and put the pastry on it.
- ⏲ Add the ham, mustard and cheese evenly on the pastry and roll up beginning from the shorter edge.
- ⏲ Cover with cling film and place in the freezer until firm for 30 minutes. Remove, and slice into 1cm thick small circles.
- ⏲ Heat your Air Fryer to 370°F and cook the rounds in it until golden brown for 10 minutes.

Grilled Cheese Delight

Preparation: 10 minutes Cooking time: 5 minutes Servings: 2

INGREDIENTS:

- ✓ 4 slices white bread
- ✓ ¼ cup butter, melted
- ✓ ½ cup sharp cheddar cheese

DIRECTIONS:

- ⏲ Preheat the Air Fryer to 360°F. Place the butter and cheese in two separate bowls.
- ⏲ Brush the butter on both sides of bread. Place the cheese on 2 of the 4 bread pieces.
- ⏲ Put together the grilled cheese and add to the Air Fryer cooking basket.
- ⏲ Cook until the cheese has melted and is golden brown or for 5 to 7 minutes.

Roti Prata Mini Sausage Rolls

Preparation: 5 minutes Cooking time: 15 minutes Servings: 4

INGREDIENTS:

- ✓ 1 packet of Roti prata

- ✓ **10 mini beef sausage**

DIRECTIONS:

- ⏱ Slice the prata into triangles. Roll each sausage in a prata triangle until all are well wrapped.
- ⏱ Heat your Air Fryer to 356°F and place the rolls in the fryer basket. Bake them for 15 minutes until crispy, turning the rolls halfway through.

Filo Covered Apple Pie

Preparation: 20 minutes Cooking time: 8 minutes Servings: 10

INGREDIENTS:

- ✓ **3 large apples, finely chopped**
- ✓ **6 teaspoons of sugar**
- ✓ **6 ounces of melted butter**
- ✓ **10 sheets of filo pastry**
- ✓ **2 teaspoons of cinnamon**
- ✓ **2 teaspoons of flour**
- ✓ **½ teaspoon cloves, ground**
- ✓ **½ teaspoon nutmeg, ground**
- ✓ **3 teaspoons of lemon juice**

DIRECTIONS:

- ⏱ Mix the apples, flour, lemon juice, cloves, cinnamon, nutmeg and sugar together in a bowl.
- ⏱ Place the filo pastry on a clean surface, unroll and brush gently with butter.
- ⏱ Spoon some apple filling and place on the filo sheets about 2" away from the base. Fold the base of the sheet and then a third of the length over the filling. Roll-up the entire filling with the filo sheet to form a triangle shape, brushing the edges with butter.
- ⏱ Coat all sides of the filo triangles with the melted butter and sprinkle some sugar on top.
- ⏱ Heat your Air Fryer to 320°F and cook the apple pies in batches for 8 minutes depending on the size. Remove when they appear light brown and crisp. Serve while warm.

Air Fried Cheeseburgers

Preparation: 5 minutes Cooking time: 10 minutes Servings: 2

INGREDIENTS:

- ✓ **2 slices of Cheddar Cheese**
- ✓ **2 bread rolls**
- ✓ **½ pound of ground beef**
- ✓ **½ teaspoon of black pepper, ground**

- ✓ **2 tablespoons of melted butter**
- ✓ **2 teaspoons of salt**

DIRECTIONS:

- ⏱ Heat your Air Fryer to 390°F.
- ⏱ Mold the ground beef to form 2 patties. Sprinkle with pepper and salt.
- ⏱ Slice the bread rolls from the center and place each patties in it.
- ⏱ Put the burgers in the cooking basket and cook for about 11 minutes. Add the cheddar cheese on the patties and cook for another 1 minute until the cheese melts.

Puff Pastry Banana Rolls

Preparation: 10 minutes Cooking time: 10 minutes Servings: 3

INGREDIENTS:

- ✓ **2 puff pastry sheets**
- ✓ **3 medium sized bananas, peeled**

DIRECTIONS:

- ⏱ Cut the pastry sheets into thin strips. Twine two strips to form a cord. Make as many cords as needed.
- ⏱ Wind the bananas with the cords until the entire banana is covered with the pastry.
- ⏱ Heat your airfyer to 356°F and cook the wrapped bananas for about 10 minutes until golden.

Curried Veggie Samosa

Preparation: 15 minutes Cooking time: 10 minutes Servings: 3

INGREDIENTS:

- ✓ **2 large potatoes, peeled, boiled in salted water and mashed**
- ✓ **3 sheets puff pastry**
- ✓ **1/2 cup onion, diced**
- ✓ **2 garlic cloves, minced**
- ✓ **2 tablespoons ginger, grated**
- ✓ **1/2 cup carrot, diced**
- ✓ **1/2 cup green peas**
- ✓ **1 teaspoon garam masala**
- ✓ **1 tablespoons curry powder Salt and pepper to taste**

DIRECTIONS

- Sauté the onion, carrots, garlic and ginger in a saucepan until tender and add to the mashed potatoes.
- Add the spices and the green peas, and salt and pepper to taste.
- Now cut the puff pastry sheets into quarters and then each of the quarters into a circular shape.
- Place two tablespoons of filling into each pastry circle and moisten edges with water. Fold the pastry in half and seal edges well using a fork.
- Preheat the Air Fryer to 390 degrees. Working in batches, fry samosas for 5 minutes each until golden brown and crispy

Crunchy Sweet Potato Sticks

Preparation: 5 minutes Cooking time: 10 minutes Servings: 1

INGREDIENTS:

- ✓ 1 medium sized sweet potato Salt to taste
- ✓ 1 teaspoon of coconut oil
- ✓ 1 tablespoon of aioli

DIRECTIONS:

- Heat your Air Fryer to 200°F.
- Cut the sweet potato into sticks and toss in the coconut oil.
- Place the potato sticks into the cooking basket and fry for 10 minutes until they turn crisp.
- Add the salt and serve with aioli.

Corn with Lime and Cheese

Preparation time: 10 minutes Cooking time: 15 minutes Servings: 2

INGREDIENTS:

- ✓ 2 corns on the cob, husks removed
- ✓ A drizzle of olive oil
- ✓ ½ cup feta cheese, grated
- ✓ 2 teaspoons sweet paprika
- ✓ Juice from 2 limes

DIRECTIONS:

- Rub corn with oil and paprika, place in your air fryer and cook at 400 degrees F for 15 minutes, flipping once.
- Divide corn on plates, sprinkle cheese on top, drizzle lime juice and serve as a side dish.
- Enjoy!

Nutrition: calories 200, fat 5, fiber 2, carbs 6, protein 6

Hasselback Potatoes

Preparation time: 10 minutes Cooking time: 20 minutes Servings: 2

INGREDIENTS:

- ✓ 2 potatoes, peeled and thinly sliced almost all the way horizontally
- ✓ 2 tablespoons olive oil
- ✓ 1 teaspoon garlic, minced
- ✓ Salt and black pepper to the taste
- ✓ ½ teaspoon oregano, dried
- ✓ ½ teaspoon basil, dried
- ✓ ½ teaspoon sweet paprika

DIRECTIONS:

- In a bowl, mix oil with garlic, salt, pepper, oregano, basil and paprika and whisk really well.
- Rub potatoes with this mix, place them in your air fryer's basket and fry them at 360 degrees F for 20 minutes.
- Divide them on plates and serve as a side dish.
- Enjoy!

Nutrition: calories 172, fat 6, fiber 6, carbs 9, protein 6

Brussels Sprouts Side Dish

Preparation time: 10 minutes Cooking time: 15 minutes Servings: 4

INGREDIENTS:

- ✓ 1 pound Brussels sprouts, trimmed and halved Salt and black pepper to the taste
- ✓ 6 teaspoons olive oil
- ✓ ½ teaspoon thyme, chopped
- ✓ ½ cup mayonnaise
- ✓ 2 tablespoons roasted garlic, crushed

DIRECTIONS:

- In your air fryer, mix Brussels sprouts with salt, pepper and oil, toss well and cook them at 390 degrees F for 15 minutes.
- Meanwhile, in a bowl, mix thyme with mayo and garlic and whisk well.
- Divide Brussels sprouts on plates, drizzle garlic sauce all over and serve as a side dish.
- Enjoy!

Nutrition: calories 172, fat 6, fiber 8, carbs 12, protein 6

Creamy Air Fried Potato Side Dish

Preparation time: 10 minutes Cooking time: 1 hour and 20 minutes

Servings: 2

INGREDIENTS:

- ✓ **1 big potato**
- ✓ **2 bacon strips, cooked and chopped**
- ✓ **1 teaspoon olive oil**
- ✓ **1/3 cup cheddar cheese, shredded**
- ✓ **1 tablespoon green onions, chopped**
- ✓ **Salt and black pepper to the taste**
- ✓ **1 tablespoon butter**
- ✓ **2 tablespoons heavy cream**

DIRECTIONS:

- ⏱ Rub potato with oil, season with salt and pepper, place in preheated air fryer and cook at 400 degrees F for 30 minutes.
- ⏱ Flip potato, cook for 30 minutes more, transfer to a cutting board, cool it down, slice in half lengthwise and scoop pulp in a bowl.
- ⏱ Add bacon, cheese, butter, heavy cream, green onions, salt and pepper, stir well and stuff potato skins with this mix.
- ⏱ Return potatoes to your air fryer and cook them at 400 degrees F for 20 minutes.
- ⏱ Divide among plates and serve as a side dish.
- ⏱ Enjoy!

Nutrition: calories 172, fat 5, fiber 7, carbs 9, protein 4

Green Beans Side Dish

Preparation time: 10 minutes Cooking time: 25 minutes Servings: 4

INGREDIENTS:

- ✓ **1 and ½ pounds green beans, trimmed and steamed for 2 minutes Salt and black pepper to the taste ½ pound shallots, chopped**
- ✓ **¼ cup almonds, toasted**
- ✓ **2 tablespoons olive oil**

DIRECTIONS:

- ⏱ In your air fryer's basket, mix green beans with salt, pepper, shallots, almonds and oil, toss well and cook at 400 degrees F for 25 minutes.
- ⏱ Divide among plates and serve as a side dish.
- ⏱ Enjoy!

Nutrition: calories 152, fat 3, fiber 6, carbs 7, protein 4

Roasted Pumpkin

Preparation time: 10 minutes Cooking time: 12 minutes Servings: 4

INGREDIENTS:

- ✓ **1 and ½ pound pumpkin, deseeded, sliced and roughly chopped**
- ✓ **3 garlic cloves, minced**
- ✓ **1 tablespoon olive oil**
- ✓ **A pinch of sea salt**
- ✓ **A pinch of brown sugar**
- ✓ **A pinch of nutmeg, ground**
- ✓ **A pinch of cinnamon powder**

DIRECTIONS:

- ⏱ In your air fryer's basket, mix pumpkin with garlic, oil, salt, brown sugar, cinnamon and nutmeg, toss well, cover and cook at 370 degrees F for 12 minutes.
- ⏱ Divide among plates and serve as a side dish.
- ⏱ Enjoy!

Nutrition: calories 200, fat 5, fiber 4, carbs 7, protein 4

Parmesan Mushrooms

Preparation time: 10 minutes Cooking time: 15 minutes Servings: 3

INGREDIENTS:

- ✓ **9 button mushroom caps**
- ✓ **3 cream cracker slices, crumbled**
- ✓ **1 egg white**
- ✓ **2 tablespoons parmesan, grated**
- ✓ **1 teaspoon Italian seasoning**
- ✓ **A pinch of salt and black pepper**
- ✓ **1 tablespoon butter, melted**

DIRECTIONS:

- ⏱ In a bowl, mix crackers with egg white, parmesan, Italian seasoning, butter, salt and pepper, stir well and stuff mushrooms with this mix.
- ⏱ Arrange mushrooms in your air fryer's basket and cook them at 360 degrees F for 15 minutes.
- ⏱ Divide among plates and serve as a side dish.
- ⏱ Enjoy!

Nutrition: calories 124, fat 4, fiber 4, carbs 7, protein 3

Vermouth Mushrooms

Preparation time: 10 minutes Cooking time: 25 minutes Servings: 4

INGREDIENTS:

- ✓ **1 tablespoon olive oil**
- ✓ **2 pounds white mushrooms**
- ✓ **2 tablespoons white vermouth**
- ✓ **2 teaspoons herbs de Provence**
- ✓ **2 garlic cloves, minced**

DIRECTIONS:

- In your air fryer, mix oil with mushrooms, herbs de Provence and garlic, toss and cook at 350 degrees F for 20 minutes.
- Add vermouth, toss and cook for 5 minutes more.
- Divide among plates and serve as a side dish.
- Enjoy!

Nutrition: calories 121, fat 2, fiber 5, carbs 7, protein 4

Roasted Parsnips

Preparation time: 10 minutes Cooking time: 40 minutes Servings: 6

INGREDIENTS:

- ✓ **2 pounds parsnips, peeled and cut into medium chunks**
- ✓ **2 tablespoons maple syrup**
- ✓ **1 tablespoon parsley flakes, dried**
- ✓ **1 tablespoon olive oil**

DIRECTIONS:

- Preheat your air fryer at 360 degrees F, add oil and heat it up as well.
- Add parsnips, parsley flakes and maple syrup, toss and cook them for 40 minutes.
- Divide among plates and serve as a side dish.
- Enjoy!

Nutrition: calories 124, fat 3, fiber 3, carbs 7, protein 4

Barley Risotto

Preparation time: 10 minutes Cooking time: 30 minutes Servings: 8

INGREDIENTS:

- ✓ **5 cups veggie stock**
- ✓ **3 tablespoons olive oil**
- ✓ **2 yellow onions, chopped**
- ✓ **2 garlic cloves, minced**
- ✓ **¾ pound barley**
- ✓ **3 ounces mushrooms, sliced**
- ✓ **2 ounces skim milk**

- ✓ **1 teaspoon thyme, dried**
- ✓ **1 teaspoon tarragon, dried**
- ✓ **Salt and black pepper to the taste**
- ✓ **2 pounds sweet potato, peeled and chopped**

DIRECTIONS:

- Put stock in a pot, add barley, stir, bring to a boil over medium heat and cook for 15 minutes.
- Heat up your air fryer at 350 degrees F, add oil and heat it up.
- Add barley, onions, garlic, mushrooms, milk, salt, pepper, tarragon and sweet potato, stir and cook for 15 minutes more.
- Divide among plates and serve as a side dish.
- Enjoy!

Nutrition: calories 124, fat 4, fiber 4, carbs 6, protein 4

Glazed Beets

Preparation time: 10 minutes Cooking time: 40 minutes Servings: 8

INGREDIENTS:

- ✓ **3 pounds small beets, trimmed**
- ✓ **4 tablespoons maple syrup**
- ✓ **1 tablespoon duck fat**

DIRECTIONS:

- Heat up your air fryer at 360 degrees F, add duck fat and heat it up.
- Add beets and maple syrup, toss and cook for 40 minutes.
- Divide among plates and serve as a side dish.
- Enjoy!

Nutrition: calories 121, fat 3, fiber 2, carbs 3, protein 4

Beer Risotto

Preparation time: 10 minutes Cooking time: 30 minutes Servings: 4

INGREDIENTS:

- ✓ **2 tablespoons olive oil**
- ✓ **2 yellow onions, chopped**
- ✓ **1 cup mushrooms, sliced**
- ✓ **1 teaspoon basil, dried**
- ✓ **1 teaspoon oregano, dried**
- ✓ **1 and ½ cups rice**
- ✓ **2 cups beer**
- ✓ **2 cups chicken stock**

- ✓ 1 tablespoon butter
- ✓ ½ cup parmesan, grated

DIRECTIONS:

- In a dish that fits your air fryer, mix oil with onions, mushrooms, basil and oregano and stir.
- Add rice, beer, butter, stock and butter, stir again, place in your air fryer's basket and cook at 350 degrees F for 30 minutes.
- Divide among plates and serve with grated parmesan on top as a side dish. Enjoy!

Nutrition: calories 142, fat 4, fiber 4, carbs 6, protein 4

Cauliflower Rice

Preparation time: 10 minutes Cooking time: 40 minutes Servings: 8

INGREDIENTS:

- ✓ 1 tablespoon peanut oil
- ✓ 1 tablespoon sesame oil
- ✓ 4 tablespoons soy sauce
- ✓ 3 garlic cloves, minced
- ✓ 1 tablespoon ginger, grated
- ✓ Juice from ½ lemon
- ✓ 1 cauliflower head, riced
- ✓ 9 ounces water chestnuts, drained
- ✓ ¾ cup peas
- ✓ 15 ounces mushrooms, chopped
- ✓ 1 egg, whisked

DIRECTIONS:

- In your air fryer, mix cauliflower rice with peanut oil, sesame oil, soy sauce, garlic, ginger and lemon juice, stir, cover and cook at 350 degrees F for 20 minutes.
- Add chestnuts, peas, mushrooms and egg, toss and cook at 360 degrees F for 20 minutes more.
- Divide among plates and serve for breakfast.
- Enjoy!

Nutrition: calories 142, fat 3, fiber 2, carbs 6, protein 4

Carrots and Rhubarb

Preparation time: 10 minutes Cooking time: 40 minutes Servings: 4

INGREDIENTS:

- ✓ 1 pound baby carrots
- ✓ 2 teaspoons walnut oil
- ✓ 1 pound rhubarb, roughly chopped

- ✓ 1 orange, peeled, cut into medium segments and zest grated
- ✓ ½ cup walnuts, halved
- ✓ ½ teaspoon stevia

DIRECTIONS:

- Put the oil in your air fryer, add carrots, toss and fry them at 380 degrees F for 20 minutes.
- Add rhubarb, orange zest, stevia and walnuts, toss and cook for 20 minutes more.
- Add orange segments, toss and serve as a side dish.
- Enjoy!

Nutrition: calories 172, fat 2, fiber 3, carbs 4, protein 4

Roasted Eggplant

Preparation time: 10 minutes Cooking time: 20 minutes Servings: 6

INGREDIENTS:

- ✓ 1 and ½ pounds eggplant, cubed
- ✓ 1 tablespoon olive oil
- ✓ 1 teaspoon garlic powder
- ✓ 1 teaspoon onion powder
- ✓ 1 teaspoon sumac
- ✓ 2 teaspoons za'atar
- ✓ Juice from ½ lemon
- ✓ 2 bay leaves

DIRECTIONS:

- In your air fryer, mix eggplant cubes with oil, garlic powder, onion powder, sumac, za'atar, lemon juice and bay leaves, toss and cook at 370 degrees F for 20 minutes.
- Divide among plates and serve as a side dish.
- Enjoy!

Nutrition: calories 172, fat 4, fiber 7, carbs 12, protein 3

Delicious Air Fried Broccoli

Preparation time: 10 minutes Cooking time: 20 minutes Servings: 4

INGREDIENTS:

- ✓ 1 tablespoon duck fat
- ✓ 1 broccoli head, florets separated
- ✓ 3 garlic cloves, minced
- ✓ Juice from ½ lemon
- ✓ 1 tablespoon sesame seeds

DIRECTIONS:

- Heat up your air fryer at 350 degrees F, add duck fat and heat as well.
- Add broccoli, garlic, lemon juice and sesame seeds, toss and cook for 20 minutes.
- Divide among plates and serve as a side dish.
- Enjoy!

Nutrition: calories 132, fat 3, fiber 3, carbs 6, protein 4

Onion Rings Side Dish

Preparation time: 10 minutes Cooking time: 10 minutes Servings: 3

INGREDIENTS:

- ✓ 1 onion cut into medium slices and rings separated
- ✓ 1 and ¼ cups white flour
- ✓ A pinch of salt
- ✓ 1 egg
- ✓ 1 cup milk
- ✓ 1 teaspoon baking powder
- ✓ ¾ cup bread crumbs

DIRECTIONS:

- In a bowl, mix flour with salt and baking powder, stir, dredge onion rings in this mix and place them on a separate plate.
- Add milk and egg to flour mix and whisk well.
- Dip onion rings in this mix, dredge them in breadcrumbs, put them in your air fryer's basket and cook them at 360 degrees F for 10 minutes.
- Divide among plates and serve as a side dish for a steak.
- Enjoy!

Nutrition: calories 140, fat 8, fiber 20, carbs 12, protein 3

Rice and Sausage Side Dish

Preparation time: 10 minutes Cooking time: 20 minutes Servings: 4

INGREDIENTS:

- ✓ 2 cups white rice, already boiled
- ✓ 1 tablespoon butter
- ✓ Salt and black pepper to the taste
- ✓ 4 garlic cloves, minced
- ✓ 1 pork sausage, chopped
- ✓ 2 tablespoons carrot, chopped
- ✓ 3 tablespoons cheddar cheese, grated
- ✓ 2 tablespoons mozzarella cheese, shredded

DIRECTIONS:

- Heat up your air fryer at 350 degrees F, add butter, melt it, add garlic, stir and brown for 2 minutes.
- Add sausage, salt, pepper, carrots and rice, stir and cook at 350 degrees F for 10 minutes.
- Add cheddar and mozzarella, toss, divide among plates and serve as a side dish.
- Enjoy!

Nutrition: calories 240, fat 12, fiber 5, carbs 20, protein 13

Potatoes Patties

Preparation time: 10 minutes Cooking time: 8 minutes Servings: 4

INGREDIENTS:

- ✓ 4 potatoes, cubed, boiled and mashed
- ✓ 1 cup parmesan, grated
- ✓ Salt and black pepper to the taste
- ✓ A pinch of nutmeg
- ✓ 2 egg yolks
- ✓ 2 tablespoons white flour
- ✓ 3 tablespoons chives, chopped

For the breading:

- ✓ ¼ cup white flour
- ✓ 3 tablespoons vegetable oil
- ✓ 2 eggs, whisked
- ✓ ¼ cup bread crumbs

DIRECTIONS:

- In a bowl, mix mashed potatoes with egg yolks, salt, pepper, nutmeg, parmesan, chives and 2 tablespoons flour, stir well, shape medium cakes and place them on a plate.
- In another bowl, mix vegetable oil with bread crumbs and stir,.
- Put whisked eggs in a third bowl and ¼ cup flour in a forth one.
- Dip cakes in flour, then in eggs and in breadcrumbs at the end, place them in your air fryer's basket, cook them at 390 degrees F for 8 minutes, divide among plates and serve as a side dish.
- Enjoy!

Nutrition: calories 140, fat 3, fiber 4, carbs 17, protein 4

Simple Potato Chips

Preparation time: 30 minutes Cooking time: 30 minutes Servings: 4

INGREDIENTS:

- ✓ 4 potatoes, scrubbed, peeled into thin chips, soaked in water for 30 minutes, drained and pat dried
- ✓ Salt the taste
- ✓ 1 tablespoon olive oil
- ✓ 2 teaspoons rosemary, chopped

DIRECTIONS:

- In a bowl, mix potato chips with salt and oil toss to coat, place them in your air fryer's basket and cook at 330 degrees F for 30 minutes.
- Divide among plates, sprinkle rosemary all over and serve as a side dish.
- Enjoy!

Nutrition: calories 200, fat 4, fiber 4, carbs 14, protein 5

Avocado Fries

Preparation time: 10 minutes Cooking time: 10 minutes Servings: 4

INGREDIENTS:

- ✓ 1 avocado, pitted, peeled, sliced and cut into medium fries
- ✓ Salt and black pepper to the taste
- ✓ ½ cup panko bread crumbs
- ✓ 1 tablespoon lemon juice
- ✓ 1 egg, whisked
- ✓ 1 tablespoon olive oil

DIRECTIONS:

- In a bowl, mix panko with salt and pepper and stir.
- In another bowl, mix egg with a pinch of salt and whisk.
- In a third bowl, mix avocado fries with lemon juice and oil and toss.
- Dip fries in egg, then in panko, place them in your air fryer's basket and cook at 390 degrees F for 10 minutes, shaking halfway. Divide among plates and serve as a side dish.
- Enjoy!

Nutrition: calories 130, fat 11, fiber 3, carbs 16, protein 4

Veggie Fries

Preparation time: 10 minutes Cooking time: 30 minutes Servings: 4

INGREDIENTS:

- ✓ 4 parsnips, cut into medium sticks
- ✓ 2 sweet potatoes cut into medium sticks
- ✓ 4 mixed carrots cut into medium sticks
- ✓ Salt and black pepper to the taste
- ✓ 2 tablespoons rosemary, chopped
- ✓ 2 tablespoons olive oil
- ✓ 1 tablespoon flour
- ✓ ½ teaspoon garlic powder

DIRECTIONS:

- Put veggie fries in a bowl, add oil, garlic powder, salt, pepper, flour and rosemary and toss to coat.
- Put sweet potatoes in your preheated air fryer, cook them for 10 minutes at 350 degrees F and transfer them to a platter.
- Put parsnip fries in your air fryer, cook for 5 minutes and transfer over potato fries.
- Put carrot fries in your air fryer, cook for 15 minutes at 350 degrees F and transfer to the platter with the other fries.
- Divide veggie fries on plates and serve them as a side dish.
- Enjoy!

Nutrition: calories 100, fat 0, fiber 4, carbs 7, protein 4

Air Fried Creamy Cabbage

Preparation time: 10 minutes Cooking time: 20 minute Servings: 4

INGREDIENTS:

- ✓ 1 green cabbage head, chopped
- ✓ 1 yellow onion, chopped
- ✓ Salt and black pepper to the taste
- ✓ 4 bacon slices, chopped
- ✓ 1 cup whipped cream
- ✓ 2 tablespoons cornstarch

DIRECTIONS:

- Put cabbage, bacon and onion in your air fryer.
- In a bowl, mix cornstarch with cream, salt and pepper, stir and add over cabbage.
- Toss, cook at 400 degrees F for 20 minutes, divide among plates and serve as a side dish.
- Enjoy!

Nutrition: calories 208, fat 10, fiber 3, carbs 16, protein 5

Tortilla Chips

Preparation time: 10 minutes Cooking time: 6 minutes Servings: 4

INGREDIENTS:

- ✓ **8 corn tortillas, cut into triangles**
- ✓ **Salt and black pepper to the taste**
- ✓ **1 tablespoon olive oil**
- ✓ **A pinch of garlic powder**
- ✓ **A pinch of sweet paprika**

DIRECTIONS:

- ⏱ In a bowl, mix tortilla chips with oil, add salt, pepper, garlic powder and paprika, toss well, place them in your air fryer's basket and cook them at 400 degrees F for 6 minutes.
- ⏱ Serve them as a side for a fish dish.
- ⏱ Enjoy!

Nutrition: calories 53, fat 1, fiber 1, carbs 6, protein 4

Zucchini Croquettes

Preparation time: 10 minutes Cooking time: 10 minutes Servings: 4

INGREDIENTS:

- ✓ **1 carrot, grated**
- ✓ **1 zucchini, grated**
- ✓ **2 slices of bread, crumbled**
- ✓ **1 egg**
- ✓ **Salt and black pepper to the taste**
- ✓ **½ teaspoon sweet paprika**
- ✓ **1 teaspoon garlic, minced**
- ✓ **2 tablespoons parmesan cheese, grated**
- ✓ **1 tablespoon corn flour**

DIRECTIONS:

- ⏱ Put zucchini in a bowl, add salt, leave aside for 10 minutes, squeeze excess water and transfer them to another bowl.
- ⏱ Add carrots, salt, pepper, paprika, garlic, flour, parmesan, egg and bread crumbs, stir well, shape 8 croquettes, place them in your air fryer and cook at 360 degrees F for 10 minutes.
- ⏱ Divide among plates and serve as a side dish
- ⏱ Enjoy!

Nutrition: calories 100, fat 3, fiber 1, carbs 7, protein 4

Creamy Potatoes

Preparation time: 10 minutes Cooking time: 20 minutes Servings: 4

INGREDIENTS:

- ✓ **1 an ½ pounds potatoes, peeled and cubed**

- ✓ **2 tablespoons olive oil**
- ✓ **Salt and black pepper to the taste**
- ✓ **1 tablespoon hot paprika**
- ✓ **1 cup Greek yogurt**

DIRECTIONS:

- ⏱ Put potatoes in a bowl, add water to cover, leave aside for 10 minutes, drain, pat dry them, transfer to another bowl, add salt, pepper, paprika and half of the oil and toss them well.
- ⏱ Put potatoes in your air fryer's basket and cook at 360 degrees F for 20 minutes.
- ⏱ In a bowl, mix yogurt with salt, pepper and the rest of the oil and whisk.
- ⏱ Divide potatoes on plates, drizzle yogurt dressing all over, toss them and serve as a side dish.
- ⏱ Enjoy!

Nutrition: calories 170, fat 3, fiber 5, carbs 20, protein 5

Mushroom Cakes

Preparation time: 10 minutes Cooking time: 8 minutes Servings: 8

INGREDIENTS:

- ✓ **4 ounces mushrooms, chopped**
- ✓ **1 yellow onion, chopped**
- ✓ **Salt and black pepper to the taste**
- ✓ **½ teaspoon nutmeg, ground**
- ✓ **2 tablespoons olive oil**
- ✓ **1 tablespoon butter**
- ✓ **1 and ½ tablespoon flour**
- ✓ **1 tablespoon bread crumbs**
- ✓ **14 ounces milk**

DIRECTIONS:

- ⏱ Heat up a pan with the butter over medium high heat, add onion and mushrooms, stir, cook for 3 minutes, add flour, stir well again and take off heat.
- ⏱ Add milk gradually, salt, pepper and nutmeg, stir and leave aside to cool down completely.
- ⏱ In a bowl, mix oil with bread crumbs and whisk.
- ⏱ Take spoonfuls of the mushroom filling, add to breadcrumbs mix, coat well, shape patties out of this mix, place them in your air fryer's basket and cook at 400 degrees F for 8 minutes.
- ⏱ Divide among plates and serve as a side for a steak
- ⏱ Enjoy!

Nutrition: calories 192, fat 2, fiber 1, carbs 16, protein 6

Creamy Roasted Peppers Side Dish

Preparation time: 10 minutes Cooking time: 10 minutes Servings: 4

INGREDIENTS:

- ✓ 1 tablespoon lemon juice
- ✓ 1 red bell pepper
- ✓ 1 green bell pepper
- ✓ 1 yellow bell pepper
- ✓ 1 lettuce head, cut into strips
- ✓ 1 ounce rocket leaves
- ✓ Salt and black pepper to the taste
- ✓ 3 tablespoons Greek yogurt
- ✓ 2 tablespoons olive oil

DIRECTIONS:

- ⏱ Place bell peppers in your air fryer's basket, cook at 400 degrees F for 10 minutes, transfer to a bowl, leave aside for 10 minutes, peel them, discard seeds, cut them in strips, transfer to a larger bowl, add rocket leaves and lettuce strips and toss.
- ⏱ In a bowl, mix oil with lemon juice, yogurt, salt and pepper and whisk well.
- ⏱ Add this over bell peppers mix, toss to coat, divide among plates and serve as a side salad.
- ⏱ Enjoy!

Nutrition: calories 170, fat 1, fiber 1, carbs 2, protein 6

Greek Veggie Side Dish

Preparation time: 10 minutes Cooking time: 45 minutes Servings: 4

INGREDIENTS:

- ✓ 1 eggplant, sliced
- ✓ 1 zucchini, sliced
- ✓ 2 red bell peppers, chopped
- ✓ 2 garlic cloves, minced
- ✓ 3 tablespoons olive oil
- ✓ 1 bay leaf
- ✓ 1 thyme spring, chopped
- ✓ 2 onions, chopped
- ✓ 4 tomatoes, cut into quarters
- ✓ Salt and black pepper to the taste

DIRECTIONS:

- ⏱ In your air fryer's pan, mix eggplant slices with zucchini ones, bell peppers, garlic, oil, bay leaf, thyme, onions, tomatoes, salt and pepper, toss and cook them at 300 degrees F for 35 minutes.
- ⏱ Divide among plates and serve as a side dish.
- ⏱ Enjoy!

Nutrition: calories 200, fat 1, fiber 3, carbs 7, protein 6

Yellow Squash and Zucchinis Side Dish

Preparation time: 10 minutes Cooking time: 35 minutes Servings: 4

INGREDIENTS:

- ✓ 6 teaspoons olive oil
- ✓ 1 pound zucchinis, sliced
- ✓ ½ pound carrots, cubed
- ✓ 1 yellow squash, halved, deseeded and cut into chunks
- ✓ Salt and white pepper to the taste
- ✓ 1 tablespoon tarragon, chopped

DIRECTIONS:

- ⏱ In your air fryer's basket, mix zucchinis with carrots, squash, salt, pepper and oil, toss well and cook at 400 degrees F for 25 minutes.
- ⏱ Divide them on plates and serve as a side dish with tarragon sprinkled on top.
- ⏱ Enjoy!

Nutrition: calories 160, fat 2, fiber 1, carbs 5, protein 5

Flavored Cauliflower Side Dish

Preparation time: 10 minutes Cooking time: 10 minutes Servings: 4

INGREDIENTS:

- ✓ 12 cauliflower florets, steamed
- ✓ Salt and black pepper to the taste
- ✓ ¼ teaspoon turmeric powder
- ✓ 1 and ½ teaspoon red chili powder
- ✓ 1 tablespoon ginger, grated
- ✓ 2 teaspoons lemon juice
- ✓ 3 tablespoons white flour
- ✓ 2 tablespoons water
- ✓ Cooking spray
- ✓ ½ teaspoon corn flour

DIRECTIONS:

- In a bowl, mix chili powder with turmeric powder, ginger paste, salt, pepper, lemon juice, white flour, corn flour and water, stir, add cauliflower, toss well and transfer them to your air fryer's basket.
- Coat them with cooking spray, cook them at 400 degrees F for 10 minutes, divide among plates and serve as a side dish.
- Enjoy!

Nutrition: calories 70, fat 1, fiber 2, carbs 12, protein 3

Coconut Cream Potato es

Preparation time: 10 minutes Cooking time: 20 minutes Servings: 4

INGREDIENTS:

- ✓ 2 eggs, whisked
- ✓ Salt and black pepper to the taste
- ✓ 1 tablespoon cheddar cheese, grated
- ✓ 1 tablespoon flour
- ✓ 2 potatoes, sliced
- ✓ 4 ounces coconut cream

DIRECTIONS:

- Place potato slices in your air fryer's basket and cook at 360 degrees F for 10 minutes.
- Meanwhile, in a bowl, mix eggs with coconut cream, salt, pepper and flour.
- Arrange potatoes in your air fryer's pan, add coconut cream mix over them, sprinkle cheese, return to air fryer's basket and cook at 400 degrees F for 10 minutes more.
- Divide among plates and serve as a side dish.
- Enjoy!

Nutrition: calories 170, fat 4, fiber 1, carbs 15, protein 17

Cajun Onion Wedges

Preparation time: 10 minutes Cooking time: 15 minutes Servings: 4

INGREDIENTS:

- ✓ 2 big white onions, cut into wedges
- ✓ Salt and black pepper to the taste
- ✓ 2 eggs
- ✓ ¼ cup milk
- ✓ 1/3 cup panko
- ✓ A drizzle of olive oil
- ✓ 1 and ½ teaspoon paprika
- ✓ 1 teaspoon garlic powder

- ✓ ½ teaspoon Cajun seasoning

DIRECTIONS:

- In a bowl, mix panko with Cajun seasoning and oil and stir.
- In another bowl, mix egg with milk, salt and pepper and stir.
- Sprinkle onion wedges with paprika and garlic powder, dip them in egg mix, then in bread crumbs mix, place in your air fryer's basket, cook at 360 degrees F for 10 minutes, flip and cook for 5 minutes more.
- Divide among plates and serve as a side dish.
- Enjoy!

Nutrition: calories 200, fat 2, fiber 2, carbs 14, protein 7

Wild Rice Pilaf

Preparation time: 10 minutes Cooking time: 25 minutes Servings: 12

INGREDIENTS:

- ✓ 1 shallot, chopped
- ✓ 1 teaspoon garlic, minced
- ✓ A drizzle of olive oil
- ✓ 1 cup farro
- ✓ ¾ cup wild rice
- ✓ 4 cups chicken stock
- ✓ Salt and black pepper to the taste
- ✓ 1 tablespoon parsley, chopped
- ✓ ½ cup hazelnuts, toasted and chopped
- ✓ ¾ cup cherries, dried
- ✓ Chopped chives for serving

DIRECTIONS:

- In a dish that fits your air fryer, mix shallot with garlic, oil, faro, wild rice, stock, salt, pepper, parsley, hazelnuts and cherries, stir, place in your air fryer's basket and cook at 350 degrees F for 25 minutes.
- Divide among plates and serve as a side dish.
- Enjoy!

Nutrition: calories 142, fat 4, fiber 4, carbs 16, protein 4

Pumpkin Ri ce

Preparation time: 5 minutes Cooking time: 30 minutes Servings: 4

INGREDIENTS:

- ✓ 2 tablespoons olive oil

- ✓ 1 small yellow onion, chopped
- ✓ 2 garlic cloves, minced
- ✓ 12 ounces white rice
- ✓ 4 cups chicken stock
- ✓ 6 ounces pumpkin puree
- ✓ ½ teaspoon nutmeg
- ✓ 1 teaspoon thyme, chopped
- ✓ ½ teaspoon ginger, grated
- ✓ ½ teaspoon cinnamon powder
- ✓ ½ teaspoon allspice
- ✓ 4 ounces heavy cream

DIRECTIONS:

- In a dish that fits your air fryer, mix oil with onion, garlic, rice, stock, pumpkin puree, nutmeg, thyme, ginger, cinnamon, allspice and cream, stir well, place in your air fryer's basket and cook at 360 degrees F for 30 minutes.
- Divide among plates and serve as a side dish.
- Enjoy!

Nutrition: calories 261, fat 6, fiber 7, carbs 29, protein 4

Colored Veggie Rice

Preparation time: 10 minutes Cooking time: 25 minutes Servings: 4

INGREDIENTS:

- ✓ 2 cups basmati rice
- ✓ 1 cup mixed carrots, peas, corn and green beans
- ✓ 2 cups water
- ✓ ½ teaspoon green chili, minced
- ✓ ½ teaspoon ginger, grated
- ✓ 3 garlic cloves, minced
- ✓ 2 tablespoons butter
- ✓ 1 teaspoon cinnamon powder
- ✓ 1 tablespoon cumin seeds
- ✓ 2 bay leaves
- ✓ 3 whole cloves
- ✓ 5 black peppercorns
- ✓ 2 whole cardamoms
- ✓ 1 tablespoon sugar
- ✓ Salt to the taste

DIRECTIONS:

- Put the water in a heat proof dish that fits your air fryer, add rice, mixed veggies, green chili, grated ginger, garlic cloves, cinnamon, cloves, butter, cumin seeds, bay leaves, cardamoms, black peppercorns, salt and sugar, stir, put in your air fryer's basket and cook at 370 degrees F for 25 minutes.
- Divide among plates and serve as a side dish.

Enjoy!

Nutrition: calories 283, fat 4, fiber 8, carbs 34, protein 14

Potato Casserole

Preparation time: 15 minutes Cooking time: 40 minutes Servings: 4

INGREDIENTS:

- ✓ 3 pounds sweet potatoes, scrubbed
- ✓ ¼ cup milk
- ✓ ½ teaspoon nutmeg, ground
- ✓ 2 tablespoons white flour
- ✓ ¼ teaspoon allspice, ground
- ✓ Salt to the taste

For the topping:

- ✓ ½ cup almond flour
- ✓ ½ cup walnuts, soaked, drained and ground
- ✓ ¼ cup pecans, soaked, drained and ground
- ✓ ¼ cup coconut, shredded
- ✓ 1 tablespoon chia seeds
- ✓ ¼ cup sugar
- ✓ 1 teaspoon cinnamon powder
- ✓ 5 tablespoons butter

DIRECTIONS:

- Place potatoes in your air fryer's basket, prick them with a fork and cook at 360 degrees F for 30 minutes.
- Meanwhile, in a bowl, mix almond flour with pecans, walnuts, ¼ cup coconut, ¼ cup sugar, chia seeds, 1 teaspoon cinnamon and the butter and stir everything.
- Transfer potatoes to a cutting board, cool them, peel and place them in a baking dish that fits your air fryer.
- Add milk, flour, salt, nutmeg and allspice and stir
- Add crumble mix you've made earlier on top, place dish in your air fryer's basket and cook at 400 degrees F for 8 minutes.
- Divide among plates and serve as a side dish.
- Enjoy!

Nutrition: calories 162, fat 4, fiber 8, carbs 18, protein 4

Lemony Artichokes

Preparation time: 10 minutes Cooking time: 15 minutes Servings: 4

INGREDIENTS:

- ✓ 2 medium artichokes, trimmed and halved Cooking spray
- ✓ 2 tablespoons lemon juice
- ✓ Salt and black pepper to the taste

DIRECTIONS:

- Grease your air fryer with cooking spray, add artichokes, drizzle lemon juice and sprinkle salt and black pepper and cook them at 380 degrees F for 15 minutes.
- Divide them on plates and serve as a side dish.
- Enjoy!

Nutrition: calories 121, fat 3, fiber 6, carbs 9, protein 4

Cauliflower and Broccoli Delight

Preparation time: 10 minutes Cooking time: 7 minutes Servings: 4

INGREDIENTS:

- ✓ 2 cauliflower heads, florets separated and steamed
- ✓ 1 broccoli head, florets separated and steamed Zest from
- ✓ 1 orange, grated Juice from 1 orange
- ✓ A pinch of hot pepper flakes
- ✓ 4 anchovies
- ✓ 1 tablespoon capers, chopped
- ✓ Salt and black pepper to the taste
- ✓ 4 tablespoons olive oil

DIRECTIONS:

- In a bowl, mix orange zest with orange juice, pepper flakes, anchovies, capers salt, pepper and olive oil and whisk well.
- Add broccoli and cauliflower, toss well, transfer them to your air fryer's basket and cook at 400 degrees F for 7 minutes.
- Divide among plates and serve as a side dish with some of the orange vinaigrette drizzled on top.
- Enjoy!

Nutrition: calories 300, fat 4, fiber 7, carbs 28, protein 4

Garlic Beet Wedges

Preparation time: 10 minutes Cooking time: 15 minutes Servings: 4

INGREDIENTS:

- ✓ 4 beets, washed, peeled and cut into large wedges
- ✓ 1 tablespoon olive oil
- ✓ Salt and black to the taste
- ✓ 2 garlic cloves, minced
- ✓ 1 teaspoon lemon juice

DIRECTIONS:

- In a bowl, mix beets with oil, salt, pepper, garlic and lemon juice, toss well, transfer to your air fryer's basket and cook them at 400 degrees F for 15 minutes.
- Divide beets wedges on plates and serve as a side dish.
- Enjoy!

Nutrition: calories 182, fat 6, fiber 3, carbs 8, protein 2

Fried Red Cabbage

Preparation time: 10 minutes Cooking time: 15 minutes Servings: 4

INGREDIENTS:

- ✓ 4 garlic cloves, minced
- ✓ ½ cup yellow onion, chopped
- ✓ 1 tablespoon olive oil
- ✓ 6 cups red cabbage, chopped
- ✓ 1 cup veggie stock
- ✓ 1 tablespoon apple cider vinegar
- ✓ 1 cup applesauce
- ✓ Salt and black pepper to the taste

DIRECTIONS:

- In a heat proof dish that fits your air fryer, mix cabbage with onion, garlic, oil, stock, vinegar, applesauce, salt and pepper, toss really well, place dish in your air fryer's basket and cook at 380 degrees F for 15 minutes.
- Divide among plates and serve as a side dish.
- Enjoy!

Nutrition: calories 172, fat 7, fiber 7, carbs 14, protein 5

Artichokes and Tarragon Sauce

Preparation time: 10 minutes Cooking time: 18 minutes Servings: 4

INGREDIENTS:

- ✓ **4 artichokes, trimmed**
- ✓ **2 tablespoons tarragon, chopped**
- ✓ **2 tablespoons chicken stock**
- ✓ **Lemon zest from 2 lemons, grated**
- ✓ **2 tablespoons lemon juice**
- ✓ **1 celery stalk, chopped**
- ✓ **½ cup olive oil**
- ✓ **Salt to the taste**

DIRECTIONS:

- ⏱ In your food processor, mix tarragon, chicken stock, lemon zest, lemon juice, celery, salt and olive oil and pulse very well.
- ⏱ In a bowl, mix artichokes with tarragon and lemon sauce, toss well, transfer them to your air fryer's basket and cook at 380 degrees F for 18 minutes.
- ⏱ Divide artichokes on plates, drizzle the rest of the sauce all over and serve as a side dish.
- ⏱ Enjoy!

Nutrition: calories 215, fat 3, fiber 8, carbs 28, protein 6

Brussels Sprouts and Pomegranate Seeds Side Dish

Preparation time: 5 minutes Cooking time: 10 minutes Servings: 4

INGREDIENTS:

- ✓ **1 pound Brussels sprouts, trimmed and halved Salt and black pepper to the taste**
- ✓ **1 cup pomegranate seeds**
- ✓ **¼ cup pine nuts, toasted**

- ✓ **1 tablespoons olive oil**
- ✓ **2 tablespoons veggie stock**

DIRECTIONS:

- ⏱ In a heat proof dish that fits your air fryer, mix Brussels sprouts with salt, pepper, pomegranate seeds, pine nuts, oil and stock, stir, place in your air fryer's basket and cook at 390 degrees F for 10 minutes.
- ⏱ Divide among plates and serve as a side dish.
- ⏱ Enjoy!

Nutrition: calories 152, fat 4, fiber 7, carbs 12, protein 3

Crispy Brussels Sprouts and Potatoes

Preparation time: 10 minutes Cooking time: 8 minutes Servings: 4

INGREDIENTS:

- ✓ **1 and ½ pounds Brussels sprouts, washed and trimmed**
- ✓ **1 cup new potatoes, chopped**
- ✓ **1 and ½ tablespoons bread crumbs**
- ✓ **Salt and black pepper to the taste**
- ✓ **1 and ½ tablespoons butter**

DIRECTIONS:

- ⏱ Put Brussels sprouts and potatoes in your air fryer's pan, add bread crumbs, salt, pepper and butter, toss well and cook at 400 degrees F for 8 minutes.
- ⏱ Divide among plates and serve as a side dish.
- ⏱ Enjoy!

Nutrition: calories 152, fat 3, fiber 7, carbs 17, protein 4

Air Fryer Snack and Appetizer Recipes

Banana Chips

Preparation time: 10 minutes Cooking time: 15 minutes Servings: 4

INGREDIENTS:

- ✓ **4 bananas, peeled and sliced**
- ✓ **A pinch of salt**
- ✓ **½ teaspoon turmeric powder**
- ✓ **½ teaspoon chaat masala**
- ✓ **1 teaspoon olive oil**

DIRECTIONS:

- In a bowl, mix banana slices with salt, turmeric, chaat masala and oil, toss and leave aside for 10 minutes.
- Transfer banana slices to your preheated air fryer at 360 degrees F and cook them for 15 minutes flipping them once.
- Serve as a snack.
- Enjoy!

Nutrition: calories 121, fat 1, fiber 2, carbs 3, protein 3

Spring Rolls

Preparation time: 10 minutes Cooking time: 25 minutes Servings: 8

INGREDIENTS:

- ✓ **2 cups green cabbage, shredded**
- ✓ **2 yellow onions, chopped**
- ✓ **1 carrot, grated**
- ✓ **½ chili pepper, minced**
- ✓ **1 tablespoon ginger, grated**
- ✓ **3 garlic cloves, minced**
- ✓ **1 teaspoon sugar**
- ✓ **Salt and black pepper to the taste**
- ✓ **1 teaspoon soy sauce**
- ✓ **2 tablespoons olive oil**
- ✓ **10 spring roll sheets**
- ✓ **2 tablespoons corn flour**
- ✓ **2 tablespoons water**

DIRECTIONS:

- Heat up a pan with the oil over medium heat, add cabbage, onions, carrots, chili pepper, ginger, garlic, sugar, salt, pepper and soy sauce, stir well, cook for 2-3 minutes, take off heat and cool down.
- Cut spring roll sheets in squares, divide cabbage mix on each and roll them.
- In a bowl, mix corn flour with water, stir well and seal spring rolls with this mix.
- Place spring rolls in your air fryer's basket and cook them at 360 degrees F for 10 minutes.
- Flip roll and cook them for 10 minutes more.
- Arrange on a platter and serve them as an appetizer.
- Enjoy!

Nutrition: calories 214, fat 4, fiber 4, carbs 12, protein 4

Crispy Radish Chips

Preparation time: 10 minutes Cooking time: 10 minutes Servings: 4

INGREDIENTS:

- ✓ **Cooking spray**
- ✓ **15 radishes, sliced**
- ✓ **Salt and black pepper to the taste**
- ✓ **1 tablespoon chives, chopped**

DIRECTIONS:

- Arrange radish slices in your air fryer's basket, spray them with cooking oil, season with salt and black pepper to the taste, cook them at 350 degrees F for 10 minutes, flipping them halfway, transfer to bowls and serve with chives sprinkled on top.
- Enjoy!

Nutrition: calories 80, fat 1, fiber 1, carbs 1, protein 1

Crab Sticks

Preparation time: 10 minutes Cooking time: 12 minutes Servings: 4

INGREDIENTS:

- ✓ **10 crabsticks, halved**
- ✓ **2 teaspoons sesame oil**
- ✓ **2 teaspoons Cajun seasoning**

DIRECTIONS:

- Put crab sticks in a bowl, add sesame oil and Cajun seasoning, toss, transfer them to your air fryer's basket and cook at 350 degrees F for 12 minutes.
- Arrange on a platter and serve as an appetizer.
- Enjoy!

Nutrition: calories 110, fat 0, fiber 1, carbs 4, protein 2

Air Fried Dill Pickles

Preparation time: 10 minutes Cooking time: 5 minutes Servings: 4

INGREDIENTS:

- ✓ **16 ounces jarred dill pickles, cut into wedges and pat dried ½ cup white flour**
- ✓ **1 egg**
- ✓ **¼ cup milk**
- ✓ **½ teaspoon garlic powder**
- ✓ **½ teaspoon sweet paprika**
- ✓ **Cooking spray**
- ✓ **¼ cup ranch sauce**

DIRECTIONS:

- ⊙ In a bowl, combine milk with egg and whisk well.
- ⊙ In a second bowl, mix flour with salt, garlic powder and paprika and stir as well
- ⊙ Dip pickles in flour, then in egg mix and again in flour and place them in your air fryer.
- ⊙ Grease them with cooking spray, cook pickle wedges at 400 degrees F for 5 minutes, transfer to a bowl and serve with ranch sauce on the side.
- ⊙ Enjoy!

Nutrition: calories 109, fat 2, fiber 2, carbs 10, protein 4

Chickpeas Snack

Preparation time: 10 minutes Cooking time: 10 minutes Servings: 4

INGREDIENTS:

- ✓ **15 ounces canned chickpeas, drained**
- ✓ **½ teaspoon cumin, ground**
- ✓ **1 tablespoon olive oil**
- ✓ **1 teaspoon smoked paprika**
- ✓ **Salt and black pepper to the taste**

DIRECTIONS:

- ⊙ In a bowl, mix chickpeas with oil, cumin, paprika, salt and pepper, toss to coat, place them in your fryer's basket and cook at 390 degrees F for 10 minutes.
- ⊙ Divide into bowls and serve as a snack.
- ⊙ Enjoy!

Nutrition: calories 140, fat 1, fiber 6, carbs 20, protein 6

Cauliflower Bars

Preparation time: 10 minutes Cooking time: 25 minutes Servings: 12

INGREDIENTS:

- ✓ **1 big cauliflower head, florets separated**
- ✓ **½ cup mozzarella, shredded**

- ✓ **¼ cup egg whites**
- ✓ **1 teaspoon Italian seasoning**
- ✓ **Salt and black pepper to the taste**

DIRECTIONS:

- ⊙ Put cauliflower florets in your food processor, pulse well, spread on a lined baking sheet that fits your air fryer, introduce in the fryer and cook at 360 degrees F for 10 minutes.
- ⊙ Transfer cauliflower to a bowl, add salt, pepper, cheese, egg whites and Italian seasoning, stir really well, spread this into a rectangle pan that fits your air fryer, press well, introduce in the fryer and cook at 360 degrees F for 15 minutes more.
- ⊙ Cut into 12 bars, arrange them on a platter and serve as a snack
- ⊙ Enjoy!

Nutrition: calories 50, fat 1, fiber 2, carbs 3, protein 3

Air Fried Banana Chips

Preparation: 15 minutes Cooking time: 15 minutes Servings: 4

INGREDIENTS:

- ✓ **3 medium sized bananas, peeled**
- ✓ **1 teaspoon of vegetable oil**
- ✓ **½ teaspoon of Chaat masala seasoning**
- ✓ **½ teaspoon of Turmeric powder**
- ✓ **1 teaspoon of salt**

DIRECTIONS:

- ⊙ Add about 1½ cups of water to the turmeric powder and a little salt. Slice the bananas into the turmeric mixture to prevent it from getting black and to give it a yellow color. Soak the bananas for 10 minutes and then drain off and dry.
- ⊙ Heat your airfryer to 356°F for 5 minutes Add the oil on the chips and toss lightly. Fry for 15 minutes in the airfryer. Remove from fryer and add the salt and seasoning. Serve immediately or preserve in an airtight container.

Air Fried Rosemary Chips

Preparation: 40 minutes Cooking time: 30 minutes Servings: 4

INGREDIENTS:

- ✓ **2 teaspoons of finely chopped rosemary**
- ✓ **4 russet potatoes**
- ✓ **3 teaspoons of olive oil**
- ✓ **¼ teaspoon of salt**

DIRECTIONS:

- ◷ Peel potatoes and slice them into thin chips. Soak them in water for 30 minutes, drain and then pat dry with paper towel.
- ◷ Heat your airfryer to about 330°F.
- ◷ Pour the olive oil into the potato chips and toss until all the potatoes are coated.
- ◷ Put the potatoes into the fryer basket and air fry for 30 minutes until golden and crisp. Shake often to during cooking to ensure the potatoes are evenly cooked.
- ◷ Remove from fryer, add the rosemary and salt and toss to mix.

Pesto Crackers

Preparation time: 10 minutes Cooking time: 17 minutes Servings: 6

INGREDIENTS:

- ✓ ½ teaspoon baking powder
- ✓ Salt and black pepper to the taste
- ✓ 1 and ¼ cups flour
- ✓ ¼ teaspoon basil, dried
- ✓ 1 garlic clove, minced
- ✓ 2 tablespoons basil pesto
- ✓ 3 tablespoons butter

DIRECTIONS:

- ◷ In a bowl, mix salt, pepper, baking powder, flour, garlic, cayenne, basil, pesto and butter and stir until you obtain a dough.
- ◷ Spread this dough on a lined baking sheet that fits your air fryer, introduce in the fryer at 325 degrees F and bake for 17 minutes.
- ◷ Leave aside to cool down, cut crackers and serve them as a snack.
- ◷ Enjoy!

Nutrition: calories 200, fat 20, fiber 1, carbs 4, protein 7

Pumpkin Muffins

Preparation time: 10 minutes Cooking time: 15 minutes Servings: 18

INGREDIENTS:

- ✓ ¼ cup butter
- ✓ ¾ cup pumpkin puree
- ✓ 2 tablespoons flaxseed meal
- ✓ ¼ cup flour

- ✓ ½ cup sugar
- ✓ ½ teaspoon nutmeg, ground
- ✓ 1 teaspoon cinnamon powder
- ✓ ½ teaspoon baking soda
- ✓ 1 egg
- ✓ ½ teaspoon baking powder

DIRECTIONS:

- ◷ In a bowl, mix butter with pumpkin puree and egg and blend well.
- ◷ Add flaxseed meal, flour, sugar, baking soda, baking powder, nutmeg and cinnamon and stir well.
- ◷ Spoon this into a muffin pan that fits your fryer introduce in the fryer at 350 degrees F and bake for 15 minutes.
- ◷ Serve muffins cold as a snack.
- ◷ Enjoy!

Nutrition: calories 50, fat 3, fiber 1, carbs 2, protein 2

Zucchini Chips

Preparation time: 10 minutes Cooking time: 1 hour Servings: 6

INGREDIENTS:

- ✓ 3 zucchinis, thinly sliced
- ✓ Salt and black pepper to the taste
- ✓ 2 tablespoons olive oil
- ✓ 2 tablespoons balsamic vinegar

DIRECTIONS:

- ◷ In a bowl, mix oil with vinegar, salt and pepper and whisk well.
- ◷ Add zucchini slices, toss to coat well, introduce in your air fryer and cook at 200 degrees F for 1 hour.
- ◷ Serve zucchini chips cold as a snack.
- ◷ Enjoy!

Nutrition: calories 40, fat 3, fiber 7, carbs 3, protein 7

Beef Jerky Snack

Preparation time: 2 hours Cooking time: 1 hour and 30 minutes

Servings: 6

INGREDIENTS:

- ✓ 2 cups soy sauce
- ✓ ½ cup Worcestershire sauce
- ✓ 2 tablespoons black peppercorns
- ✓ 2 tablespoons black pepper
- ✓ 2 pounds beef round, sliced

DIRECTIONS:

- 🕐 In a bowl, mix soy sauce with black peppercorns, black pepper and Worcestershire sauce and whisk well.
- 🕐 Add beef slices, toss to coat and leave aside in the fridge for 6 hours.
- 🕐 Introduce beef rounds in your air fryer and cook them at 370 degrees F for 1 hour and 30 minutes.
- 🕐 Transfer to a bowl and serve cold.
- 🕐 Enjoy!

Nutrition: calories 300, fat 12, fiber 4, carbs 3, protein 8

Honey Party Wings

Preparation time: 1 hour and 10 minutes Cooking time: 12 minutes

Servings: 8

INGREDIENTS:

- ✓ **16 chicken wings, halved**
- ✓ **2 tablespoons soy sauce**
- ✓ **2 tablespoons honey**
- ✓ **Salt and black pepper to the taste**
- ✓ **2 tablespoons lime juice**

DIRECTIONS:

- 🕐 In a bowl, mix chicken wings with soy sauce, honey, salt, pepper and lime juice, toss well and keep in the fridge for 1 hour.
- 🕐 Transfer chicken wings to your air fryer and cook them at 360 degrees F for 12 minutes, flipping them halfway.
- 🕐 Arrange them on a platter and serve as an appetizer.
- 🕐 Enjoy!

Nutrition: calories 211, fat 4, fiber 7, carbs 14, protein 3

Salmon Party Patties

Preparation time: 10 minutes Cooking time: 22 minutes Servings: 4

INGREDIENTS:

- ✓ **3 big potatoes, boiled, drained and mashed**
- ✓ **1 big salmon fillet, skinless, boneless**
- ✓ **2 tablespoons parsley, chopped**
- ✓ **2 tablespoon dill, chopped**
- ✓ **Salt and black pepper to the taste**
- ✓ **1 egg**
- ✓ **2 tablespoons bread crumbs**
- ✓ **Cooking spray**

DIRECTIONS:

- 🕐 Place salmon in your air fryer's basket and cook for 10 minutes at 360 degrees F.
- 🕐 Transfer salmon to a cutting board, cool it down, flake it and put it in a bowl.
- 🕐 Add mashed potatoes, salt, pepper, dill, parsley, egg and bread crumbs, stir well and shape 8 patties out of this mix.
- 🕐 Place salmon patties in your air fryer's basket, spry them with cooking oil, cook at 360 degrees F for 12 minutes, flipping them halfway, transfer them to a platter and serve as an appetizer.
- 🕐 Enjoy!

Nutrition: calories 231, fat 3, fiber 7, carbs 14, protein 4

Sausage Balls

Preparation time: 10 minutes Cooking time: 15 minutes Servings: 9

INGREDIENTS:

- ✓ **4 ounces sausage meat, ground**
- ✓ **Salt and black pepper to the taste**
- ✓ **1 teaspoon sage**
- ✓ **½ teaspoon garlic, minced**
- ✓ **1 small onion, chopped**
- ✓ **3 tablespoons breadcrumbs**

DIRECTIONS:

- 🕐 In a bowl, mix sausage with salt, pepper, sage, garlic, onion and breadcrumbs, stir well and shape small balls out of this mix.
- 🕐 Put them in your air fryer's basket, cook at 360 degrees F for 15 minutes, divide into bowls and serve as a snack.
- 🕐 Enjoy!

Nutrition: calories 130, fat 7, fiber 1, carbs 13, protein 4

Chicken Dip

Preparation time: 10 minutes Cooking time: 25 minutes Servings: 10

INGREDIENTS:

- ✓ **3 tablespoons butter, melted**
- ✓ **1 cup yogurt**
- ✓ **12 ounces cream cheese**
- ✓ **2 cups chicken meat, cooked and shredded**
- ✓ **2 teaspoons curry powder**
- ✓ **4 scallions, chopped**

- ✓ 6 ounces Monterey jack cheese, grated
- ✓ 1/3 cup raisins
- ✓ ¼ cup cilantro, chopped
- ✓ ½ cup almonds, sliced
- ✓ Salt and black pepper to the taste
- ✓ ½ cup chutney

DIRECTIONS:

- In a bowl mix cream cheese with yogurt and whisk using your mixer.
- Add curry powder, scallions, chicken meat, raisins, cheese, cilantro, salt and pepper and stir everything.
- Spread this into a baking dish that fist your air fryer, sprinkle almonds on top, place in your air fryer, bake at 300 degrees for 25 minutes, divide into bowls, top with chutney and serve as an appetizer.
- Enjoy!

Nutrition: calories 240, fat 10, fiber 2, carbs 24, protein 12

Coconut Chicken Bites

Preparation time: 10 minutes Cooking time: 13 minutes Servings: 4

INGREDIENTS:

- ✓ 2 teaspoons garlic powder
- ✓ 2 eggs
- ✓ Salt and black pepper to the taste
- ✓ ¾ cup panko bread crumbs
- ✓ ¾ cup coconut, shredded
- ✓ Cooking spray
- ✓ 8 chicken tenders

DIRECTIONS:

In a bowl, mix eggs with salt, pepper and garlic powder and whisk well.

- In another bowl, mix coconut with panko and stir well.
- Dip chicken tenders in eggs mix and then coat in coconut one well.
- Spray chicken bites with cooking spray, place them in your air fryer's basket and cook them at 350 degrees F for 10 minutes.
- Arrange them on a platter and serve as an appetizer.
- Enjoy!

Nutrition: calories 252, fat 4, fiber 2, carbs 14, protein 24

Buffalo Cauliflower Snack

Preparation time: 10 minutes Cooking time: 15 minutes Servings: 4

INGREDIENTS:

- ✓ 4 cups cauliflower florets
- ✓ 1 cup panko bread crumbs
- ✓ ¼ cup butter, melted
- ✓ ¼ cup buffalo sauce
- ✓ Mayonnaise for serving

DIRECTIONS:

- In a bowl, mix buffalo sauce with butter and whisk well.
- Dip cauliflower florets in this mix and coat them in panko bread crumbs.
- Place them in your air fryer's basket and cook at 350 degrees F for 15 minutes.
- Arrange them on a platter and serve with mayo on the side.
- Enjoy!

Nutrition: calories 241, fat 4, fiber 7, carbs 8, protein 4

Banana Snack

Preparation time: 10 minutes Cooking time: 5 minutes Servings: 8

INGREDIENTS:

- ✓ 16 baking cups crust
- ✓ ¼ cup peanut butter
- ✓ ¾ cup chocolate chips
- ✓ 1 banana, peeled and sliced into 16 pieces
- ✓ 1 tablespoon vegetable oil

DIRECTIONS:

- Put chocolate chips in a small pot, heat up over low heat, stir until it melts and take off heat.
- In a bowl, mix peanut butter with coconut oil and whisk well.
- Spoon 1 teaspoon chocolate mix in a cup, add 1 banana slice and top with 1 teaspoon butter mix
- Repeat with the rest of the cups, place them all into a dish that fits your air fryer, cook at 320 degrees F for 5 minutes, transfer to a freezer and keep there until you serve them as a snack.
- Enjoy!

Nutrition: calories 70, fat 4, fiber 1, carbs 10, protein 1

Potato Spread

Preparation time: 10 minutes Cooking time: 10 minutes Servings: 10

INGREDIENTS:

- ✓ 19 ounces canned garbanzo beans, drained
- ✓ 1 cup sweet potatoes, peeled and chopped ¼ cup tahini
- ✓ 2 tablespoons lemon juice
- ✓ 1 tablespoon olive oil
- ✓ 5 garlic cloves, minced
- ✓ ½ teaspoon cumin, ground
- ✓ 2 tablespoons water
- ✓ A pinch of salt and white pepper

DIRECTIONS:

- ⏱ Put potatoes in your air fryer's basket, cook them at 360 degrees F for 15 minutes, cool them down, peel, put them in your food processor and pulse well. basket,
- ⏱ Add sesame paste, garlic, beans, lemon juice, cumin, water and oil and pulse really well.
- ⏱ Add salt and pepper, pulse again, divide into bowls and serve.
- ⏱ Enjoy!

Nutrition: calories 200, fat 3, fiber 10, carbs 20, protein 11

Mexican Apple Snack

Preparation time: 10 minutes Cooking time: 5 minutes Servings: 4

INGREDIENTS:

- ✓ 3 big apples, cored, peeled and cubed
- ✓ 2 teaspoons lemon juice
- ✓ ¼ cup pecans, chopped
- ✓ ½ cup dark chocolate chips
- ✓ ½ cup clean caramel sauce

DIRECTIONS:

- ⏱ In a bowl, mix apples with lemon juice, stir and transfer to a pan that fits your air fryer.
- ⏱ Add chocolate chips, pecans, drizzle the caramel sauce, toss, introduce in your air fryer and cook at 320 degrees F for 5 minutes.
- ⏱ Toss gently, divide into small bowls and serve right away as a snack.
- ⏱ Enjoy!

Nutrition: calories 200, fat 4, fiber 3, carbs 20, protein 3

Shrimp Muffins

Preparation time: 10 minutes Cooking time: 26 minutes Servings: 6

INGREDIENTS:

- ✓ 1 spaghetti squash, peeled and halved
- ✓ 2 tablespoons mayonnaise
- ✓ 1 cup mozzarella, shredded
- ✓ 8 ounces shrimp, peeled, cooked and chopped
- ✓ 1 and ½ cups panko
- ✓ 1 teaspoon parsley flakes
- ✓ 1 garlic clove, minced
- ✓ Salt and black pepper to the taste
- ✓ Cooking spray

DIRECTIONS:

- ⏱ Put squash halves in your air fryer, cook at 350 degrees F for 16 minutes, leave aside to cool down and scrape flesh into a bowl.
- ⏱ Add salt, pepper, parsley flakes, panko, shrimp, mayo and mozzarella and stir well.
- ⏱ Spray a muffin tray that fits your air fryer with cooking spray and divide squash and shrimp mix in each cup.
- ⏱ Introduce in the fryer and cook at 360 degrees F for 10 minutes.
- ⏱ Arrange muffins on a platter and serve as a snack.
- ⏱ Enjoy!

Nutrition: calories 60, fat 2, fiber 0.4, carbs 4, protein 4

Zucchini Cakes

Preparation time: 10 minutes Cooking time: 12 minutes Servings: 12

INGREDIENTS:

- ✓ Cooking spray
- ✓ ½ cup dill, chopped
- ✓ 1 egg
- ✓ ½ cup whole wheat flour
- ✓ Salt and black pepper to the taste
- ✓ 1 yellow onion, chopped
- ✓ 2 garlic cloves, minced
- ✓ 3 zucchinis, grated

DIRECTIONS:

- In a bowl, mix zucchinis with garlic, onion, flour, salt, pepper, egg and dill, stir well, shape small patties out of this mix, spray them with cooking spray, place them in your air fryer's basket and cook at 370 degrees F for 6 minutes on each side.
- Serve them as a snack right away.
- Enjoy!

Nutrition: calories 60, fat 1, fiber 2, carbs 6, protein 2

Sweet Popcorn

Preparation time: 5 minutes Cooking time: 10 minutes Servings: 4

INGREDIENTS:

- ✓ 2 tablespoons corn kernels
- ✓ 2 and ½ tablespoons butter
- ✓ 2 ounces brown sugar

DIRECTIONS:

- Put corn kernels in your air fryer's pan, cook at 400 degrees F for 6 minutes, transfer them to a tray, spread and leave aside for now.
- Heat up a pan over low heat, add butter, melt it, add sugar and stir until it dissolves.
- Add popcorn, toss to coat, take off heat and spread on the tray again.
- Cool down, divide into bowls and serve as a snack.
- Enjoy!

Nutrition: calories 70, fat 0.2, fiber 0, carbs 1, protein 1

Apple Chips

Preparation time: 10 minutes Cooking time: 10 minutes Servings: 2

INGREDIENTS:

- ✓ 1 apple, cored and sliced
- ✓ A pinch of salt
- ✓ ½ teaspoon cinnamon powder
- ✓ 1 tablespoon white sugar

DIRECTIONS:

- In a bowl, mix apple slices with salt, sugar and cinnamon, toss, transfer to your air fryer's basket, cook for 10 minutes at 390 degrees F flipping once.
- Divide apple chips in bowls and serve as a snack.
- Enjoy!

Nutrition: calories 70, fat 0, fiber 4, carbs 3, protein 1

Bread Sticks

Preparation time: 10 minutes Cooking time: 10 minutes Servings: 2

INGREDIENTS:

- ✓ 4 bread slices, each cut into 4 sticks
- ✓ 2 eggs
- ✓ ¼ cup milk
- ✓ 1 teaspoon cinnamon powder
- ✓ 1 tablespoon honey
- ✓ ¼ cup brown sugar
- ✓ A pinch of nutmeg

DIRECTIONS:

- In a bowl, mix eggs with milk, brown sugar, cinnamon, nutmeg and honey and whisk well.
- Dip bread sticks in this mix, place them in your air fryer's basket and cook at 360 degrees F for 10 minutes.
- Divide bread sticks into bowls and serve as a snack.
- Enjoy!

Nutrition: calories 140, fat 1, fiber 4, carbs 8, protein 4

Crispy Shrimp

Preparation time: 10 minutes Cooking time: 5 minutes Servings: 4

INGREDIENTS:

- ✓ 12 big shrimp, deveined and peeled
- ✓ 2 egg whites
- ✓ 1 cup coconut, shredded
- ✓ 1 cup panko bread crumbs
- ✓ 1 cup white flour
- ✓ Salt and black pepper to the taste

DIRECTIONS:

- In a bowl, mix panko with coconut and stir.
- Put flour, salt and pepper in a second bowl and whisk egg whites in a third one.
- Dip shrimp in flour, egg whites mix and coconut, place them all in your air fryer's basket, cook at 350 degrees F for 10 minutes flipping halfway.
- Arrange on a platter and serve as an appetizer.
- Enjoy!

Nutrition: calories 140, fat 4, fiber 0, carbs 3, protein 4

Cajun Shrimp Appetizer

Preparation time: 10 minutes Cooking time: 5 minutes Servings: 2

INGREDIENTS:

- ✓ 20 tiger shrimp, peeled and deveined
- ✓ Salt and black pepper to the taste
- ✓ ½ teaspoon old bay seasoning

- ✓ 1 tablespoon olive oil
- ✓ ¼ teaspoon smoked paprika

DIRECTIONS:

- In a bowl, mix shrimp with oil, salt, pepper, old bay seasoning and paprika and toss to coat.
- Place shrimp in your air fryer's basket and cook at 390 degrees F for 5 minutes.
- Arrange them on a platter and serve as an appetizer.
- Enjoy!

Nutrition: calories 162, fat 6, fiber 4, carbs 8, protein 14

Crispy Fish Sticks

Preparation time: 10 minutes Cooking time: 12 minutes Servings: 2

INGREDIENTS:

- ✓ 4 ounces bread crumbs
- ✓ 4 tablespoons olive oil
- ✓ 1 egg, whisked
- ✓ 4 white fish filets, boneless, skinless and cut into medium sticks Salt and black pepper to the taste

DIRECTIONS:

- In a bowl, mix bread crumbs with oil and stir well.
- Put egg in a second bowl, add salt and pepper and whisk well.
- Dip fish stick in egg and them in bread crumb mix, place them in your air fryer's basket and cook at 360 degrees F for 12 minutes.
- Arrange fish sticks on a platter and serve as an appetizer.
- Enjoy!

Nutrition: calories 160, fat 3, fiber 5, carbs 12, protein 3

Fish Nuggets

Preparation time: 10 minutes Cooking time: 12 minutes Servings: 4

INGREDIENTS:

- ✓ 28 ounces fish fillets, skinless and cut into medium pieces Salt and black pepper to the taste
- ✓ 5 tablespoons flour
- ✓ 1 egg, whisked
- ✓ 5 tablespoons water
- ✓ 3 ounces panko bread crumbs
- ✓ 1 tablespoon garlic powder
- ✓ 1 tablespoon smoked paprika
- ✓ 4 tablespoons homemade mayonnaise

- ✓ Lemon juice from ½ lemon
- ✓ 1 teaspoon dill, dried
- ✓ Cooking spray

DIRECTIONS:

- In a bowl, mix flour with water and stir well.
- Add egg, salt and pepper and whisk well.
- In a second bowl, mix panko with garlic powder and paprika and stir well.
- Dip fish pieces in flour and egg mix and then in panko mix, place them in your air fryer's basket, spray them with cooking oil and cook at 400 degrees F for 12 minutes.
- Meanwhile, in a bowl mix mayo with dill and lemon juice and whisk well.
- Arrange fish nuggets on a platter and serve with dill mayo on the side.
- Enjoy!

Nutrition: calories 332, fat 12, fiber 6, carbs 17, protein 15

Shrimp and Chestnut Rolls

Preparation time: 10 minutes Cooking time: 15 minutes Servings: 4

INGREDIENTS:

- ✓ ½ pound already cooked shrimp, chopped 8 ounces water chestnuts, chopped
- ✓ ½ pounds shiitake mushrooms, chopped
- ✓ 2 cups cabbage, chopped
- ✓ 2 tablespoons olive oil
- ✓ 1 garlic clove, minced
- ✓ 1 teaspoon ginger, grated
- ✓ 3 scallions, chopped
- ✓ Salt and black pepper to the taste
- ✓ 1 tablespoon water
- ✓ 1 egg yolk
- ✓ 6 spring roll wrappers

DIRECTIONS:

- Heat up a pan with the oil over medium high heat, add cabbage, shrimp, chestnuts, mushrooms, garlic, ginger, scallions, salt and pepper, stir and cook for 2 minutes.
- In a bowl, mix egg with water and stir well.
- Arrange roll wrappers on a working surface, divide shrimp and veggie mix on them, seal edges with egg wash, place them all in your air fryer's basket, cook at 360 degrees F for 15 minutes, transfer to a platter and serve as an appetizer.

Nutrition: calories 140, fat 3, fiber 1, carbs 12, protein 3

Seafood Appetizer

Preparation time: 10 minutes Cooking time: 25 minutes Servings: 4

INGREDIENTS:

- ✓ ½ cup yellow onion, chopped
- ✓ 1 cup green bell pepper, chopped
- ✓ 1 cup celery, chopped
- ✓ 1 cup baby shrimp, peeled and deveined
- ✓ 1 cup crabmeat, flaked
- ✓ 1 cup homemade mayonnaise
- ✓ 1 teaspoon Worcestershire sauce
- ✓ Salt and black pepper to the taste
- ✓ 2 tablespoons bread crumbs
- ✓ 1 tablespoon butter
- ✓ 1 teaspoon sweet paprika

DIRECTIONS:

- ⏱ In a bowl, mix shrimp with crab meat, bell pepper, onion, mayo, celery, salt and pepper and stir.
- ⏱ Add Worcestershire sauce, stir again and pour everything into a baking dish that fits your air fryer.
- ⏱ Sprinkle bread crumbs and add butter, introduce in your air fryer and cook at 320 degrees F for 25 minutes, shaking halfway.
- ⏱ Divide into bowl and serve with paprika sprinkled on top as an appetizer.
- ⏱ Enjoy!

Nutrition: calories 200, fat 1, fiber 2, carbs 5, protein 1

Salmon Meatballs

Preparation time: 10 minutes Cooking time: 12 minutes Servings: 4

INGREDIENTS:

- ✓ 3 tablespoons cilantro, minced
- ✓ 1 pound salmon, skinless and chopped
- ✓ 1 small yellow onion, chopped
- ✓ 1 egg white
- ✓ Salt and black pepper to the taste
- ✓ 2 garlic cloves, minced
- ✓ ½ teaspoon paprika
- ✓ ¼ cup panko
- ✓ ½ teaspoon oregano, ground
- ✓ Cooking spray

DIRECTIONS:

- ⏱ In your food processor, mix salmon with onion, cilantro, egg white, garlic cloves, salt, pepper, paprika and oregano and stir well.
- ⏱ Add panko, blend again and shape meatballs from this mix using your palms.
- ⏱ Place them in your air fryer's basket, spray them with cooking spray and cook at 320 degrees F for 12 minutes shaking the fryer halfway.
- ⏱ Arrange meatballs on a platter and serve them as an appetizer.
- ⏱ Enjoy!

Nutrition: calories 289, fat 12, fiber 3, carbs 22, protein 23

Easy Chicken Wings

Preparation time: 10 minutes Cooking time: 1 hours Servings: 2

INGREDIENTS:

- ✓ 16 pieces chicken wings
- ✓ Salt and black pepper to the taste
- ✓ ¼ cup butter
- ✓ ¾ cup potato starch
- ✓ ¼ cup honey
- ✓ 4 tablespoons garlic, minced

DIRECTIONS:

- ⏱ In a bowl, mix chicken wings with salt, pepper and potato starch, toss well, transfer to your air fryer's basket, cook them at 380 degrees F for 25 minutes and at 400 degrees F for 5 minutes more.
- ⏱ Meanwhile, heat up a pan with the butter over medium high heat, melt it, add garlic, stir, cook for 5 minutes and then mix with salt, pepper and honey.
- ⏱ Whisk well, cook over medium heat for 20 minutes and take off heat.
- ⏱ Arrange chicken wings on a platter, drizzle honey sauce all over and serve as an appetizer.
- ⏱ Enjoy!

Nutrition: calories 244, fat 7, fiber 3, carbs 19, protein 8

Chicken Breast Rolls

Preparation time: 10 minutes Cooking time: 22 minutes Servings: 4

INGREDIENTS:

- ✓ 2 cups baby spinach

- ✓ **4 chicken breasts, boneless and skinless**
- ✓ **1 cup sun dried tomatoes, chopped**
- ✓ **Salt and black pepper to the taste**
- ✓ **1 and ½ tablespoons Italian seasoning**
- ✓ **4 mozzarella slices**
- ✓ **A drizzle of olive oil**

DIRECTIONS:

- ⏱ Flatten chicken breasts using a meat tenderizer, divide tomatoes, mozzarella and spinach, season with salt, pepper and Italian seasoning, roll and seal them.
- ⏱ Place them in your air fryer's basket, drizzle some oil over them and cook at 375 degrees F for 17 minutes, flipping once.
- ⏱ Arrange chicken rolls on a platter and serve them as an appetizer.
- ⏱ Enjoy!

Nutrition: calories 300, fat 1, fiber 4, carbs 7, protein 10

Crispy Chicken Breast Sticks

Preparation time: 10 minutes Cooking time: 16 minutes Servings: 4

INGREDIENTS:

- ✓ **¾ cup white flour**
- ✓ **1 pound chicken breast, skinless, boneless and cut into medium sticks**
- ✓ **1 teaspoon sweet paprika**
- ✓ **1 cup panko bread crumbs**
- ✓ **1 egg, whisked**
- ✓ **Salt and black pepper to the taste**
- ✓ **½ tablespoon olive oil**
- ✓ **Zest from 1 lemon, grated**

DIRECTIONS:

- ⏱ In a bowl, mix paprika with flour, salt, pepper and lemon zest and stir.
- ⏱ Put whisked egg in another bowl and the panko breadcrumbs in a third one.
- ⏱ Dredge chicken pieces in flour, egg and panko and place them in your lined air fryer's basket, drizzle the oil over them, cook at 400 degrees F for 8 minutes, flip and cook for 8 more minutes.
- ⏱ Arrange them on a platter and serve as a snack.
- ⏱ Enjoy!

Nutrition: calories 254, fat 4, fiber 7, carbs 20, protein 22

Beef Roll s

Preparation time: 10 minutes Cooking time: 14 minutes Servings: 4

INGREDIENTS:

- ✓ **2 pounds beef steak, opened and flattened with a meat tenderizer Salt and black pepper to the taste**
- ✓ **1 cup baby spinach**
- ✓ **3 ounces red bell pepper, roasted and chopped**
- ✓ **6 slices provolone cheese**
- ✓ **3 tablespoons pesto**

DIRECTIONS:

- ⏱ Arrange flattened beef steak on a cutting board, spread pesto all over, add cheese in a single layer, add bell peppers, spinach, salt and pepper to the taste.
- ⏱ Roll your steak, secure with toothpicks, season again with salt and pepper, place roll in your air fryer's basket and cook at 400 degrees F for 14 minutes, rotating roll halfway.
- ⏱ Leave aside to cool down, cut into 2 inch smaller rolls, arrange on a platter and serve them as an appetizer.
- ⏱ Enjoy!

Nutrition: calories 230, fat 1, fiber 3, carbs 12, protein 10

Empanadas

Preparation time: 10 minutes Cooking time: 25 minutes Servings: 4

INGREDIENTS:

- ✓ **1 package empanada shells**
- ✓ **1 tablespoon olive oil**
- ✓ **1 pound beef meat, ground**
- ✓ **1 yellow onion, chopped**
- ✓ **Salt and black pepper to the taste**
- ✓ **2 garlic cloves, minced**
- ✓ **½ teaspoon cumin, ground**
- ✓ **¼ cup tomato salsa**
- ✓ **1 egg yolk whisked with 1 tablespoon water**
- ✓ **1 green bell pepper, chopped**

DIRECTIONS:

- ⏱ Heat up a pan with the oil over medium high heat, add beef and brown on all sides.
- ⏱ Add onion, garlic, salt, pepper, bell pepper and tomato salsa, stir and cook for 15 minutes.

- Divide cooked meat in empanada shells, brush them with egg wash and seal.
- Place them in your air fryer's steamer basket and cook at 350 degrees F for 10 minutes.
- Arrange on a platter and serve as an appetizer.
- Enjoy!

Nutrition: calories 274, fat 17, fiber 14, carbs 20, protein 7

Greek Lamb Meatballs

Preparation time: 10 minutes Cooking time: 8 minutes Servings: 10

INGREDIENTS:

- ✓ 4 ounces lamb meat, minced
- ✓ Salt and black pepper to the taste
- ✓ 1 slice of bread, toasted and crumbled
- ✓ 2 tablespoons feta cheese, crumbled
- ✓ ½ tablespoon lemon peel, grated
- ✓ 1 tablespoon oregano, chopped

DIRECTIONS:

- In a bowl, combine meat with bread crumbs, salt, pepper, feta, oregano and lemon peel, stir well, shape 10 meatballs and place them in you air fryer.
- Cook at 400 degrees F for 8 minutes, arrange them on a platter and serve as an appetizer.
- Enjoy!

Nutrition: calories 234, fat 12, fiber 2, carbs 20, protein 30

Beef Party Rolls

Preparation time: 10 minutes Cooking time: 15 minutes Servings: 4

INGREDIENTS:

- ✓ 14 ounces beef stock
- ✓ 7 ounces white wine
- ✓ 4 beef cutlets
- ✓ Salt and black pepper to the taste
- ✓ 8 sage leaves
- ✓ 4 ham slices
- ✓ 1 tablespoon butter, melted

DIRECTIONS:

- Heat up a pan with the stock over medium high heat, add wine, cook until it reduces, take off heat and divide into small bowls
- Season cutlets with salt and pepper, cover with sage and roll each in ham slices.
- Brush rolls with butter, place them in your air fryer's basket and cook at 400 degrees F for 15 minutes.

- Arrange rolls on a platter and serve them with the gravy on the side.
- Enjoy!

Nutrition: calories 260, fat 12, fiber 1, carbs 22, protein 21

Pork Rolls

Preparation time: 10 minutes Cooking time: 40 minutes Servings: 4

INGREDIENTS:

- ✓ 1 15 ounces pork fillet
- ✓ ½ teaspoon chili powder
- ✓ 1 teaspoon cinnamon powder
- ✓ 1 garlic clove, minced
- ✓ Salt and black pepper to the taste
- ✓ 2 tablespoons olive oil
- ✓ 1 and ½ teaspoon cumin, ground
- ✓ 1 red onion, chopped
- ✓ 3 tablespoons parsley, chopped

DIRECTIONS:

- In a bowl, mix cinnamon with garlic, salt, pepper, chili powder, oil, onion, parsley and cumin and stir well
- Put pork fillet on a cutting board, flatten it using a meat tenderizer. And use a meat tenderizer to flatten it.
- Spread onion mix on pork, roll tight, cut into medium rolls, place them in your preheated air fryer at 360 degrees F and cook them for 35 minutes.
- Arrange them on a platter and serve as an appetizer
- Enjoy!

Nutrition: calories 304, fat 12, fiber 1, carbs 15, protein 23

Beef Patties

Preparation time: 10 minutes Cooking time: 8 minutes Servings: 4

INGREDIENTS:

- ✓ 14 ounces beef, minced
- ✓ 2 tablespoons ham, cut into strips
- ✓ 1 leek, chopped
- ✓ 3 tablespoons bread crumbs
- ✓ Salt and black pepper to the taste
- ✓ ½ teaspoon nutmeg, ground

DIRECTIONS:

- In a bowl, mix beef with leek, salt, pepper, ham, breadcrumbs and nutmeg, stir well and shape small patties out of this mix.
- Place them in your air fryer's basket, cook at 400 degrees F for 8 minutes, arrange on a platter and serve as an appetizer.
- Enjoy!

Nutrition: calories 260, fat 12, fiber 3, carbs 12, protein 21

Roasted Bell Pepper Rolls

Preparation time: 10 minutes Cooking time: 10 minutes Servings: 8

INGREDIENTS:

- ✓ 1 yellow bell pepper, halved
- ✓ 1 orange bell pepper, halved
- ✓ Salt and black pepper to the taste
- ✓ 4 ounces feta cheese, crumbled
- ✓ 1 green onion, chopped
- ✓ 2 tablespoons oregano, chopped

DIRECTIONS:

- In a bowl, mix cheese with onion, oregano, salt and pepper and whisk well.
- Place bell pepper halves in your air fryer's basket, cook at 400 degrees F for 10 minutes, transfer to a cutting board, cool down and peel.
- Divide cheese mix on each bell pepper half, roll, secure with toothpicks, arrange on a platter and serve as an appetizer.
- Enjoy!

Nutrition: calories 170, fat 1, fiber 2, carbs 8, protein 5

Stuffed Peppers

Preparation time: 10 minutes Cooking time: 8 minutes Servings: 8

INGREDIENTS:

- ✓ 8 small bell peppers, tops cut off and seeds removed
- ✓ 1 tablespoon olive oil
- ✓ Salt and black pepper to the taste
- ✓ 3.5 ounces goat cheese, cut into 8 pieces

DIRECTIONS:

- In a bowl, mix cheese with oil with salt and pepper and toss to coat.
- Stuff each pepper with goat cheese, place them in your air fryer's basket, cook at 400 degrees F for 8 minutes, arrange on a platter and serve as an appetizer.

- Enjoy!

Nutrition: calories 120, fat 1, fiber 1, carbs 12, protein 8

Herbed Tomatoes Appetizer

Preparation time: 10 minutes Cooking time: 20 minutes Servings: 2

INGREDIENTS:

- ✓ 2 tomatoes, halved
- ✓ Cooking spray
- ✓ Salt and black pepper to the taste
- ✓ 1 teaspoon parsley, dried
- ✓ 1 teaspoon basil, dried
- ✓ 1 teaspoon oregano, dried
- ✓ 1 teaspoon rosemary, dried

DIRECTIONS:

- Spray tomato halves with cooking oil, season with salt, pepper, parsley, basil, oregano and rosemary over them.
- Place them in your air fryer's basket and cook at 320 degrees F for 20 minutes.
- Arrange them on a platter and serve as an appetizer.
- Enjoy!

Nutrition: calories 100, fat 1, fiber 1, carbs 4, protein 1

Olives B alls

Preparation time: 10 minutes Cooking time: 4 minutes Servings: 6

INGREDIENTS:

- ✓ 8 black olives, pitted and minced
- ✓ Salt and black pepper to the taste
- ✓ 2 tablespoons sun dried tomato pesto
- ✓ 14 pepperoni slices, chopped
- ✓ 4 ounces cream cheese
- ✓ 1 tablespoons basil, chopped

DIRECTIONS:

- In a bowl, mix cream cheese with salt, pepper, basil, pepperoni, pesto and black olives, stir well and shape small balls out of this mix.
- Place them in your air fryer's basket, cook at 350 degrees F for 4 minutes, arrange on a platter and serve as a snack.
- Enjoy!

Nutrition: calories 100, fat 1, fiber 0, carbs 8, protein 3

Jalapeno Balls

Preparation time: 10 minutes Cooking time: 4 minutes Servings: 3

INGREDIENTS:

- ✓ 3 bacon slices, cooked and crumbled
- ✓ 3 ounces cream cheese
- ✓ ¼ teaspoon onion powder
- ✓ Salt and black pepper to the taste
- ✓ 1 jalapeno pepper, chopped
- ✓ ½ teaspoon parsley, dried
- ✓ ¼ teaspoon garlic powder

DIRECTIONS:

- ⏱ In a bowl, mix cream cheese with jalapeno pepper, onion and garlic powder, parsley, bacon salt and pepper and stir well.
- ⏱ Shape small balls out of this mix, place them in your air fryer's basket, cook at 350 degrees F for 4 minutes, arrange on a platter and serve as an appetizer.
- ⏱ Enjoy!

Nutrition: calories 172, fat 4, fiber 1, carbs 12, protein 5

Wrapped Shrimp

Preparation time: 10 minutes Cooking time: 8 minutes Servings: 16

INGREDIENTS:

- ✓ 2 tablespoons olive oil
- ✓ 10 ounces already cooked shrimp, peeled and deveined
- ✓ 1 tablespoons mint, chopped
- ✓ 1/3 cup blackberries, ground
- ✓ 11 prosciutto sliced
- ✓ 1/3 cup red wine

DIRECTIONS:

- ⏱ Wrap each shrimp in a prosciutto slices, drizzle the oil over them, rub well, place in your preheated air fryer at 390 degrees F and fry them for 8 minutes.
- ⏱ Meanwhile, heat up a pan with ground blackberries over medium heat, add mint and wine, stir, cook for 3 minutes and take off heat.
- ⏱ Arrange shrimp on a platter, drizzle blackberries sauce over them and serve as an appetizer.
- ⏱ Enjoy!

Nutrition: calories 224, fat 12, fiber 2, carbs 12, protein 14

Broccoli Patties

Preparation time: 10 minutes Cooking time: 10 minutes Servings: 12

INGREDIENTS:

- ✓ 4 cups broccoli florets
- ✓ 1 and ½ cup almond flour
- ✓ 1 teaspoon paprika
- ✓ Salt and black pepper to the taste
- ✓ 2 eggs
- ✓ ¼ cup olive oil
- ✓ 2 cups cheddar cheese, grated
- ✓ 1 teaspoon garlic powder
- ✓ ½ teaspoon apple cider vinegar
- ✓ ½ teaspoon baking soda

DIRECTIONS:

- ⏱ Put broccoli florets in your food processor, add salt and pepper, blend well and transfer to a bowl.
- ⏱ Add almond flour, salt, pepper, paprika, garlic powder, baking soda, cheese, oil, eggs and vinegar, stir well and shape 12 patties out of this mix.
- ⏱ Place them in your preheated air fryer's basket and cook at 350 degrees F for 10 minutes.
- ⏱ Arrange patties on a platter and serve as an appetizer.
- ⏱ Enjoy!

Nutrition: calories 203, fat 12, fiber 2, carbs 14, protein 2

Different Stuffed Peppers

Preparation time: 10 minutes Cooking time: 20 minutes Servings: 6

INGREDIENTS:

- ✓ 1 pound mini bell peppers, halved
- ✓ Salt and black pepper to the taste
- ✓ 1 teaspoon garlic powder
- ✓ 1 teaspoon sweet paprika
- ✓ ½ teaspoon oregano, dried
- ✓ ¼ teaspoon red pepper flakes
- ✓ 1 pound beef meat, ground
- ✓ 1 and ½ cups cheddar cheese, shredded

- ✓ 1 tablespoons chili powder
- ✓ 1 teaspoon cumin, ground
- ✓ Sour cream for serving

DIRECTIONS:

- In a bowl, mix chili powder with paprika, salt, pepper, cumin, oregano, pepper flakes and garlic powder and stir.
- Heat up a pan over medium heat, add beef, stir and brown for 10 minutes.
- Add chili powder mix, stir, take off heat and stuff pepper halves with this mix.
- Sprinkle cheese all over, place peppers in your air fryer's basket and cook them at 350 degrees F for 6 minutes.
- Arrange peppers on a platter and serve them with sour cream on the side.
- Enjoy!

Nutrition: calories 170, fat 22, fiber 3, carbs 6, protein 27

Cheesy Zucchini Snack

Preparation time: 10 minutes Cooking time: 8 minutes Servings: 4

INGREDIENTS:

- ✓ 1 cup mozzarella, shredded
- ✓ ¼ cup tomato sauce
- ✓ 1 zucchini, sliced
- ✓ Salt and black pepper to the taste
- ✓ A pinch of cumin
- ✓ Cooking spray

DIRECTIONS:

- Arrange zucchini slices in your air fryer's basket, spray them with cooking oil, spread tomato sauce all over, them, season with salt, pepper, cumin, sprinkle mozzarella at the end and cook them at 320 degrees F for 8 minutes.
- Arrange them on a platter and serve as a snack.
- Enjoy!

Nutrition: calories 150, fat 4, fiber 2, carbs 12, protein 4

Spinach Balls

Preparation time: 10 minutes Cooking time: 7 minutes Servings: 30

INGREDIENTS:

- ✓ 4 tablespoons butter, melted
- ✓ 2 eggs
- ✓ 1 cup flour

- ✓ 16 ounces spinach
- ✓ 1/3 cup feta cheese, crumbled
- ✓ ¼ teaspoon nutmeg, ground
- ✓ 1/3 cup parmesan, grated
- ✓ Salt and black pepper to the taste
- ✓ 1 tablespoon onion powder
- ✓ 3 tablespoons whipping cream
- ✓ 1 teaspoon garlic powder

DIRECTIONS:

- In your blender, mix spinach with butter, eggs, flour, feta cheese, parmesan, nutmeg, whipping cream, salt, pepper, onion and garlic pepper, blend very well and keep in the freezer for 10 minutes.
- Shape 30 spinach balls, place them in your air fryer's basket and cook at 300 degrees F for 7 minutes.
- Serve as a party appetizer.
- Enjoy!

Nutrition: calories 60, fat 5, fiber 1, carbs 1, protein 2

Mushrooms Appetizer

Preparation time: 10 minutes Cooking time: 10 minutes Servings: 4

INGREDIENTS:

- ✓ ¼ cup mayonnaise
- ✓ 1 teaspoon garlic powder
- ✓ 1 small yellow onion, chopped
- ✓ 24 ounces white mushroom caps
- ✓ Salt and black pepper to the taste
- ✓ 1 teaspoon curry powder
- ✓ 4 ounces cream cheese, soft
- ✓ ¼ cup sour cream
- ✓ ½ cup Mexican cheese, shredded
- ✓ 1 cup shrimp, cooked, peeled, deveined and chopped

DIRECTIONS:

- In a bowl, mix mayo with garlic powder, onion, curry powder, cream cheese, sour cream, Mexican cheese, shrimp, salt and pepper to the taste and whisk well.
- Stuff mushrooms with this mix, place them in your air fryer's basket and cook at 300 degrees F for 10 minutes.
- Arrange on a platter and serve as an appetizer.
- Enjoy!

Nutrition: calories 200, fat 20, fiber 3, carbs 16, protein 14

Cheesy Party Wings

Preparation time: 10 minutes Cooking time: 12 minutes Servings: 6

INGREDIENTS:

- ✓ **6 pound chicken wings, halved**
- ✓ **Salt and black pepper to the taste**
- ✓ **½ teaspoon Italian seasoning**
- ✓ **2 tablespoons butter**
- ✓ **½ cup parmesan cheese, grated**
- ✓ **A pinch of red pepper flakes, crushed**
- ✓ **1 teaspoon garlic powder**
- ✓ **1 egg**

DIRECTIONS:

- Arrange chicken wings in your air fryer's basket and cook at 390 degrees F and cook for 9 minutes.
- Meanwhile, in your blender, mix butter with cheese, egg, salt, pepper, pepper flakes, garlic powder and Italian seasoning and blend very well.
- Take chicken wings out, pour cheese sauce over them, toss to coat well and cook in your air fryer's basket at 390 degrees F for 3 minutes.
- Serve them as an appetizer.
- Enjoy!

Nutrition: calories 204, fat 8, fiber 1, carbs 18, protein 14

Cheese Sticks

Preparation time: 1 hour and 10 minutes Cooking time: 8 minutes

Servings: 16

INGREDIENTS:

- ✓ **2 eggs, whisked**
- ✓ **Salt and black pepper to the taste**
- ✓ **8 mozzarella cheese strings, cut into halves**
- ✓ **1 cup parmesan, grated**
- ✓ **1 tablespoon Italian seasoning**
- ✓ **Cooking spray**
- ✓ **1 garlic clove, minced**

DIRECTIONS:

- In a bowl, mix parmesan with salt, pepper, Italian seasoning and garlic and stir well.
- Put whisked eggs in another bowl.
- Dip mozzarella sticks in egg mixture, then in cheese mix.

- Dip them again in egg and in parmesan mix and keep them in the freezer for 1 hour.
- Spray cheese sticks with cooking oil, place them in your air fryer's basket and cook at 390 degrees F for 8 minutes flipping them halfway.
- Arrange them on a platter and serve as an appetizer.
- Enjoy!

Nutrition: calories 140, fat 5, fiber 1, carbs 3, protein 4

Sweet Bacon Snack

Preparation time: 10 minutes Cooking time: 30 minutes Servings: 16

INGREDIENTS:

- ✓ **½ teaspoon cinnamon powder**
- ✓ **16 bacon slices**
- ✓ **1 tablespoon avocado oil**
- ✓ **3 ounces dark chocolate**
- ✓ **1 teaspoon maple extract**

DIRECTIONS:

- Arrange bacon slices in your air fryer's basket, sprinkle cinnamon mix over them and cook them at 300 degrees F for 30 minutes.
- Heat up a pot with the oil over medium heat, add chocolate and stir until it melts.
- Add maple extract, stir, take off heat and leave aside to cool down a bit.
- Take bacon strips out of the oven, leave them to cool down, dip each in chocolate mix, place them on a parchment paper and leave them to cool down completely.
- Serve cold as a snack.
- Enjoy!

Nutrition: calories 200, fat 4, fiber 5, carbs 12, protein 3

Chicken Rolls

Preparation time: 2 hours and 10 minutes Cooking time: 10 minutes

Servings: 12

INGREDIENTS:

- ✓ **4 ounces blue cheese, crumbled**
- ✓ **2 cups chicken, cooked and chopped**
- ✓ **Salt and black pepper to the taste**
- ✓ **2 green onions, chopped**
- ✓ **2 celery stalks, finely chopped**
- ✓ **½ cup tomato sauce**
- ✓ **12 egg roll wrappers**

- ✓ **Cooking spray**

DIRECTIONS:

- In a bowl, mix chicken meat with blue cheese, salt, pepper, green onions, celery and tomato sauce, stir well and keep in the fridge for 2 hours.
- Place egg wrappers on a working surface, divide chicken mix on them, roll and seal edges.
- Place rolls in your air fryer's basket, spray them with cooking oil and cook at 350 degrees F for 10 minutes, flipping them halfway.
- Enjoy!

Nutrition: calories 220, fat 7, fiber 2, carbs 14, protein 10

Tasty Kale and Celery Crackers

Preparation time: 10 minutes Cooking time: 20 minutes Servings: 6

INGREDIENTS:

- ✓ **2 cups flax seed, ground**
- ✓ **2 cups flax seed, soaked overnight and drained**
- ✓ **4 bunches kale, chopped**
- ✓ **1 bunch basil, chopped**
- ✓ **½ bunch celery, chopped**
- ✓ **4 garlic cloves, minced**
- ✓ **1/3 cup olive oil**

DIRECTIONS:

- In your food processor mix ground flaxseed with celery, kale, basil and garlic and blend well.
- Add oil and soaked flaxseed and blend again, spread in your air fryer's pan, cut into medium crackers and cook them at 380 degrees F for 20 minutes.
- Divide into bowls and serve as an appetizer.
- Enjoy!

Nutrition: calories 143, fat 1, fiber 2, carbs 8, protein 4

Egg White Chips

Preparation time: 5 minutes Cooking time: 8 minutes Servings: 2

INGREDIENTS:

- ✓ **½ tablespoon water**
- ✓ **2 tablespoons parmesan, shredded**
- ✓ **4 eggs whites**
- ✓ **Salt and black pepper to the taste**

DIRECTIONS:

- In a bowl, mix egg whites with salt, pepper and water and whisk well.

- Spoon this into a muffin pan that fits your air fryer, sprinkle cheese on top, introduce in your air fryer and cook at 350 degrees F for 8 minutes.
- Arrange egg white chips on a platter and serve as a snack.
- Enjoy!

Nutrition: calories 180, fat 2, fiber 1, carbs 12, protein 7

Tuna Cakes

Preparation time: 10 minutes Cooking time: 10 minutes Servings: 12

INGREDIENTS:

- ✓ **15 ounces canned tuna, drain and flaked**
- ✓ **3 eggs**
- ✓ **½ teaspoon dill, dried**
- ✓ **1 teaspoon parsley, dried**
- ✓ **½ cup red onion, chopped**
- ✓ **1 teaspoon garlic powder**
- ✓ **Salt and black pepper to the taste**
- ✓ **Cooking spray**

DIRECTIONS:

- In a bowl, mix tuna with salt, pepper, dill, parsley, onion, garlic powder and eggs, stir well and shape medium cakes out of this mix.
- Place tuna cakes in your air fryer's basket, spray them with cooking oil and cook at 350 degrees F for 10 minutes, flipping them halfway.
- Arrange them on a platter and serve as an appetizer.
- Enjoy!

Nutrition: calories 140, fat 2, fiber 1, carbs 8, protein 6

Calamari and Shrimp Snack

Preparation time: 10 minutes Cooking time: 20 minutes Servings: 1

INGREDIENTS:

- ✓ **8 ounces calamari, cut into medium rings**
- ✓ **7 ounces shrimp, peeled and deveined**
- ✓ **1 eggs**
- ✓ **3 tablespoons white flour**
- ✓ **1 tablespoon olive oil**
- ✓ **2 tablespoons avocado, chopped**
- ✓ **1 teaspoon tomato paste**
- ✓ **1 tablespoon mayonnaise**

- ✓ **A splash of Worcestershire sauce**
- ✓ **1 teaspoon lemon juice**
- ✓ **Salt and black pepper to the taste**
- ✓ **½ teaspoon turmeric powder**

DIRECTIONS:

- In a bowl, whisk egg with oil, add calamari rings and shrimp and toss to coat.
- In another bowl, mix flour with salt, pepper and turmeric and stir.
- Dredge calamari and shrimp in this mix, place them in your air fryer's basket and cook at 350 degrees F for 9 minutes, flipping them once.
- Meanwhile, in a bowl, mix avocado with mayo and tomato paste and mash using a fork.
- Add Worcestershire sauce, lemon juice, salt and pepper and stir well.
- Arrange calamari and shrimp on a platter and serve with the sauce on the side.
- Enjoy!

Nutrition: calories 288, fat 23, fiber 3, carbs 10, protein 15

Air Fryer Fish and Seafood Recipes

Cod Steaks with Plum Sauce

Preparation time: 10 minutes Cooking time: 20 minutes Servings: 2

INGREDIENTS:

- ✓ **2 big cod steaks**
- ✓ **Salt and black pepper to the taste**
- ✓ **½ teaspoon garlic powder**
- ✓ **½ teaspoon ginger powder**
- ✓ **¼ teaspoon turmeric powder**
- ✓ **1 tablespoon plum sauce**
- ✓ **Cooking spray**

DIRECTIONS:

- ⏱ Season cod steaks with salt and pepper, spray them with cooking oil, add garlic powder, ginger powder and turmeric powder and rub well.
- ⏱ Place cod steaks in your air fryer and cook at 360 degrees F for 15 minutes, flipping them after 7 minutes.
- ⏱ Heat up a pan over medium heat, add plum sauce, stir and cook for 2 minutes.
- ⏱ Divide cod steaks on plates, drizzle plum sauce all over and serve.
- ⏱ Enjoy!

Nutrition: calories 250, fat 7, fiber 1, carbs 14, protein 12

Flavored Air Fried Salmon

Preparation time: 1 hour Cooking time: 8 minutes Servings: 2

INGREDIENTS:

- ✓ **2 salmon fillets**
- ✓ **2 tablespoons lemon juice**
- ✓ **Salt and black pepper to the taste**
- ✓ **½ teaspoon garlic powder**
- ✓ **1/3 cup water**
- ✓ **1/3 cup soy sauce**
- ✓ **3 scallions, chopped**
- ✓ **1/3 cup brown sugar**
- ✓ **2 tablespoons olive oil**

DIRECTIONS:

- ⏱ In a bowl, mix sugar with water, soy sauce, garlic powder, salt, pepper, oil and lemon juice, whisk well, add salmon fillets, toss to coat and leave aside in the fridge for 1 hour.

- ⏱ Transfer salmon fillets to the fryer's basket and cook at 360 degrees F for 8 minutes flipping them halfway.
- ⏱ Divide salmon on plates, sprinkle scallions on top and serve right away.
- ⏱ Enjoy!

Nutrition: calories 300, fat 12, fiber 10, carbs 23, protein 20

Salmon with Capers and Mash

Preparation time: 10 minutes Cooking time: 20 minutes Servings: 4

INGREDIENTS:

- ✓ **4 salmon fillets, skinless and boneless**
- ✓ **1 tablespoon capers, drained**
- ✓ **Salt and black pepper to the taste**
- ✓ **Juice from 1 lemon**
- ✓ **2 teaspoons olive oil**

For the potato mash:

- ✓ **2 tablespoons olive oil**
- ✓ **1 tablespoon dill, dried**
- ✓ **1 pound potatoes, chopped**
- ✓ **½ cup milk**

DIRECTIONS:

- ⏱ Put potatoes in a pot, add water to cover, add some salt, bring to a boil over medium high heat, cook for 15 minutes, drain, transfer to a bowl, mash with a potato masher, add 2 tablespoons oil, dill, salt, pepper and milk, whisk well and leave aside for now.
- ⏱ Season salmon with salt and pepper, drizzle 2 teaspoons oil over them, rub, transfer to your air fryer's basket, add capers on top, cook at 360 degrees F and cook for 8 minutes.
- ⏱ Divide salmon and capers on plates, add mashed potatoes on the side, drizzle lemon juice all over and serve.
- ⏱ Enjoy!

Nutrition: calories 300, fat 17, fiber 8, carbs 12, protein 18

Lemony Saba Fish

Preparation time: 10 minutes Cooking time: 8 minutes Servings: 1

INGREDIENTS:

- ✓ **4 Saba fish fillet, boneless**
- ✓ **Salt and black pepper to the taste**
- ✓ **3 red chili pepper, chopped**
- ✓ **2 tablespoons lemon juice**

- ✓ **2 tablespoon olive oil**
- ✓ **2 tablespoon garlic, minced**

DIRECTIONS:

- ⏱ Season fish fillets with salt and pepper and put in a bowl.
- ⏱ Add lemon juice, oil, chili and garlic toss to coat, transfer fish to your air fryer and cook at 360 degrees F for 8 minutes, flipping halfway.
- ⏱ Divide among plates and serve with some fries.
- ⏱ Enjoy!

Nutrition: calories 300, fat 4, fiber 8, carbs 15, protein 15

Asian Halibut

Preparation time: 30 minutes Cooking time: 10 minutes Servings: 3

INGREDIENTS:

- ✓ **1 pound halibut steaks**
- ✓ **2/3 cup soy sauce**
- ✓ **¼ cup sugar**
- ✓ **2 tablespoons lime juice**
- ✓ **½ cup mirin**
- ✓ **¼ teaspoon red pepper flakes, crushed**
- ✓ **¼ cup orange juice**
- ✓ **¼ teaspoon ginger, grated**
- ✓ **1 garlic clove, minced**

DIRECTIONS:

- ⏱ Put soy sauce in a pan, heat up over medium heat, add mirin, sugar, lime and orange juice, pepper flakes, ginger and garlic, stir well, bring to a boil and take off heat.
- ⏱ Transfer half of the marinade to a bowl, add halibut, toss to coat and leave aside in the fridge for 30 minutes.
- ⏱ Transfer halibut to your air fryer and cook at 390 degrees F for 10 minutes, flipping once.
- ⏱ Divide halibut steaks on plates, drizzle the rest of the marinade all over and serve hot.
- ⏱ Enjoy!

Nutrition: calories 286, fat 5, fiber 12, carbs 14, protein 23

Cod and Vinaigrette

Preparation time: 10 minutes Cooking time: 15 minutes Servings: 4

INGREDIENTS:

- ✓ **4 cod fillets, skinless and boneless**
- ✓ **12 cherry tomatoes, halved**

- ✓ **8 black olives, pitted and roughly chopped**
- ✓ **2 tablespoons lemon juice**
- ✓ **Salt and black pepper to the taste**
- ✓ **2 tablespoons olive oil**
- ✓ **Cooking spray**
- ✓ **1 bunch basil, chopped**

DIRECTIONS:

- ⏱ Season cod with salt and pepper to the taste, place in your air fryer's basket and cook at 360 degrees F for 10 minutes, flipping after 5 minutes.
- ⏱ Meanwhile, heat up a pan with the oil over medium heat, add tomatoes, olives and lemon juice, stir, bring to a simmer, add basil, salt and pepper, stir well and take off heat.
- ⏱ Divide fish on plates and serve with the vinaigrette drizzled on top.
- ⏱ Enjoy!

Nutrition: calories 300, fat 5, fiber 8, carbs 12, protein 8

Shrimp and Crab Mix

Preparation time: 10 minutes Cooking time: 25 minutes Servings: 4

INGREDIENTS:

- ✓ **½ cup yellow onion, chopped**
- ✓ **1 cup green bell pepper, chopped**
- ✓ **1 cup celery, chopped**
- ✓ **1 pound shrimp, peeled and deveined**
- ✓ **1 cup crabmeat, flaked**
- ✓ **1 cup mayonnaise**
- ✓ **1 teaspoon Worcestershire sauce**
- ✓ **Salt and black pepper to the taste**
- ✓ **2 tablespoons breadcrumbs**
- ✓ **1 tablespoon butter, melted**
- ✓ **1 teaspoon sweet paprika**

DIRECTIONS:

- ⏱ In a bowl, mix shrimp with crab meat, bell pepper, onion, mayo, celery, salt, pepper and Worcestershire sauce, toss well and transfer to a pan that fits your air fryer.
- ⏱ Sprinkle bread crumbs and paprika, add melted butter, place in your air fryer and cook at 320 degrees F for 25 minutes, shaking halfway.
- ⏱ Divide among plates and serve right away.
- ⏱ Enjoy!

Nutrition: calories 200, fat 13, fiber 9, carbs 17, protein 19

Seafood Casserole

Preparation time: 10 minutes Cooking time: 40 minutes Servings: 6

INGREDIENTS:

- ✓ 6 tablespoons butter
- ✓ 2 ounces mushrooms, chopped
- ✓ 1 small green bell pepper, chopped
- ✓ 1 celery stalk, chopped
- ✓ 2 garlic cloves, minced
- ✓ 1 small yellow onion, chopped
- ✓ Salt and black pepper to the taste
- ✓ 4 tablespoons flour
- ✓ ½ cup white wine
- ✓ 1 and ½ cups milk
- ✓ ½ cup heavy cream
- ✓ 4 sea scallops, sliced
- ✓ 4 ounces haddock, skinless, boneless and cut into small pieces 4 ounces lobster meat, already cooked and cut into small pieces ½ teaspoon mustard powder
- ✓ 1 tablespoon lemon juice
- ✓ 1/3 cup bread crumbs
- ✓ Salt and black pepper to the taste
- ✓ 3 tablespoons cheddar cheese, grated
- ✓ A handful parsley, chopped
- ✓ 1 teaspoon sweet paprika

DIRECTIONS:

- Heat up a pan with 4 tablespoons butter over medium high heat, add bell pepper, mushrooms, celery, garlic, onion and wine, stir and cook for 10 minutes
- Add flour, cream and milk, stir well and cook for 6 minutes.
- Add lemon juice, salt, pepper, mustard powder, scallops, lobster meat and haddock, stir well, take off heat and transfer to a pan that fits your air fryer.
- In a bowl, mix the rest of the butter with bread crumbs, paprika and cheese and sprinkle over seafood mix.
- Transfer pan to your air fryer and cook at 360 degrees F for 16 minutes.

- Divide among plates and serve with parsley sprinkled on top.
- Enjoy!

Nutrition: calories 270, fat 32, fiber 14, carbs 15, protein 23

Trout Fillet and Orange Sauce

Preparation time: 10 minutes Cooking time: 10 minutes Servings: 4

INGREDIENTS:

- ✓ 4 trout fillets, skinless and boneless
- ✓ 4 spring onions, chopped
- ✓ 1 tablespoon olive oil
- ✓ 1 tablespoon ginger, minced
- ✓ Salt and black pepper to the taste
- ✓ Juice and zest from 1 orange

DIRECTIONS:

- Season trout fillets with salt, pepper, rub them with the olive oil, place in a pan that fits your air fryer, add ginger, green onions, orange zest and juice, toss well, place in your air fryer and cook at 360 degrees F for 10 minutes.
- Divide fish and sauce on plates and serve right away.
- Enjoy!

Nutrition: calories 239, fat 10, fiber 7, carbs 18, protein 23

Cod Fillets and Peas

Preparation time: 10 minutes Cooking time: 10 minutes Servings: 4

INGREDIENTS:

- ✓ 4 cod fillets, boneless
- ✓ 2 tablespoons parsley, chopped
- ✓ 2 cups peas
- ✓ 4 tablespoons wine
- ✓ ½ teaspoon oregano, dried
- ✓ ½ teaspoon sweet paprika
- ✓ 2 garlic cloves, minced
- ✓ Salt and pepper to the taste

DIRECTIONS:

- In your food processor mix garlic with parsley, salt, pepper, oregano, paprika and wine and blend well.
- Rub fish with half of this mix, place in your air fryer and cook at 360 degrees F for 10 minutes.

- Meanwhile, put peas in a pot, add water to cover, add salt, bring to a boil over medium high heat, cook for 10 minutes, drain and divide among plates.
- Also divide fish on plates, spread the rest of the herb dressing all over and serve.
- Enjoy!

Nutrition: calories 261, fat 8, fiber 12, carbs 20, protein 22

Thyme and Parsley Salmon

Preparation time: 10 minutes Cooking time: 15 minutes Servings: 4

INGREDIENTS:

- ✓ **4 salmon fillets, boneless**
- ✓ **Juice from 1 lemon**
- ✓ **1 yellow onion, chopped**
- ✓ **3 tomatoes, sliced**
- ✓ **4 thyme springs**
- ✓ **4 parsley springs**
- ✓ **3 tablespoons extra virgin olive oil**
- ✓ **Salt and black pepper to the taste**

DIRECTIONS:

- Drizzle 1 tablespoon oil in a pan that fits your air fryer,, add a layer of tomatoes, salt and pepper, drizzle 1 more tablespoon oil, add fish, season them with salt and pepper, drizzle the rest of the oil, add thyme and parsley springs, onions, lemon juice, salt and pepper, place in your air fryer's basket and cook at 360 degrees F for 12 minutes shaking once.
- Divide everything on plates and serve right away.
- Enjoy!

Nutrition: calories 242, fat 9, fiber 12, carbs 20, protein 31

Battered & Crispy Fish Tacos

Preparation: 10minutes Cooking time: 10 minutes Servings: 2

INGREDIENTS:

- ✓ **11/2 cup Flour Corn tortillas Peach salsa Cilantro**
- ✓ **Fresh halibut, slice into strips**
- ✓ **1 can of beer**
- ✓ **2 tablespoons Vegetable Oil**
- ✓ **1 teaspoon baking powder**
- ✓ **1 teaspoon Salt Cholula sauce Avocado Cream (recipe below)**

DIRECTIONS:

- Lay out the corn tortillas topped with peach salsa on a plate and set aside.
- Combine 1 cup of flour, beer and baking powder until it forms a pancake like consistency.
- Toss the fish in the remaining flour then dip in the beer batter mixture until well coated.
- Place on preheated Air Fryer rack and cook 6-8 minutes or until golden at 200°F.
- Place the fish on top of the salsa mixture topped with avocado cream, cilantro and Cholula sauce.
- To Make The Avocado Cream:
- 1 large avocado 3/4 cup buttermilk Juice from 1/2 lime Combine in a blender until smooth.

Steamed Salmon & Dill Dip

Preparation: 15 minutes Cooking time: 10 minutes Servings: 2

INGREDIENTS:

- ✓ **¾ pound of salmon, cut in half**
- ✓ **8 tablespoons of sour cream**
- ✓ **2 teaspoons of olive oil**
- ✓ **6 teaspoons of finely chopped dill**
- ✓ **8 tablespoons of Greek Yogurt**
- ✓ **¼ teaspoons of salt**

DIRECTIONS:

- Heat your Air Fryer to 285°F. Add a cup of cool water at the base of your Air Fryer.
- Coat each portion of the salmon with olive oil and season with salt.
- Place into the fryer basket and cook for about 11 minutes.
- While cooking the fish, mix the sour cream, salt, yogurt and dill in a bowl.
- Remove the fish from the Air Fryer and garnish with a pinch of dill and serve with the dill dip.

Salmon And Potato Fishcakes

Preparation: 63 minutes Cooking time: 7 minutes Servings: 4

INGREDIENTS:

- ✓ **14 ounces of potatoes, cooked and mashed**
- ✓ **4 tablespoons of chopped parsley**
- ✓ **½ pound of salmon, cooked and shredded**
- ✓ **¼ cup of flour**
- ✓ **1 ounce of capers**
- ✓ **1 lemon zest Salt and pepper to taste Oil spray**

DIRECTIONS:

- Mix the mashed potatoes with the salmon, capers, parsley and zest. Add salt and pepper and mix thoroughly.
- Mold into cakes and coat with flour. Refrigerate for an hour until firm.
- Preheat the Air Fryer to 356°F.
- Put the fishcakes into the air fryer basket, spray oil on them and bake for about 7 minutes.

Crab And Vegetable Croquettes

Preparation: 30 minutes Cooking time: 20 minutes Servings: 6

INGREDIENTS:

- ✓ 4 tablespoons of finely chopped bell pepper
- ✓ 4 tablespoons of mayonnaise
- ✓ 4 tablespoons of finely chopped onions
- ✓ 4 tablespoons of sour cream
- ✓ 16 ounces of lump crabmeat
- ✓ 1 teaspoon of vegetable oil
- ✓ ½ teaspoon of lemon juice
- ✓ ½ teaspoon of salt
- ✓ ½ teaspoon of finely chopped parsley
- ✓ ½ teaspoon of ground pepper
- ✓ 2 egg whites
- ✓ 6 teaspoons of finely chopped celery
- ✓ ¼ teaspoon of finely chopped tarragon
- ✓ ¼ teaspoon of finely chopped chives
- ✓ 1 cup of breadcrumbs
- ✓ 1 cup of flour

DIRECTIONS:

- Mix the onions, vegetable oil, celery and peppers in a pot and place over medium heat. Sweat for 5 minutes until translucent. Turn off heat and set aside to cool.
- Transfer the mixture into a mixing bowl and add the crabmeat, chives, tarragon, mayonnaise, ground pepper, lemon juice, sour cream, and parsley. Mix thoroughly and mold into small balls.
- Heat your Air Fryer to 390°F.
- Mix the breadcrumbs and salt together and set aside. Put the egg white and flour into separate bowls.
- Put the molded balls into the flour, then dip into egg whites and finally roll them in the breadcrumbs to coat evenly.

- Place half of the balls in the fryer basket and cook for 10 minutes until golden. Do same for the second batch until all the croquettes are cooked.

Coconut Coated Fish Cakes With Mango Sauce

Preparation: 20 minutes Cooking time: 14 minutes Servings: 4

INGREDIENTS:

- ✓ 18 ounces of white fish fillet
- ✓ 1 green onion, finely chopped
- ✓ 1 mango, peeled, cubed
- ✓ 4 tablespoons of ground coconut
- ✓ 1½ ounces of parsley, finely chopped
- ✓ 1½ teaspoons of ground fresh red chili
- ✓ 1 lime, juice and zest
- ✓ 1 egg
- ✓ 1 teaspoon of salt

DIRECTIONS:

- Add ½ ounce of parsley, ½ teaspoon of ground chili, half of the lime juice and zest to the mango cubes and mix thoroughly.
- Using a food processor, puree the fish and add the salt, egg, and the rest of the lime zest, lime juice and chili. Stir in the green onions, 2 tablespoons of coconut and the rest of the parsley.
- Put the rest of the coconut in a shallow dish. Mold the fish mixture into 12 round cakes. Place the cakes in the coconut to coat them.
- Put half of the cakes into the fryer basket and bake for 7 minutes at 356°F. Remove when cakes are golden and bake the second batch of cakes.
- Serve the cakes with the mango salsa.

Teriyaki Glazed Halibut Steak

Preparation: 30 minutes Cooking time: 10-15 minutes Servings: 3

INGREDIENTS

- ✓ 1 pound halibut steak For The Marinade:
- ✓ 2/3 cup low sodium soy sauce
- ✓ ½ cup mirin
- ✓ 2 tablespoons lime juice
- ✓ ¼ cup sugar
- ✓ ¼ cup orange juice
- ✓ ¼ teaspoon ginger ground

- ✓ ¼ teaspoon crushed red pepper flakes
- ✓ 1 each garlic clove (smashed)

DIRECTIONS

- ◔ Place all the Ingredients for the teriyaki glaze/marinade in a sauce pan. Bring to a boil and lessen by half, then let it cool.
- ◔ When it cools, pour half of the glaze/marinade into a Ziploc bag together with the halibut then refrigerate for 30 minutes.
- ◔ Preheat the Air Fryer to 390°F. Place the marinated halibut into the Air Fryer and cook 10-12 minutes. Brush some of the glaze that's left over the halibut steak.
- ◔ Spread over white rice with basil/mint chutney.

Salmon And Potato Patties

Preparation: 10 minutes Cooking time: 29 minutes Servings: 8

INGREDIENTS:

- ✓ 7 ounces of salmon
- ✓ 1 cup of breadcrumbs
- ✓ 3 russet potatoes (about
- ✓ 7 ounce each) peeled, chopped
- ✓ 1 egg, whisked
- ✓ 4 ounces of frozen vegetables, parboiled and drained
- ✓ 1 tablespoon of finely chopped parsley
- ✓ ½ teaspoon of black pepper
- ✓ 1 teaspoon of dill Salt to taste
- ✓ Oil spray

DIRECTIONS:

- ◔ Put the chopped potatoes into boiling water and cook for 10-12 minutes. Drain off water completely. Mash the potatoes with a wooden mixer and place in a refrigerator to cool.
- ◔ Heat your air fryer to 356°F for 5 minutes. Put in the salmon and grill for 5 minutes. Remove and flake the salmon using a fork.
- ◔ Take the mashed potatoes out of the refrigerator and add the salmon, vegetables, black pepper, salt, dill and parsley and mix together. Add the whisked egg and stir.
- ◔ Mold into 8 patties and coat the patties with the breadcrumbs. Spray the patties with oil using oil spray.
- ◔ Place them into the air fryer and cook for about 12 minutes or until golden. You can serve with mayo and lemon with a salad.

Air Fried Crumbed Fish

Preparation: 10 minutes Cooking time: 12 minutes Servings: 2

INGREDIENTS

- ✓ 4 fish fillets
- ✓ 5 oz. breadcrumbs
- ✓ 4 tablespoons vegetable oil
- ✓ 1 egg, whisked
- ✓ 1 lemon, to serve

DIRECTIONS

- ◔ Preheat air fryer to 350 degrees F. Combine breadcrumbs and stir well until crumbly and loose.
- ◔ Dip the fish fillets into the egg, shake off residual then dip into breadcrumb mix, ensuring that it is thoroughly and evenly coated.
- ◔ Lay in the air fryer gently and cook for 12 minutes. Serve with lemon.

Fried Fish With Onions

Preparation: 40 minutes Cooking time: 40 minutes Servings: 2

INGREDIENTS

- ✓ ½ pound fish fillets, wash & cubed
- ✓ ½ onion, minced
- ✓ 1 clove garlic, minced
- ✓ 1 tablespoon oil
- ✓ 1 tablespoon chili paste
- ✓ 1½ tablespoon soy sauce
- ✓ 1 tablespoon sugar
- ✓ ¼ cup water
- ✓ 1/2 tablespoon salt
- ✓ 2 tablespoon vinegar

DIRECTIONS:

- ◔ Marinate fish cubes with salt for 30 minutes. Preheat Air Fryer to 390F. Layer the fish with oil, and place in the air fryer. Cook for 15 minutes.
- ◔ Meanwhile, add the oil, chili paste, onion and garlic to a small pan. Turn heat to medium and stirfry for 5 minutes until the onions are translucent.
- ◔ Remove fish from the air fryer, and place in the pan. Now add the water, soy sauce, sugar, salt and vinegar. Lower heat, cover and simmer for 10 minutes.
- ◔ Finally, set heat to high. Remove when sauce thickens.

Cod Fish Nuggets

Nutrition: calories 300, fat 12, fiber 9, carbs 27, protein 24

Preparation: 15 minutes Cooking time: 10 minutes Servings: 4

INGREDIENTS

- ✓ 1 pound cod, cut lengthwise into strips of 1-inch by 5

For The Breading:

- ✓ 1 cup all-purpose flour
- ✓ 2 tablespoons olive oil ¾ cup panko breadcrumbs
- ✓ 2 eggs, beaten
- ✓ 1 pinch salt

DIRECTIONS

- ⏱ Preheat the Air Fryer to 390°F. Blend the panko, breadcrumbs, olive oil and salt in a food processor.
- ⏱ Set aside the panko mixture, flour and eggs in three separate bowls.
- ⏱ Place cod pieces into the flour, the eggs and the breadcrumbs, pressing firmly to ensure that the breadcrumbs stick to the fish. Shake any excess breadcrumbs off.
- ⏱ Add the cod nuggets to the cooking basket and cook 8 to 10 minutes until golden brown.

Trout and Butter Sauce

Preparation time: 10 minutes Cooking time: 10 minutes Servings: 4

INGREDIENTS:

- ✓ 4 trout fillets, boneless
- ✓ Salt and black pepper to the taste
- ✓ 3 teaspoons lemon zest, grated
- ✓ 3 tablespoons chives, chopped
- ✓ 6 tablespoons butter
- ✓ 2 tablespoons olive oil
- ✓ 2 teaspoons lemon juice

DIRECTIONS:

- ⏱ Season trout with salt and pepper, drizzle the olive oil, rub, transfer to your air fryer and cook at 360 degrees F for 10 minutes, flipping once.
- ⏱ Meanwhile, heat up a pan with the butter over medium heat, add salt, pepper, chives, lemon juice and zest, whisk well, cook for 1-2 minutes and take off heat
- ⏱ Divide fish fillets on plates, drizzle butter sauce all over and serve.
- ⏱ Enjoy!

Creamy Salmon

Preparation time: 10 minutes Cooking time: 10 minutes Servings: 4

INGREDIENTS:

- ✓ 4 salmon fillets, boneless
- ✓ 1 tablespoons olive oil
- ✓ Salt and black pepper to the taste
- ✓ 1/3 cup cheddar cheese, grated
- ✓ 1 and ½ teaspoon mustard
- ✓ ½ cup coconut cream

DIRECTIONS:

- ⏱ Season salmon with salt and pepper, drizzle the oil and rub well.
- ⏱ In a bowl, mix coconut cream with cheddar, mustard, salt and pepper and stir well.
- ⏱ Transfer salmon to a pan that fits your air fryer, add coconut cream mix, introduce in your air fryer and cook at 320 degrees F for 10 minutes.
- ⏱ Divide among plates and serve.
- ⏱ Enjoy!

Nutrition: calories 200, fat 6, fiber 14, carbs 17, protein 20

Salmon and Avocado Salsa

Preparation time: 30 minutes Cooking time: 10 minutes Servings: 4

INGREDIENTS:

- ✓ 4 salmon fillets
- ✓ 1 tablespoon olive oil
- ✓ Salt and black pepper to the taste
- ✓ 1 teaspoon cumin, ground
- ✓ 1 teaspoon sweet paprika
- ✓ ½ teaspoon chili powder
- ✓ 1 teaspoon garlic powder

For the salsa:

- ✓ 1 small red onion, chopped
- ✓ 1 avocado, pitted, peeled and chopped
- ✓ 2 tablespoons cilantro, chopped
- ✓ Juice from 2 limes
- ✓ Salt and black pepper to the taste

DIRECTIONS:

- In a bowl, mix salt, pepper, chili powder, onion powder, paprika and cumin, stir, rub salmon with this mix, drizzle the oil, rub again, transfer to your air fryer and cook at 350 degrees F for 5 minutes on each side.
- Meanwhile, in a bowl, mix avocado with red onion, salt, pepper, cilantro and lime juice and stir.
- Divide fillets on plates, top with avocado salsa and serve.
- Enjoy!

Nutrition: calories 300, fat 14, fiber 4, carbs 18, protein 16

Tasty Air Fried Cod

Preparation time: 10 minutes Cooking time: 12 minutes Servings: 4

INGREDIENTS:

- ✓ **2 cod fish, 7 ounces each**
- ✓ **A drizzle of sesame oil**
- ✓ **Salt and black pepper to the taste**
- ✓ **1 cup water**
- ✓ **1 teaspoon dark soy sauce**
- ✓ **4 tablespoons light soy sauce**
- ✓ **1 tablespoon sugar**
- ✓ **3 tablespoons olive oil**
- ✓ **4 ginger slices**
- ✓ **3 spring onions, chopped**
- ✓ **2 tablespoons coriander, chopped**

DIRECTIONS:

- Season fish with salt, pepper, drizzle sesame oil, rub well and leave aside for 10 minutes.
- Add fish to your air fryer and cook at 356 degrees F for 12 minutes.
- Meanwhile, heat up a pot with the water over medium heat, add dark and light soy sauce and sugar, stir, bring to a simmer and take off heat.
- Heat up a pan with the olive oil over medium heat, add ginger and green onions, stir, cook for a few minutes and take off heat.
- Divide fish on plates, top with ginger and green onions, drizzle soy sauce mix, sprinkle coriander and serve right away.
- Enjoy!

Nutrition: calories 300, fat 17, fiber 8, carbs 20, protein 22

Delicious Catfish

Preparation time: 10 minutes Cooking time: 20 minutes Servings: 4

INGREDIENTS:

- ✓ **4 cat fish fillets**
- ✓ **Salt and black pepper to the taste**
- ✓ **A pinch of sweet paprika**
- ✓ **1 tablespoon parsley, chopped**
- ✓ **1 tablespoon lemon juice**
- ✓ **1 tablespoon olive oil**

DIRECTIONS:

- Season catfish fillets with salt, pepper, paprika, drizzle oil, rub well, place in your air fryer's basket and cook at 400 degrees F for 20 minutes, flipping the fish after 10 minutes.
- Divide fish on plates, drizzle lemon juice all over, sprinkle parsley and serve.
- Enjoy!

Nutrition: calories 253, fat 6, fiber 12, carbs 26, protein 22

Cod Fillets with Fennel and Grapes Salad

Preparation time: 10 minutes Cooking time: 15 minutes Servings: 2

INGREDIENTS:

- ✓ **2 black cod fillets, boneless**
- ✓ **1 tablespoon olive oil**
- ✓ **Salt and black pepper to the taste**
- ✓ **1 fennel bulb, thinly sliced**
- ✓ **1 cup grapes, halved**
- ✓ **½ cup pecans**

DIRECTIONS:

- Drizzle half of the oil over fish fillets, season with salt and pepper, rub well, place fillets in your air fryer's basket, cook for 10 minutes at 400 degrees F and transfer to a plate.
- In a bowl, mix pecans with grapes, fennel, the rest of the oil, salt and pepper, toss to coat, add to a pan that fits your air fryer and cook at 400 degrees F for 5 minutes.
- Divide cod on plates, add fennel and grapes mix on the side and serve.
- Enjoy!

Nutrition: calories 300, fat 4, fiber 2, carbs 32, protein 22

Tabasco Shrimp

Preparation time: 10 minutes Cooking time: 10 minutes Servings: 4

INGREDIENTS:

- ✓ 1 pound shrimp, peeled and deveined
- ✓ 1 teaspoon red pepper flakes
- ✓ 2 tablespoon olive oil
- ✓ 1 teaspoon Tabasco sauce
- ✓ 2 tablespoons water
- ✓ 1 teaspoon oregano, dried
- ✓ Salt and black pepper to the taste
- ✓ ½ teaspoon parsley, dried
- ✓ ½ teaspoon smoked paprika

DIRECTIONS:

- In a bowl, mix oil with water, Tabasco sauce, pepper flakes, oregano, parsley, salt, pepper, paprika and shrimp and toss well to coat.
- Transfer shrimp to your preheated air fryer at 370 degrees F and cook for 10 minutes shaking the fryer once.
- Divide shrimp on plates and serve with a side salad.
- Enjoy!

Nutrition: calories 200, fat 5, fiber 6, carbs 13, protein 8

Buttered Shrimp Skewers

Preparation time: 10 minutes Cooking time: 6 minutes Servings: 2

INGREDIENTS:

- ✓ 8 shrimps, peeled and deveined
- ✓ 4 garlic cloves, minced
- ✓ Salt and black pepper to the taste
- ✓ 8 green bell pepper slices
- ✓ 1 tablespoon rosemary, chopped
- ✓ 1 tablespoon butter, melted

DIRECTIONS:

- In a bowl, mix shrimp with garlic, butter, salt, pepper, rosemary and bell pepper slices, toss to coat and leave aside for 10 minutes.
- Arrange 2 shrimp and 2 bell pepper slices on a skewer and repeat with the rest of the shrimp and bell pepper pieces.
- Place them all in your air fryer's basket and cook at 360 degrees F for 6 minutes.
- Divide among plates and serve right away.
- Enjoy!

Nutrition: calories 140, fat 1, fiber 12, carbs 15, protein 7

Asian Salmon

Preparation time: 1 hour Cooking time: 15 minutes Servings: 2

INGREDIENTS:

- ✓ 2 medium salmon fillets
- ✓ 6 tablespoons light soy sauce
- ✓ 3 teaspoons mirin
- ✓ 1 teaspoon water
- ✓ 6 tablespoons honey

DIRECTIONS:

- In a bowl, mix soy sauce with honey, water and mirin, whisk well, add salmon, rub well and leave aside in the fridge for 1 hour.
- Transfer salmon to your air fryer and cook at 360 degrees F for 15 minutes, flipping them after 7 minutes.
- Meanwhile, put the soy marinade in a pan, heat up over medium heat, whisk well, cook for 2 minutes and take off heat.
- Divide salmon on plates, drizzle marinade all over and serve.
- Enjoy!

Nutrition: calories 300, fat 12, fiber 8, carbs 13, protein 24

Italian Barramundi Fillets and Tomato Salsa

Preparation time: 10 minutes Cooking time: 8 minutes Servings: 4

INGREDIENTS:

- ✓ 2 barramundi fillets, boneless
- ✓ 1 tablespoon olive oil+ 2 teaspoons
- ✓ 2 teaspoons Italian seasoning
- ✓ ¼ cup green olives, pitted and chopped
- ✓ ¼ cup cherry tomatoes, chopped
- ✓ ¼ cup black olives, chopped
- ✓ 1 tablespoon lemon zest
- ✓ 2 tablespoons lemon zest
- ✓ Salt and black pepper to the taste
- ✓ 2 tablespoons parsley, chopped

DIRECTIONS:

- Rub fish with salt, pepper, Italian seasoning and 2 teaspoons olive oil, transfer to your air fryer and cook at 360 degrees F for 8 minutes, flipping them halfway.
- In a bowl, mix tomatoes with black olives, green olives, salt, pepper, lemon zest and lemon juice, parsley and 1 tablespoon olive oil and toss well

- ⏱ Divide fish on plates, add tomato salsa on top and serve.
- ⏱ Enjoy!

Nutrition: calories 270, fat 4, fiber 2, carbs 18, protein 27

Creamy Shrimp and Veggies

Preparation time: 10 minutes Cooking time: 30 minutes Servings: 4

INGREDIENTS:

- ✓ 8 ounces mushrooms, chopped
- ✓ 1 asparagus bunch, cut into medium pieces
- ✓ 1 pound shrimp, peeled and deveined
- ✓ Salt and black pepper to the taste
- ✓ 1 spaghetti squash, cut into halves
- ✓ 2 tablespoons olive oil
- ✓ 2 teaspoons Italian seasoning
- ✓ 1 yellow onion, chopped
- ✓ 1 teaspoon red pepper flakes, crushed
- ✓ ¼ cup butter, melted
- ✓ 1 cup parmesan cheese, grated
- ✓ 2 garlic cloves, minced
- ✓ 1 cup heavy cream

DIRECTIONS:

- ⏱ Place squash halves in you air fryer's basket, cook at 390 degrees F for 17 minutes, transfer to a cutting board, scoop insides and transfer to a bowl.
- ⏱ Put water in a pot, add some salt, bring to a boil over medium heat, add asparagus, steam for a couple of minutes, transfer to a bowl filled with ice water, drain and leave aside as well.
- ⏱ Heat up a pan that fits your air fryer with the oil over medium heat, add onions and mushrooms, stir and cook for 7 minutes.
- ⏱ Add pepper flakes, Italian seasoning, salt, pepper, squash, asparagus, shrimp, melted butter, cream, parmesan and garlic, toss and cook in your air fryer at 360 degrees F for 6 minutes.
- ⏱ Divide everything on plates and serve.
- ⏱ Enjoy!

Nutrition: calories 325, fat 6, fiber 5, carbs 14, protein 13

Tuna and Chimichuri Sauce

Preparation time: 10 minutes Cooking time: 8 minutes Servings: 4

INGREDIENTS:

- ✓ ½ cup cilantro, chopped
- ✓ 1/3 cup olive oil+ 2 tablespoons
- ✓ 1 small red onion, chopped
- ✓ 3 tablespoon balsamic vinegar
- ✓ 2 tablespoons parsley, chopped
- ✓ 2 tablespoons basil, chopped
- ✓ 1 jalapeno pepper, chopped
- ✓ 1 pound sushi tuna steak
- ✓ Salt and black pepper to the taste
- ✓ 1 teaspoon red pepper flakes
- ✓ 1 teaspoon thyme, chopped
- ✓ 3 garlic cloves, minced
- ✓ 2 avocados, pitted, peeled and sliced
- ✓ 6 ounces baby arugula

DIRECTIONS:

- ⏱ In a bowl, mix 1/3 cup oil with jalapeno, vinegar, onion, cilantro, basil, garlic, parsley, pepper flakes, thyme, salt and pepper, whisk well and leave aside for now.
- ⏱ Season tuna with salt and pepper, rub with the rest of the oil, place in your air fryer and cook at 360 degrees F for 3 minutes on each side.
- ⏱ Mix arugula with half of the chimichuri mix you've made and toss to coat.
- ⏱ Divide arugula on plates, slice tuna and also divide among plates, top with the rest of the chimichuri and serve.
- ⏱ Enjoy!

Nutrition: calories 276, fat 3, fiber 1, carbs 14, protein 20

Squid and Guacamole

Preparation time: 10 minutes Cooking time: 6 minutes Servings: 2

INGREDIENTS:

- ✓ 2 medium squids, tentacles separated and tubes scored lengthwise
- ✓ 1 tablespoon olive oil
- ✓ Juice from 1 lime
- ✓ Salt and black pepper to the taste

For the guacamole:

- ✓ 2 avocados, pitted, peeled and chopped
- ✓ 1 tablespoon coriander, chopped
- ✓ 2 red chilies, chopped

- ✓ 1 tomato, chopped
- ✓ 1 red onion, chopped
- ✓ Juice from 2 limes

DIRECTIONS:

- Season squid and squid tentacles with salt, pepper, drizzle the olive oil all over, put in your air fryer's basket and cook at 360 degrees F for 3 minutes on each side.
- Transfer squid to a bowl, drizzle lime juice all over and toss.
- Meanwhile, put avocado in a bowl, mash with a fork, add coriander, chilies, tomato, onion and juice from 2 limes and toss.
- Divide squid on plates, top with guacamole and serve.
- Enjoy!

Nutrition: calories 500, fat 43, fiber 6, carbs 7, protein 20

Shrimp and Cauliflower

Preparation time: 10 minutes Cooking time: 12 minutes Servings: 2

INGREDIENTS:

- ✓ 1 tablespoon butter
- ✓ Cooking spray
- ✓ 1 cauliflower head, riced
- ✓ 1 pound shrimp, peeled and deveined
- ✓ ¼ cup heavy cream
- ✓ 8 ounces mushrooms, roughly chopped
- ✓ A pinch of red pepper flakes
- ✓ Salt and black pepper to the taste
- ✓ 2 garlic cloves, minced
- ✓ 4 bacon slices, cooked and crumbled
- ✓ ½ cup beef stock
- ✓ 1 tablespoon parsley, finely chopped
- ✓ 1 tablespoon chives, chopped

DIRECTIONS:

- Season shrimp with salt and pepper, spray with cooking oil, place in your air fryer and cook at 360 degrees F for 7 minutes.
- Meanwhile, heat up a pan with the butter over medium heat, add mushrooms, stir and cook for 3-4 minutes.
- Add garlic, cauliflower rice, pepper flakes, stock, cream, chives, parsley, salt and pepper, stir, cook for a few minutes and take off heat.

- Divide shrimp on plates, add cauliflower mix on the side, sprinkle bacon on top and serve.
- Enjoy!

Nutrition: calories 245, fat 7, fiber 4, carbs 6, protein 20

Stuffed Salmon

Preparation time: 10 minutes Cooking time: 20 minutes Servings: 2

INGREDIENTS:

- ✓ 2 salmon fillets, skinless and boneless
- ✓ 1 tablespoon olive oil
- ✓ 5 ounces tiger shrimp, peeled, deveined and chopped
- ✓ 6 mushrooms, chopped
- ✓ 3 green onions, chopped
- ✓ 2 cups spinach, torn
- ✓ ¼ cup macadamia nuts, toasted and chopped Salt and black pepper to the taste

DIRECTIONS:

- Heat up a pan with half of the oil over medium high heat, add mushrooms, onions, salt and pepper, stir and cook for 4 minutes.
- Add macadamia nuts, spinach and shrimp, stir, cook for 3 minutes and take off heat.
- Make an incision lengthwise in each salmon fillet, season with salt and pepper, divide spinach and shrimp mix into incisions and rub with the rest of the olive oil.
- Place in your air fryer's basket and cook at 360 degrees F and cook for 10 minutes, flipping halfway.
- Divide stuffed salmon on plates and serve.
- Enjoy!

Nutrition: calories 290, fat 15, fiber 3, carbs 12, protein 31

Mustard Salmon

Preparation time: 10 minutes Cooking time: 10 minutes Servings: 1

INGREDIENTS:

- ✓ 1 big salmon fillet, boneless
- ✓ Salt and black pepper to the taste
- ✓ 2 tablespoons mustard
- ✓ 1 tablespoon coconut oil

- ✓ 1 tablespoon maple extract

DIRECTIONS:

- In a bowl, mix maple extract with mustard, whisk well, season salmon with salt and pepper and brush salmon with this mix.
- Spray some cooking spray over fish, place in your air fryer and cook at 370 degrees F for 10 minutes, flipping halfway.
- Serve with a tasty side salad.
- Enjoy!

Nutrition: calories 300, fat 7, fiber 14, carbs 16, protein 20

Flavored Jamaican Salmon

Preparation time: 10 minutes Cooking time: 10 minutes Servings: 4

INGREDIENTS:

- ✓ 2 teaspoons sriracha sauce
- ✓ 4 teaspoons sugar
- ✓ 3 scallions, chopped
- ✓ Salt and black pepper to the taste
- ✓ 2 teaspoons olive oil
- ✓ 4 teaspoons apple cider vinegar
- ✓ 3 teaspoons avocado oil
- ✓ 4 medium salmon fillets, boneless
- ✓ 4 cups baby arugula
- ✓ 2 cups cabbage, shredded
- ✓ 1 and ½ teaspoon Jamaican jerk seasoning ¼ cup pepitas, toasted
- ✓ 2 cups radish, julienned

DIRECTIONS:

- In a bowl, mix sriracha with sugar, whisk and transfer 2 teaspoons to another bowl.
- Combine 2 teaspoons sriracha mix with the avocado oil, olive oil, vinegar, salt and pepper and whisk well.
- Sprinkle jerk seasoning over salmon, rub with sriracha and sugar mix and season with salt and pepper.
- Transfer to your air fryer and cook at 360 degrees F for 10 minutes, flipping once.
- In a bowl, mix radishes with cabbage, arugula, salt, pepper, sriracha and vinegar mix and toss well.
- Divide salmon and radish mix on plates, sprinkle pepitas and scallions on top and serve.
- Enjoy!

Nutrition: calories 290, fat 6, fiber 12, carbs 17, protein 10

Swordfish and Mango Salsa

Preparation time: 10 minutes Cooking time: 6 minutes Servings: 2

INGREDIENTS:

- ✓ 2 medium swordfish steaks
- ✓ Salt and black pepper to the taste
- ✓ 2 teaspoons avocado oil
- ✓ 1 tablespoon cilantro, chopped
- ✓ 1 mango, chopped
- ✓ 1 avocado, pitted, peeled and chopped
- ✓ A pinch of cumin
- ✓ A pinch of onion powder
- ✓ A pinch of garlic powder
- ✓ 1 orange, peeled and sliced
- ✓ ½ tablespoon balsamic vinegar

DIRECTIONS:

- Season fish steaks with salt, pepper, garlic powder, onion powder and cumin and rub with half of the oil, place in your air fryer and cook at 360 degrees F for 6 minutes, flipping halfway.
- Meanwhile, in a bowl, mix avocado with mango, cilantro, balsamic vinegar, salt, pepper and the rest of the oil and stir well.
- Divide fish on plates, top with mango salsa and serve with orange slices on the side.
- Enjoy!

Nutrition: calories 200, fat 7, fiber 2, carbs 14, protein 14

Salmon and Orange Marmalade

Preparation time: 10 minutes Cooking time: 15 minutes Servings: 4

INGREDIENTS:

- ✓ 1 pound wild salmon, skinless, boneless and cubed
- ✓ 2 lemons, sliced
- ✓ ¼ cup balsamic vinegar
- ✓ ¼ cup orange juice
- ✓ 1/3 cup orange marmalade
- ✓ A pinch of salt and black pepper

DIRECTIONS:

- Heat up a pot with the vinegar over medium heat, add marmalade and orange juice, stir, bring to a simmer, cook for 1 minute and take off heat.

- Thread salmon cubes and lemon slices on skewers, season with salt and black pepper, brush them with half of the orange marmalade mix, arrange in your air fryer's basket and cook at 360 degrees F for 3 minutes on each side.
- Brush skewers with the rest of the vinegar mix, divide among plates and serve right away with a side salad.
- Enjoy!

Nutrition: calories 240, fat 9, fiber 12, carbs 14, protein 10

Chili Salmon

Preparation time: 10 minutes Cooking time: 15 minutes Servings: 12

INGREDIENTS:

- ✓ **1 and ¼ cups coconut, shredded**
- ✓ **1 pound salmon, cubed**
- ✓ **1/3 cup flour**
- ✓ **A pinch of salt and black pepper**
- ✓ **1 egg**
- ✓ **2 tablespoons olive oil**
- ✓ **¼ cup water**
- ✓ **4 red chilies, chopped**
- ✓ **3 garlic cloves, minced**
- ✓ **¼ cup balsamic vinegar**
- ✓ **½ cup honey**

DIRECTIONS:

- In a bowl, mix flour with a pinch of salt and stir.
- In another bowl, mix egg with black pepper and whisk.
- Put coconut in a third bowl.
- Dip salmon cubes in flour, egg and coconut, put them in your air fryer's basket, cook at 370 degrees F for 8 minutes, shaking halfway and divide among plates.
- Heat up a pan with the water over medium high heat, add chilies, cloves, vinegar and honey, stir very well, bring to a boil, simmer for a couple of minutes, drizzle over salmon and serve.
- Enjoy!

Nutrition: calories 220, fat 12, fiber 2, carbs 14, protein 13

Salmon and Lemon Relish

Preparation time: 10 minutes Cooking time: 30 minutes Servings: 2

INGREDIENTS:

- ✓ **2 salmon fillets, boneless**

- ✓ **Salt and black pepper to the taste**
- ✓ **1 tablespoon olive oil**

For the relish:

- ✓ **1 tablespoon lemon juice**
- ✓ **1 shallot, chopped**
- ✓ **1 Meyer lemon, cut in wedges and then sliced**
- ✓ **2 tablespoons parsley, chopped**
- ✓ **¼ cup olive oil**

DIRECTIONS:

- Season salmon with salt and pepper, rub with 1 tablespoon oil, place in your air fryer's basket and cook at 320 degrees F for 20 minutes, flipping the fish halfway.
- Meanwhile, in a bowl, mix shallot with the lemon juice, a pinch of salt and black pepper, stir and leave aside for 10 minutes.
- In a separate bowl, mix marinated shallot with lemon slices, salt, pepper, parsley and ¼ cup oil and whisk well.
- Divide salmon on plates, top with lemon relish and serve.
- Enjoy!

Nutrition: calories 200, fat 3, fiber 3, carbs 23, protein 19

Salmon and Avocado Sauce

Preparation time: 10 minutes Cooking time: 10 minutes Servings: 4

INGREDIENTS:

- ✓ **1 avocado, pitted, peeled and chopped**
- ✓ **4 salmon fillets, boneless**
- ✓ **¼ cup cilantro, chopped**
- ✓ **1/3 cup coconut milk**
- ✓ **1 tablespoon lime juice**
- ✓ **1 tablespoon lime zest, grated**
- ✓ **1 teaspoon onion powder**
- ✓ **1 teaspoon garlic powder**
- ✓ **Salt and black pepper to the taste**

DIRECTIONS:

- Season salmon fillets with salt, black pepper and lime zest, rub well, put in your air fryer, cook at 350 degrees F for 9 minutes, flipping once and divide among plates.
- In your food processor, mix avocado with cilantro, garlic powder, onion powder, lime juice, salt, pepper

and coconut milk, blend well, drizzle over salmon and serve right away.

🕐 Enjoy!

Nutrition: calories 260, fat 7, fiber 20, carbs 28, protein 18

Crusted Salmon

Preparation time: 10 minutes Cooking time: 10 minutes Servings: 4

INGREDIENTS:

- ✓ **1 cup pistachios, chopped**
- ✓ **4 salmon fillets**
- ✓ **¼ cup lemon juice**
- ✓ **2 tablespoons honey**
- ✓ **1 teaspoon dill, chopped**
- ✓ **Salt and black pepper to the taste**
- ✓ **1 tablespoon mustard**

DIRECTIONS:

🕐 In a bowl, mix pistachios with mustard, honey, lemon juice, salt, black pepper and dill, whisk and spread over salmon.

🕐 Put in your air fryer and cook at 350 degrees F for 10 minutes.

🕐 Divide among plates and serve with a side salad.

🕐 Enjoy!

Nutrition: calories 300, fat 17, fiber 12, carbs 20, protein 22

Stuffed Calamari

Preparation time: 10 minutes Cooking time: 25 minutes Servings: 4

INGREDIENTS:

- ✓ **4 big calamari, tentacles separated and chopped and tubes reserved**
- ✓ **2 tablespoons parsley, chopped**
- ✓ **5 ounces kale, chopped**
- ✓ **2 garlic cloves, minced**
- ✓ **1 red bell pepper, chopped**
- ✓ **1 tablespoon olive oil**
- ✓ **2 ounces canned tomato puree**
- ✓ **1 yellow onion, chopped**
- ✓ **Salt and black pepper to the taste**

DIRECTIONS:

🕐 Heat up a pan with the oil over medium heat, add onion and garlic, stir and cook for 2 minutes.

🕐 Add bell pepper, tomato puree, calamari tentacles, kale, salt and pepper, stir, cook for 10 minutes and take off heat. stir and cook for 3 minutes.

🕐 Stuff calamari tubes with this mix, secure with toothpicks, put in your air fryer and cook at 360 degrees F for 20 minutes.

🕐 Divide calamari on plates, sprinkle parsley all over and serve.

🕐 Enjoy!

Nutrition: calories 322, fat 10, fiber 14, carbs 14, protein 22

Salmon and Chives Vinaigrette

Preparation time: 10 minutes Cooking time: 12 minutes Servings: 4

INGREDIENTS:

- ✓ **2 tablespoons dill, chopped**
- ✓ **4 salmon fillets, boneless**
- ✓ **2 tablespoons chives, chopped**
- ✓ **1/3 cup maple syrup**
- ✓ **1 tablespoon olive oil**
- ✓ **3 tablespoons balsamic vinegar**
- ✓ **Salt and black pepper to the taste**

DIRECTIONS:

🕐 Season fish with salt and pepper, rub with the oil, place in your air fryer and cook at 350 degrees F for 8 minutes, flipping once.

🕐 Heat up a small pot with the vinegar over medium heat, add maple syrup, chives and dill, stir and cook for 3 minutes.

🕐 Divide fish on plates and serve with chives vinaigrette on top.

🕐 Enjoy!

Nutrition: calories 270, fat 3, fiber 13, carbs 25, protein 10

Roasted Cod and Prosciutto

Preparation time: 10 minutes Cooking time: 10 minutes Servings: 4

INGREDIENTS:

- ✓ **1 tablespoon parsley, chopped**
- ✓ **4 medium cod filets**
- ✓ **¼ cup butter, melted**
- ✓ **2 garlic cloves, minced**
- ✓ **2 tablespoons lemon juice**
- ✓ **3 tablespoons prosciutto, chopped**
- ✓ **1 teaspoon Dijon mustard**

- ✓ 1 shallot, chopped
- ✓ Salt and black pepper to the taste

DIRECTIONS:

- ⓘ In a bowl, mix mustard with butter, garlic, parsley, shallot, lemon juice, prosciutto, salt and pepper and whisk well.
- ⓘ Season fish with salt and pepper, spread prosciutto mix all over, put in your air fryer and cook at 390 degrees F for 10 minutes.
- ⓘ Divide among plates and serve.
- ⓘ Enjoy!

Nutrition: calories 200, fat 4, fiber 7, carbs 12, protein 6

Halibut and Sun Dried Tomatoes Mix

Preparation time: 10 minutes Cooking time: 10 minutes Servings: 2

INGREDIENTS:

- ✓ 2 medium halibut fillets
- ✓ 2 garlic cloves, minced
- ✓ 2 teaspoons olive oil
- ✓ Salt and black pepper to the taste
- ✓ 6 sun dried tomatoes, chopped
- ✓ 2 small red onions, sliced
- ✓ 1 fennel bulb, sliced
- ✓ 9 black olives, pitted and sliced
- ✓ 4 rosemary springs, chopped
- ✓ ½ teaspoon red pepper flakes, crushed

DIRECTIONS:

- ⓘ Season fish with salt, pepper, rub with garlic and oil and put in a heat proof dish that fits your air fryer.
- ⓘ Add onion slices, sun dried tomatoes, fennel, olives, rosemary and sprinkle pepper flakes, transfer to your air fryer and cook at 380 degrees F for 10 minutes.
- ⓘ Divide fish and veggies on plates and serve.
- ⓘ Enjoy!

Nutrition: calories 300, fat 12, fiber 9, carbs 18, protein 30

Black Cod and Plum Sauce

Preparation time: 10 minutes Cooking time: 15 minutes Servings: 2

INGREDIENTS:

- ✓ 1 egg white
- ✓ ½ cup red quinoa, already cooked
- ✓ 2 teaspoons whole wheat flour
- ✓ 4 teaspoons lemon juice

- ✓ ½ teaspoon smoked paprika
- ✓ 1 teaspoon olive oil
- ✓ 2 medium black cod fillets, skinless and boneless
- ✓ 1 red plum, pitted and chopped
- ✓ 2 teaspoons raw honey
- ✓ ¼ teaspoon black peppercorns, crushed
- ✓ 2 teaspoons parsley
- ✓ ¼ cup water

DIRECTIONS:

- ⓘ In a bowl, mix 1 teaspoon lemon juice with egg white, flour and ¼ teaspoon paprika and whisk well.
- ⓘ Put quinoa in a bowl and mix it with 1/3 of egg white mix.
- ⓘ Put the fish into the bowl with the remaining egg white mix and toss to coat.
- ⓘ Dip fish in quinoa mix, coat well and leave aside for 10 minutes.
- ⓘ Heat up a pan with 1 teaspoon oil over medium heat, add peppercorns, honey and plum, stir, bring to a simmer and cook for 1 minute.
- ⓘ Add the rest of the lemon juice, the rest of the paprika and the water, stir well and simmer for 5 minutes.
- ⓘ Add parsley, stir, take sauce off heat and leave aside for now.
- ⓘ Put fish in your air fryer and cook at 380 degrees F for 10 minutes
- ⓘ Arrange fish on plates, drizzle plum sauce on top and serve.
- ⓘ Enjoy!

Nutrition: calories 324, fat 14, fiber 22, carbs 27, protein 22

Fish and Couscous

Preparation time: 10 minutes Cooking time: 15 minutes Servings: 4

INGREDIENTS:

- ✓ 2 red onions, chopped
- ✓ Cooking spray
- ✓ 2 small fennel bulbs, cored and sliced
- ✓ ¼ cup almonds, toasted and sliced
- ✓ Salt and black pepper to the taste
- ✓ 2 and ½ pounds sea bass, gutted
- ✓ 5 teaspoons fennel seeds
- ✓ ¾ cup whole wheat couscous, cooked

DIRECTIONS:

- Season fish with salt and pepper, spray with cooking spray, place in your air fryer and cook at 350 degrees F for 10 minutes.
- Meanwhile, spray a pan with some cooking oil and heat it up over medium heat.
- Add fennel seeds to this pan, stir and toast them for 1 minute.
- Add onion, salt, pepper, fennel bulbs, almonds and couscous, stir, cook for 2-3 minutes and divide among plates.
- Add fish next to couscous mix and serve right away.
- Enjoy!

Nutrition: calories 354, fat 7, fiber 10, carbs 20, protein 30

Chinese Cod

Preparation time: 10 minutes Cooking time: 10 minutes Servings: 2

INGREDIENTS:

- ✓ **2 medium cod fillets, boneless**
- ✓ **1 teaspoon peanuts, crushed**
- ✓ **2 teaspoons garlic powder**
- ✓ **1 tablespoon light soy sauce**
- ✓ **½ teaspoon ginger, grated**

DIRECTIONS:

- Put fish fillets in a heat proof dish that fits your air fryer, add garlic powder, soy sauce and ginger, toss well, put in your air fryer and cook at 350 degrees F for 10 minutes.
- Divide fish on plates, sprinkle peanuts on top and serve.
- Enjoy!

Nutrition: calories 254, fat 10, fiber 11, carbs 14, protein 23

Cod with Pearl Onions

Preparation time: 10 minutes Cooking time: 15 minutes Servings: 2

INGREDIENTS:

- ✓ **14 ounces pearl onions**
- ✓ **2 medium cod fillets**
- ✓ **1 tablespoon parsley, dried**
- ✓ **1 teaspoon thyme, dried**
- ✓ **Black pepper to the taste**
- ✓ **8 ounces mushrooms, sliced**

DIRECTIONS:

- Put fish in a heat proof dish that fits your air fryer, add onions, parsley, mushrooms, thyme and black

pepper, toss well, put in your air fryer and cook at 350 degrees F and cook for 15 minutes.
- Divide everything on plates and serve.
- Enjoy!

Nutrition: calories 270, fat 14, fiber 8, carbs 14, protein 22

Hawaiian Salmon

Preparation time: 10 minutes Cooking time: 10 minutes Servings: 2

INGREDIENTS:

- ✓ **20 ounces canned pineapple pieces and juice ½ teaspoon ginger, grated**
- ✓ **2 teaspoons garlic powder**
- ✓ **1 teaspoon onion powder**
- ✓ **1 tablespoon balsamic vinegar**
- ✓ **2 medium salmon fillets, boneless**
- ✓ **Salt and black pepper to the taste**

DIRECTIONS:

- Season salmon with garlic powder, onion powder, salt and black pepper, rub well, transfer to a heat proof dish that fits your air fryer, add ginger and pineapple chunks and toss them really gently.
- Drizzle the vinegar all over, put in your air fryer and cook at 350 degrees F for 10 minutes.
- Divide everything on plates and serve..
- Enjoy!

Nutrition: calories 200, fat 8, fiber 12, carbs 17, protein 20

Salmon and Avocado Salad

Preparation time: 10 minutes Cooking time: 20 minutes Servings: 4

INGREDIENTS:

- ✓ **2 medium salmon fillets**
- ✓ **¼ cup melted butter**
- ✓ **4 ounces mushrooms, sliced**
- ✓ **Sea salt and black pepper to the taste**
- ✓ **12 cherry tomatoes, halved**
- ✓ **2 tablespoons olive oil**
- ✓ **8 ounces lettuce leaves, torn**
- ✓ **1 avocado, pitted, peeled and cubed**
- ✓ **1 jalapeno pepper, chopped**
- ✓ **5 cilantro springs, chopped**
- ✓ **2 tablespoons white wine vinegar**
- ✓ **1 ounce feta cheese, crumbled**

DIRECTIONS:

- Place salmon on a lined baking sheet, brush with 2 tablespoons melted butter, season with salt and pepper, broil for 15 minutes over medium heat and then keep warm.
- Meanwhile, heat up a pan with the rest of the butter over medium heat, add mushrooms, stir and cook for a few minutes.
- Put tomatoes in a bowl, add salt, pepper and 1 tablespoon olive oil and toss to coat.
- In a salad bowl, mix salmon with mushrooms, lettuce, avocado, tomatoes, jalapeno and cilantro.
- Add the rest of the oil, vinegar, salt and pepper, sprinkle cheese on top and serve.

Enjoy!

Nutrition: calories 235, fat 6, fiber 8, carbs 19, protein 5

Salmon and Greek Yogurt Sauce

Preparation time: 10 minutes Cooking time: 20 minutes Servings: 2

INGREDIENTS:

- ✓ 2 medium salmon fillets
- ✓ 1 tablespoon basil, chopped
- ✓ 6 lemon slices
- ✓ Sea salt and black pepper to the taste
- ✓ 1 cup Greek yogurt
- ✓ 2 teaspoons curry powder
- ✓ A pinch of cayenne pepper
- ✓ 1 garlic clove, minced
- ✓ ½ teaspoon cilantro, chopped
- ✓ ½ teaspoon mint, chopped

DIRECTIONS:

- Place each salmon fillet on a parchment paper piece, make 3 splits in each and stuff them with basil.
- Season with salt and pepper, top each fillet with 3 lemon slices, fold parchment, seal edges, introduce in the oven at 400 degrees F and bake for 20 minutes.
- Meanwhile, in a bowl, mix yogurt with cayenne pepper, salt to the taste, garlic, curry, mint and cilantro and whisk well.
- Transfer fish to plates, drizzle the yogurt sauce you've just prepared on top and serve right away!
- Enjoy!

Nutrition: calories 242, fat 1, fiber 2, carbs 3, protein 3

Special Salmon

Preparation time: 10 minutes Cooking time: 25 minutes Servings: 4

INGREDIENTS:

- ✓ 1 pound medium beets, sliced
- ✓ 6 tablespoons olive oil
- ✓ 1 and ½ pounds salmon fillets, skinless and boneless Salt and pepper to the taste
- ✓ 1 tablespoon chives, chopped
- ✓ 1 tablespoon parsley, chopped
- ✓ 1 tablespoon fresh tarragon, chopped
- ✓ 3 tablespoon shallots, chopped
- ✓ 1 tablespoon grated lemon zest
- ✓ ¼ cup lemon juice
- ✓ 4 cups mixed baby greens

DIRECTIONS:

- In a bowl, mix beets with ½ tablespoon oil and toss to coat.
- Season them with salt and pepper, arrange them on a baking sheet, introduce in the oven at 450 degrees F and bake for 20 minutes.
- Take beets out of the oven, add salmon on top, brush it with the rest if the oil and season with salt and pepper.
- In a bowl, mix chives with parsley and tarragon and sprinkle 1 tablespoon of this mix over salmon.
- Introduce in the oven again and bake for 15 minutes.
- Meanwhile, in a boil with shallots with lemon peel, salt, pepper and lemon juice and the rest of the herbs mixture and stir gently.
- Combine 2 tablespoons of shallots dressing with mixed greens and toss gently.
- Take salmon out of the oven, arrange on plates, add beets and greens on the side, drizzle the rest of the shallot dressing on top and serve right away.
- Enjoy!

Nutrition: calories 312, fat 2, fiber 2, carbs 2, protein 4

Spanish Salmon

Preparation time: 10 minutes Cooking time: 15 minutes Servings: 6

INGREDIENTS:

- ✓ 2 cups bread croutons
- ✓ 3 red onions, cut into medium wedges

- ✓ ¾ cup green olives, pitted
- ✓ 3 red bell peppers, cut into medium wedges ½ teaspoon smoked paprika Salt and black pepper to the taste
- ✓ 5 tablespoons olive oil
- ✓ 6 medium salmon fillets, skinless and boneless
- ✓ 2 tablespoons parsley, chopped

DIRECTIONS:

- In a heat proof dish that fits your air fryer, mix bread croutons with onion wedges, bell pepper ones, olives, salt, pepper, paprika and 3 tablespoons olive oil, toss well, place in your air fryer and cook at 356 degrees F for 7 minutes.
- Rub salmon with the rest of the oil, add over veggies and cook at 360 degrees F for 8 minutes.
- Divide fish and veggie mix on plates, sprinkle parsley all over and serve.
- Enjoy!

Nutrition: calories 321, fat 8, fiber 14, carbs 27, protein 22

Marinated Salmon

Preparation time: 1 hour Cooking time: 20 minutes Servings: 6

INGREDIENTS:

- ✓ 1 whole salmon
- ✓ 1 tablespoon dill, chopped
- ✓ 1 tablespoon tarragon, chopped
- ✓ 1 tablespoon garlic, minced
- ✓ Juice from 2 lemons
- ✓ 1 lemon, sliced
- ✓ A pinch of salt and black pepper

DIRECTIONS:

- In a large fish, mix fish with salt, pepper and lemon juice, toss well and keep in the fridge for 1 hour.
- Stuff salmon with garlic and lemon slices, place in your air fryer's basket and cook at 320 degrees F for 25 minutes.
- Divide among plates and serve with a tasty coleslaw on the side.
- Enjoy!

Nutrition: calories 300, fat 8, fiber 9, carbs 19, protein 27

Delicious Red Snapper

Preparation time: 30 minutes Cooking time: 15 minutes Servings: 4

INGREDIENTS:

- ✓ 1 big red snapper, cleaned and scored
- ✓ Salt and black pepper to the taste
- ✓ 3 garlic cloves, minced
- ✓ 1 jalapeno, chopped
- ✓ ¼ pound okra, chopped
- ✓ 1 tablespoon butter
- ✓ 2 tablespoons olive oil
- ✓ 1 red bell pepper, chopped
- ✓ 2 tablespoons white wine
- ✓ 2 tablespoons parsley, chopped

DIRECTIONS:

- In a bowl, mix jalapeno, wine with garlic, stir well and rub snapper with this mix.
- Season fish with salt and pepper and leave it aside for 30 minutes.
- Meanwhile, heat up a pan with 1 tablespoon butter over medium heat, add bell pepper and okra, stir and cook for 5 minutes.
- Stuff red snapper's belly with this mix, also add parsley and rub with the olive oil.
- Place in preheated air fryer and cook at 400 degrees F for 15 minutes, flipping the fish halfway.
- Divide among plates and serve.
- Enjoy!

Nutrition: calories 261, fat 7, fiber 18, carbs 28, protein 18

Snapper Fillets and Veggies

Preparation time: 10 minutes Cooking time: 14 minutes Servings: 2

INGREDIENTS:

- ✓ 2 red snapper fillets, boneless
- ✓ 1 tablespoon olive oil
- ✓ ½ cup red bell pepper, chopped
- ✓ ½ cup green bell pepper, chopped
- ✓ ½ cup leeks, chopped
- ✓ Salt and black pepper to the taste
- ✓ 1 teaspoon tarragon, dried
- ✓ A splash of white wine

DIRECTIONS:

- In a heat proof dish that fits your air fryer, mix fish fillets with salt, pepper, oil, green bell pepper, red bell pepper, leeks, tarragon and wine, toss well everything, introduce in preheated air fryer at 350 degrees F and cook for 14 minutes, flipping fish fillets halfway.

🕐 Divide fish and veggies on plates and serve warm.

🕐 Enjoy!

Nutrition: calories 300, fat 12, fiber 8, carbs 29, protein 12

Air Fried Branzino

Preparation time: 10 minutes Cooking time: 10 minutes Servings: 4

INGREDIENTS:

- ✓ **Zest from 1 lemon, grated**
- ✓ **Zest from 1 orange, grated**
- ✓ **Juice from ½ lemon**
- ✓ **Juice from ½ orange**
- ✓ **Salt and black pepper to the taste**
- ✓ **4 medium branzino fillets, boneless**
- ✓ **½ cup parsley, chopped**
- ✓ **2 tablespoons olive oil**
- ✓ **A pinch of red pepper flakes, crushed**

DIRECTIONS:

🕐 In a large bowl, mix fish fillets with lemon zest, orange zest, lemon juice, orange juice, salt, pepper, oil and pepper flakes, toss really well, transfer fillets to your preheated air fryer at 350 degrees F and bake for 10 minutes, flipping fillets once.

🕐 Divide fish on plates, sprinkle with parsley and serve right away.

🕐 Enjoy!

Nutrition: calories 261, fat 8, fiber 12, carbs 21, protein 12

Lemon Sole and Swiss Chard

Preparation time: 10 minutes Cooking time: 14 minutes Servings: 4

INGREDIENTS:

- ✓ **1 teaspoon lemon zest, grated**
- ✓ **4 white bread slices, quartered**
- ✓ **¼ cup walnuts, chopped**
- ✓ **¼ cup parmesan, grated**
- ✓ **4 tablespoons olive oil**
- ✓ **4 sole fillets, boneless**
- ✓ **Salt and black pepper to the taste**
- ✓ **4 tablespoons butter**
- ✓ **¼ cup lemon juice**

- ✓ **3 tablespoons capers**
- ✓ **2 garlic cloves, minced**
- ✓ **2 bunches Swiss chard, chopped**

DIRECTIONS:

🕐 In your food processor, mix bread with walnuts, cheese and lemon zest and pulse well.

🕐 Add half of the olive oil, pulse really well again and leave aside for now.

🕐 Heat up a pan with the butter over medium heat, add lemon juice, salt, pepper and capers, stir well, add fish and toss it.

🕐 Transfer fish to your preheated air fryer's basket, top with bread mix you've made at the beginning and cook at 350 degrees F for 14 minutes.

🕐 Meanwhile, heat up another pan with the rest of the oil, add garlic, Swiss chard, salt and pepper, stir gently, cook for 2 minutes and take off heat.

🕐 Divide fish on plates and serve with sautéed chard on the side.

🕐 Enjoy!

Nutrition: calories 321, fat 7, fiber 18, carbs 27, protein 12

Salmon and Blackberry Glaze

Preparation time: 10 minutes Cooking time: 33 minutes Servings: 4

INGREDIENTS:

- ✓ **1 cup water**
- ✓ **1 inch ginger piece, grated**
- ✓ **Juice from ½ lemon**
- ✓ **12 ounces blackberries**
- ✓ **1 tablespoon olive oil**
- ✓ **¼ cup sugar**
- ✓ **4 medium salmon fillets, skinless**
- ✓ **Salt and black pepper to the taste**

DIRECTIONS:

🕐 Heat up a pot with the water over medium high heat, add ginger, lemon juice and blackberries, stir, bring to a boil, cook for 4-5 minutes, take off heat, strain into a bowl, return to pan and combine with sugar.

🕐 Stir this mix, bring to a simmer over medium low heat and cook for 20 minutes.

🕐 Leave blackberry sauce to cool down, brush salmon with it, season with salt and pepper, drizzle olive oil all over and rub fish well.

🕐 Place fish in your preheated air fryer at 350 degrees F and cook for 10 minutes, flipping fish fillets once.

- Divide among plates, drizzle some of the remaining blackberry sauce all over and serve.
- Enjoy!

Nutrition: calories 312, fat 4, fiber 9, carbs 19, protein 14

Oriental Fish

Preparation time: 10 minutes Cooking time: 12 minutes Servings: 4

INGREDIENTS:

- ✓ 2 pounds red snapper fillets, boneless
- ✓ Salt and black pepper to the taste
- ✓ 3 garlic cloves, minced
- ✓ 1 yellow onion, chopped
- ✓ 1 tablespoon tamarind paste
- ✓ 1 tablespoon oriental sesame oil
- ✓ 1 tablespoon ginger, grated
- ✓ 2 tablespoons water
- ✓ ½ teaspoon cumin, ground
- ✓ 1 tablespoon lemon juice
- ✓ 3 tablespoons mint, chopped

DIRECTIONS:

- In your food processor, mix garlic with onion, salt, pepper, tamarind paste, sesame oil, ginger, water and cumin, pulse well and rub fish with this mix.
- Place fish in your preheated air fryer at 320 degrees F and cook for 12 minutes, flipping fish halfway.
- Divide fish on plates, drizzle lemon juice all over, sprinkle mint and serve right away.
- Enjoy!

Nutrition: calories 241, fat 8, fiber 16, carbs 17, protein 12

Delicious French Cod

Preparation time: 10 minutes Cooking time: 22 minutes Servings: 4

INGREDIENTS:

- ✓ 2 tablespoons olive oil
- ✓ 1 yellow onion, chopped
- ✓ ½ cup white wine
- ✓ 2 garlic cloves, minced
- ✓ 14 ounces canned tomatoes, stewed
- ✓ 3 tablespoons parsley, chopped
- ✓ 2 pounds cod, boneless
- ✓ Salt and black pepper to the taste

- ✓ 2 tablespoons butter

DIRECTIONS:

- Heat up a pan with the oil over medium heat, add garlic and onion, stir and cook for 5 minutes.
- Add wine, stir and cook for 1 minute more.
- Add tomatoes, stir, bring to a boil, cook for 2 minutes, add parsley, stir again and take off heat.
- Pour this mix into a heat proof dish that fits your air fryer, add fish, season it with salt and pepper and cook in your fryer at 350 degrees F for 14 minutes.
- Divide fish and tomatoes mix on plates and serve.
- Enjoy!

Nutrition: calories 231, fat 8, fiber 12, carbs 26, protein 14

Special Catfish Fillets

Preparation time: 10 minutes Cooking time: 12 minutes Servings: 4

INGREDIENTS:

- ✓ 2 catfish fillets
- ✓ ½ teaspoon garlic, minced
- ✓ 2 ounces butter
- ✓ 4 ounces Worcestershire sauce
- ✓ ½ teaspoon jerk seasoning
- ✓ 1 teaspoon mustard
- ✓ 1 tablespoon balsamic vinegar
- ✓ ¾ cup catsup
- ✓ Salt and black pepper to the taste
- ✓ 1 tablespoon parsley, chopped

DIRECTIONS:

- Heat up a pan with the butter over medium heat, add Worcestershire sauce, garlic, jerk seasoning, mustard, catsup, vinegar, salt and pepper, stir well, take off heat and add fish fillets.
- Toss well, leave aside for 10 minutes, drain fillets, transfer them to your preheated air fryer's basket at 350 degrees F and cook for 8 minutes, flipping fillets halfway.
- Divide among plates, sprinkle parsley on top and serve right away. Enjoy!

Nutrition: calories 351, fat 8, fiber 16, carbs 27, protein 17

Coconut Tilapia

Preparation time: 10 minutes Cooking time: 10 minutes Servings: 4

INGREDIENTS:

- ✓ **4 medium tilapia fillets**
- ✓ **Salt and black pepper to the taste**
- ✓ **½ cup coconut milk**
- ✓ **1 teaspoon ginger, grated**
- ✓ **½ cup cilantro, chopped**
- ✓ **2 garlic cloves, chopped**
- ✓ **½ teaspoon garam masala**
- ✓ **Cooking spray**
- ✓ **½ jalapeno, chopped**

DIRECTIONS:

- In your food processor, mix coconut milk with salt, pepper, cilantro, ginger, garlic, jalapeno and garam masala and pulse really well.
- Spray fish with cooking spray, spread coconut mix all over, rub well, transfer to your air fryer's basket and cook at 400 degrees F for 10 minutes.
- Divide among plates and serve hot.
- Enjoy!

Nutrition: calories 200, fat 5, fiber 6, carbs 25, protein 26

Tilapia and Chives Sauce

Preparation time: 10 minutes Cooking time: 8 minutes Servings: 4

INGREDIENTS:

- ✓ **4 medium tilapia fillets**
- ✓ **Cooking spray**
- ✓ **Salt and black pepper to the taste**
- ✓ **2 teaspoons honey**
- ✓ **¼ cup Greek yogurt**
- ✓ **Juice from 1 lemon**
- ✓ **2 tablespoons chives, chopped**

DIRECTIONS:

- Season fish with salt and pepper, spray with cooking spray, place in preheated air fryer 350 degrees F and cook for 8 minutes, flipping halfway.
- Meanwhile, in a bowl, mix yogurt with honey, salt, pepper, chives and lemon juice and whisk really well.
- Divide air fryer fish on plates, drizzle yogurt sauce all over and serve right away.
- Enjoy!

Nutrition: calories 261, fat 8, fiber 18, carbs 24, protein 21

Honey Sea Bass

Preparation time: 10 minutes Cooking time: 10 minutes Servings: 2

INGREDIENTS:

- ✓ **2 sea bass fillets**
- ✓ **Zest from ½ orange, grated**
- ✓ **Juice from ½ orange**
- ✓ **A pinch of salt and black pepper**
- ✓ **2 tablespoons mustard**
- ✓ **2 teaspoons honey**
- ✓ **2 tablespoons olive oil**
- ✓ **½ pound canned lentils, drained**
- ✓ **A small bunch of dill, chopped**
- ✓ **2 ounces watercress**
- ✓ **A small bunch of parsley, chopped**

DIRECTIONS:

- Season fish fillets with salt and pepper, add orange zest and juice, rub with 1 tablespoon oil, with honey and mustard, rub, transfer to your air fryer and cook at 350 degrees F for 10 minutes, flipping halfway.
- Meanwhile, put lentils in a small pot, warm it up over medium heat, add the rest of the oil, watercress, dill and parsley, stir well and divide among plates.
- Add fish fillets and serve right away.
- Enjoy!

Nutrition: calories 212, fat 8, fiber 12, carbs 9, protein 17

Tasty Pollock

Preparation time: 10 minutes Cooking time: 15 minutes Servings: 6

INGREDIENTS:

- ✓ **½ cup sour cream**
- ✓ **4 Pollock fillets, boneless**
- ✓ **¼ cup parmesan, grated**
- ✓ **2 tablespoons butter, melted**
- ✓ **Salt and black pepper to the taste**
- ✓ **Cooking spray**

DIRECTIONS:

- In a bowl, mix sour cream with butter, parmesan, salt and pepper and whisk well.
- Spray fish with cooking spray and season with salt and pepper.

- Spread sour cream mix on one side of each Pollock fillet, arrange them in your preheated air fryer at 320 degrees F and cook them for 15 minutes.
- Divide Pollock fillets on plates and serve with a tasty side salad.
- Enjoy!

Nutrition: calories 300, fat 13, fiber 3, carbs 14, protein 44

Creamy Chicken, Rice and Peas

Preparation time: 10 minutes Cooking time: 30 minutes Servings: 4

INGREDIENTS:

- ✓ **1 pound chicken breasts, skinless, boneless and cut into quarters**
- ✓ **1 cup white rice, already cooked**
- ✓ **Salt and black pepper to the taste**
- ✓ **1 tablespoon olive oil**
- ✓ **3 garlic cloves, minced**
- ✓ **1 yellow onion, chopped**
- ✓ **½ cup white wine**
- ✓ **¼ cup heavy cream**
- ✓ **1 cup chicken stock**
- ✓ **¼ cup parsley, chopped**
- ✓ **2 cups peas, frozen**
- ✓ **1 and ½ cups parmesan, grated**

DIRECTIONS:

- Season chicken breasts with salt and pepper, drizzle half of the oil over them, rub well, put in your air fryer's basket and cook them at 360 degrees F for 6 minutes.
- Heat up a pan with the rest of the oil over medium high heat, add garlic, onion, wine, stock, salt, pepper and heavy cream, stir, bring to a simmer and cook for 9 minutes.
- Transfer chicken breasts to a heat proof dish that fits your air fryer, add peas, rice and cream mix over them, toss, sprinkle parmesan and parsley all over, place in your air fryer and cook at 420 degrees F for 10 minutes.
- Divide among plates and serve hot.
- Enjoy!

Nutrition: calories 313, fat 12, fiber 14, carbs 27, protein 44

Italian Chicken

Preparation time: 10 minutes Cooking time: 16 minutes Servings: 4

INGREDIENTS:

- ✓ **5 chicken thighs**
- ✓ **1 tablespoon olive oil**
- ✓ **2 garlic cloves, minced**

- ✓ **1 tablespoon thyme, chopped**
- ✓ **½ cup heavy cream**
- ✓ **¾ cup chicken stock**
- ✓ **1 teaspoon red pepper flakes, crushed**
- ✓ **¼ cup parmesan, grated**
- ✓ **½ cup sun dried tomatoes**
- ✓ **2 tablespoons basil, chopped**
- ✓ **Salt and black pepper to the taste**

DIRECTIONS:

- Season chicken with salt and pepper, rub with half of the oil, place in your preheated air fryer at 350 degrees F and cook for 4 minutes.
- Meanwhile, heat up a pan with the rest of the oil over medium high heat, add thyme garlic, pepper flakes, sun dried tomatoes, heavy cream, stock, parmesan, salt and pepper, stir, bring to a simmer, take off heat and transfer to a dish that fits your air fryer.
- Add chicken thighs on top, introduce in your air fryer and cook at 320 degrees F for 12 minutes.
- Divide among plates and serve with basil sprinkled on top.
- Enjoy!

Nutrition: calories 272, fat 9, fiber 12, carbs 37, protein 23

Honey Duck Breast s

Preparation time: 10 minutes Cooking time: 22 minutes Servings: 2

INGREDIENTS:

- ✓ **1 smoked duck breast, halved**
- ✓ **1 teaspoon honey**
- ✓ **1 teaspoon tomato paste**
- ✓ **1 tablespoon mustard**
- ✓ **½ teaspoon apple vinegar**

DIRECTIONS:

- In a bowl, mix honey with tomato paste, mustard and vinegar, whisk well, add duck breast pieces, toss to coat well, transfer to your air fryer and cook at 370 degrees F for 15 minutes.
- Take duck breast out of the fryer, add to honey mix, toss again, return to air fryer and cook at 370 degrees F for 6 minutes more.
- Divide among plates and serve with a side salad.
- Enjoy!

Nutrition: calories 274, fat 11, fiber 13, carbs 22, protein 13

Chinese Duck Legs

Preparation time: 10 minutes Cooking time: 36 minutes Servings: 2

INGREDIENTS:

- ✓ 2 duck legs
- ✓ 2 dried chilies, chopped
- ✓ 1 tablespoon olive oil
- ✓ 2 star anise
- ✓ 1 bunch spring onions, chopped
- ✓ 4 ginger slices
- ✓ 1 tablespoon oyster sauce
- ✓ 1 tablespoon soy sauce
- ✓ 1 teaspoon sesame oil
- ✓ 14 ounces water
- ✓ 1 tablespoon rice wine

DIRECTIONS:

- ⏲ Heat up a pan with the oil over medium high heat, add chili, star anise, sesame oil, rice wine, ginger, oyster sauce, soy sauce and water, stir and cook for 6 minutes.
- ⏲ Add spring onions and duck legs, toss to coat, transfer to a pan that fits your air fryer, put in your air fryer and cook at 370 degrees F for 30 minutes.
- ⏲ Divide among plates and serve.
- ⏲ Enjoy!

Nutrition: calories 300, fat 12, fiber 12, carbs 26, protein 18

Chinese Stuffed Chicke n

Preparation time: 10 minutes Cooking time: 35 minutes Servings: 8

INGREDIENTS:

- ✓ 1 whole chicken
- ✓ 10 wolfberries
- ✓ 2 red chilies, chopped
- ✓ 4 ginger slices
- ✓ 1 yam, cubed
- ✓ 1 teaspoon soy sauce
- ✓ Salt and white pepper to the taste
- ✓ 3 teaspoons sesame oil

DIRECTIONS:

- ⏲ Season chicken with salt, pepper, rub with soy sauce and sesame oil and stuff with wolfberries, yam cubes, chilies and ginger.
- ⏲ Place in your air fryer, cook at 400 degrees F for 20 minutes and then at 360 degrees F for 15 minutes.
- ⏲ Carve chicken, divide among plates and serve.
- ⏲ Enjoy!

Nutrition: calories 320, fat 12, fiber 17, carbs 22, protein 12

Easy Chicken Thighs and Baby Potatoes

Preparation time: 10 minutes Cooking time: 30 minutes Servings: 4

INGREDIENTS:

- ✓ 8 chicken thighs
- ✓ 2 tablespoons olive oil
- ✓ 1 pound baby potatoes, halved
- ✓ 2 teaspoons oregano, dried
- ✓ 2 teaspoons rosemary, dried
- ✓ ½ teaspoon sweet paprika
- ✓ Salt and black pepper to the taste
- ✓ 2 garlic cloves, minced
- ✓ 1 red onion, chopped
- ✓ 2 teaspoons thyme, chopped

DIRECTIONS:

- ⏲ In a bowl, mix chicken thighs with potatoes, salt, pepper, thyme, paprika, onion, rosemary, garlic, oregano and oil.
- ⏲ Toss to coat, spread everything in a heat proof dish that fits your air fryer and cook at 400 degrees F for 30 minutes, shaking halfway.
- ⏲ Divide among plates and serve.
- ⏲ Enjoy!

Nutrition: calories 364, fat 14, fiber 13, carbs 21, protein 34

Chicken and Capers

Preparation time: 10 minutes Cooking time: 20 minutes Servings: 2

INGREDIENTS:

- ✓ 4 chicken thighs
- ✓ 3 tablespoons capers
- ✓ 4 garlic cloves, minced

- ✓ **3 tablespoons butter, melted**
- ✓ **Salt and black pepper to the taste**
- ✓ **½ cup chicken stock**
- ✓ **1 lemon, sliced**
- ✓ **4 green onions, chopped**

DIRECTIONS:

- Brush chicken with butter, sprinkle salt and pepper to the taste, place them in a baking dish that fits your air fryer.
- Also add capers, garlic, chicken stock and lemon slices, toss to coat, introduce in your air fryer and cook at 370 degrees F for 20 minutes, shaking halfway.
- Sprinkle green onions, divide among plates and serve.
- Enjoy!

Nutrition: calories 200, fat 9, fiber 10, carbs 17, protein 7

Chicken and Creamy Mushrooms

Preparation time: 10 minutes Cooking time: 30 minutes Servings: 8

INGREDIENTS:

- ✓ **8 chicken thighs**
- ✓ **Salt and black pepper to the taste**
- ✓ **8 ounces cremini mushrooms, halved**
- ✓ **3 garlic cloves, minced**
- ✓ **3 tablespoons butter, melted**
- ✓ **1 cup chicken stock**
- ✓ **¼ cup heavy cream**
- ✓ **½ teaspoon basil, dried**
- ✓ **½ teaspoon thyme, dried**
- ✓ **½ teaspoon oregano, dried**
- ✓ **1 tablespoon mustard**
- ✓ **¼ cup parmesan, grated**

DIRECTIONS:

- Rub chicken pieces with 2 tablespoons butter, season with salt and pepper, put in your air fryer's basket, cook at 370 degrees F for 5 minutes and leave aside in a bowl for now.
- Meanwhile, heat up a pan with the rest of the butter over medium high heat, add mushrooms and garlic, stir and cook for 5 minutes.
- Add salt, pepper, stock, oregano, thyme and basil, stir well and transfer to a heat proof dish that fits your air fryer.

- Add chicken, toss everything, put in your air fryer and cook at 370 degrees F for 20 minutes.
- Add mustard, parmesan and heavy cream, toss everything again, cook for 5 minutes more, divide among plates and serve.
- Enjoy!

Nutrition: calories 340, fat 10, fiber 13, carbs 22, protein 12

Duck and Plum Sauce

Preparation time: 10 minutes Cooking time: 32 minutes Servings: 2

INGREDIENTS:

- ✓ **2 duck breasts**
- ✓ **1 tablespoon butter, melted**
- ✓ **1 star anise**
- ✓ **1 tablespoon olive oil**
- ✓ **1 shallot, chopped**
- ✓ **9 ounces red plumps, stoned, cut into small wedges**
- ✓ **2 tablespoons sugar**
- ✓ **2 tablespoons red wine**
- ✓ **1 cup beef stock**

DIRECTIONS:

- Heat up a pan with the olive oil over medium heat, add shallot, stir and cook for 5 minutes,
- Add sugar and plums, stir and cook until sugar dissolves.
- Add stock and wine, stir, cook for 15 minutes, take off heat and keep warm for now.
- Score duck breasts, season with salt and pepper, rub with melted butter, transfer to a heat proof dish that fits your air fryer, add star anise and plum sauce, introduce in your air fryer and cook at 360 degrees F for 12 minutes.
- Divide everything on plates and serve.
- Enjoy!

Nutrition: calories 400, fat 25, fiber 12, carbs 29, protein 44

Air Fried Japanese Duck Breasts

Preparation time: 10 minutes Cooking time: 20 minutes Servings: 6

INGREDIENTS:

- ✓ **6 duck breasts, boneless**
- ✓ **4 tablespoons soy sauce**
- ✓ **1 and ½ teaspoon five spice powder**
- ✓ **2 tablespoons honey**
- ✓ **Salt and black pepper to the taste**

- ✓ **20 ounces chicken stock**
- ✓ **4 ginger slices**
- ✓ **4 tablespoons hoisin sauce**
- ✓ **1 teaspoon sesame oil**

DIRECTIONS:

- ○ In a bowl, mix five spice powder with soy sauce, salt, pepper and honey, whisk, add duck breasts, toss to coat and leave aside for now.
- ○ Heat up a pan with the stock over medium high heat, hoisin sauce, ginger and sesame oil, stir well, cook for 2-3 minutes more, take off heat and leave aside.
- ○ Put duck breasts in your air fryer and cook them at 400 degrees F for 15 minutes.
- ○ Divide among plates, drizzle hoisin and ginger sauce all over them and serve.
- ○ Enjoy!

Nutrition: calories 336, fat 12, fiber 1, carbs 25, protein 33

Easy Duck Breasts

Preparation time: 10 minutes Cooking time: 40 minutes Servings: 6

INGREDIENTS:

- ✓ **6 duck breasts, halved**
- ✓ **Salt and black pepper to the taste**
- ✓ **3 tablespoons flour**
- ✓ **6 tablespoons butter, melted**
- ✓ **2 cups chicken stock**
- ✓ **½ cup white wine**
- ✓ **¼ cup parsley, chopped**
- ✓ **2 cups mushrooms, chopped**

DIRECTIONS:

- ○ Season duck breasts with salt and pepper, place them in a bowl, add melted butter, toss and transfer to another bowl.
- ○ Combine melted butter with flour, wine, salt, pepper and chicken stock and stir well.
- ○ Arrange duck breasts in a baking dish that fits your air fryer, pour the sauce over them, add parsley and mushrooms, introduce in your air fryer and cook at 350 degrees F for 40 minutes.
- ○ Divide among plates and serve.
- ○ Enjoy!

Nutrition: calories 320, fat 28, fiber 12, carbs 12, protein 42

Duck Breasts with Endives

Preparation time: 10 minutes Cooking time: 25 minutes Servings: 4

INGREDIENTS:

- ✓ **2 duck breasts**
- ✓ **Salt and black pepper to the taste**
- ✓ **1 tablespoon sugar**
- ✓ **1 tablespoon olive oil**
- ✓ **6 endives, julienned**
- ✓ **2 tablespoons cranberries**
- ✓ **8 ounces white wine**
- ✓ **1 tablespoons garlic, minced**
- ✓ **2 tablespoons heavy cream**

DIRECTIONS:

- ○ Score duck breasts and season them with salt and pepper, put in preheated air fryer and cook at 350 degrees F for 20 minutes, flipping them halfway.
- ○ Meanwhile, heat up a pan with the oil over medium heat, add sugar and endives, stir and cook for 2 minutes.
- ○ Add salt, pepper, wine, garlic, cream and cranberries, stir and cook for 3 minutes.
- ○ Divide duck breasts on plates, drizzle the endives sauce all over and serve.
- ○ Enjoy!

Nutrition: calories 400, fat 12, fiber 32, carbs 29, protein 28

Creamy Coconut Chicken

Preparation time: 2 hours Cooking time: 25 minutes Servings: 4

INGREDIENTS:

- ✓ **4 big chicken legs**
- ✓ **5 teaspoons turmeric powder**
- ✓ **2 tablespoons ginger, grated**
- ✓ **Salt and black pepper to the taste**
- ✓ **4 tablespoons coconut cream**

DIRECTIONS:

- ○ In a bowl, mix cream with turmeric, ginger, salt and pepper, whisk, add chicken pieces, toss them well and leave aside for 2 hours.
- ○ Transfer chicken to your preheated air fryer, cook at 370 degrees F for 25 minutes, divide among plates and serve with a side salad.
- ○ Enjoy!

Nutrition: calories 300, fat 4, fiber 12, carbs 22, protein 20

Chinese Chicken Wings

Preparation time: 2 hours Cooking time: 15 minutes Servings: 6

INGREDIENTS:

- ✓ 16 chicken wings
- ✓ 2 tablespoons honey
- ✓ 2 tablespoons soy sauce
- ✓ Salt and black pepper to the taste
- ✓ ¼ teaspoon white pepper
- ✓ 3 tablespoons lime juice

DIRECTIONS:

- In a bowl, mix honey with soy sauce, salt, black and white pepper and lime juice, whisk well, add chicken pieces, toss to coat and keep in the fridge for 2 hours.
- Transfer chicken to your air fryer, cook at 370 degrees F for 6 minutes on each side, increase heat to 400 degrees F and cook for 3 minutes more.
- Serve hot.
- Enjoy!

Nutrition: calories 372, fat 9, fiber 10, carbs 37, protein 24

Herbed Chicken

Preparation time: 30 minutes Cooking time: 40 minutes Servings: 4

INGREDIENTS:

- ✓ 1 whole chicken
- ✓ Salt and black pepper to the taste
- ✓ 1 teaspoon garlic powder
- ✓ 1 teaspoon onion powder
- ✓ ½ teaspoon thyme, dried
- ✓ 1 teaspoon rosemary, dried
- ✓ 1 tablespoon lemon juice
- ✓ 2 tablespoons olive oil

DIRECTIONS:

- Season chicken with salt and pepper, rub with thyme, rosemary, garlic powder and onion powder, rub with lemon juice and olive oil and leave aside for 30 minutes.
- Put chicken in your air fryer and cook at 360 degrees F for 20 minutes on each side.
- Leave chicken aside to cool down, carve and serve.
- Enjoy!

Nutrition: calories 390, fat 10, fiber 5, carbs 22, protein 20

Delicious Spicy Drumsticks

Preparation: 2 minutes Cooking time: 18 minutes Servings: 4

INGREDIENTS:

- ✓ 4 chicken drumsticks
- ✓ 6 teaspoons of Montreal chicken spices
- ✓ 6 teaspoons of ground black pepper
- ✓ 1 teaspoon of olive oil
- ✓ 1 teaspoon of salt
- ✓ 6 teaspoons of chicken seasoning (your choice)

DIRECTIONS:

- Mix all the spices and seasonings in a bowl. Brush the chicken with olive oil.
- Rub the spices on the chicken. Ensure the spices stick firmly to the drumsticks.
- Heat your Air Fryer to 200°F for 3 minutes. Put the chicken into the fryer and cook for 10 minutes.
- Turn down the heat to 150°F and cook again for 8 minutes.

Spicy Garlic Chicken Nuggets

Preparation: 20 minutes Cooking time: 20 minutes Servings: 2

INGREDIENTS:

- ✓ 1 eggs, whisked
- ✓ 2 chicken breast halves, boneless, skinless,
- ✓ ½ pound of flour
- ✓ 3 tablespoons of garlic powder
- ✓ 1 tablespoon of black pepper
- ✓ 1 teaspoon of salt

DIRECTIONS:

- Mix the garlic, salt, pepper and flour in a shallow dish. Put the whisked egg in a separate bowl.
- Preheat the Air Fryer at 356°F.
- Cut the chicken into small pieces and dip them into the eggs and then coat with the flour mixture. Shake off any excess flour coating and place the chicken in a plate.
- Put the chicken pieces into the Air Fryer and cook until golden for 20 minutes. Shake the chicken halfway through.

Onion And Parsley Turkey Rolls

Preparation: 15 minutes Cooking time: 40 minutes Servings: 4

INGREDIENTS:

- ✓ 1 pound of turkey breast fillets
- ✓ 6 teaspoons of olive oil
- ✓ 1 teaspoon of cinnamon

- ✓ 1 clove of garlic, crushed
- ✓ 1 small sized onion, finely chopped
- ✓ 1 teaspoon of salt
- ✓ 1½ ounces of parsley, finely chopped
- ✓ 1½ teaspoon of ground cumin
- ✓ ½ teaspoon of ground chili

DIRECTIONS:

- ⏱ Place the turkey fillets on a chopping board with the smaller side facing you and cut through horizontally up to about 2/3 of the length. Fold open the slit and cut through again to form a long strip of meat.
- ⏱ Mix the chili, garlic, cumin, pepper, cinnamon and salt together in a large bowl. Stir in the olive oil. Remove 1 tablespoon of the mixture and set aside in a small bowl.
- ⏱ Add the parsley and onion to the mixture in the large bowl and stir.
- ⏱ Heat your Air Fryer to 356°F.
- ⏱ Spread the herb mixture on the surface of the meat and roll firmly beginning from the shorter end. Tie the roll with a string at about an inch interval. Coat the outside of the meat rolls with the spice mixture that was set aside.
- ⏱ Place in the air fryer and cook for 40 minutes.

Crispy Chicken Fillets

Preparation: 10 minutes Cooking time: 15 minutes Servings: 3

INGREDIENTS:

- ✓ 12 ounces of chicken fillets
- ✓ 1 teaspoon of ground black pepper
- ✓ 2 tablespoons of vegetable oil
- ✓ 8 tablespoons of breadcrumbs
- ✓ 4 ounces of flour
- ✓ 2 eggs, whisked
- ✓ ½ teaspoon salt

DIRECTIONS:

- ⏱ Heat your Air Fryer up to 330°F.
- ⏱ Add the salt, pepper and oil to the breadcrumbs then mix thoroughly.
- ⏱ Put the flour and egg into shallow bowls. Place the chicken in the flour, shake off excess and then dip into the whisked eggs and then coat evenly with breadcrumbs pressing to ensure that the breadcrumbs stick.
- ⏱ Shake off excess and place into the basket of the Air Fryer. Cook for 10 minutes and then increase heat to

390°F. Finally, cook for another 5 minutes until golden.

Sweet Potatoes & Creamy Crisp Chicken Airfry

Preparation: 15 minutes Cooking time: 40 minutes Servings: 2

INGREDIENTS:

- ✓ ¼ cup of flour, seasoned with salt and pepper
- ✓ 1 cup of buttermilk
- ✓ 1 teaspoon of garlic, finely copped
- ✓ 1 egg, whisked (5-ounce) chicken breast
- ✓ ½ teaspoon of pepper
- ✓ 7 ounces of breadcrumbs
- ✓ 2 medium sized sweet potatoes
- ✓ 3 teaspoons of smoked paprika
- ✓ 3 teaspoons of vegetable oil Salt and pepper to taste

DIRECTIONS:

- ⏱ Put the pepper, garlic and buttermilk into the bowl of chicken breasts, cover and leave to marinate in the fridge overnight.
- ⏱ Preheat the Air Fryer to 374°F for about 3 minutes.
- ⏱ Rub off the marinade from the chicken and dip the chicken into the seasoned flour, then into the egg and lastly the breadcrumbs. Ensure the coating sticks firmly to the chicken.
- ⏱ Fry the chicken in the air fryer for 20 minutes until well cooked. Remove from the fryer.
- ⏱ Peel the sweet potatoes and slice into chips, 1cm thick. Add the oil and paprika to the chips and toss.
- ⏱ Place the chips into the fryer and fry for 20 minutes at 374°F. Shake at about 6 minutes intervals. Season chips with salt and pepper when ready.

Mushroom & Chicken Noodles With Glasswort And Sesame

Preparation: 30 minutes Cooking time: 17 minutes Servings: 4

INGREDIENTS:

- ✓ 14 ounces of chicken thigh fillets, cut to pieces
- ✓ 14 ounces of noodles, cooked
- ✓ 2 cloves of garlic
- ✓ 2/3 cup of chestnut mushrooms

- ✓ 2/3 cup of shiitake mushrooms
- ✓ 1/4 cup of soy sauce
- ✓ 6 teaspoons of sesame oil
- ✓ 3 teaspoons of sesame seeds
- ✓ 7 ounces of glasswort
- ✓ 3 ounces of bean sprouts
- ✓ 1 teaspoon sambal
- ✓ 1 medium sized onion, thinly sliced Krupuk

DIRECTIONS:

- Mix the soy sauce, garlic and sambal to form a marinade and soak the chicken pieces in it to absorb.
- Add 3 teaspoons of oil to the cooked noodles.
- Heat the Air Fryer to 392°F. Place the chicken pieces in the fryer basket and sprinkle with oil. Cook for 6 minutes, shaking at intervals.
- Add the onion, mushrooms, glasswort and bean sprouts. Cook for another 5 minutes. Put in the noodles and cook further for 5 minutes. Finally, add the krupuk at the last minute.
- Remove from the Air Fryer and sprinkle with sesame seed.

Prawn Chicken Drumettes

Preparation: 15 minutes Cooking time: 15 minutes Servings: 3

INGREDIENTS:

- ✓ 10½ ounces of chicken drumettes
- ✓ 1 teaspoon of sesame oil
- ✓ 1 teaspoon of ginger juice
- ✓ 6 teaspoons of vegetable oil ¾ teaspoon of sugar
- ✓ 3 teaspoons of prawn paste
- ✓ ½ teaspoon of Shaoxing wine

DIRECTIONS:

- Mix the sesame oil, ginger juice, sugar, prawn paste and shaoxing wine together to form the marinade. Soak the chicken in the marinade for an hour or overnight in the refrigerator.
- Preheat your Air Fryer for 5 minutes at 356°F.
- Brush the chicken lightly with vegetable oil and arrange in a single layer in the fryer basket. Cook for 8 minutes, turn the chicken over and cook for another 7 minutes until golden.

Asian Popcorn Chicken

Preparation: 30 minutes Cooking time: 15 minutes Servings: 2

INGREDIENTS

- ✓ 1 lbs. chicken breast chicken thigh, boneless
- ✓ 1 clove garlic, medium, minced
- ✓ 1 tablespoon soy sauce
- ✓ 2 green onions, minced
- ✓ ¼ teaspoon of pepper
- ✓ ¼ teaspoon of chili pepper
- ✓ ¼ t teaspoon of five spice
- ✓ ½ teaspoon of sweet potato starch or corn starch
- ✓ 1 cup sweet potato starch/corn starch
- ✓ 1 egg
- ✓ ¼ cup water Breadcrumbs

DIRECTIONS:

- Wash the chicken and dice. Put the washed and minced green onions and garlic in a medium bowl. Add the chili pepper, five spice powder, pepper, soy sauce and starch, mixing well.
- Place chicken into the bowl and ensure the pieces are fully coated on all the sides. Leave the chicken to marinate in the bowl for at least 30 minutes or overnight if you like.
- Preheat the air fryer to 390F. Beat 1 egg with water in a small ball, add starch and mix thoroughly.
- Coat the chicken with the starch, pressing with hands, so it does not fall off. Place in the air fryer and cook for 12 minutes. Served, tossed with salt and pepper.

Herbal Chicken With Purple Sweet Potato

Preparation: 5minutes Cooking time: 22 minutes Servings: 2

INGREDIENTS:

- ✓ 1/2 portion of chicken, halved
- ✓ 1 teaspoon olive
- ✓ 1 tablespoon herbs chicken spices, (Seahs Emperor) Handful of purple sweet potato; brushed clean and pat dry Handful of salad green

DIRECTION:

- Trim the chicken then rinse and pat dry. Marinate with olive oil and herb chicken spices for 1 hour or overnight in the refrigerator.
- Place the sweet potato in the Air Fryer basket, set temperature to 350°F and cook for 10 minutes.

- ⏱ Arrange the marinated chicken on the Air Fryer basket and cook another 12 minutes.
- ⏱ During the last 4 to 5 minutes, check the color of the chicken to make sure they are nicely brown then keep cooking.
- ⏱ Leave the food for 1-2 minutes in the Air Fryer before removing and serving with salad greens.

Tasty And Spicy Chicken Jerks

Preparation: 38 minutes Cooking time: 18 minutes Servings: 5

INGREDIENTS:

- ✓ 6 teaspoons of vegetable oil
- ✓ 1 teaspoon of white pepper
- ✓ 3 teaspoons of chopped fresh thyme
- ✓ 6 cloves of garlic, finely diced
- ✓ 1 teaspoon of cinnamon
- ✓ 4 green onions, finely chopped
- ✓ 2½ ounces of lime juice
- ✓ 3 teaspoons of grated ginger
- ✓ 1 habanera pepper, seeded and finely chopped
- ✓ 1 teaspoon cayenne pepper
- ✓ 6 teaspoons of sugar
- ✓ 30 chicken wings
- ✓ 8 tablespoons of red wine vinegar
- ✓ 6 teaspoons of soy sauce
- ✓ 1 teaspoon of salt

DIRECTIONS:

- ⏱ Add up all the Ingredients in a large bowl, ensuring that the chicken is well covered with the spices and seasonings. Pour into a large re- sealable bag and leave to marinate in a refrigerator for 2-24 hours.
- ⏱ Heat your Air fryer to 390°F.
- ⏱ Remove the chicken wings from bag, discard the liquid and dry the wings with a disposable paper towel.
- ⏱ Put the wings into the fryer basket and fry for 18 minutes. Shake the chicken halfway through.
- ⏱ Serve with ranch dressing.

Chicken Parmesan

Preparation time: 10 minutes Cooking time: 15 minutes Servings: 4

INGREDIENTS:

- ✓ 2 cups panko bread crumbs
- ✓ ¼ cup parmesan, grated
- ✓ ½ teaspoon garlic powder
- ✓ 2 cups white flour
- ✓ 1 egg, whisked
- ✓ 1 and ½ pounds chicken cutlets, skinless and boneless Salt and black pepper to the taste
- ✓ 1 cup mozzarella, grated
- ✓ 2 cups tomato sauce
- ✓ 3 tablespoons basil, chopped

DIRECTIONS:

- ⏱ In a bowl, mix panko with parmesan and garlic powder and stir.
- ⏱ Put flour in a second bowl and the egg in a third.
- ⏱ Season chicken with salt and pepper, dip in flour, then in egg mix and in panko.
- ⏱ Put chicken pieces in your air fryer and cook them at 360 degrees F for 3 minutes on each side.
- ⏱ Transfer chicken to a baking dish that fits your air fryer, add tomato sauce and top with mozzarella, introduce in your air fryer and cook at 375 degrees F for 7 minutes.
- ⏱ Divide among plates, sprinkle basil on top and serve.
- ⏱ Enjoy!

Nutrition: calories 304, fat 12, fiber 11, carbs 22, protein 15

Mexican Chicken

Preparation time: 10 minutes Cooking time: 20 minutes Servings: 4

INGREDIENTS:

- ✓ 16 ounces salsa verde
- ✓ 1 tablespoon olive oil
- ✓ Salt and black pepper to the taste
- ✓ 1 pound chicken breast, boneless and skinless
- ✓ 1 and ½ cup Monterey Jack cheese, grated ¼ cup cilantro, chopped
- ✓ 1 teaspoon garlic powder

DIRECTIONS:

- ⏱ Pour salsa verde in a baking dish that fits your air fryer, season chicken with salt, pepper, garlic powder, brush with olive oil and place it over your salsa verde.
- ⏱ Introduce in your air fryer and cook at 380 degrees F for 20 minutes.
- ⏱ Sprinkle cheese on top and cook for 2 minutes more.
- ⏱ Divide among plates and serve hot.
- ⏱ Enjoy!

Nutrition: calories 340, fat 18, fiber 14, carbs 32, protein 18

Chicken Breas ts and Tomatoes Sauce

Preparation time: 10 minutes Cooking time: 20 minutes Servings: 4

INGREDIENTS:

- ✓ 1 red onion, chopped
- ✓ 4 chicken breasts, skinless and boneless
- ✓ ¼ cup balsamic vinegar
- ✓ 14 ounces canned tomatoes, chopped
- ✓ Salt and black pepper to the taste
- ✓ ¼ cup parmesan, grated
- ✓ ¼ teaspoon garlic powder
- ✓ Cooking spray

DIRECTIONS:

- Spray a baking dish that fits your air fryer with cooking oil, add chicken, season with salt, pepper, balsamic vinegar, garlic powder, tomatoes and cheese, toss, introduce in your air fryer and cook at 400 degrees F for 20 minutes.
- Divide among plates and serve hot.
- Enjoy!

Nutrition: calories 250, fat 12, fiber 12, carbs 19, protein 28

Chicken and Asparagus

Preparation time: 10 minutes Cooking time: 20 minutes Servings: 4

INGREDIENTS:

- ✓ 8 chicken wings, halved
- ✓ 8 asparagus spears
- ✓ Salt and black pepper to the taste
- ✓ 1 tablespoon rosemary, chopped
- ✓ 1 teaspoon cumin, ground

DIRECTIONS:

- Pat dry chicken wings, season with salt, pepper, cumin and rosemary, put them in your air fryer's basket and cook at 360 degrees F for 20 minutes.
- Meanwhile, heat up a pan over medium heat, add asparagus, add water to cover, steam for a few minutes, transfer to a bowl filled with ice water, drain and arrange on plates.

- Add chicken wings on the side and serve.
- Enjoy!

Nutrition: calories 270, fat 8, fiber 12, carbs 24, protein 22

Chicken Thighs and Apple Mix

Preparation time: 12 hours Cooking time: 30 minutes Servings: 4

INGREDIENTS:

- ✓ 8 chicken thighs, bone in and skin on
- ✓ Salt and black pepper to the taste
- ✓ 1 tablespoon apple cider vinegar
- ✓ 3 tablespoons onion, chopped
- ✓ 1 tablespoon ginger, grated
- ✓ ½ teaspoon thyme, dried
- ✓ 3 apples, cored and cut into quarters
- ✓ ¾ cup apple juice
- ✓ ½ cup maple syrup

DIRECTIONS:

- In a bowl, mix chicken with salt, pepper, vinegar, onion, ginger, thyme, apple juice and maple syrup, toss well, cover and keep in the fridge for 12 hours.
- Transfer this whole mix to a baking dish that fits your air fryer, add apple pieces, place in your air fryer and cook at 350 degrees F for 30 minutes.
- Divide among plates and serve warm.
- Enjoy!

Nutrition: calories 314, fat 8, fiber 11, carbs 34, protein 22

Chicken and Parsley Sauce

Preparation time: 30 minutes Cooking time: 25 minutes Servings: 6

INGREDIENTS:

- ✓ 1 cup parsley, chopped
- ✓ 1 teaspoon oregano, dried
- ✓ ½ cup olive oil
- ✓ ¼ cup red wine
- ✓ 4 garlic cloves
- ✓ A pinch of salt
- ✓ A drizzle of maple syrup
- ✓ 12 chicken thighs

DIRECTIONS:

- In your food processor, mix parsley with oregano, garlic, salt, oil, wine and maple syrup and pulse really well.

- In a bowl, mix chicken with parsley sauce, toss well and keep in the fridge for 30 minutes.
- Drain chicken, transfer to your air fryer's basket and cook at 380 degrees F for 25 minutes, flipping chicken once.
- Divide chicken on plates, drizzle parsley sauce all over and serve.
- Enjoy!

Nutrition: calories 354, fat 10, fiber 12, carbs 22, protein 17

Chicken and Lentils Casserole

Preparation time: 10 minutes Cooking time: 1 hour Servings: 8

INGREDIENTS:

- ✓ 1 and ½ cups green lentils
- ✓ 3 cups chicken stock
- ✓ 2 pound chicken breasts, skinless, boneless and chopped Salt and cayenne pepper to the taste
- ✓ 3 teaspoons cumin, ground
- ✓ Cooking spray
- ✓ 5 garlic cloves, minced
- ✓ 1 yellow onion, chopped
- ✓ 2 red bell peppers, chopped
- ✓ 14 ounces canned tomatoes, chopped
- ✓ 2 cups corn
- ✓ 2 cups Cheddar cheese, shredded
- ✓ 2 tablespoons jalapeno pepper, chopped
- ✓ 1 tablespoon garlic powder
- ✓ 1 cup cilantro, chopped

DIRECTIONS:

- Put the stock in a pot, add some salt, add lentils, stir, bring to a boil over medium heat, cover and simmer for 35 minutes.
- Meanwhile, spray chicken pieces with some cooking spray, season with salt, cayenne pepper and 1 teaspoon cumin, put them in your air fryer's basket and cook them at 370 degrees for 6 minutes, flipping half way.
- Transfer chicken to a heat proof dish that fits your air fryer, add bell peppers, garlic, tomatoes, onion, salt, cayenne and 1 teaspoon cumin.
- Drain lentils and add them to the chicken mix as well.
- Add jalapeno pepper, garlic powder, the rest of the cumin, corn, half of the cheese and half of the cilantro, introduce in your air fryer and cook at 320 degrees F for 25 minutes.

- Sprinkle the rest of the cheese and the remaining cilantro, divide chicken casserole on plates and serve.
- Enjoy!

Nutrition: calories 344, fat 11, fiber 12, carbs 22, protein 33

Fall Air Fried Chicken Mix

Preparation time: 10 minutes Cooking time: 20 minutes Servings: 8

INGREDIENTS:

- ✓ 3 pounds chicken breasts, skinless and boneless
- ✓ 1 yellow onion, chopped
- ✓ 1 garlic clove, minced
- ✓ Salt and black pepper to the taste
- ✓ 10 white mushrooms, halved
- ✓ 1 tablespoon olive oil
- ✓ 1 red bell pepper, chopped
- ✓ 1 green bell pepper
- ✓ 2 tablespoons mozzarella cheese, shredded Cooking spray

DIRECTIONS:

- Season chicken with salt and pepper, rub with garlic, spray with cooking spray, place in your preheated air fryer and cook at 390 degrees F for 12 minutes.
- Meanwhile, heat up a pan with the oil over medium heat, add onion, stir and sauté for 2 minutes.
- Add mushrooms, garlic and bell peppers, stir and cook for 8 minutes.
- Divide chicken on plates, add mushroom mix on the side, sprinkle cheese while chicken is still hot and serve right away.
- Enjoy!

Nutrition: calories 305, fat 12, fiber 11, carbs 26, protein 32

Chicken Salad

Preparation time: 10 minutes Cooking time: 10 minutes Servings: 4

INGREDIENTS:

- ✓ 1 pound chicken breast, boneless, skinless and halved Cooking spray
- ✓ Salt and black pepper to the taste
- ✓ ½ cup feta cheese, cubed
- ✓ 2 tablespoons lemon juice

- ✓ 1 and ½ teaspoons mustard
- ✓ 1 tablespoon olive oil
- ✓ 1 and ½ teaspoons red wine vinegar
- ✓ ½ teaspoon anchovies, minced
- ✓ ¾ teaspoon garlic, minced
- ✓ 1 tablespoon water
- ✓ 8 cups lettuce leaves, cut into strips
- ✓ 4 tablespoons parmesan, grated

DIRECTIONS:

- Spray chicken breasts with cooking oil, season with salt and pepper, introduce in your air fryer's basket and cook at 370 degrees F for 10 minutes, flipping halfway.
- Transfer chicken beasts to a cutting board, shred using 2 forks, put in a salad bowl and mix with lettuce leaves.
- In your blender, mix feta cheese with lemon juice, olive oil, mustard, vinegar, garlic, anchovies, water and half of the parmesan and blend very well.
- Add this over chicken mix, toss, sprinkle the rest of the parmesan and serve.
- Enjoy!

Nutrition: calories 312, fat 6, fiber 16, carbs 22, protein 26

Chicken and Green Onions Sauce

Preparation time: 10 minutes Cooking time: 16 minutes Servings: 4

INGREDIENTS:

- ✓ 10 green onions, roughly chopped
- ✓ 1 inch piece ginger root, chopped
- ✓ 4 garlic cloves, minced
- ✓ 2 tablespoons fish sauce
- ✓ 3 tablespoons soy sauce
- ✓ 1 teaspoon Chinese five spice
- ✓ 10 chicken drumsticks
- ✓ 1 cup coconut milk
- ✓ Salt and black pepper to the taste
- ✓ 1 teaspoon butter, melted
- ✓ ¼ cup cilantro, chopped
- ✓ 1 tablespoon lime juice

DIRECTIONS:

- In your food processor, mix green onions with ginger, garlic, soy sauce, fish sauce, five spice, salt, pepper, butter and coconut milk and pulse well.
- In a bowl, mix chicken with green onions mix, toss well, transfer everything to a pan that fits your air fryer and cook at 370 degrees F for 16 minutes, shaking the fryer once.
- Divide among plates, sprinkle cilantro on top, drizzle lime juice and serve with a side salad.
- Enjoy!

Nutrition: calories 321, fat 12, fiber 12, carbs 22, protein 20

Chicken Cacciatore

Preparation time: 10 minutes Cooking time: 20 minutes Servings: 4

INGREDIENTS:

- ✓ Salt and black pepper to the taste
- ✓ 8 chicken drumsticks, bone-in
- ✓ 1 bay leaf
- ✓ 1 teaspoon garlic powder
- ✓ 1 yellow onion, chopped
- ✓ 28 ounces canned tomatoes and juice, crushed
- ✓ 1 teaspoon oregano, dried
- ✓ ½ cup black olives, pitted and sliced

DIRECTIONS:

- In a heat proof dish that fits your air fryer, mix chicken with salt, pepper, garlic powder, bay leaf, onion, tomatoes and juice, oregano and olives, toss, introduce in your preheated air fryer and cook at 365 degrees F for 20 minutes.
- Divide among plates and serve.
- Enjoy!

Nutrition: calories 300, fat 12, fiber 8, carbs 20, protein 24

Chicken Wings and Mint Sauce

Preparation time: 20 minutes Cooking time: 16 minutes Servings: 6

INGREDIENTS:

- ✓ 18 chicken wings, halved
- ✓ 1 tablespoon turmeric powder
- ✓ 1 tablespoon cumin, ground
- ✓ 1 tablespoon ginger, grated
- ✓ 1 tablespoon coriander, ground
- ✓ 1 tablespoon sweet paprika
- ✓ Salt and black pepper to the taste

- ✓ **2 tablespoons olive oil**

For the mint sauce:

- ✓ **Juice from ½ lime**
- ✓ **1 cup mint leaves**
- ✓ **1 small ginger piece, chopped**
- ✓ **¾ cup cilantro**
- ✓ **1 tablespoon olive oil**
- ✓ **1 tablespoon water**
- ✓ **Salt and black pepper to the taste**
- ✓ **1 Serrano pepper, chopped**

DIRECTIONS:

- ⏱ In a bowl, mix 1 tablespoon ginger with cumin, coriander, paprika, turmeric, salt, pepper, cayenne and 2 tablespoons oil and stir well.
- ⏱ Add chicken wings pieces to this mix, toss to coat well and keep in the fridge for 10 minutes.
- ⏱ Transfer chicken to your air fryer's basket and cook at 370 degrees F for 16 minutes, flipping them halfway.
- ⏱ In your blender, mix mint with cilantro, 1 small ginger pieces, juice from ½ lime, 1 tablespoon olive oil, salt, pepper, water and Serrano pepper and blend very well.
- ⏱ Divide chicken wings on plates, drizzle mint sauce all over and serve.
- ⏱ Enjoy!

Nutrition: calories 300, fat 15, fiber 11, carbs 27, protein 16

Lemon Chicken

Preparation time: 10 minutes Cooking time: 30 minutes Servings: 6

INGREDIENTS:

- ✓ **1 whole chicken, cut into medium pieces**
- ✓ **1 tablespoon olive oil**
- ✓ **Salt and black pepper to the taste**
- ✓ **Juice from 2 lemons**
- ✓ **Zest from 2 lemons, grated**

DIRECTIONS:

- ⏱ Season chicken with salt, pepper, rub with oil and lemon zest, drizzle lemon juice, put in your air fryer and cook at 350 degrees F for 30 minutes, flipping chicken pieces halfway.
- ⏱ Divide among plates and serve with a side salad.
- ⏱ Enjoy!

Nutrition: calories 334, fat 24, fiber 12, carbs 26, protein 20

Chicken and Simple Coconut Sauce

Preparation time: 10 minutes Cooking time: 12 minutes Servings: 6

INGREDIENTS:

- ✓ **1 tablespoon olive oil**
- ✓ **3 and ½ pounds chicken breasts**
- ✓ **1 cup chicken stock**
- ✓ **1 and ¼ cups yellow onion, chopped**
- ✓ **1 tablespoon lime juice**
- ✓ **¼ cup coconut milk**
- ✓ **2 teaspoons sweet paprika**
- ✓ **1 teaspoon red pepper flakes**
- ✓ **2 tablespoons green onions, chopped**
- ✓ **Salt and black pepper to the taste**

DIRECTIONS:

- ⏱ Heat up a pan that fits your air fryer with the oil over medium high heat, add onions, stir and cook for 4 minutes.
- ⏱ Add stock, coconut milk, pepper flakes, paprika, lime juice, salt and pepper and stir well.
- ⏱ Add chicken to the pan, add more salt and pepper, toss, introduce in your air fryer and cook at 360 degrees F for 12 minutes.
- ⏱ Divide chicken and sauce on plates and serve.
- ⏱ Enjoy!

Nutrition: calories 320, fat 13, fiber 13, carbs 32, protein 23

Chicken and Black Olives Sauce

Preparation time: 10 minutes Cooking time: 8 minutes Servings: 2

INGREDIENTS:

- ✓ **1 chicken breast cut into 4 pieces**
- ✓ **2 tablespoons olive oil**
- ✓ **3 garlic cloves, minced**

For the sauce:

- ✓ **1 cup black olives, pitted**
- ✓ **Salt and black pepper to the taste**
- ✓ **2 tablespoons olive oil**
- ✓ **¼ cup parsley, chopped**
- ✓ **1 tablespoons lemon juice**

DIRECTIONS:

- In your food processor, mix olives with salt, pepper, 2 tablespoons olive oil, lemon juice and parsley, blend very well and transfer to a bowl.
- Season chicken with salt and pepper, rub with the oil and garlic, place in your preheated air fryer and cook at 370 degrees F for 8 minutes.
- Divide chicken on plates, top with olives sauce and serve.
- Enjoy!

Nutrition: calories 270, fat 12, fiber 12, carbs 23, protein 22

Cheese Crusted Chicken

Preparation time: 10 minutes Cooking time: 15 minutes Servings: 4

INGREDIENTS:

- ✓ 4 bacon slices, cooked and crumbled
- ✓ 4 chicken breasts, skinless and boneless
- ✓ 1 tablespoon water
- ✓ ½ cup avocado oil
- ✓ 1 egg, whisked
- ✓ Salt and black pepper to the taste
- ✓ 1 cup asiago cheese, shredded
- ✓ ¼ teaspoon garlic powder
- ✓ 1 cup parmesan cheese, grated

DIRECTIONS:

- In a bowl, mix parmesan with garlic, salt and pepper and stir.
- In another bowl, mix egg with water and whisk well.
- Season chicken with salt and pepper and dip each pieces into egg and then into cheese mix.
- Add chicken to your air fryer and cook at 320 degrees F for 15 minutes.
- Divide chicken on plates, sprinkle bacon and asiago cheese on top and serve.
- Enjoy!

Nutrition: calories 400, fat 22, fiber 12, carbs 32, protein 47

Pepperoni Chicken

Preparation time: 10 minutes Cooking time: 22 minutes Servings: 6

INGREDIENTS:

- ✓ 14 ounces tomato paste
- ✓ 1 tablespoon olive oil
- ✓ 4 medium chicken breasts, skinless and boneless

    Salt and black pepper to the taste
- ✓ 1 teaspoon oregano, dried

- ✓ 6 ounces mozzarella, sliced
- ✓ 1 teaspoon garlic powder
- ✓ 2 ounces pepperoni, sliced

DIRECTIONS:

- In a bowl, mix chicken with salt, pepper, garlic powder and oregano and toss.
- Put chicken in your air fryer, cook at 350 degrees F for 6 minutes and transfer to a pan that fits your air fryer.
- Add mozzarella slices on top, spread tomato paste, top with pepperoni slices, introduce in your air fryer and cook at 350 degrees F for 15 minutes more.
- Divide among plates and serve.
- Enjoy!

Nutrition: calories 320, fat 10, fiber 16, carbs 23, protein 27

Chicken and Creamy Veggie Mix

Preparation time: 10 minutes Cooking time: 30 minutes Servings: 6

INGREDIENTS:

- ✓ 2 cups whipping cream
- ✓ 40 ounces chicken pieces, boneless and skinless
- ✓ 3 tablespoons butter, melted
- ✓ ½ cup yellow onion, chopped
- ✓ ¾ cup red peppers, chopped
- ✓ 29 ounces chicken stock
- ✓ Salt and black pepper to the taste
- ✓ 1 bay leaf
- ✓ 8 ounces mushrooms, chopped
- ✓ 17 ounces asparagus, trimmed
- ✓ 3 teaspoons thyme, chopped

DIRECTIONS:

- Heat up a pan with the butter over medium heat, add onion and peppers, stir and cook for 3 minutes.
- Add stock, bay leaf, salt and pepper, bring to a boil and simmer for 10 minutes.
- Add asparagus, mushrooms, chicken, cream, thyme, salt and pepper to the taste, stir, introduce in your air fryer and cook at 360 degrees F for 15 minutes.
- Divide chicken and veggie mix on plates and serve.
- Enjoy!

Nutrition: calories 360, fat 27, fiber 13, carbs 24, protein 47

Turkey Quarters and Veggies

Preparation time: 10 minutes Cooking time: 34 minutes Servings: 4

INGREDIENTS:

- ✓ **1 yellow onion, chopped**
- ✓ **1 carrot, chopped**
- ✓ **3 garlic cloves, minced**
- ✓ **2 pounds turkey quarters**
- ✓ **1 celery stalk, chopped**
- ✓ **1 cup chicken stock**
- ✓ **2 tablespoons olive oil**
- ✓ **2 bay leaves**
- ✓ **½ teaspoon rosemary, dried**
- ✓ **½ teaspoon sage, dried**
- ✓ **½ teaspoon thyme, dried**
- ✓ **Salt and black pepper to the taste**

DIRECTIONS:

- ⏲ Rub turkey quarters with salt, pepper, half of the oil, thyme, sage, rosemary and thyme, put in your air fryer and cook at 360 degrees F for 20 minutes.
- ⏲ In a pan that fits your air fryer, mix onion with carrot, garlic, celery, the rest of the oil, stock, bay leaves, salt and pepper and toss.
- ⏲ Add turkey, introduce everything in your air fryer and cook at 360 degrees F for 14 minutes more.
- ⏲ Divide everything on plates and serve.
- ⏲ Enjoy!

Nutrition: calories 362, fat 12, fiber 16, carbs 22, protein 17

Chicken and Garlic Sauce

Preparation time: 10 minutes Cooking time: 20 minutes Servings: 4

INGREDIENTS:

- ✓ **1 tablespoon butter, melted**
- ✓ **4 chicken breasts, skin on and bone-in**
- ✓ **1 tablespoon olive oil**
- ✓ **Salt and black pepper to the taste**
- ✓ **40 garlic cloves, peeled and chopped**
- ✓ **2 thyme springs**
- ✓ **¼ cup chicken stock**
- ✓ **2 tablespoons parsley, chopped**
- ✓ **¼ cup dry white wine**

DIRECTIONS:

- ⏲ Season chicken breasts with salt and pepper, rub with the oil, place in your air fryer, cook at 360

degrees F for 4 minutes on each side and transfer to a heat proof dish that fits your air fryer.
- ⏲ Add melted butter, garlic, thyme, stock, wine and parsley, toss, introduce in your air fryer and cook at 350 degrees F for 15 minutes more.
- ⏲ Divide everything on plates and serve.
- ⏲ Enjoy!

Nutrition: calories 227, fat 9, fiber 13, carbs 22, protein 12

Turkey, Peas and Mushrooms Casserole

Preparation time: 10 minutes Cooking time: 20 minutes Servings: 4

INGREDIENTS:

- ✓ **2 pounds turkey breasts, skinless, boneless Salt and black pepper to the taste**
- ✓ **1 yellow onion, chopped**
- ✓ **1 celery stalk, chopped**
- ✓ **½ cup peas**
- ✓ **1 cup chicken stock**
- ✓ **1 cup cream of mushrooms soup**
- ✓ **1 cup bread cubes**

DIRECTIONS:

- ⏲ In a pan that fits your air fryer, mix turkey with salt, pepper, onion, celery, peas and stock, introduce in your air fryer and cook at 360 degrees F for 15 minutes.
- ⏲ Add bread cubes and cream of mushroom soup, stir toss and cook at 360 degrees F for 5 minutes more.
- ⏲ Divide among plates and serve hot.
- ⏲ Enjoy!

Nutrition: calories 271, fat 9, fiber 9, carbs 16, protein 7

Tasty Chicken Thighs

Preparation time: 10 minutes Cooking time: 20 minutes Servings: 6

INGREDIENTS:

- ✓ **2 and ½ pounds chicken thighs**
- ✓ **Salt and black pepper to the taste**
- ✓ **5 green onions, chopped**
- ✓ **2 tablespoons sesame oil**
- ✓ **1 tablespoon sherry wine**
- ✓ **½ teaspoon white vinegar**
- ✓ **1 tablespoon soy sauce**

✓ ¼ teaspoon sugar

DIRECTIONS:

- Season chicken with salt and pepper, rub with half of the sesame oil, add to your air fryer and cook at 360 degrees F for 20 minutes.
- Meanwhile, heat up a pan with the rest of the oil over medium high heat, add green onions, sherry wine, vinegar, soy sauce and sugar, toss, cover and cook for 10 minutes
- Shred chicken using 2 forks divide among plates, drizzle sauce all over
- and serve.
- Enjoy!

Nutrition: calories 321, fat 8, fiber 12, carbs 36, protein 24

Chicken Tenders and Flavored Sauce

Preparation time: 10 minutes Cooking time: 10 minutes Servings: 6

INGREDIENTS:

- ✓ 1 teaspoon chili powder
- ✓ 2 teaspoon garlic powder
- ✓ 1 teaspoon onion powder
- ✓ 1 teaspoon sweet paprika
- ✓ Salt and black pepper to the taste
- ✓ 2 tablespoons butter
- ✓ 2 tablespoons olive oil
- ✓ 2 pounds chicken tenders
- ✓ 2 tablespoons cornstarch
- ✓ ½ cup chicken stock
- ✓ 2 cups heavy cream
- ✓ 2 tablespoons water
- ✓ 2 tablespoons parsley, chopped

DIRECTIONS:

- In a bowl, mix garlic powder with onion powder, chili, salt, pepper and paprika, stir, add chicken and toss.
- Rub chicken tenders with oil, place in your air fryer and cook at 360 degrees F for 10 minutes.
- Meanwhile, heat up a pan with the butter over medium high heat, add cornstarch, stock, cream, water and parsley, stir, cover and cook for 10 minutes.
- Divide chicken on plates, drizzle sauce all over and serve.
- Enjoy!

Nutrition: calories 351, fat 12, fiber 9, carbs 20, protein 17

Duck and Veggies

Preparation time: 10 minutes Cooking time: 20 minutes Servings: 8

INGREDIENTS:

- ✓ 1 duck, chopped in medium pieces
- ✓ 3 cucumbers, chopped
- ✓ 3 tablespoon white wine
- ✓ 2 carrots, chopped
- ✓ 1 cup chicken stock
- ✓ 1 small ginger piece, grated
- ✓ Salt and black pepper to the taste

DIRECTIONS:

- In a pan that fits your air fryer, mix duck pieces with cucumbers, wine, carrots, ginger, stock, salt and pepper, toss, introduce in your air fryer and cook at 370 degrees F for 20 minutes.
- Divide everything on plates and serve.
- Enjoy!

Nutrition: calories 200, fat 10, fiber 8, carbs 20, protein 22

Chicken and Apricot Sauce

Preparation time: 10 minutes Cooking time: 20 minutes Servings: 4

INGREDIENTS:

- ✓ 1 whole chicken, cut into medium pieces Salt and black pepper to the taste
- ✓ 1 tablespoon olive oil
- ✓ ½ teaspoon smoked paprika
- ✓ ¼ cup white wine
- ✓ ½ teaspoon marjoram, dried
- ✓ ¼ cup chicken stock
- ✓ 2 tablespoons white vinegar
- ✓ ¼ cup apricot preserves
- ✓ 1 and ½ teaspoon ginger, grated
- ✓ 2 tablespoons honey

DIRECTIONS:

- Season chicken with salt, pepper, marjoram and paprika, toss to coat, add oil, rub well, place in your air fryer and cook at 360 degrees F for 10 minutes.
- Transfer chicken to a pan that fits your air fryer, add stock, wine, vinegar, ginger, apricot preserves and honey, toss, put in your air fryer and cook at 360 degrees F for 10 minutes more.

- Divide chicken and apricot sauce on plates and serve.
- Enjoy!

Nutrition: calories 200, fat 7, fiber 19, carbs 20, protein 14

Chicken and Cauliflower Rice Mix

Preparation time: 10 minutes Cooking time: 20 minutes Servings: 6

INGREDIENTS:

- ✓ 3 bacon slices, chopped
- ✓ 3 carrots, chopped
- ✓ 3 pounds chicken thighs, boneless and skinless
- ✓ 2 bay leaves
- ✓ ¼ cup red wine vinegar
- ✓ 4 garlic cloves, minced
- ✓ Salt and black pepper to the taste
- ✓ 4 tablespoons olive oil
- ✓ 1 tablespoon garlic powder
- ✓ 1 tablespoon Italian seasoning
- ✓ 24 ounces cauliflower rice
- ✓ 1 teaspoon turmeric powder
- ✓ 1 cup beef stock

DIRECTIONS:

- Heat up a pan that fits your air fryer over medium high heat, add bacon, carrots, onion and garlic, stir and cook for 8 minutes.
- Add chicken, oil, vinegar, turmeric, garlic powder, Italian seasoning and bay leaves, stir, introduce in your air fryer and cook at 360 degrees F for 12 minutes.
- Add cauliflower rice and stock, stir, cook for 6 minutes more, divide among plates and serve.
- Enjoy!

Nutrition: calories 340, fat 12, fiber 12, carbs 16, protein 8

Chicken and Spinach Salad

Preparation time: 10 minutes Cooking time: 12 minutes Servings: 2

INGREDIENTS:

- ✓ 2 teaspoons parsley, dried
- ✓ 2 chicken breasts, skinless and boneless
- ✓ ½ teaspoon onion powder
- ✓ 2 teaspoons sweet paprika
- ✓ ½ cup lemon juice

- ✓ Salt and black pepper to the taste
- ✓ 5 cups baby spinach
- ✓ 8 strawberries, sliced
- ✓ 1 small red onion, sliced
- ✓ 2 tablespoons balsamic vinegar
- ✓ 1 avocado, pitted, peeled and chopped
- ✓ ¼ cup olive oil
- ✓ 1 tablespoon tarragon, chopped

DIRECTIONS:

- Put chicken in a bowl, add lemon juice, parsley, onion powder and paprika and toss.
- Transfer chicken to your air fryer and cook at 360 degrees F for 12 minutes.
- In a bowl, mix spinach, onion, strawberries and avocado and toss.
- In another bowl, mix oil with vinegar, salt, pepper and tarragon, whisk well, add to the salad and toss.
- Divide chicken on plates, add spinach salad on the side and serve. Enjoy!

Nutrition: calories 240, fat 5, fiber 13, carbs 25, protein 22

Chicke n and Chestnuts Mix

Preparation time: 10 minutes Cooking time: 12 minutes Servings: 2

INGREDIENTS:

- ✓ ½ pound chicken pieces
- ✓ 1 small yellow onion, chopped
- ✓ 2 teaspoons garlic, minced
- ✓ A pinch of ginger, grated
- ✓ A pinch of allspice, ground
- ✓ 4 tablespoons water chestnuts
- ✓ 2 tablespoons soy sauce
- ✓ 2 tablespoons chicken stock
- ✓ 2 tablespoons balsamic vinegar
- ✓ 2 tortillas for serving

DIRECTIONS:

- In a pan that fits your air fryer, mix chicken meat with onion, garlic, ginger, allspice, chestnuts, soy sauce, stock and vinegar, stir, transfer to your air fryer and cook at 360 degrees F for 12 minutes.
- Divide everything on plates and serve.

Nutrition: calories 301, fat 12, fiber 7, carbs 24, protein 12

Cider Glazed Chicken

Preparation time: 10 minutes Cooking time: 14 minutes Servings: 4

INGREDIENTS:

- ✓ **1 sweet potato, cubed**
- ✓ **2 apples, cored and sliced**
- ✓ **1 tablespoon olive oil**
- ✓ **1 tablespoon rosemary, chopped**
- ✓ **Salt and black pepper to the taste**
- ✓ **6 chicken thighs, bone in and skin on**
- ✓ **2/3 cup apple cider**
- ✓ **1 tablespoon mustard**
- ✓ **2 tablespoons honey**
- ✓ **1 tablespoon butter**

DIRECTIONS:

- ⏲ Heat up a pan that fits your air fryer with half of the oil over medium high heat, add cider, honey, butter and mustard, whisk well, bring to a simmer, take off heat, add chicken and toss really well.
- ⏲ In a bowl, mix potato cubes with rosemary, apples, salt, pepper and the rest of the oil, toss well and add to chicken mix.
- ⏲ Place pan in your air fryer and cook at 390 degrees F for 14 minutes.
- ⏲ Divide everything on plates and serve.
- ⏲ Enjoy!

Nutrition: calories 241, fat 7, fiber 12, carbs 28, protein 22

Veggie Stuffed Chicken Breasts

Preparation time: 10 minutes Cooking time: 15 minutes Servings: 4

INGREDIENTS:

- ✓ **4 chicken breasts, skinless and boneless**
- ✓ **2 tablespoons olive oil**
- ✓ **Salt and black pepper to the taste**
- ✓ **1 zucchini, chopped**
- ✓ **1 teaspoon Italian seasoning**
- ✓ **2 yellow bell peppers, chopped**
- ✓ **3 tomatoes, chopped**
- ✓ **1 red onion, chopped**
- ✓ **1 cup mozzarella, shredded**

DIRECTIONS:

- ⏲ Mix a slit on each chicken breast creating a pocket, season with salt and pepper and rub them with olive oil.
- ⏲ In a bowl, mix zucchini with Italian seasoning, bell peppers, tomatoes and onion and stir.
- ⏲ Stuff chicken breasts with this mix, sprinkle mozzarella over them, place them in your air fryer's basket and cook at 350 degrees F for 15 minutes.
- ⏲ Divide among plates and serve.
- ⏲ Enjoy!

Nutrition: calories 300, fat 12, fiber 7, carbs 22, protein 18

Greek Chicken

Preparation time: 10 minutes Cooking time: 15 minutes Servings: 4

INGREDIENTS:

- ✓ **2 tablespoons olive oil**
- ✓ **Juice from 1 lemon**
- ✓ **1 teaspoon oregano, dried**
- ✓ **3 garlic cloves, minced**
- ✓ **1 pound chicken thighs**
- ✓ **Salt and black pepper to the taste**
- ✓ **½ pound asparagus, trimmed**
- ✓ **1 zucchini, roughly chopped**
- ✓ **1 lemon sliced**

DIRECTIONS:

- ⏲ In a heat proof dish that fits your air fryer, mix chicken pieces with oil, lemon juice, oregano, garlic, salt, pepper, asparagus, zucchini and lemon slices, toss, introduce in preheated air fryer and cook at 380 degrees F for 15 minutes.
- ⏲ Divide everything on plates and serve.
- ⏲ Enjoy!

Nutrition: calories 300, fat 8, fiber 12, carbs 20, protein 18

Duck Breasts with Red Wine and Orange Sauce

Preparation time: 10 minutes Cooking time: 35 minutes Servings: 4

INGREDIENTS:

- ✓ **½ cup honey**
- ✓ **2 cups orange juice**
- ✓ **4 cups red wine**
- ✓ **2 tablespoons sherry vinegar**

- ✓ 2 cups chicken stock
- ✓ 2 teaspoons pumpkin pie spice
- ✓ 2 tablespoons butter
- ✓ 2 duck breasts, skin on and halved
- ✓ 2 tablespoons olive oil
- ✓ Salt and black pepper to the taste

DIRECTIONS:

- ⏱ Heat up a pan with the orange juice over medium heat, add honey, stir well and cook for 10 minutes.
- ⏱ Add wine, vinegar, stock, pie spice and butter, stir well, cook for 10 minutes more and take off heat.
- ⏱ Season duck breasts with salt and pepper, rub with olive oil, place in preheated air fryer at 370 degrees F and cook for 7 minutes on each side.
- ⏱ Divide duck breasts on plates, drizzle wine and orange juice all over and serve right away.
- ⏱ Enjoy!

Nutrition: calories 300, fat 8, fiber 12, carbs 24, protein 11

Duck Breast with Fig Sauce

Preparation time: 10 minutes Cooking time: 20 minutes Servings: 4

INGREDIENTS:

- ✓ 2 duck breasts, skin on, halved
- ✓ 1 tablespoon olive oil
- ✓ ½ teaspoon thyme, chopped
- ✓ ½ teaspoon garlic powder
- ✓ ¼ teaspoon sweet paprika
- ✓ Salt and black pepper to the taste
- ✓ 1 cup beef stock
- ✓ 3 tablespoons butter, melted
- ✓ 1 shallot, chopped
- ✓ ½ cup port wine
- ✓ 4 tablespoons fig preserves
- ✓ 1 tablespoon white flour

DIRECTIONS:

- ⏱ Season duck breasts with salt and pepper, drizzle half of the melted butter, rub well, put in your air fryer's basket and cook at 350 degrees F for 5 minutes on each side.

- ⏱ Meanwhile, heat up a pan with the olive oil and the rest of the butter over medium high heat, add shallot, stir and cook for 2 minutes.
- ⏱ Add thyme, garlic powder, paprika, stock, salt, pepper, wine and figs, stir and cook for 7-8 minutes.
- ⏱ Add flour, stir well, cook until sauce thickens a bit and take off heat.
- ⏱ Divide duck breasts on plates, drizzle figs sauce all over and serve. Enjoy!

Nutrition: calories 246, fat 12, fiber 4, carbs 22, protein 3

Duck Breasts and Raspberry Sauce

Preparation time: 10 minutes Cooking time: 15 minutes Servings: 4

INGREDIENTS:

- ✓ 2 duck breasts, skin on and scored
- ✓ Salt and black pepper to the taste
- ✓ Cooking spray
- ✓ ½ teaspoon cinnamon powder
- ✓ ½ cup raspberries
- ✓ 1 tablespoon sugar
- ✓ 1 teaspoon red wine vinegar
- ✓ ½ cup water

DIRECTIONS:

- ⏱ Season duck breasts with salt and pepper, spray them with cooking spray, put in preheated air fryer skin side down and cook at 350 degrees F for 10 minutes.
- ⏱ Heat up a pan with the water over medium heat, add raspberries, cinnamon, sugar and wine, stir, bring to a simmer, transfer to your blender, puree and return to pan.
- ⏱ Add air fryer duck breasts to pan as well, toss to coat, divide among plates and serve right away.
- ⏱ Enjoy!

Nutrition: calories 456, fat 22, fiber 4, carbs 14, protein 45

Duck and Cherries

Preparation time: 10 minutes Cooking time: 20 minutes Servings: 4

INGREDIENTS:

- ✓ ½ cup sugar
- ✓ ¼ cup honey
- ✓ 1/3 cup balsamic vinegar
- ✓ 1 teaspoon garlic, minced
- ✓ 1 tablespoon ginger, grated

- ✓ 1 teaspoon cumin, ground
- ✓ ½ teaspoon clove, ground
- ✓ ½ teaspoon cinnamon powder
- ✓ 4 sage leaves, chopped
- ✓ 1 jalapeno, chopped
- ✓ 2 cups rhubarb, sliced
- ✓ ½ cup yellow onion, chopped
- ✓ 2 cups cherries, pitted
- ✓ 4 duck breasts, boneless, skin on and scored Salt and black pepper to the taste

DIRECTIONS:

- Season duck breast with salt and pepper, put in your air fryer and cook at 350 degrees F for 5 minutes on each side.
- Meanwhile, heat up a pan over medium heat, add sugar, honey, vinegar, garlic, ginger, cumin, clove, cinnamon, sage, jalapeno, rhubarb, onion and cherries, stir, bring to a simmer and cook for 10 minutes.
- Add duck breasts, toss well, divide everything on plates and serve. Enjoy!

Nutrition: calories 456, fat 13, fiber 4, carbs 64, protein 31

Easy Duck Breasts

Preparation time: 10 minutes Cooking time: 15 minutes Servings: 4

INGREDIENTS:

- ✓ 4 duck breasts, skinless and boneless
- ✓ 4 garlic heads, peeled, tops cut off and quartered
- ✓ 2 tablespoons lemon juice
- ✓ Salt and black pepper to the taste
- ✓ ½ teaspoon lemon pepper
- ✓ 1 and ½ tablespoon olive oil

DIRECTIONS:

In a bowl, mix duck breasts with garlic, lemon juice, salt, pepper, lemon pepper and olive oil and toss everything. Transfer duck and garlic to your air fryer and cook at 350 degrees F for 15 minutes.

Divide duck breasts and garlic on plates and serve.
Enjoy!

Nutrition: calories 200, fat 7, fiber 1, carbs 11, protein 17

Duck and Tea Sauce

Preparation time: 10 minutes Cooking time: 20 minutes Servings: 4

INGREDIENTS:

- ✓ 2 duck breast halves, boneless
- ✓ 2 and ¼ cup chicken stock
- ✓ ¾ cup shallot, chopped
- ✓ 1 and ½ cup orange juice
- ✓ Salt and black pepper to the taste
- ✓ 3 teaspoons earl gray tea leaves
- ✓ 3 tablespoons butter, melted
- ✓ 1 tablespoon honey

DIRECTIONS:

- Season duck breast halves with salt and pepper, put in preheated air fryer and cook at 360 degrees F for 10 minutes.
- Meanwhile, heat up a pan with the butter over medium heat, add shallot, stir and cook for 2-3 minutes.
- Add stock, stir and cook for another minute.
- Add orange juice, tea leaves and honey, stir, cook for 2-3 minutes more and strain into a bowl.
- Divide duck on plates, drizzle tea sauce all over and serve.
- Enjoy!

Nutrition: calories 228, fat 11, fiber 2, carbs 20, protein 12

Marinated Duck Breasts

Preparation time: 1 day Cooking time: 15 minutes Servings: 2

INGREDIENTS:

- ✓ 2 duck breasts
- ✓ 1 cup white wine
- ✓ ¼ cup soy sauce
- ✓ 2 garlic cloves, minced
- ✓ 6 tarragon springs
- ✓ Salt and black pepper to the taste
- ✓ 1 tablespoon butter
- ✓ ¼ cup sherry wine

DIRECTIONS:

- In a bowl, mix duck breasts with white wine, soy sauce, garlic, tarragon, salt and pepper, toss well and keep in the fridge for 1 day.
- Transfer duck breasts to your preheated air fryer at 350 degrees F and cook for 10 minutes, flipping halfway.
- Meanwhile, pour the marinade in a pan, heat up over medium heat, add butter and sherry, stir, bring to a simmer, cook for 5 minutes and take off heat.
- Divide duck breasts on plates, drizzle sauce all over and serve.
- Enjoy!

Nutrition: calories 475, fat 12, fiber 3, carbs 10, protein 48

Chicken Breasts with Passion Fruit Sauce

Preparation time: 10 minutes Cooking time: 10 minutes Servings: 4

INGREDIENTS:

- ✓ 4 chicken breasts
- ✓ Salt and black pepper to the taste
- ✓ 4 passion fruits, halved, deseeded and pulp reserved
- ✓ 1 tablespoon whiskey
- ✓ 2 star anise
- ✓ 2 ounces maple syrup
- ✓ 1 bunch chives, chopped

DIRECTIONS:

- Heat up a pan with the passion fruit pulp over medium heat, add whiskey, star anise, maple syrup and chives, stir well, simmer for 5-6 minutes and take off heat.
- Season chicken with salt and pepper, put in preheated air fryer and cook at 360 degrees F for 10 minutes, flipping halfway.
- Divide chicken on plates, heat up the sauce a bit, drizzle it over chicken and serve.
- Enjoy!

Nutrition: calories 374, fat 8, fiber 22, carbs 34, protein 37

Chicken Breasts and BBQ Chili Sauce

Preparation time: 10 minutes Cooking time: 20 minutes Servings: 6

INGREDIENTS:

- ✓ 2 cups chili sauce

- ✓ 2 cups ketchup
- ✓ 1 cup pear jelly
- ✓ ¼ cup honey
- ✓ ½ teaspoon liquid smoke
- ✓ 1 teaspoon chili powder
- ✓ 1 teaspoon mustard powder
- ✓ 1 teaspoon sweet paprika
- ✓ Salt and black pepper to the taste
- ✓ 1 teaspoon garlic powder
- ✓ 6 chicken breasts, skinless and boneless

DIRECTIONS:

- Season chicken breasts with salt and pepper, put in preheated air fryer and cook at 350 degrees F for 10 minutes.
- Meanwhile, heat up a pan with the chili sauce over medium heat, add ketchup, pear jelly, honey, liquid smoke, chili powder, mustard powder, sweet paprika, salt, pepper and the garlic powder, stir, bring to a simmer and cook for 10 minutes.
- Add air fried chicken breasts, toss well, divide among plates and serve. Enjoy!

Nutrition: calories 473, fat 13, fiber 7, carbs 39, protein 33

Duck Breasts And Mango Mix

Preparation time: 1 hour Cooking time: 10 minutes Servings: 4

INGREDIENTS:

- ✓ 4 duck breasts
- ✓ 1 and ½ tablespoons lemongrass, chopped
- ✓ 3 tablespoons lemon juice
- ✓ 2 tablespoons olive oil
- ✓ Salt and black pepper to the taste
- ✓ 3 garlic cloves, minced

For the mango mix:

- ✓ 1 mango, peeled and chopped
- ✓ 1 tablespoon coriander, chopped
- ✓ 1 red onion, chopped
- ✓ 1 tablespoon sweet chili sauce
- ✓ 1 and ½ tablespoon lemon juice
- ✓ 1 teaspoon ginger, grated
- ✓ ¾ teaspoon sugar

DIRECTIONS:

In a bowl, mix duck breasts with salt, pepper, lemongrass, 3 tablespoons lemon juice, olive oil and garlic, toss well, keep in the fridge for 1 hour, transfer to your air fryer and cook at 360 degrees F for 10 minutes, flipping once.

Meanwhile, in a bowl, mix mango with coriander, onion, chili sauce, lemon juice, ginger and sugar and toss well.

Divide duck on plates, add mango mix on the side and serve.

Enjoy!

Nutrition: calories 465, fat 11, fiber 4, carbs 29, protein 38

Quick Creamy Chicken Casserole

Preparation time: 10 minutes Cooking time: 12 minutes Servings: 4

INGREDIENTS:

- ✓ 10 ounces spinach, chopped
- ✓ 4 tablespoons butter
- ✓ 3 tablespoons flour
- ✓ 1 and ½ cups milk
- ✓ ½ cup parmesan, grated
- ✓ ½ cup heavy cream
- ✓ Salt and black pepper to the taste
- ✓ 2 cup chicken breasts, skinless, boneless and cubed
- ✓ 1 cup bread crumbs

DIRECTIONS:

- Heat up a pan with the butter over medium heat, add flour and stir well.
- Add milk, heavy cream and parmesan, stir well, cook for 1-2 minutes more and take off heat.
- In a pan that fits your air fryer, spread chicken and spinach.
- Add salt and pepper and toss.

- Add cream mix and spread, sprinkle bread crumbs on top, introduce in your air fryer and cook at 350 for 12 minutes.
- Divide chicken and spinach mix on plates and serve.
- Enjoy!

Nutrition: calories 321, fat 9, fiber 12, carbs 22, protein 17

Chicken and Peaches

Preparation time: 10 minutes Cooking time: 30 minutes Servings: 6

INGREDIENTS:

- ✓ 1 whole chicken, cut into medium pieces
- ✓ ¾ cup water
- ✓ 1/3 cup honey
- ✓ Salt and black pepper to the taste
- ✓ ¼ cup olive oil
- ✓ 4 peaches, halved

DIRECTIONS:

- Put the water in a pot, bring to a simmer over medium heat, add honey, whisk really well and leave aside.
- Rub chicken pieces with the oil, season with salt and pepper, place in your air fryer's basket and cook at 350 degrees F for 10 minutes.
- Brush chicken with some of the honey mix, cook for 6 minutes more, flip again, brush one more time with the honey mix and cook for 7 minutes more.
- Divide chicken pieces on plates and keep warm.
- Brush peaches with what's left of the honey marinade, place them in your air fryer and cook them for 3 minutes.
- Divide among plates next to chicken pieces and serve.
- Enjoy!

Nutrition: calories 430, fat 14, fiber 3, carbs 15, protein 20

Tea Glazed Chicken

Preparation time: 10 minutes Cooking time: 30 minutes Servings: 6

INGREDIENTS:

- ✓ ½ cup apricot preserves
- ✓ ½ cup pineapple preserves
- ✓ 6 chicken legs
- ✓ 1 cup hot water
- ✓ 6 black tea bags
- ✓ 1 tablespoon soy sauce
- ✓ 1 onion, chopped

- ✓ ¼ teaspoon red pepper flakes
- ✓ 1 tablespoon olive oil
- ✓ Salt and black pepper to the taste
- ✓ 6 chicken legs

DIRECTIONS:

- ⏱ Put the hot water in a bowl, add tea bags, leave aside covered for 10 minutes, discard bags at the end and transfer tea to another bowl.
- ⏱ Add soy sauce, pepper flakes, apricot and pineapple preserves, whisk really well and take off heat.
- ⏱ Season chicken with salt and pepper, rub with oil, put in your air fryer and cook at 350 degrees F for 5 minutes.
- ⏱ Spread onion on the bottom of a baking dish that fits your air fryer, add chicken pieces, drizzle the tea glaze on top, introduce in your air fryer and cook at 320 degrees F for 25 minutes.
- ⏱ Divide everything on plates and serve.
- ⏱ Enjoy!

Nutrition: calories 298, fat 14, fiber 1, carbs 14, protein 30

Chicken and Radish Mix

Preparation time: 10 minutes Cooking time: 30 minutes Servings: 4

INGREDIENTS:

- ✓ 4 chicken things, bone-in
- ✓ Salt and black pepper to the taste
- ✓ 1 tablespoon olive oil
- ✓ 1 cup chicken stock
- ✓ 6 radishes, halved
- ✓ 1 teaspoon sugar
- ✓ 3 carrots, cut into thin sticks
- ✓ 2 tablespoon chives, chopped

DIRECTIONS:

- ⏱ Heat up a pan that fits your air fryer over medium heat, add stock, carrots, sugar and radishes, stir gently, reduce heat to medium, cover pot partly and simmer for 20 minutes.
- ⏱ Rub chicken with olive oil, season with salt and pepper, put in your air fryer and cook at 350 degrees F for 4 minutes.
- ⏱ Add chicken to radish mix, toss, introduce everything in your air fryer, cook for 4 minutes more, divide among plates and serve.
- ⏱ Enjoy!

Nutrition: calories 237, fat 10, fiber 4, carbs 19, protein 29

Air Fryer Meat Recipes

Indian Pork

Preparation time: 35 minutes Cooking time: 10 minutes Servings: 4

INGREDIENTS:

- ✓ **1 teaspoon ginger powder**
- ✓ **2 teaspoons chili paste**
- ✓ **2 garlic cloves, minced**
- ✓ **14 ounces pork chops, cubed**
- ✓ **1 shallot, chopped**
- ✓ **1 teaspoon coriander, ground**
- ✓ **7 ounces coconut milk**
- ✓ **2 tablespoons olive oil**
- ✓ **3 ounces peanuts, ground**
- ✓ **3 tablespoons soy sauce**
- ✓ **Salt and black pepper to the taste**

DIRECTIONS:

- ⏱ In a bowl, mix ginger with 1 teaspoon chili paste, half of the garlic, half of the soy sauce and half of the oil, whisk, add meat, toss and leave aside for 10 minutes.
- ⏱ Transfer meat to your air fryer's basket and cook at 400 degrees F for 12 minutes, turning halfway.
- ⏱ Meanwhile, heat up a pan with the rest of the oil over medium high heat, add shallot, the rest of the garlic, coriander, coconut milk, the rest of the peanuts, the rest of the chili paste and the rest of the soy sauce, stir and cook for 5 minutes.
- ⏱ Divide pork on plates, spread coconut mix on top and serve.
- ⏱ Enjoy!

Nutrition: calories 423, fat 11, fiber 4, carbs 42, protein 18

Lamb and Creamy Brussels Sprouts

Preparation time: 10 minutes Cooking time: 1 hour and 10 minutes

Servings: 4

INGREDIENTS:

- ✓ **2 pounds leg of lamb, scored**
- ✓ **2 tablespoons olive oil**
- ✓ **1 tablespoon rosemary, chopped**
- ✓ **1 tablespoon lemon thyme, chopped**
- ✓ **1 garlic clove, minced**
- ✓ **1 and ½ pounds Brussels sprouts, trimmed**
- ✓ **1 tablespoon butter, melted**
- ✓ **½ cup sour cream**
- ✓ **Salt and black pepper to the taste**

DIRECTIONS:

- ⏱ Season leg of lamb with salt, pepper, thyme and rosemary, brush with oil, place in your air fryer's basket, cook at 300 degrees F for 1 hour, transfer to a plate and keep warm.
- ⏱ In a pan that fits your air fryer, mix Brussels sprouts with salt, pepper, garlic, butter and sour cream, toss, put in your air fryer and cook at 400 degrees F for 10 minutes.
- ⏱ Divide lamb on plates, add Brussels sprouts on the side and serve.
- ⏱ Enjoy!

Nutrition: calories 440, fat 23, fiber 0, carbs 2, protein 49

Beef Fillets with Garlic Mayo

Preparation time: 10 minutes Cooking time: 40 minutes Servings: 8

INGREDIENTS:

- ✓ **1 cup mayonnaise**
- ✓ **1/3 cup sour cream**
- ✓ **2 garlic cloves, minced**
- ✓ **3 pounds beef fillet**
- ✓ **2 tablespoons chives, chopped**
- ✓ **2 tablespoons mustard**
- ✓ **2 tablespoons mustard**
- ✓ **¼ cup tarragon, chopped**
- ✓ **Salt and black pepper to the taste**

DIRECTIONS:

- ⏱ Season beef with salt and pepper to the taste, place in your air fryer, cook at 370 degrees F for 20 minutes, transfer to a plate and leave aside for a few minutes.
- ⏱ In a bowl, mix garlic with sour cream, chives, mayo, some salt and pepper, whisk and leave aside.
- ⏱ In another bowl, mix mustard with Dijon mustard and tarragon, whisk, add beef, toss, return to your air fryer and cook at 350 degrees F for 20 minutes more.
- ⏱ Divide beef on plates, spread garlic mayo on top and serve.
- ⏱ Enjoy!

Nutrition: calories 400, fat 12, fiber 2, carbs 27, protein 19

Mustard Marina ted Beef

Preparation time: 10 minutes Cooking time: 45 minutes Servings: 6

INGREDIENTS:

- ✓ **6 bacon strips**
- ✓ **2 tablespoons butter**
- ✓ **3 garlic cloves, minced**
- ✓ **Salt and black pepper to the taste**
- ✓ **1 tablespoon horseradish**
- ✓ **1 tablespoon mustard**
- ✓ **3 pounds beef roast**
- ✓ **1 and ¾ cup beef stock**
- ✓ **¾ cup red wine**

DIRECTIONS:

- In a bowl, mix butter with mustard, garlic, salt, pepper and horseradish, whisk and rub beef with this mix.
- Arrange bacon strips on a cutting board, place beef on top, fold bacon around beef, transfer to your air fryer's basket, cook at 400 degrees F for 15 minutes and transfer to a pan that fits your fryer.
- Add stock and wine to beef, introduce pan in your air fryer and cook at 360 degrees F for 30 minutes more.
- Carve beef, divide among plates and serve with a side salad.
- Enjoy!

Nutrition: calories 500, fat 9, fiber 4, carbs 29, protein 36

Creamy Pork

Preparation time: 10 minutes Cooking time: 22 minutes Servings: 6

INGREDIENTS:

- ✓ **2 pounds pork meat, boneless and cubed**
- ✓ **2 yellow onions, chopped**
- ✓ **1 tablespoon olive oil**
- ✓ **1 garlic clove, minced**
- ✓ **3 cups chicken stock**
- ✓ **2 tablespoons sweet paprika**
- ✓ **Salt and black pepper to the taste**
- ✓ **2 tablespoons white flour**
- ✓ **1 and ½ cups sour cream**
- ✓ **2 tablespoons dill, chopped**

DIRECTIONS:

- In a pan that fits your air fryer, mix pork with salt, pepper and oil, toss, introduce in your air fryer and cook at 360 degrees F for 7 minutes.
- Add onion, garlic, stock, paprika, flour, sour cream and dill, toss and cook at 370 degrees F for 15 minutes more.
- Divide everything on plates and serve right away.
- Enjoy!

Nutrition: calories 300, fat 4, fiber 10, carbs 26, protein 34

Marinated Pork Chops and Onions

Preparation time: 24 hours Cooking time: 25 minutes Servings: 6

INGREDIENTS:

- ✓ **2 pork chops**
- ✓ **¼ cup olive oil**
- ✓ **2 yellow onions, sliced**
- ✓ **2 garlic cloves, minced**
- ✓ **2 teaspoons mustard**
- ✓ **1 teaspoon sweet paprika**
- ✓ **Salt and black pepper to the taste**
- ✓ **½ teaspoon oregano, dried**
- ✓ **½ teaspoon thyme, dried**
- ✓ **A pinch of cayenne pepper**

DIRECTIONS:

- In a bowl, mix oil with garlic, mustard, paprika, black pepper, oregano, thyme and cayenne and whisk well.
- Combine onions with meat and mustard mix, toss to coat, cover and keep in the fridge for 1 day.
- Transfer meat and onions mix to a pan that fits your air fryer and cook at 360 degrees F for 25 minutes.
- Divide everything on plates and serve.
- Enjoy!

Nutrition: calories 384, fat 4, fiber 4, carbs 17, protein 25

Simple Braised Pork

Preparation time: 40 minutes Cooking time: 40 minutes Servings: 4

INGREDIENTS:

- ✓ **2 pounds pork loin roast, boneless and cubed**
- ✓ **4 tablespoons butter, melted**
- ✓ **Salt and black pepper to the taste**
- ✓ **2 cups chicken stock**
- ✓ **½ cup dry white wine**

- ✓ **2 garlic cloves, minced**
- ✓ **1 teaspoon thyme, chopped**
- ✓ **1 thyme spring**
- ✓ **1 bay leaf**
- ✓ **½ yellow onion, chopped**
- ✓ **2 tablespoons white flour**
- ✓ **½ pound red grapes**

DIRECTIONS:

- Season pork cubes with salt and pepper, rub with 2 tablespoons melted butter, put in your air fryer and cook at 370 degrees F for 8 minutes.
- Meanwhile, heat up a pan that fits your air fryer with 2 tablespoons butter over medium high heat, add garlic and onion, stir and cook for 2 minutes.
- Add wine, stock, salt, pepper, thyme, flour and bay leaf, stir well, bring to a simmer and take off heat.
- Add pork cubes and grapes, toss, introduce in your air fryer and cook at 360 degrees F for 30 minutes more.
- Divide everything on plates and serve.
- Enjoy!

Nutrition: calories 320, fat 4, fiber 5, carbs 29, protein 38

Pork with Couscous

Preparation time: 10 minutes Cooking time: 35 minutes Servings: 6

INGREDIENTS:

- ✓ **2 and ½ pounds pork loin, boneless and trimmed ¾ cup chicken stock**
- ✓ **2 tablespoons olive oil**
- ✓ **½ tablespoon sweet paprika**
- ✓ **2 and ¼ teaspoon sage, dried**
- ✓ **½ tablespoon garlic powder**
- ✓ **¼ teaspoon rosemary, dried**
- ✓ **¼ teaspoon marjoram, dried**
- ✓ **1 teaspoon basil, dried**
- ✓ **1 teaspoon oregano, dried**
- ✓ **Salt and black pepper to the taste**
- ✓ **2 cups couscous, cooked**

DIRECTIONS:

- In a bowl, mix oil with stock, paprika, garlic powder, sage, rosemary, thyme, marjoram, oregano, salt and pepper to the taste, whisk well, add pork loin, toss well and leave aside for 1 hour.

- Transfer everything to a pan that fits your air fryer and cook at 370 degrees F for 35 minutes.
- Divide among plates and serve with couscous on the side.
- Enjoy!

Nutrition: calories 310, fat 4, fiber 6, carbs 37, protein 34

Flavored Rib Eye Steak

Preparation time: 10 minutes Cooking time: 20 minutes Servings: 4

INGREDIENTS:

- ✓ **2 pounds rib eye steak**
- ✓ **Salt and black pepper to the taste**
- ✓ **1 tablespoons olive oil**

For the rub:

- ✓ **3 tablespoons sweet paprika**
- ✓ **2 tablespoons onion powder**
- ✓ **2 tablespoons garlic powder**
- ✓ **1 tablespoon brown sugar**
- ✓ **2 tablespoons oregano, dried**
- ✓ **1 tablespoon cumin, ground**
- ✓ **1 tablespoon rosemary, dried**

DIRECTIONS:

- In a bowl, mix paprika with onion and garlic powder, sugar, oregano, rosemary, salt, pepper and cumin, stir and rub steak with this mix.
- Season steak with salt and pepper, rub again with the oil, put in your air fryer and cook at 400 degrees F for 20 minutes, flipping them halfway.
- Transfer steak to a cutting board, slice and serve with a side salad.
- Enjoy!

Nutrition: calories 320, fat 8, fiber 7, carbs 22, protein 21

Chinese Steak and Broccoli

Preparation time: 45 minutes Cooking time: 12 minutes Servings: 4

INGREDIENTS:

- ✓ **¾ pound round steak, cut into strips**
- ✓ **1 pound broccoli florets**
- ✓ **1/3 cup oyster sauce**
- ✓ **2 teaspoons sesame oil**
- ✓ **1 teaspoon soy sauce**

- ✓ 1 teaspoon sugar
- ✓ 1/3 cup sherry
- ✓ 1 tablespoon olive oil
- ✓ 1 garlic clove, minced

DIRECTIONS:

- ⓘ In a bowl, mix sesame oil with oyster sauce, soy sauce, sherry and sugar, stir well, add beef, toss and leave aside for 30 minutes.
- ⓘ Transfer beef to a pan that fits your air fryer, also add broccoli, garlic and oil, toss everything and cook at 380 degrees F for 12 minutes.
- ⓘ Divide among plates and serve.
- ⓘ Enjoy!

Nutrition: calories 330, fat 12, fiber 7, carbs 23, protein 23

Provencal Pork

Preparation time: 10 minutes Cooking time: 15 minutes Servings: 2

INGREDIENTS:

- ✓ 1 red onion, sliced
- ✓ 1 yellow bell pepper, cut into strips
- ✓ 1 green bell pepper, cut into strips
- ✓ Salt and black pepper to the taste
- ✓ 2 teaspoons Provencal herbs
- ✓ ½ tablespoon mustard
- ✓ 1 tablespoon olive oil
- ✓ 7 ounces pork tenderloin

DIRECTIONS:

- ⓘ In a baking dish that fits your air fryer, mix yellow bell pepper with green bell pepper, onion, salt, pepper, Provencal herbs and half of the oil and toss well.
- ⓘ Season pork with salt, pepper, mustard and the rest of the oil, toss well and add to veggies.
- ⓘ Introduce everything in your air fryer, cook at 370 degrees F for 15 minutes, divide among plates and serve.
- ⓘ Enjoy!

Nutrition: calories 300, fat 8, fiber 7, carbs 21, protein 23

Beef S trips with Snow Peas and Mushrooms

Preparation time: 10 minutes Cooking time: 22 minutes Servings: 2

INGREDIENTS:

- ✓ 2 beef steaks, cut into strips
- ✓ Salt and black pepper to the taste
- ✓ 7 ounces snow peas
- ✓ 8 ounces white mushrooms, halved
- ✓ 1 yellow onion, cut into rings
- ✓ 2 tablespoons soy sauce
- ✓ 1 teaspoon olive oil

DIRECTIONS:

- ⓘ In a bowl, mix olive oil with soy sauce, whisk, add beef strips and toss.
- ⓘ In another bowl, mix snow peas, onion and mushrooms with salt, pepper and the oil, toss well, put in a pan that fits your air fryer and cook at 350 degrees F for 16 minutes.
- ⓘ Add beef strips to the pan as well and cook at 400 degrees F for 6 minutes more.
- ⓘ Divide everything on plates and serve.
- ⓘ Enjoy!

Nutrition: calories 235, fat 8, fiber 2, carbs 22, protein 24

Garlic Lamb Chops

Preparation time: 10 minutes Cooking time: 10 minutes Servings: 4

INGREDIENTS:

- ✓ 3 tablespoons olive oil
- ✓ 8 lamb chops
- ✓ Salt and black pepper to the taste
- ✓ 4 garlic cloves, minced
- ✓ 1 tablespoon oregano, chopped
- ✓ 1 tablespoon coriander, chopped

DIRECTIONS:

- ⓘ In a bowl, mix oregano with salt, pepper, oil, garlic and lamb chops and toss to coat.
- ⓘ Transfer lamb chops to your air fryer and cook at 400 degrees F for 10 minutes.
- ⓘ Divide lamb chops on plates and serve with a side salad.
- ⓘ Enjoy!

Nutrition: calories 231, fat 7, fiber 5, carbs 14, protein 23

Crispy Lamb

Preparation time: 10 minutes Cooking time: 30 minutes Servings: 4

INGREDIENTS:

- ✓ 1 tablespoon bread crumbs

- ✓ 2 tablespoons macadamia nuts, toasted and crushed
- ✓ 1 tablespoon olive oil
- ✓ 1 garlic clove, minced
- ✓ 28 ounces rack of lamb
- ✓ Salt and black pepper to the taste
- ✓ 1 egg,
- ✓ 1 tablespoon rosemary, chopped

DIRECTIONS:

- In a bowl, mix oil with garlic and stir well.
- Season lamb with salt, pepper and brush with the oil.
- In another bowl, mix nuts with breadcrumbs and rosemary.
- Put the egg in a separate bowl and whisk well.
- Dip lamb in egg, then in macadamia mix, place them in your air fryer's basket, cook at 360 degrees F and cook for 25 minutes, increase heat to 400 degrees F and cook for 5 minutes more.
- Divide among plates and serve right away.
- Enjoy!

Nutrition: calories 230, fat 2, fiber 2, carbs 10, protein 12

Simple Air Fried Pork Shoulder

Preparation time: 30 minutes Cooking time: 1 hour and 20 minutes

Servings: 6

INGREDIENTS:

- ✓ 3 tablespoons garlic, minced
- ✓ 3 tablespoons olive oil
- ✓ 4 pounds pork shoulder
- ✓ Salt and black pepper to the taste

DIRECTIONS:

- In a bowl, mix olive oil with salt, pepper and oil, whisk well and brush pork shoulder with this mix.
- Place in preheated air fryer and cook at 390 degrees F for 10 minutes.
- Reduce heat to 300 degrees F and roast pork for 1 hour and 10 minutes.
- Slice pork shoulder, divide among plates and serve with a side salad. Enjoy!

Nutrition: calories 221, fat 4, fiber 4, carbs 7, protein 10

Fennel Flavored Pork Roast

Preparation time: 10 minutes Cooking time: 1 hour Servings: 10

INGREDIENTS:

- ✓ 5 and ½ pounds pork loin roast, trimmed Salt and black pepper to the taste
- ✓ 3 garlic cloves, minced
- ✓ 2 tablespoons rosemary, chopped
- ✓ 1 teaspoon fennel, ground
- ✓ 1 tablespoon fennel seeds
- ✓ 2 teaspoons red pepper, crushed
- ✓ ¼ cup olive oil

DIRECTIONS:

- In your food processor mix garlic with fennel seeds, fennel, rosemary, red pepper, some black pepper and the olive oil and blend until you obtain a paste.
- Spread 2 tablespoons garlic paste on pork loin, rub well, season with salt and pepper, introduce in your preheated air fryer and cook at 350 degrees F for 30 minutes.
- Reduce heat to 300 degrees F and cook for 15 minutes more.
- Slice pork, divide among plates and serve.
- Enjoy!

Nutrition: calories 300, fat 14, fiber 9, carbs 26, protein 22

Beef Brisket and Onion Sauce

Preparation time: 10 minutes Cooking time: 2 hours Servings: 6

INGREDIENTS:

- ✓ 1 pound yellow onion, chopped
- ✓ 4 pounds beef brisket
- ✓ 1 pound carrot, chopped
- ✓ 8 earl grey tea bags
- ✓ ½ pound celery, chopped
- ✓ Salt and black pepper to the taste
- ✓ 4 cups water

For the sauce:

- ✓ 16 ounces canned tomatoes, chopped
- ✓ ½ pound celery, chopped
- ✓ 1 ounce garlic, minced
- ✓ 4 ounces vegetable oil
- ✓ 1 pound sweet onion, chopped
- ✓ 1 cup brown sugar
- ✓ 8 earl grey tea bags

- ✓ **1 cup white vinegar**

DIRECTIONS:

- ◔ Put the water in a heat proof dish that fits your air fryer, add 1 pound onion, 1 pound carrot, ½ pound celery, salt and pepper, stir and bring to a simmer over medium high heat.
- ◔ Add beef brisket and 8 tea bags, stir, transfer to your air fryer and cook at 300 degrees F for 1 hour and 30 minutes.
- ◔ Meanwhile, heat up a pan with the vegetable oil over medium high heat, add 1 pound onion, stir and sauté for 10 minutes.
- ◔ Add garlic, ½ pound celery, tomatoes, sugar, vinegar, salt, pepper and 8 tea bags, stir, bring to a simmer, cook for 10 minutes and discard tea bags.
- ◔ Transfer beef brisket to a cutting board, slice, divide among plates, drizzle onion sauce all over and serve.
- ◔ Enjoy!

Nutrition: calories 400, fat 12, fiber 4, carbs 38, protein 34

Beef and Green Onions Marinade

Preparation time: 10 minutes Cooking time: 20 minutes Servings: 4

INGREDIENTS:

- ✓ **1 cup green onion, chopped**
- ✓ **1 cup soy sauce**
- ✓ **½ cup water**
- ✓ **¼ cup brown sugar**
- ✓ **¼ cup sesame seeds**
- ✓ **5 garlic cloves, minced**
- ✓ **1 teaspoon black pepper**
- ✓ **1 pound lean beef**

DIRECTIONS:

- ◔ In a bowl, mix onion with soy sauce, water, sugar, garlic, sesame seeds and pepper, whisk, add meat, toss and leave aside for 10 minutes.
- ◔ Drain beef, transfer to your preheated air fryer and cook at 390 degrees F for 20 minutes.
- ◔ Slice, divide among plates and serve with a side salad.
- ◔ Enjoy!

Nutrition: calories 329, fat 8, fiber 12, carbs 26, protein 22

Garlic and Bell Pepper Beef

Preparation time: 30 minutes Cooking time: 30 minutes Servings: 4

INGREDIENTS:

- ✓ **11 ounces steak fillets, sliced**

- ✓ **4 garlic cloves, minced**
- ✓ **2 tablespoons olive oil**
- ✓ **1 red bell pepper, cut into strips**
- ✓ **Black pepper to the taste**
- ✓ **1 tablespoon sugar**
- ✓ **2 tablespoons fish sauce**
- ✓ **2 teaspoons corn flour**
- ✓ **½ cup beef stock**
- ✓ **4 green onions, sliced**

DIRECTIONS:

- ◔ In a pan that fits your air fryer mix beef with oil, garlic, black pepper and bell pepper, stir, cover and keep in the fridge for 30 minutes.
- ◔ Put the pan in your preheated air fryer and cook at 360 degrees F for 14 minutes.
- ◔ In a bowl, mix sugar with fish sauce, stir well, pour over beef and cook at 360 degrees F for 7 minutes more.
- ◔ Add stock mixed with corn flour and green onions, toss and cook at 370 degrees F for 7 minutes more.
- ◔ Divide everything on plates and serve.
- ◔ Enjoy!

Nutrition: calories 343, fat 3, fiber 12, carbs 26, protein 38

Marinated Lamb and Veggies

Preparation time: 10 minutes Cooking time: 30 minutes Servings: 4

INGREDIENTS:

- ✓ **1 carrot, chopped**
- ✓ **1 onion, sliced**
- ✓ **½ tablespoon olive oil**
- ✓ **3 ounces bean sprouts**
- ✓ **8 ounces lamb loin, sliced**

For the marinade:

- ✓ **1 garlic clove, minced**
- ✓ **½ apple, grated**
- ✓ **Salt and black pepper to the taste**
- ✓ **1 small yellow onion, grated**
- ✓ **1 tablespoon ginger, grated**
- ✓ **5 tablespoons soy sauce**
- ✓ **1 tablespoons sugar**

- ✓ **2 tablespoons orange juice**

DIRECTIONS:

- In a bowl, mix 1 grated onion with the apple, garlic, 1 tablespoon ginger, soy sauce, orange juice, sugar and black pepper, whisk well, add lamb and leave aside for 10 minutes.
- Heat up a pan that fits your air fryer with the olive oil over medium high heat, add 1 sliced onion, carrot and bean sprouts, stir and cook for 3 minutes.
- Add lamb and the marinade, transfer pan to your preheated air fryer and cook at 360 degrees F for 25 minutes.
- Divide everything into bowls and serve.
- Enjoy!

Nutrition: calories 265, fat 3, fiber 7, carbs 18, protein 22

Creamy Lamb

Preparation time: 1 day Cooking time: 1 hour Servings: 8

INGREDIENTS:

- ✓ **5 pounds leg of lamb**
- ✓ **2 cups low fat buttermilk**
- ✓ **2 tablespoons mustard**
- ✓ **½ cup butter**
- ✓ **2 tablespoons basil, chopped**
- ✓ **2 tablespoons tomato paste**
- ✓ **2 garlic cloves, minced**
- ✓ **Salt and black pepper to the taste**
- ✓ **1 cup white wine**
- ✓ **1 tablespoon cornstarch mixed with 1 tablespoon water ½ cup sour cream**

DIRECTIONS:

- Put lamb roast in a big dish, add buttermilk, toss to coat, cover and keep in the fridge for 24 hours.
- Pat dry lamb and put in a pan that fits your air fryer.
- In a bowl, mix butter with tomato paste, mustard, basil, rosemary, salt, pepper and garlic, whisk well, spread over lamb, introduce everything in your air fryer and cook at 300 degrees F for 1 hour.
- Slice lamb, divide among plates, leave aside for now and heat up cooking juices from the pan on your stove.
- Add wine, cornstarch mix, salt, pepper and sour cream, stir, take off heat, drizzle this sauce over lamb and serve.
- Enjoy!

Nutrition: calories 287, fat 4, fiber 7, carbs 19, protein 25

Air Fryer Lamb Shanks

Preparation time: 10 minutes Cooking time: 45 minutes Servings: 4

INGREDIENTS:

- ✓ **4 lamb shanks**
- ✓ **1 yellow onion, chopped**
- ✓ **1 tablespoon olive oil**
- ✓ **4 teaspoons coriander seeds, crushed**
- ✓ **2 tablespoons white flour**
- ✓ **4 bay leaves**
- ✓ **2 teaspoons honey**
- ✓ **5 ounces dry sherry**
- ✓ **2 and ½ cups chicken stock**
- ✓ **Salt and pepper to the taste**

DIRECTIONS:

- Season lamb shanks with salt and pepper, rub with half of the oil, put in your air fryer and cook at 360 degrees F for 10 minutes.
- Heat up a pan that fits your air fryer with the rest of the oil over medium high heat, add onion and coriander, stir and cook for 5 minutes.
- Add flour, sherry, stock, honey and bay leaves, salt and pepper, stir, bring to a simmer, add lamb, introduce everything in your air fryer and cook at 360 degrees F for 30 minutes.
- Divide everything on plates and serve.
- Enjoy!

Nutrition: calories 283, fat 4, fiber 2, carbs 17, protein 26

Lamb Roast and Potatoes

Preparation time: 10 minutes Cooking time: 45 minutes Servings: 6

INGREDIENTS:

- ✓ **4 pounds lamb roast**
- ✓ **1 spring rosemary**
- ✓ **3 garlic cloves, minced**
- ✓ **6 potatoes, halved**
- ✓ **½ cup lamb stock**
- ✓ **4 bay leaves**
- ✓ **Salt and black pepper to the taste**

DIRECTIONS:

- Put potatoes in a dish that fits your air fryer, add lamb, garlic, rosemary spring, salt, pepper, bay leaves

and stock, toss, introduce in your air fryer and cook at 360 degrees F for 45 minutes.
- ⏱ Slice lamb, divide among plates and serve with potatoes and cooking juices.
- ⏱ Enjoy!

Nutrition: calories 273, fat 4, fiber 12, carbs 25, protein 29

Lemony Lamb Leg

Preparation time: 10 minutes Cooking time: 1 hour Servings: 6

INGREDIENTS:

- ✓ **4 pounds lamb leg**
- ✓ **2 tablespoons olive oil**
- ✓ **2 springs rosemary, chopped**
- ✓ **2 tablespoons parsley, chopped**
- ✓ **2 tablespoons oregano, chopped**
- ✓ **Salt and black pepper to the taste**
- ✓ **1 tablespoon lemon rind, grated**
- ✓ **3 garlic cloves, minced**
- ✓ **2 tablespoons lemon juice**
- ✓ **2 pounds baby potatoes**
- ✓ **1 cup beef stock**

DIRECTIONS:

- ⏱ Make small cuts all over lamb, insert rosemary springs and season with salt and pepper.
- ⏱ In a bowl, mix 1 tablespoon oil with oregano, parsley, garlic, lemon juice and rind, stir and rub lamb with this mix.
- ⏱ Heat up a pan that fits your air fryer with the rest of the oil over medium high heat, add potatoes, stir and cook for 3 minutes.
- ⏱ Add lamb and stock, stir, introduce in your air fryer and cook at 360 degrees F for 1 hour.
- ⏱ Divide everything on plates and serve.
- ⏱ Enjoy!

Nutrition: calories 264, fat 4, fiber 12, carbs 27, protein 32

Beef Curry

Preparation time: 10 minutes Cooking time: 45 minutes Servings: 4

INGREDIENTS:

- ✓ **2 pounds beef steak, cubed**
- ✓ **2 tablespoons olive oil**
- ✓ **3 potatoes, cubed**

- ✓ **1 tablespoon wine mustard**
- ✓ **2 and ½ tablespoons curry powder**
- ✓ **2 yellow onions, chopped**
- ✓ **2 garlic cloves, minced**
- ✓ **10 ounces canned coconut milk**
- ✓ **2 tablespoons tomato sauce**
- ✓ **Salt and black pepper to the taste**

DIRECTIONS:

- ⏱ Heat up a pan that fits your air fryer with the oil over medium high heat, add onions and garlic, stir and cook for 4 minutes.
- ⏱ Add potatoes and mustard, stir and cook for 1 minute.
- ⏱ Add beef, curry powder, salt, pepper, coconut milk and tomato sauce, stir, transfer to your air fryer and cook at 360 degrees F for 40 minutes.
- ⏱ Divide into bowls and serve.
- ⏱ Enjoy!

Nutrition: calories 432, fat 16, fiber 4, carbs 20, protein 27

Beef Roast and Wine Sauce

Preparation time: 10 minutes Cooking time: 45 minutes Servings: 6

INGREDIENTS:

- ✓ **3 pounds beef roast**
- ✓ **Salt and black pepper to the taste**
- ✓ **17 ounces beef stock**
- ✓ **3 ounces red wine**
- ✓ **½ teaspoon chicken salt**
- ✓ **½ teaspoon smoked paprika**
- ✓ **1 yellow onion, chopped**
- ✓ **4 garlic cloves, minced**
- ✓ **3 carrots, chopped**
- ✓ **5 potatoes, chopped**

DIRECTIONS:

- ⏱ In a bowl, mix salt, pepper, chicken salt and paprika, stir, rub beef with this mix and put it in a big pan that fits your air fryer.
- ⏱ Add onion, garlic, stock, wine, potatoes and carrots, introduce in your air fryer and cook at 360 degrees F for 45 minutes.
- ⏱ Divide everything on plates and serve.
- ⏱ Enjoy!

Nutrition: calories 304, fat 20, fiber 7, carbs 20, protein 32

Beef and Cabbage Mix

Preparation time: 10 minutes Cooking time: 40 minutes Servings: 6

INGREDIENTS:

- ✓ 2 and ½ pounds beef brisket
- ✓ 1 cup beef stock
- ✓ 2 bay leaves
- ✓ 3 garlic cloves, chopped
- ✓ 4 carrots, chopped
- ✓ 1 cabbage head, cut into medium wedges Salt and black pepper to the taste
- ✓ 3 turnips, cut into quarters

DIRECTIONS:

- ⏱ Put beef brisket and stock in a large pan that fits your air fryer, season beef with salt and pepper, add garlic and bay leaves, carrots, cabbage, potatoes and turnips, toss, introduce in your air fryer and cook at 360 degrees F and cook for 40 minutes.
- ⏱ Divide among plates and serve.
- ⏱ Enjoy!

Nutrition: calories 353, fat 16, fiber 7, carbs 20, protein 24

Lamb Shanks and Carrots

Preparation time: 10 minutes Cooking time: 45 minutes Servings: 4

INGREDIENTS:

- ✓ 4 lamb shanks
- ✓ 2 tablespoons olive oil
- ✓ 1 yellow onion, finely chopped
- ✓ 6 carrots, roughly chopped
- ✓ 2 garlic cloves, minced
- ✓ 2 tablespoons tomato paste
- ✓ 1 teaspoon oregano, dried
- ✓ 1 tomato, roughly chopped
- ✓ 2 tablespoons water
- ✓ 4 ounces red wine
- ✓ Salt and black pepper to the taste

DIRECTIONS:

- ⏱ Season lamb with salt and pepper, rub with oil, put in your air fryer and cook at 360 degrees F for 10 minutes.

- ⏱ In a pan that fits your air fryer, mix onion with carrots, garlic, tomato paste, tomato, oregano, wine and water and toss.
- ⏱ Add lamb, toss, introduce in your air fryer and cook at 370 degrees F for 35 minutes.
- ⏱ Divide everything on plates and serve.
- ⏱ Enjoy!

Nutrition: calories 432, fat 17, fiber 8, carbs 17, protein 43

Tasty Lamb Ribs

Preparation time: 15 minutes Cooking time: 40 minutes Servings: 8

INGREDIENTS:

- ✓ 8 lamb ribs
- ✓ 4 garlic cloves, minced
- ✓ 2 carrots, chopped
- ✓ 2 cups veggie stock
- ✓ 1 tablespoon rosemary, chopped
- ✓ 2 tablespoons extra virgin olive oil
- ✓ Salt and black pepper to the taste
- ✓ 3 tablespoons white flour

DIRECTIONS:

- ⏱ Season lamb ribs with salt and pepper, rub with oil and garlic, put in preheated air fryer and cook at 360 degrees F for 10 minutes.
- ⏱ In a heat proof dish that fits your fryer, mix stock with flour and whisk well.
- ⏱ Add rosemary, carrots and lamb ribs, place in your air fryer and cook at 350 degrees F for 30 minutes.
- ⏱ Divide lamb mix on plates and serve hot.
- ⏱ Enjoy!

Nutrition: calories 302, fat 7, fiber 2, carbs 22, protein 27

Oriental Air Fried Lamb

Preparation time: 10 minutes Cooking time: 42 minutes Servings: 8

INGREDIENTS:

- ✓ 2 and ½ pounds lamb shoulder, chopped
- ✓ 3 tablespoons honey
- ✓ 3 ounces almonds, peeled and chopped
- ✓ 9 ounces plumps, pitted
- ✓ 8 ounces veggie stock
- ✓ 2 yellow onions, chopped
- ✓ 2 garlic cloves, minced

- ✓ Salt and black pepper to the tastes
- ✓ 1 teaspoon cumin powder
- ✓ 1 teaspoon turmeric powder
- ✓ 1 teaspoon ginger powder
- ✓ 1 teaspoon cinnamon powder
- ✓ 3 tablespoons olive oil

DIRECTIONS:

- ① In a bowl, mix cinnamon powder with ginger, cumin, turmeric, garlic, olive oil and lamb, toss to coat, place in your preheated air fryer and cook at 350 degrees F for 8 minutes.
- ① Transfer meat to a dish that fits your air fryer, add onions, stock, honey and plums, stir, introduce in your air fryer and cook at 350 degrees F for 35 minutes.
- ① Divide everything on plates and serve with almond sprinkled on top.
- ① Enjoy!

Nutrition: calories 432, fat 23, fiber 6, carbs 30, protein 20

Short Ribs and Special Sauce

Preparation time: 10 minutes Cooking time: 36 minutes Servings: 4

INGREDIENTS:

- ✓ 2 green onions, chopped
- ✓ 1 teaspoon vegetable oil
- ✓ 3 garlic cloves, minced
- ✓ 3 ginger slices
- ✓ 4 pounds short ribs
- ✓ ½ cup water
- ✓ ½ cup soy sauce
- ✓ ¼ cup rice wine
- ✓ ¼ cup pear juice
- ✓ 2 teaspoons sesame oil

DIRECTIONS:

- ① Heat up a pan that fits your air fryer with the oil over medium heat, add green onions, ginger and garlic, stir and cook for 1 minute.
- ① Add ribs, water, wine, soy sauce, sesame oil and pear juice, stir, introduce in your air fryer and cook at 350 degrees F for 35 minutes.
- ① Divide ribs and sauce on plates and serve.
- ① Enjoy!

Nutrition: calories 321, fat 12, fiber 4, carbs 20, protein 14

Short Ribs and Beer Sauce

Preparation time: 15 minutes Cooking time: 45 minutes Servings: 6

INGREDIENTS:

- ✓ 4 pounds short ribs, cut into small pieces
- ✓ 1 yellow onion, chopped
- ✓ Salt and black pepper to the taste
- ✓ ¼ cup tomato paste
- ✓ 1 cup dark beer
- ✓ 1 cup chicken stock
- ✓ 1 bay leaf
- ✓ 6 thyme springs, chopped
- ✓ 1 Portobello mushroom, dried

DIRECTIONS:

- ① Heat up a pan that fits your air fryer over medium heat, add tomato paste, onion, stock, beer, mushroom, bay leaves and thyme and bring to a simmer.
- ① Add ribs, introduce in your air fryer and cook at 350 degrees F for 40 minutes.
- ① Divide everything on plates and serve.
- ① Enjoy!

Nutrition: calories 300, fat 7, fiber 8, carbs 18, protein 23

Roasted Pork Belly and Apple Sauce

Preparation time: 10 minutes Cooking time: 40 minutes Servings: 6

INGREDIENTS:

- ✓ 2 tablespoons sugar
- ✓ 1 tablespoon lemon juice
- ✓ 1 quart water
- ✓ 17 ounces apples, cored and cut into wedges
- ✓ 2 pounds pork belly, scored
- ✓ Salt and black pepper to the taste
- ✓ A drizzle of olive oil

DIRECTIONS:

- ① In your blender, mix water with apples, lemon juice and sugar, pulse well, transfer to a bowl, add meat, toss well, drain, put in your air fryer and cook at 400 degrees F for 40 minutes.
- ① Pour the sauce in a pot, heat up over medium heat and simmer for 15 minutes.
- ① Slice pork belly, divide among plates, drizzle the sauce all over and serve.

⏱ Enjoy!

Nutrition: calories 456, fat 34, fiber 4, carbs 10, protein 25

Stuffed Pork Steaks

Preparation time: 10 minutes Cooking time: 20 minutes Servings: 4

INGREDIENTS:

- ✓ Zest from 2 limes, grated
- ✓ Zest from 1 orange, grated
- ✓ Juice from 1 orange
- ✓ Juice from 2 limes
- ✓ 4 teaspoons garlic, minced
- ✓ ¾ cup olive oil
- ✓ 1 cup cilantro, chopped
- ✓ 1 cup mint, chopped
- ✓ 1 teaspoon oregano, dried
- ✓ Salt and black pepper to the taste
- ✓ 2 teaspoons cumin, ground
- ✓ 4 pork loin steaks
- ✓ 2 pickles, chopped
- ✓ 4 ham slices
- ✓ 6 Swiss cheese slices
- ✓ 2 tablespoons mustard

DIRECTIONS:

- ⏱ In your food processor, mix lime zest and juice with orange zest and juice, garlic, oil, cilantro, mint, oregano, cumin, salt and pepper and blend well.
- ⏱ Season steaks with salt and pepper, place them into a bowl, add marinade and toss to coat.
- ⏱ Place steaks on a working surface, divide pickles, cheese, mustard and ham on them, roll and secure with toothpicks.
- ⏱ Put stuffed pork steaks in your air fryer and cook at 340 degrees F for 20 minutes.
- ⏱ Divide among plates and serve with a side salad.
- ⏱ Enjoy!

Nutrition: calories 270, fat 7, fiber 2, carbs 13, protein 20

Pork Chops and Mushrooms Mix

Preparation time: 10 minutes Cooking time: 40 minutes Servings: 3

INGREDIENTS:

- ✓ 8 ounces mushrooms, sliced
- ✓ 1 teaspoon garlic powder

- ✓ 1 yellow onion, chopped
- ✓ 1 cup mayonnaise
- ✓ 3 pork chops, boneless
- ✓ 1 teaspoon nutmeg
- ✓ 1 tablespoon balsamic vinegar
- ✓ ½ cup olive oil

DIRECTIONS:

- ⏱ Heat up a pan that fits your air fryer with the oil over medium heat, add mushrooms and onions, stir and cook for 4 minutes.
- ⏱ Add pork chops, nutmeg and garlic powder and brown on both sides.
- ⏱ Introduce pan your air fryer at 330 degrees F and cook for 30 minutes.
- ⏱ Add vinegar and mayo, stir, divide everything on plates and serve.
- ⏱ Enjoy!

Nutrition: calories 600, fat 10, fiber 1, carbs 8, protein 30

Beef Stuffed Squash

Preparation time: 10 minutes Cooking time: 40 minutes Servings: 2

INGREDIENTS:

- ✓ 1 spaghetti squash, pricked
- ✓ 1 pound beef, ground
- ✓ Salt and black pepper to the taste
- ✓ 3 garlic cloves, minced
- ✓ 1 yellow onion, chopped
- ✓ 1 Portobello mushroom, sliced
- ✓ 28 ounces canned tomatoes, chopped
- ✓ 1 teaspoon oregano, dried
- ✓ ¼ teaspoon cayenne pepper
- ✓ ½ teaspoon thyme, dried
- ✓ 1 green bell pepper, chopped

DIRECTIONS:

- ⏱ Put spaghetti squash in your air fryer, cook at 350 degrees F for 20 minutes, transfer to a cutting board, and cut into halves and discard seeds.
- ⏱ Heat up a pan over medium high heat, add meat, garlic, onion and mushroom, stir and cook until meat browns.
- ⏱ Add salt, pepper, thyme, oregano, cayenne, tomatoes and green pepper, stir and cook for 10 minutes.

- ⏱ Stuff squash with this beef mix, introduce in the fryer and cook at 360 degrees F for 10 minutes.
- ⏱ Divide among plates and serve.
- ⏱ Enjoy!

Nutrition: calories 260, fat 7, fiber 2, carbs 14, protein 10

Greek Beef Meatballs Salad

Preparation time: 10 minutes Cooking time: 10 minutes Servings: 6

INGREDIENTS:

- ✓ ¼ cup milk
- ✓ 17 ounces beef, ground
- ✓ 1 yellow onion, grated
- ✓ 5 bread slices, cubed
- ✓ 1 egg, whisked
- ✓ ¼ cup parsley, chopped
- ✓ Salt and black pepper to the taste
- ✓ 2 garlic cloves, minced
- ✓ ¼ cup mint, chopped
- ✓ 2 and ½ teaspoons oregano, dried
- ✓ 1 tablespoon olive oil
- ✓ Cooking spray
- ✓ 7 ounces cherry tomatoes, halved
- ✓ 1 cup baby spinach
- ✓ 1 and ½ tablespoons lemon juice
- ✓ 7 ounces Greek yogurt

DIRECTIONS:

- ⏱ Put torn bread in a bowl, add milk, soak for a few minutes, squeeze and transfer to another bowl.
- ⏱ Add beef, egg, salt, pepper, oregano, mint, parsley, garlic and onion, stir and shape medium meatballs out of this mix.
- ⏱ Spray them with cooking spray, place them in your air fryer and cook at 370 degrees F for 10 minutes.
- ⏱ In a salad bowl, mix spinach with cucumber and tomato.
- ⏱ Add meatballs, the oil, some salt, pepper, lemon juice and yogurt, toss and serve.
- ⏱ Enjoy!

Nutrition: calories 200, fat 4, fiber 8, carbs 13, protein 27

Beef Patties and Mushroom Sauce

Preparation time: 10 minutes Cooking time: 25 minutes Servings: 6

INGREDIENTS:

- ✓ 2 pounds beef, ground
- ✓ Salt and black pepper to the taste
- ✓ ½ teaspoon garlic powder
- ✓ 1 tablespoon soy sauce
- ✓ ¼ cup beef stock
- ✓ ¾ cup flour
- ✓ 1 tablespoon parsley, chopped
- ✓ 1 tablespoon onion flakes

<u>For the sauce:</u>

- ✓ 1 cup yellow onion, chopped
- ✓ 2 cups mushrooms, sliced
- ✓ 2 tablespoons bacon fat
- ✓ 2 tablespoons butter
- ✓ ½ teaspoon soy sauce
- ✓ ¼ cup sour cream
- ✓ ½ cup beef stock
- ✓ Salt and black pepper to the taste

DIRECTIONS:

- ⏱ In a bowl, mix beef with salt, pepper, garlic powder, 1 tablespoon soy sauce, ¼ cup beef stock, flour, parsley and onion flakes, stir well, shape 6 patties, place them in your air fryer and cook at 350 degrees F for 14 minutes.
- ⏱ Meanwhile, heat up a pan with the butter and the bacon fat over medium heat, add mushrooms, stir and cook for 4 minutes.
- ⏱ Add onions, stir and cook for 4 minutes more.
- ⏱ Add ½ teaspoon soy sauce, sour cream and ½ cup stock, stir well, bring to a simmer and take off heat.
- ⏱ Divide beef patties on plates and serve with mushroom sauce on top.
- ⏱ Enjoy!

Nutrition: calories 435, fat 23, fiber 4, carbs 6, protein 32

Beef Casserole

Preparation time: 30 minutes Cooking time: 35 minutes Servings: 12

INGREDIENTS:

- ✓ 1 tablespoon olive oil
- ✓ 2 pounds beef, ground
- ✓ 2 cups eggplant, chopped
- ✓ Salt and black pepper to the taste

- ✓ 2 teaspoons mustard
- ✓ 2 teaspoons gluten free Worcestershire sauce
- ✓ 28 ounces canned tomatoes, chopped
- ✓ 2 cups mozzarella, grated
- ✓ 16 ounces tomato sauce
- ✓ 2 tablespoons parsley, chopped
- ✓ 1 teaspoon oregano, dried

DIRECTIONS:

- In a bowl, mix eggplant with salt, pepper and oil and toss to coat.
- In another bowl, mix beef with salt, pepper, mustard and Worcestershire sauce, stir well and spread on the bottom of a pan that fits your air fryer.
- Add eggplant mix, tomatoes, tomato sauce, parsley, oregano and sprinkle mozzarella at the end.
- Introduce in your air fryer and cook at 360 degrees F for 35 minutes
- Divide among plates and serve hot.
- Enjoy!

Nutrition: calories 200, fat 12, fiber 2, carbs 16, protein 15

Lamb and Spinach Mix

Preparation time: 10 minutes Cooking time: 35 minutes Servings: 6

INGREDIENTS:

- ✓ 2 tablespoons ginger, grated
- ✓ 2 garlic cloves, minced
- ✓ 2 teaspoons cardamom, ground
- ✓ 1 red onion, chopped
- ✓ 1 pound lamb meat, cubed
- ✓ 2 teaspoons cumin powder
- ✓ 1 teaspoon garam masala
- ✓ ½ teaspoon chili powder
- ✓ 1 teaspoon turmeric
- ✓ 2 teaspoons coriander, ground
- ✓ 1 pound spinach
- ✓ 14 ounces canned tomatoes, chopped

DIRECTIONS:

- In a heat proof dish that fits your air fryer, mix lamb with spinach, tomatoes, ginger, garlic, onion, cardamom, cloves, cumin, garam masala, chili, turmeric and coriander, stir, introduce in preheated air fryer and cook at 360 degrees F for 35 minutes
- Divide into bowls and serve.

- Enjoy!

Nutrition: calories 160, fat 6, fiber 3, carbs 17, protein 20

Lamb and Lemon Sauce

Preparation time: 10 minutes Cooking time: 30 minutes Servings: 4

INGREDIENTS:

- ✓ 2 lamb shanks
- ✓ Salt and black pepper to the taste
- ✓ 2 garlic cloves, minced
- ✓ 4 tablespoons olive oil
- ✓ Juice from ½ lemon
- ✓ Zest from ½ lemon
- ✓ ½ teaspoon oregano, dried

DIRECTIONS:

- Season lamb with salt, pepper, rub with garlic, put in your air fryer and cook at 350 degrees F for 30 minutes.
- Meanwhile, in a bowl, mix lemon juice with lemon zest, some salt and pepper, the olive oil and oregano and whisk very well.
- Shred lamb, discard bone, divide among plates, drizzle the lemon dressing all over and serve.
- Enjoy!

Nutrition: calories 260, fat 7, fiber 3, carbs 15, protein 12

Lamb and Green Pesto

Preparation time: 1 hour Cooking time: 45 minutes Servings: 4

INGREDIENTS:

- ✓ 1 cup parsley
- ✓ 1 cup mint
- ✓ 1 small yellow onion, roughly chopped
- ✓ 1/3 cup pistachios, chopped
- ✓ 1 teaspoon lemon zest, grated
- ✓ 5 tablespoons olive oil
- ✓ Salt and black pepper to the taste
- ✓ 2 pounds lamb riblets
- ✓ ½ onion, chopped
- ✓ 5 garlic cloves, minced
- ✓ Juice from 1 orange

DIRECTIONS:

- In your food processor, mix parsley with mint, onion, pistachios, lemon zest, salt, pepper and oil and blend very well.
- Rub lamb with this mix, place in a bowl, cover and leave in the fridge for 1 hour.
- Transfer lamb to a baking dish that fits your air fryer, also add garlic, drizzle orange juice and cook in your air fryer at 300 degrees F for 45 minutes.
- Divide lamb on plates and serve.
- Enjoy!

Nutrition: calories 200, fat 4, fiber 6, carbs 15, protein 7

Lamb Rack s and Fennel Mix

Preparation time: 10 minutes Cooking time: 16 minutes Servings: 4

INGREDIENTS:

- ✓ 12 ounces lamb racks
- ✓ 2 fennel bulbs, sliced
- ✓ Salt and black pepper to the taste
- ✓ 2 tablespoons olive oil
- ✓ 4 figs, cut into halves
- ✓ 1/8 cup apple cider vinegar
- ✓ 1 tablespoon brown sugar

DIRECTIONS:

- In a bowl, mix fennel with figs, vinegar, sugar and oil, toss to coat well, transfer to a baking dish that fits your air fryer, introduce in your air fryer and cook at 350 degrees F for 6 minutes.
- Season lamb with salt and pepper, add to the baking dish with the fennel mix and air fry for 10 minutes more.
- Divide everything on plates and serve.
- Enjoy!

Nutrition: calories 240, fat 9, fiber 3, carbs 15, protein 12

Burgundy Beef Mix

Preparation time: 10 minutes Cooking time: 1 hour Servings: 7

INGREDIENTS:

- ✓ 2 pounds beef chuck roast, cubed
- ✓ 15 ounces canned tomatoes, chopped
- ✓ 4 carrots, chopped
- ✓ Salt and black pepper to the taste
- ✓ ½ pounds mushrooms, sliced
- ✓ 2 celery ribs, chopped
- ✓ 2 yellow onions, chopped

- ✓ 1 cup beef stock
- ✓ 1 tablespoon thyme, chopped
- ✓ ½ teaspoon mustard powder
- ✓ 3 tablespoons almond flour
- ✓ 1 cup water

DIRECTIONS:

- Heat up a heat proof pot that fits your air fryer over medium high heat, add beef, stir and brown them for a couple of minutes.
- Add tomatoes, mushrooms, onions, carrots, celery, salt, pepper mustard, stock and thyme and stir.
- In a bowl mix water with flour, stir well, add this to the pot, toss, introduce in your air fryer and cook at 300 degrees F for 1 hour.
- Divide into bowls and serve.
- Enjoy!

Nutrition: calories 275, fat 13, fiber 4, carbs 17, protein 28

Mexican Beef Mix

Preparation time: 10 minutes Cooking time: 1 hour and 10 minutes Servings: 8

INGREDIENTS:

- ✓ 2 yellow onions, chopped
- ✓ 2 tablespoons olive oil
- ✓ 2 pounds beef roast, cubed
- ✓ 2 green bell peppers, chopped
- ✓ 1 habanero pepper, chopped
- ✓ 4 jalapenos, chopped
- ✓ 14 ounces canned tomatoes, chopped
- ✓ 2 tablespoons cilantro, chopped
- ✓ 6 garlic cloves, minced
- ✓ ½ cup water
- ✓ Salt and black pepper to the taste
- ✓ 1 and ½ teaspoons cumin, ground
- ✓ ½ cup black olives, pitted and chopped
- ✓ 1 teaspoon oregano, dried

DIRECTIONS:

- In a pan that fits your air fryer, combine beef with oil, green bell peppers, onions, jalapenos, habanero pepper, tomatoes, garlic, water, cilantro, oregano,

cumin, salt and pepper, stir, put in your air fryer and cook at 300 degrees F for 1 hour and 10 minutes.
- ⏲ Add olives, stir, divide into bowls and serve.
- ⏲ Enjoy!

Nutrition: calories 305, fat 14, fiber 4, carbs 18, protein 25

Creamy Ham and Cauliflower Mix

Preparation time: 10 minutes Cooking time: 4 hours Servings: 6

INGREDIENTS:

- ✓ 8 ounces cheddar cheese, grated
- ✓ 4 cups ham, cubed
- ✓ 14 ounces chicken stock
- ✓ ½ teaspoon garlic powder
- ✓ ½ teaspoon onion powder
- ✓ Salt and black pepper to the taste
- ✓ 4 garlic cloves, minced
- ✓ ¼ cup heavy cream
- ✓ 16 ounces cauliflower florets

DIRECTIONS:

- ⏲ In a pot that fits your air fryer, mix ham with stock, cheese, cauliflower, garlic powder, onion powder, salt, pepper, garlic and heavy cream, stir, put in your air fryer and cook at 300 degrees F for 1 hour.
- ⏲ Divide into bowls and serve.
- ⏲ Enjoy!

Nutrition: calories 320, fat 20, fiber 3, carbs 16, protein 23

Air Fried Sausage and Mushrooms

Preparation time: 10 minutes Cooking time: 40 minutes Servings: 6

INGREDIENTS:

- ✓ 3 red bell peppers, chopped
- ✓ 2 pounds pork sausage, sliced
- ✓ Salt and black pepper to the taste
- ✓ 2 pounds Portobello mushrooms, sliced
- ✓ 2 sweet onions, chopped
- ✓ 1 tablespoon brown sugar
- ✓ 1 teaspoon olive oil

DIRECTIONS:

- ⏲ In a baking dish that fits your air fryer, mix sausage slices with oil, salt, pepper, bell pepper, mushrooms,

onion and sugar, toss, introduce in your air fryer and cook at 300 degrees F for 40 minutes.
- ⏲ Divide among plates and serve right away.
- ⏲ Enjoy!

Nutrition: calories 130, fat 12, fiber 1, carbs 13, protein 18

Sausage and Kale

Preparation time: 10 minutes Cooking time: 20 minutes Servings: 4

INGREDIENTS:

- ✓ 1 cup yellow onion, chopped
- ✓ 1 and ½ pound Italian pork sausage, sliced ½ cup red bell pepper, chopped Salt and black pepper to the taste
- ✓ 5 pounds kale, chopped
- ✓ 1 teaspoon garlic, minced
- ✓ ¼ cup red hot chili pepper, chopped
- ✓ 1 cup water

DIRECTIONS:

- ⏲ In a pan that fits your air fryer, mix sausage with onion, bell pepper, salt, pepper, kale, garlic, water and chili pepper, toss, introduce in preheated air fryer and cook at 300 degrees F for 20 minutes.
- ⏲ Divide everything on plates and serve.
- ⏲ Enjoy!

Nutrition: calories 150, fat 4, fiber 1, carbs 12, protein 14

Sirloin Steaks and Pico De Gallo

Preparation time: 10 minutes Cooking time: 10 minutes Servings: 4

INGREDIENTS:

- ✓ 2 tablespoons chili powder
- ✓ 4 medium sirloin steaks
- ✓ 1 teaspoon cumin, ground
- ✓ ½ tablespoon sweet paprika
- ✓ 1 teaspoon onion powder
- ✓ 1 teaspoon garlic powder
- ✓ Salt and black pepper to the taste

For the Pico de gallo:

- ✓ 1 small red onion, chopped
- ✓ 2 tomatoes, chopped
- ✓ 2 garlic cloves, minced
- ✓ 2 tablespoons lime juice

- ✓ **1 small green bell pepper, chopped**
- ✓ **1 jalapeno, chopped**
- ✓ **¼ cup cilantro, chopped**
- ✓ **¼ teaspoon cumin, ground**

DIRECTIONS:

- In a bowl, mix chili powder with a pinch of salt, black pepper, onion powder, garlic powder, paprika and 1 teaspoon cumin, stir well, season steaks with this mix, put them in your air fryer and cook at 360 degrees F for 10 minutes.
- In a bowl, mix red onion with tomatoes, garlic, lime juice, bell pepper, jalapeno, cilantro, black pepper to the taste and ¼ teaspoon cumin and toss.
- Top steaks with this mix and serve right away
- Enjoy!

Nutrition: calories 200, fat 12, fiber 4, carbs 15, protein 18

Coffee Flavored Steaks

Preparation time: 10 minutes Cooking time: 15 minutes Servings: 4

INGREDIENTS:

- ✓ **1 and ½ tablespoons coffee, ground**
- ✓ **4 rib eye steaks**
- ✓ **½ tablespoon sweet paprika**
- ✓ **2 tablespoons chili powder**
- ✓ **2 teaspoons garlic powder**
- ✓ **2 teaspoons onion powder**
- ✓ **¼ teaspoon ginger, ground**
- ✓ **¼ teaspoon, coriander, ground**
- ✓ **A pinch of cayenne pepper**
- ✓ **Black pepper to the taste**

DIRECTIONS:

- In a bowl, mix coffee with paprika, chili powder, garlic powder, onion powder, ginger, coriander, cayenne and black pepper, stir, rub steaks with this mix, put in preheated air fryer and cook at 360 degrees F for 15 minutes.
- Divide steaks on plates and serve with a side salad.
- Enjoy!

Nutrition: calories 160, fat 10, fiber 8, carbs 14, protein 12

Filet Mignon and Mushrooms Sauce

Preparation time: 10 minutes Cooking time: 25 minutes Servings: 4

INGREDIENTS:

- ✓ **12 mushrooms, sliced**
- ✓ **1 shallot, chopped**
- ✓ **4 fillet mignons**
- ✓ **2 garlic cloves, minced**
- ✓ **2 tablespoons olive oil**
- ✓ **¼ cup Dijon mustard**
- ✓ **¼ cup wine**
- ✓ **1 and ¼ cup coconut cream**
- ✓ **2 tablespoons parsley, chopped**
- ✓ **Salt and black pepper to the taste**

DIRECTIONS:

- Heat up a pan with the oil over medium high heat, add garlic and shallots, stir and cook for 3 minutes.
- Add mushrooms, stir and cook for 4 minutes more.
- Add wine, stir and cook until it evaporates.
- Add coconut cream, mustard, parsley, a pinch of salt and black pepper to the taste, stir, cook for 6 minutes more and take off heat.
- Season fillets with salt and pepper, put them in your air fryer and cook at 360 degrees F for 10 minutes.
- Divide fillets on plates and serve with the mushroom sauce on top.
- Enjoy!

Nutrition: calories 340, fat 12, fiber 1, carbs 14, protein 23

Beef Kabobs

Preparation time: 10 minutes Cooking time: 10 minutes Servings: 4

INGREDIENTS:

- ✓ **2 red bell peppers, chopped**
- ✓ **2 pounds sirloin steak, cut into medium pieces**
- ✓ **1 red onion, chopped**
- ✓ **1 zucchini, sliced**
- ✓ **Juice form 1 lime**
- ✓ **2 tablespoons chili powder**
- ✓ **2 tablespoon hot sauce**
- ✓ **½ tablespoons cumin, ground**
- ✓ **¼ cup olive oil**
- ✓ **¼ cup salsa**
- ✓ **Salt and black pepper to the taste**

DIRECTIONS:

- In a bowl, mix salsa with lime juice, oil, hot sauce, chili powder, cumin, salt and black pepper and whisk well.
- Divide meat bell peppers, zucchini and onion on skewers, brush kabobs with the salsa mix you made earlier, put them in your preheated air fryer and cook them for 10 minutes at 370 degrees F flipping kabobs halfway.
- Divide among plates and serve with a side salad.
- Enjoy!

Nutrition: calories 170, fat 5, fiber 2, carbs 13, protein 16

Mediterranean Steaks and Scallops

Preparation time: 10 minutes Cooking time: 14 minutes Servings: 2

INGREDIENTS:

- ✓ **10 sea scallops**
- ✓ **2 beef steaks**
- ✓ **4 garlic cloves, minced**
- ✓ **1 shallot, chopped**
- ✓ **2 tablespoons lemon juice**
- ✓ **2 tablespoons parsley, chopped**
- ✓ **2 tablespoons basil, chopped**
- ✓ **1 teaspoon lemon zest**
- ✓ **¼ cup butter**
- ✓ **¼ cup veggie stock**
- ✓ **Salt and black pepper to the taste**

DIRECTIONS:

- Season steaks with salt and pepper, put them in your air fryer, cook at 360 degrees F for 10 minutes and transfer to a pan that fits the fryer.
- Add shallot, garlic, butter, stock, basil, lemon juice, parsley, lemon zest and scallops, toss everything gently and cook at 360 degrees F for 4 minutes more.
- Divide steaks and scallops on plates and serve.
- Enjoy!

Nutrition: calories 150, fat 2, fiber 2, carbs 14, protein 17

Beef Medallions Mix

Preparation time: 2 hours Cooking time: 10 minutes Servings: 4

INGREDIENTS:

- ✓ **2 teaspoons chili powder**
- ✓ **1 cup tomatoes, crushed**
- ✓ **4 beef medallions**

- ✓ **2 teaspoons onion powder**
- ✓ **2 tablespoons soy sauce**
- ✓ **Salt and black pepper to the taste**
- ✓ **1 tablespoons hot pepper**
- ✓ **2 tablespoons lime juice**

DIRECTIONS:

- In a bowl, mix tomatoes with hot pepper, soy sauce, chili powder, onion powder, a pinch of salt, black pepper and lime juice and whisk well.
- Arrange beef medallions in a dish, pour sauce over them, toss and leave them aside for 2 hours.
- Discard tomato marinade, put beef in your preheated air fryer and cook at 360 degrees F for 10 minutes.
- Divide steaks on plates and serve with a side salad.
- Enjoy!

Nutrition: calories 230, fat 4, fiber 1, carbs 13, protein 14

Balsamic Beef

Preparation time: 10 minutes Cooking time: 1 hour Servings: 6

INGREDIENTS:

- ✓ **1 medium beef roast**
- ✓ **1 tablespoon Worcestershire sauce**
- ✓ **½ cup balsamic vinegar**
- ✓ **1 cup beef stock**
- ✓ **1 tablespoons honey**
- ✓ **1 tablespoon soy sauce**
- ✓ **4 garlic cloves, minced**

DIRECTIONS:

- In a heat proof dish that fits your air fryer, mix roast with roast with Worcestershire sauce, vinegar, stock, honey, soy sauce and garlic, toss well, introduce in your air fryer and cook at 370 degrees F for 1 hour.
- Slice roast, divide among plates, drizzle the sauce all over and serve. Enjoy!

Nutrition: calories 311, fat 7, fiber 12, carbs 20, protein 16

Pork Chops and Roasted Peppers

Preparation time: 10 minutes Cooking time: 16 minutes Servings: 4

INGREDIENTS:

- ✓ **3 tablespoons olive oil**
- ✓ **3 tablespoons lemon juice**
- ✓ **1 tablespoon smoked paprika**

- ✓ **2 tablespoons thyme, chopped**
- ✓ **3 garlic cloves, minced**
- ✓ **4 pork chops, bone in**
- ✓ **Salta and black pepper to the taste**
- ✓ **2 roasted bell peppers, chopped**

DIRECTIONS:

In a pan that fits your air fryer, mix pork chops with oil, lemon juice, smoked paprika, thyme, garlic, bell peppers, salt and pepper, toss well, introduce in your air fryer and cook at 400

degrees F for 16 minutes.

- ⏱ Divide pork chops and peppers mix on plates and serve right away. Enjoy!

Nutrition: calories 321, fat 6, fiber 8, carbs 14, protein 17

Pork Chops and Green Beans

Preparation time: 10 minutes Cooking time: 15 minutes Servings: 4

INGREDIENTS:

- ✓ **4 pork chops, bone in**
- ✓ **2 tablespoons olive oil**
- ✓ **1 tablespoon sage, chopped**
- ✓ **Salt and black pepper to the taste**
- ✓ **16 ounces green beans**
- ✓ **3 garlic cloves, minced**
- ✓ **2 tablespoons parsley, chopped**

DIRECTIONS:

- ⏱ In a pan that fits your air fryer, mix pork chops with olive oil, sage, salt, pepper, green beans, garlic and parsley, toss, introduce in your air fryer and cook at 360 degrees F for 15 minutes.
- ⏱ Divide everything on plates and serve.
- ⏱ Enjoy!

Nutrition: calories 261, fat 7, fiber 9, carbs 14, protein 20

Pork Chops and Sage Sauce

Preparation time: 10 minutes Cooking time: 15 minutes Servings: 2

INGREDIENTS:

- ✓ **2 pork chops**
- ✓ **Salt and black pepper to the taste**
- ✓ **1 tablespoon olive oil**
- ✓ **2 tablespoons butter**

- ✓ **1 shallot, sliced**
- ✓ **1 handful sage, chopped**
- ✓ **1 teaspoon lemon juice**

DIRECTIONS:

- ⏱ Season pork chops with salt and pepper, rub with the oil, put in your air fryer and cook at 370 degrees F for 10 minutes, flipping them halfway.
- ⏱ Meanwhile, heat up a pan with the butter over medium heat, add shallot, stir and cook for 2 minutes.
- ⏱ Add sage and lemon juice, stir well, cook for a few more minutes and take off heat.
- ⏱ Divide pork chops on plates, drizzle sage sauce all over and serve.
- ⏱ Enjoy!

Nutrition: calories 265, fat 6, fiber 8, carbs 19, protein 12

Tasty Ham and Greens

Preparation time: 10 minutes Cooking time: 16 minutes Servings: 8

INGREDIENTS:

- ✓ **2 tablespoons olive oil**
- ✓ **4 cups ham, chopped**
- ✓ **2 tablespoons flour**
- ✓ **3 cups chicken stock**
- ✓ **5 ounces onion, chopped**
- ✓ **16 ounces collard greens, chopped**
- ✓ **14 ounces canned black eyed peas, drained ½ teaspoon red pepper, crushed**

DIRECTIONS:

- ⏱ Drizzle the oil in a pan that fits your air fryer, add ham, stock and flour and whisk.
- ⏱ Also add onion, black eyed peas, red pepper and collard greens, introduce in your air fryer and cook at 390 degrees F for 16 minutes.
- ⏱ Divide everything on plates and serve.
- ⏱ Enjoy!

Nutrition: calories 322, fat 6, fiber 8, carbs 12, protein 5

Ham and Veggie Air Fried Mix

Preparation time: 10 minutes Cooking time: 20 minutes Servings: 6

INGREDIENTS:

- ✓ **¼ cup butter**
- ✓ **¼ cup flour**
- ✓ **3 cups milk**

- ✓ **½ teaspoon thyme, dried**
- ✓ **2 cups ham, chopped**
- ✓ **6 ounces sweet peas**
- ✓ **4 ounces mushrooms, halved**
- ✓ **1 cup baby carrots**

DIRECTIONS:

- Heat up a large pan that fits your air fryer with the butter over medium heat, melt it, add flour and whisk well.
- Add milk and, well again and take off heat.
- Add thyme, ham, peas, mushrooms and baby carrots, toss, put in your air fryer and cook at 360 degrees F for 20 minutes.
- Divide everything on plates and serve.
- Enjoy!

Nutrition: calories 311, fat 6, fiber 8, carbs 12, protein 7

Air Fryer Vegetable Recipes

Beet s and Arugula Salad

Preparation time: 10 minutes Cooking time: 10 minutes Servings: 4

INGREDIENTS:

- ✓ **1 and ½ pounds beets, peeled and quartered A drizzle of olive oil**
- ✓ **2 teaspoons orange zest, grated**
- ✓ **2 tablespoons cider vinegar**
- ✓ **½ cup orange juice**
- ✓ **2 tablespoons brown sugar**
- ✓ **2 scallions, chopped**
- ✓ **2 teaspoons mustard**
- ✓ **2 cups arugula**

DIRECTIONS:

- ⏱ Rub beets with the oil and orange juice, place them in your air fryer and cook at 350 degrees F for 10 minutes.
- ⏱ Transfer beet quarters to a bowl, add scallions, arugula and orange zest and toss.
- ⏱ In a separate bowl, mix sugar with mustard and vinegar, whisk well, add to salad, toss and serve.
- ⏱ Enjoy!

Nutrition: calories 121, fat 2, fiber 3, carbs 11, protein 4

Beet , Tomato and Goat Cheese Mix

Preparation time: 30 minutes Cooking time: 14 minutes Servings: 8

INGREDIENTS:

- ✓ **8 small beets, trimmed, peeled and halved**
- ✓ **1 red onion, sliced**
- ✓ **4 ounces goat cheese, crumbled**
- ✓ **1 tablespoon balsamic vinegar**
- ✓ **Salt and black pepper to the taste**
- ✓ **2 tablespoons sugar**
- ✓ **1 pint mixed cherry tomatoes, halved**
- ✓ **2 ounces pecans**
- ✓ **2 tablespoons olive oil**

DIRECTIONS:

- ⏱ Put beets in your air fryer, season them with salt and pepper, cook at 350 degrees F for 14 minutes and transfer to a salad bowl.
- ⏱ Add onion, cherry tomatoes and pecans and toss.

- ⏱ In another bowl, mix vinegar with sugar and oil, whisk well until sugar dissolves and add to salad.
- ⏱ Also add goat cheese, toss and serve.
- ⏱ Enjoy!

Nutrition: calories 124, fat 7, fiber 5, carbs 12, protein 6

Broccoli Salad

Preparation time: 10 minutes Cooking time: 8 minutes Servings: 4

INGREDIENTS:

- ✓ **1 broccoli head, florets separated**
- ✓ **1 tablespoon peanut oil**
- ✓ **6 garlic cloves, minced**
- ✓ **1 tablespoon Chinese rice wine vinegar**
- ✓ **Salt and black pepper to the taste**

DIRECTIONS:

- ⏱ In a bowl, mix broccoli with salt, pepper and half of the oil, toss, transfer to your air fryer and cook at 350 degrees F for 8 minutes, shaking the fryer halfway.
- ⏱ Transfer broccoli to a salad bowl, add the rest of the peanut oil, garlic and rice vinegar, toss really well and serve.
- ⏱ Enjoy!

Nutrition: calories 121, fat 3, fiber 4, carbs 4, protein 4

Brussels Sprouts and Tomatoes Mix

Preparation time: 5 minutes Cooking time: 10 minutes Servings: 4

INGREDIENTS:

- ✓ **1 pound Brussels sprouts, trimmed**
- ✓ **Salt and black pepper to the taste**
- ✓ **6 cherry tomatoes, halved**
- ✓ **¼ cup green onions, chopped**
- ✓ **1 tablespoon olive oil**

DIRECTIONS:

- ⏱ Season Brussels sprouts with salt and pepper, put them in your air fryer and cook at 350 degrees F for 10 minutes.
- ⏱ Transfer them to a bowl, add salt, pepper, cherry tomatoes, green onions and olive oil, toss well and serve.
- ⏱ Enjoy!

Nutrition: calories 121, fat 4, fiber 4, carbs 11, protein 4

Brussels Sprouts and Butter Sauce

Preparation time: 4 minutes Cooking time: 10 minutes Servings: 4

INGREDIENTS:

- ✓ 1 pound Brussels sprouts, trimmed
- ✓ Salt and black pepper to the taste
- ✓ ½ cup bacon, cooked and chopped
- ✓ 1 tablespoon mustard
- ✓ 1 tablespoon butter
- ✓ 2 tablespoons dill, finely chopped

DIRECTIONS:

- ⏱ Put Brussels sprouts in your air fryer and cook them at 350 degrees F for 10 minutes.
- ⏱ Heat up a pan with the butter over medium high heat, add bacon, mustard and dill and whisk well.
- ⏱ Divide Brussels sprouts on plates, drizzle butter sauce all over and serve.
- ⏱ Enjoy!

Nutrition: calories 162, fat 8, fiber 8, carbs 14, protein 5

Cheesy Brussels Sprouts

Preparation time: 10 minutes Cooking time: 8 minutes Servings: 4

INGREDIENTS:

- ✓ 1 pound Brussels sprouts, washed
- ✓ Juice of 1 lemon
- ✓ Salt and black pepper to the taste
- ✓ 2 tablespoons butter
- ✓ 3 tablespoons parmesan, grated

DIRECTIONS:

- ⏱ Put Brussels sprouts in your air fryer, cook them at 350 degrees F for 8 minutes and transfer them to a bowl.
- ⏱ Heat up a pan with the butter over medium heat, add lemon juice, salt and pepper, whisk well and add to Brussels sprouts.
- ⏱ Add parmesan, toss until parmesan melts and serve.
- ⏱ Enjoy!

Nutrition: calories 152, fat 6, fiber 6, carbs 8, protein 12

Spicy Cabbage

Preparation time: 10 minutes Cooking time: 8 minutes Servings: 4

INGREDIENTS:

- ✓ 1 cabbage, cut into 8 wedges
- ✓ 1 tablespoon sesame seed oil
- ✓ 1 carrots, grated
- ✓ ¼ cup apple cider vinegar
- ✓ ¼ cups apple juice
- ✓ ½ teaspoon cayenne pepper
- ✓ 1 teaspoon red pepper flakes, crushed

DIRECTIONS:

- ⏱ In a pan that fits your air fryer, combine cabbage with oil, carrot, vinegar, apple juice, cayenne and pepper flakes, toss, introduce in preheated air fryer and cook at 350 degrees F for 8 minutes.
- ⏱ Divide cabbage mix on plates and serve.
- ⏱ Enjoy!

Nutrition: calories 100, fat 4, fiber 2, carbs 11, protein 7

Sweet Baby Carrots Dish

Preparation time: 10 minutes Cooking time: 10 minutes Servings: 4

INGREDIENTS:

- ✓ 2 cups baby carrots
- ✓ A pinch of salt and black pepper
- ✓ 1 tablespoon brown sugar
- ✓ ½ tablespoon butter, melted

DIRECTIONS:

- ⏱ In a dish that fits your air fryer, mix baby carrots with butter, salt, pepper and sugar, toss, introduce in your air fryer and cook at 350 degrees F for 10 minutes.
- ⏱ Divide among plates and serve.
- ⏱ Enjoy!

Nutrition: calories 100, fat 2, fiber 3, carbs 7, protein 4

Collard Greens Mix

Preparation time: 10 minutes Cooking time: 10 minutes Servings: 4

INGREDIENTS:

- ✓ 1 bunch collard greens, trimmed
- ✓ 2 tablespoons olive oil
- ✓ 2 tablespoons tomato puree
- ✓ 1 yellow onion, chopped
- ✓ 3 garlic cloves, minced
- ✓ Salt and black pepper to the taste
- ✓ 1 tablespoon balsamic vinegar

- ✓ 1 teaspoon sugar

DIRECTIONS:

- ⏱ In a dish that fits your air fryer, mix oil, garlic, vinegar, onion and tomato puree and whisk.
- ⏱ Add collard greens, salt, pepper and sugar, toss, introduce in your air fryer and cook at 320 degrees F for 10 minutes.
- ⏱ Divide collard greens mix on plates and serve.
- ⏱ Enjoy!

Nutrition: calories 121, fat 3, fiber 3, carbs 7, protein 3

Collard Greens and Turkey Wings

Preparation time: 10 minutes Cooking time: 20 minutes Servings: 6

INGREDIENTS:

- ✓ 1 sweet onion, chopped
- ✓ 2 smoked turkey wings
- ✓ 2 tablespoons olive oil
- ✓ 3 garlic cloves, minced
- ✓ 2 and ½ pounds collard greens, chopped
- ✓ Salt and black pepper to the taste
- ✓ 2 tablespoons apple cider vinegar
- ✓ 1 tablespoon brown sugar
- ✓ ½ teaspoon crushed red pepper

DIRECTIONS:

- ⏱ Heat up a pan that fits your air fryer with the oil over medium high heat, add onions, stir and cook for 2 minutes.
- ⏱ Add garlic, greens, vinegar, salt, pepper, crushed red pepper, sugar and smoked turkey, introduce in preheated air fryer and cook at 350 degrees F for 15 minutes.
- ⏱ Divide greens and turkey on plates and serve.
- ⏱ Enjoy!

Nutrition: calories 262, fat 4, fiber 8, carbs 12, protein 4

Herbed Eggplant and Zucchini Mix

Preparation time: 10 minutes Cooking time: 8 minutes Servings: 4

INGREDIENTS:

- ✓ 1 eggplant, roughly cubed
- ✓ 3 zucchinis, roughly cubed
- ✓ 2 tablespoons lemon juice
- ✓ Salt and black pepper to the taste
- ✓ 1 teaspoon thyme, dried

- ✓ 1 teaspoon oregano, dried
- ✓ 3 tablespoons olive oil

DIRECTIONS:

- ⏱ Put eggplant in a dish that fits your air fryer, add zucchinis, lemon juice, salt, pepper, thyme, oregano and olive oil, toss, introduce in your air fryer and cook at 360 degrees F for 8 minutes.
- ⏱ Divide among plates and serve right away.
- ⏱ Enjoy!

Nutrition: calories 152, fat 5, fiber 7, carbs 19, protein 5

Flavored Fennel

Preparation time: 10 minutes Cooking time: 8 minutes Servings: 4

INGREDIENTS:

- ✓ 2 fennel bulbs, cut into quarters
- ✓ 3 tablespoons olive oil
- ✓ Salt and black pepper to the taste
- ✓ 1 garlic clove, minced
- ✓ 1 red chili pepper, chopped
- ✓ ¾ cup veggie stock
- ✓ Juice from ½ lemon
- ✓ ¼ cup white wine
- ✓ ¼ cup parmesan, grated

DIRECTIONS:

- ⏱ Heat up a pan that fits your air fryer with the oil over medium high heat, add garlic and chili pepper, stir and cook for 2 minutes.
- ⏱ Add fennel, salt, pepper, stock, wine, lemon juice, and parmesan, toss to coat, introduce in your air fryer and cook at 350 degrees F for 6 minutes.
- ⏱ Divide among plates and serve right away.
- ⏱ Enjoy!

Nutrition: calories 100, fat 4, fiber 8, carbs 4, protein 4

Okra and Corn Salad

Preparation time: 10 minutes Cooking time: 12 minutes Servings: 6

INGREDIENTS:

- ✓ 1 pound okra, trimmed
- ✓ 6 scallions, chopped
- ✓ 3 green bell peppers, chopped
- ✓ Salt and black pepper to the taste

- ✓ 2 tablespoons olive oil
- ✓ 1 teaspoon sugar
- ✓ 28 ounces canned tomatoes, chopped
- ✓ 1 cup con

DIRECTIONS:

- Heat up a pan that fits your air fryer with the oil over medium high heat, add scallions and bell peppers, stir and cook for 5 minutes.
- Add okra, salt, pepper, sugar, tomatoes and corn, stir, introduce in your air fryer and cook at 360 degrees F for 7 minutes.
- Divide okra mix on plates and serve warm.
- Enjoy!

Nutrition: calories 152, fat 4, fiber 3, carbs 18, protein 4

Air Fried Leeks

Preparation time: 10 minutes Cooking time: 7 minutes Servings: 4

INGREDIENTS:

- ✓ 4 leeks, washed, ends cut off and halved
- ✓ Salt and black pepper to the taste
- ✓ 1 tablespoon butter, melted
- ✓ 1 tablespoon lemon juice

DIRECTIONS:

- Rub leeks with melted butter, season with salt and pepper, put in your air fryer and cook at 350 degrees F for 7 minutes.
- Arrange on a platter, drizzle lemon juice all over and serve.
- Enjoy!

Nutrition: calories 100, fat 4, fiber 2, carbs 6, protein 2

Crispy Potatoes and Parsley

Preparation time: 10 minutes Cooking time: 10 minutes Servings: 4

INGREDIENTS:

- ✓ 1 pound gold potatoes, cut into wedges
- ✓ Salt and black pepper to the taste
- ✓ 2 tablespoons olive
- ✓ Juice from ½ lemon
- ✓ ¼ cup parsley leaves, chopped

DIRECTIONS:

- Rub potatoes with salt, pepper, lemon juice and olive oil, put them in your air fryer and cook at 350 degrees F for 10 minutes.

- Divide among plates, sprinkle parsley on top and serve.
- Enjoy!

Nutrition: calories 152, fat 3, fiber 7, carbs 17, protein 4

Indian Turnips Salad

Preparation time: 10 minutes Cooking time: 12 minutes Servings: 4

INGREDIENTS:

- ✓ 20 ounces turnips, peeled and chopped
- ✓ 1 teaspoon garlic, minced
- ✓ 1 teaspoon ginger, grated
- ✓ 2 yellow onions, chopped
- ✓ 2 tomatoes, chopped
- ✓ 1 teaspoon cumin, ground
- ✓ 1 teaspoon coriander, ground
- ✓ 2 green chilies, chopped
- ✓ ½ teaspoon turmeric powder
- ✓ 2 tablespoons butter
- ✓ Salt and black pepper to the taste
- ✓ A handful coriander leaves, chopped

DIRECTIONS:

- Heat up a pan that fits your air fryer with the butter, melt it, add green chilies, garlic and ginger, stir and cook for 1 minute.
- Add onions, salt, pepper, tomatoes, turmeric, cumin, ground coriander and turnips, stir, introduce in your air fryer and cook at 350 degrees F for 10 minutes.
- Divide among plates, sprinkle fresh coriander on top and serve.
- Enjoy!

Nutrition: calories 100, fat 3, fiber 6, carbs 12, protein 4

Spinach Pie

Preparation time: 10 minutes Cooking time: 15 minutes Servings: 4

INGREDIENTS:

- ✓ 7 ounces flour
- ✓ 2 tablespoons butter
- ✓ 7ounces spinach
- ✓ 1 tablespoon olive oil
- ✓ 2 eggs
- ✓ 2 tablespoons milk
- ✓ 3 ounces cottage cheese

- ✓ **Salt and black pepper to the taste**
- ✓ **1 yellow onion, chopped**

DIRECTIONS:

- ☉ In your food processor, mix flour with butter, 1 egg, milk, salt and pepper, blend well, transfer to a bowl, knead, cover and leave for 10 minutes.
- ☉ Heat up a pan with the oil over medium high heat, add onion and spinach, stir and cook for 2 minutes.
- ☉ Add salt, pepper, the remaining egg and cottage cheese, stir well and take off heat.
- ☉ Divide dough in 4 pieces, roll each piece, place on the bottom of a ramekin, add spinach filling over dough, place ramekins in your air fryer's basket and cook at 360 degrees F for 15 minutes.
- ☉ Serve warm,
- ☉ Enjoy!

Nutrition: calories 250, fat 12, fiber 2, carbs 23, protein 12

Balsamic Artichokes

Preparation time: 10 minutes Cooking time: 7 minutes Servings: 4

INGREDIENTS:

- ✓ **4 big artichokes, trimmed**
- ✓ **Salt and black pepper to the taste**
- ✓ **2 tablespoons lemon juice**
- ✓ **¼ cup extra virgin olive oil**
- ✓ **2 teaspoons balsamic vinegar**
- ✓ **1 teaspoon oregano, dried**
- ✓ **2 garlic cloves, minced**

DIRECTIONS:

- ☉ Season artichokes with salt and pepper, rub them with half of the oil and half of the lemon juice, put them in your air fryer and cook at 360 degrees F for 7 minutes.
- ☉ Meanwhile, in a bowl, mix the rest of the lemon juice with vinegar, the remaining oil, salt, pepper, garlic and oregano and stir very well.
- ☉ Arrange artichokes on a platter, drizzle the balsamic vinaigrette over them and serve.
- ☉ Enjoy!

Nutrition: calories 200, fat 3, fiber 6, carbs 12, protein 4

Cheesy Artichokes

Preparation time: 10 minutes Cooking time: 6 minutes Servings: 6

INGREDIENTS:

- ✓ **14 ounces canned artichoke hearts**
- ✓ **8 ounces cream cheese**
- ✓ **16 ounces parmesan cheese, grated**
- ✓ **10 ounces spinach**
- ✓ **½ cup chicken stock**
- ✓ **8 ounces mozzarella, shredded**
- ✓ **½ cup sour cream**
- ✓ **3 garlic cloves, minced**
- ✓ **½ cup mayonnaise**
- ✓ **1 teaspoon onion powder**

DIRECTIONS:

- ☉ In a pan that fits your air fryer, mix artichokes with stock, garlic, spinach, cream cheese, sour cream, onion powder and mayo, toss, introduce in your air fryer and cook at 350 degrees F for 6 minutes.
- ☉ Add mozzarella and parmesan, stir well and serve.
- ☉ Enjoy!

Nutrition: calories 261, fat 12, fiber 2, carbs 12, protein 15

Artichokes and Special Sauce

Preparation time: 10 minutes Cooking time: 6 minutes Servings: 2

INGREDIENTS:

- ✓ **2 artichokes, trimmed**
- ✓ **A drizzle of olive oil**
- ✓ **2 garlic cloves, minced**
- ✓ **1 tablespoon lemon juice**

For the sauce:

- ✓ **¼ cup coconut oil**
- ✓ **¼ cup extra virgin olive oil**
- ✓ **3 anchovy fillets**
- ✓ **3 garlic cloves**

DIRECTIONS:

- ☉ In a bowl, mix artichokes with oil, 2 garlic cloves and lemon juice, toss well, transfer to your air fryer, cook at 350 degrees F for 6 minutes and divide among plates.
- ☉ In your food processor, mix coconut oil with anchovy, 3 garlic cloves and olive oil, blend very well, drizzle over artichokes and serve.
- ☉ Enjoy!

Nutrition: calories 261, fat 4, fiber 7, carbs 20, protein 12

Beet Salad and Parsley Dressing

Preparation time: 10 minutes Cooking time: 14 minutes Servings: 4

INGREDIENTS:

- ✓ 4 beets
- ✓ 2 tablespoons balsamic vinegar
- ✓ A bunch of parsley, chopped
- ✓ Salt and black pepper to the taste
- ✓ 1 tablespoon extra virgin olive oil
- ✓ 1 garlic clove, chopped
- ✓ 2 tablespoons capers

DIRECTIONS:

- ⏱ Put beets in your air fryer and cook them at 360 degrees F for 14 minutes.
- ⏱ Meanwhile, in a bowl, mix parsley with garlic, salt, pepper, olive oil and capers and stir very well.
- ⏱ Transfer beets to a cutting board, leave them to cool down, peel them, slice put them in a salad bowl.
- ⏱ Add vinegar, drizzle the parsley dressing all over and serve.
- ⏱ Enjoy!

Nutrition: calories 70, fat 2, fiber 1, carbs 6, protein 4

Beets and Blue Cheese Salad

Preparation time: 10 minutes Cooking time: 14 minutes Servings: 6

INGREDIENTS:

- ✓ 6 beets, peeled and quartered
- ✓ Salt and black pepper to the taste
- ✓ ¼ cup blue cheese, crumbled
- ✓ 1 tablespoon olive oil

DIRECTIONS:

- ⏱ Put beets in your air fryer, cook them at 350 degrees F for 14 minutes and transfer them to a bowl.
- ⏱ Add blue cheese, salt, pepper and oil, toss and serve.
- ⏱ Enjoy!

Nutrition: calories 100, fat 4, fiber 4, carbs 10, protein 5

Simple Stuffed Tomatoes

Preparation time: 10 minutes Cooking time: 15 minutes Servings: 4

INGREDIENTS:

- ✓ 4 tomatoes, tops cut off and pulp scooped and chopped Salt and black pepper to the taste

- ✓ 1 yellow onion, chopped
- ✓ 1 tablespoon butter
- ✓ 2 tablespoons celery, chopped
- ✓ ½ cup mushrooms, chopped
- ✓ 1 tablespoon bread crumbs
- ✓ 1 cup cottage cheese
- ✓ ¼ teaspoon caraway seeds
- ✓ 1 tablespoon parsley, chopped

DIRECTIONS:

- ⏱ Heat up a pan with the butter over medium heat, melt it, add onion and celery, stir and cook for 3 minutes.
- ⏱ Add tomato pulp and mushrooms, stir and cook for 1 minute more.
- ⏱ Add salt, pepper, crumbled bread, cheese, caraway seeds and parsley, stir, cook for 4 minutes more and take off heat.
- ⏱ Stuff tomatoes with this mix, place them in your air fryer and cook at 350 degrees F for 8 minutes.
- ⏱ Divide stuffed tomatoes on plates and serve.
- ⏱ Enjoy!

Nutrition: calories 143, fat 4, fiber 6, carbs 4, protein 4

Indian Potatoes

Preparation time: 10 minutes Cooking time: 12 minutes Servings: 4

INGREDIENTS:

- ✓ 1 tablespoon coriander seeds
- ✓ 1 tablespoon cumin seeds
- ✓ Salt and black pepper to the taste
- ✓ ½ teaspoon turmeric powder
- ✓ ½ teaspoon red chili powder
- ✓ 1 teaspoon pomegranate powder
- ✓ 1 tablespoon pickled mango, chopped
- ✓ 2 teaspoons fenugreek, dried
- ✓ 5 potatoes, boiled, peeled and cubed
- ✓ 2 tablespoons olive oil

DIRECTIONS:

- ⏱ Heat up a pan that fits your air fryer with the oil over medium heat, add coriander and cumin seeds, stir and cook for 2 minutes.
- ⏱ Add salt, pepper, turmeric, chili powder, pomegranate powder, mango, fenugreek and

potatoes, toss, introduce in your air fryer and cook at 360 degrees F for 10 minutes.
- Divide among plates and serve hot.
- Enjoy!

Nutrition: calories 251, fat 7, fiber 4, carbs 12, protein 7

Broccoli and Tomatoes Air Fried Stew

Preparation time: 10 minutes Cooking time: 20 minutes Servings: 4

INGREDIENTS:

- ✓ **1 broccoli head, florets separated**
- ✓ **2 teaspoons coriander seeds**
- ✓ **1 tablespoon olive oil**
- ✓ **1 yellow onion, chopped**
- ✓ **Salt and black pepper to the taste**
- ✓ **A pinch of red pepper, crushed**
- ✓ **1 small ginger piece, chopped**
- ✓ **1 garlic clove, minced**
- ✓ **28 ounces canned tomatoes, pureed**

DIRECTIONS:

- Heat up a pan that fits your air fryer with the oil over medium heat, add onions, salt, pepper and red pepper, stir and cook for 7 minutes.
- Add ginger, garlic, coriander seeds, tomatoes and broccoli, stir, introduce in your air fryer and cook at 360 degrees F for 12 minutes.
- Divide into bowls and serve.
- Enjoy!

Nutrition: calories 150, fat 4, fiber 2, carbs 7, protein 12

Collard Gree ns and Bacon

Preparation time: 10 minutes Cooking time: 12 minutes Servings: 4

INGREDIENTS:

- ✓ **1 pound collard greens**
- ✓ **3 bacon strips, chopped**
- ✓ **¼ cup cherry tomatoes, halved**
- ✓ **1 tablespoon apple cider vinegar**
- ✓ **2 tablespoons chicken stock**
- ✓ **Salt and black pepper to the taste**

DIRECTIONS:

- Heat up a pan that fits your air fryer over medium heat, add bacon, stir and cook 1-2 minutes

- Add tomatoes, collard greens, vinegar, stock, salt and pepper, stir, introduce in your air fryer and cook at 320 degrees F for 10 minutes.
- Divide among plates and serve.
- Enjoy!

Nutrition: calories 120, fat 3, fiber 1, carbs 3, protein 7

Sesame Mustard Greens

Preparation time: 10 minutes Cooking time: 11 minutes Servings: 4

INGREDIENTS:

- ✓ **2 garlic cloves, minced**
- ✓ **1 pound mustard greens, torn**
- ✓ **1 tablespoon olive oil**
- ✓ **½ cup yellow onion, sliced**
- ✓ **Salt and black pepper to the taste**
- ✓ **3 tablespoons veggie stock**
- ✓ **¼ teaspoon dark sesame oil**

DIRECTIONS:

- Heat up a pan that fits your air fryer with the oil over medium heat, add onions, stir and brown them for 5 minutes.
- Add garlic, stock, greens, salt and pepper, stir, introduce in your air fryer and cook at 350 degrees F for 6 minutes.
- Add sesame oil, toss to coat, divide among plates and serve.
- Enjoy!

Nutrition: calories 120, fat 3, fiber 1, carbs 3, protein 7

Radish Hash

Preparation time: 10 minutes Cooking time: 7 minutes Servings: 4

INGREDIENTS:

- ✓ **½ teaspoon onion powder**
- ✓ **1 pound radishes, sliced**
- ✓ **½ teaspoon garlic powder**
- ✓ **Salt and black pepper to the taste**
- ✓ **4 eggs**
- ✓ **1/3 cup parmesan, grated**

DIRECTIONS:

- In a bowl, mix radishes with salt, pepper, onion and garlic powder, eggs and parmesan and stir well.

- Transfer radishes to a pan that fits your air fryer and cook at 350 degrees F for 7 minutes.
- Divide hash on plates and serve.
- Enjoy!

Nutrition: calories 80, fat 5, fiber 2, carbs 5, protein 7

Delicious Zucchini Mix

Preparation time: 10 minutes Cooking time: 14 minutes Servings: 6

INGREDIENTS:

- ✓ 6 zucchinis, halved and then sliced
- ✓ Salt and black pepper to the taste
- ✓ 1 tablespoon butter
- ✓ 1 teaspoon oregano, dried
- ✓ ½ cup yellow onion, chopped
- ✓ 3 garlic cloves, minced
- ✓ 2 ounces parmesan, grated
- ✓ ¾ cup heavy cream

DIRECTIONS:

- Heat up a pan that fits your air fryer with the butter over medium high heat, add onion, stir and cook for 4 minutes.
- Add garlic, zucchinis, oregano, salt, pepper and heavy cream, toss, introduce in your air fryer and cook at 350 degrees F for 10 minutes.
- Add parmesan, stir, divide among plates and serve.
- Enjoy!

Nutrition: calories 160, fat 4, fiber 2, carbs 8, protein 8

Swiss Chard and Sausage

Preparation time: 10 minutes Cooking time: 20 minutes Servings: 8

INGREDIENTS:

- ✓ 8 cups Swiss chard, chopped
- ✓ ½ cup onion, chopped
- ✓ 1 tablespoon olive oil
- ✓ 1 garlic clove, minced
- ✓ Salt and black pepper to the taste
- ✓ 3 eggs
- ✓ 2 cups ricotta cheese
- ✓ 1 cup mozzarella, shredded
- ✓ A pinch of nutmeg
- ✓ ¼ cup parmesan, grated
- ✓ 1 pound sausage, chopped

DIRECTIONS:

- Heat up a pan that fits your air fryer with the oil over medium heat, add onions, garlic, Swiss chard, salt, pepper and nutmeg, stir, cook for 2 minutes and take off heat.
- In a bowl, whisk eggs with mozzarella, parmesan and ricotta, stir, pour over Swiss chard mix, toss, introduce in your air fryer and cook at 320 degrees F for 17 minutes.
- Divide among plates and serve.
- Enjoy!

Nutrition: calories 332, fat 13, fiber 3, carbs 14, protein 23

Swiss Chard Salad

Preparation time: 10 minutes Cooking time: 13 minutes Servings: 4

INGREDIENTS:

- ✓ 1 bunch Swiss chard, torn
- ✓ 2 tablespoons olive oil
- ✓ 1 small yellow onion, chopped
- ✓ A pinch of red pepper flakes
- ✓ ¼ cup pine nuts, toasted
- ✓ ¼ cup raisins
- ✓ 1 tablespoon balsamic vinegar
- ✓ Salt and black pepper to the taste

DIRECTIONS:

- Heat up a pan that fits your air fryer with the oil over medium heat, add chard and onions, stir and cook for 5 minutes.
- Add salt, pepper, pepper flakes, raisins, pine nuts and vinegar, stir, introduce in your air fryer and cook at 350 degrees F for 8 minutes.
- Divide among plates and serve.
- Enjoy!

Nutrition: calories 120, fat 2, fiber 1, carbs 8, protein 8

Spanish Greens

Preparation time: 10 minutes Cooking time: 8 minutes Servings: 4

INGREDIENTS:

- ✓ 1 apple, cored and chopped
- ✓ 1 yellow onion, sliced
- ✓ 3 tablespoons olive oil
- ✓ ¼ cup raisins
- ✓ 6 garlic cloves, chopped
- ✓ ¼ cup pine nuts, toasted

- ✓ ¼ cup balsamic vinegar
- ✓ 5 cups mixed spinach and chard
- ✓ Salt and black pepper to the taste
- ✓ A pinch of nutmeg

DIRECTIONS:

- ⏱ Heat up a pan that fits your air fryer with the oil over medium high heat, add onion, stir and cook for 3 minutes.
- ⏱ Add apple, garlic, raisins, vinegar, mixed spinach and chard, nutmeg, salt and pepper, stir, introduce in preheated air fryer and cook at 350 degrees F for 5 minutes.
- ⏱ Divide among plates, sprinkle pine nuts on top and serve.
- ⏱ Enjoy!

Nutrition: calories 120, fat 1, fiber 2, carbs 3, protein 6

Flavored Air Fried Tomatoes

Preparation time: 10 minutes Cooking time: 15 Servings: 8

INGREDIENTS:

- ✓ 1 jalapeno pepper, chopped
- ✓ 4 garlic cloves, minced
- ✓ 2 pounds cherry tomatoes, halved
- ✓ Salt and black pepper to the taste
- ✓ ¼ cup olive oil
- ✓ ½ teaspoon oregano, dried
- ✓ ¼ cup basil, chopped
- ✓ ½ cup parmesan, grated

DIRECTIONS:

- ⏱ In a bowl, mix tomatoes with garlic, jalapeno, season with salt, pepper and oregano and drizzle the oil, toss to coat, introduce in your air fryer and cook at 380 degrees F for 15 minutes.
- ⏱ Transfer tomatoes to a bowl, add basil and parmesan, toss and serve. Enjoy!

Nutrition: calories 140, fat 2, fiber 2, carbs 6, protein 8

Italian Eggplant Stew

Preparation time: 10 minutes Cooking time: 15 minutes Servings: 4

INGREDIENTS:

- ✓ 1 red onion, chopped
- ✓ 2 garlic cloves, chopped
- ✓ 1 bunch parsley, chopped

- ✓ Salt and black pepper to the taste
- ✓ 1 teaspoon oregano, dried
- ✓ 2 eggplants, cut into medium chunks
- ✓ 2 tablespoons olive oil
- ✓ 2 tablespoons capers, chopped
- ✓ 1 handful green olives, pitted and sliced
- ✓ 5 tomatoes, chopped
- ✓ 3 tablespoons herb vinegar

DIRECTIONS:

- ⏱ Heat up a pan that fits your air fryer with the oil over medium heat, add eggplant, oregano, salt and pepper, stir and cook for 5 minutes.
- ⏱ Add garlic, onion, parsley, capers, olives, vinegar and tomatoes, stir, introduce in your air fryer and cook at 360 degrees F for 15 minutes.
- ⏱ Divide into bowls and serve.
- ⏱ Enjoy!

Nutrition: calories 170, fat 13, fiber 3, carbs 5, protein 7

Rutabaga and Cherry Tomatoes Mix

Preparation time: 10 minutes Cooking time: 15 minutes Servings: 4

INGREDIENTS:

- ✓ 1 tablespoon shallot, chopped
- ✓ 1 garlic clove, minced
- ✓ ¾ cup cashews, soaked for a couple of hours and drained
- ✓ 2 tablespoons nutritional yeast
- ✓ ½ cup veggie stock
- ✓ Salt and black pepper to the taste
- ✓ 2 teaspoons lemon juice

For the pasta:

- ✓ 1 cup cherry tomatoes, halved
- ✓ 5 teaspoons olive oil
- ✓ ¼ teaspoon garlic powder
- ✓ 2 rutabagas, peeled and cut into thick noodles

DIRECTIONS:

- ⏱ Place tomatoes and rutabaga noodles into a pan that fits your air fryer, drizzle the oil over them, season with salt, black pepper and garlic powder, toss to coat and cook in your air fryer at 350 degrees F for 15 minutes.

- Meanwhile, in a food processor, mix garlic with shallots, cashews, veggie stock, nutritional yeast, lemon juice, a pinch of sea salt and black pepper to the taste and blend well.
- Divide rutabaga pasta on plates, top with tomatoes, drizzle the sauce over them and serve.
- Enjoy!

Nutrition: calories 160, fat 2, fiber 5, carbs 10, protein 8

Garlic Tomatoes

Preparation time: 10 minutes Cooking time: 15 minutes Servings: 4

INGREDIENTS:

- ✓ 4 garlic cloves, crushed
- ✓ 1 pound mixed cherry tomatoes
- ✓ 3 thyme springs, chopped
- ✓ Salt and black pepper to the taste
- ✓ ¼ cup olive oil

DIRECTIONS:

- In a bowl, mix tomatoes with salt, black pepper, garlic, olive oil and thyme, toss to coat, introduce in your air fryer and cook at 360 degrees F for 15 minutes.
- Divide tomatoes mix on plates and serve.
- Enjoy!

Nutrition: calories 100, fat 0, fiber 1, carbs 1, protein 6

Tomato and Basil Tart

Preparation time: 10 minutes Cooking time: 14 minutes Servings: 2

INGREDIENTS:

- ✓ 1 bunch basil, chopped
- ✓ 4 eggs
- ✓ 1 garlic clove, minced
- ✓ Salt and black pepper to the taste
- ✓ ½ cup cherry tomatoes, halved
- ✓ ¼ cup cheddar cheese, grated

DIRECTIONS:

- In a bowl, mix eggs with salt, black pepper, cheese and basil and whisk well.
- Pour this into a baking dish that fits your air fryer, arrange tomatoes on top, introduce in the fryer and cook at 320 degrees F for 14 minutes.
- Slice and serve right away.
- Enjoy!

Nutrition: calories 140, fat 1, fiber 1, carbs 2, protein 10

Zucchini Noodles Delight

Preparation time: 10 minutes Cooking time: 20 minutes Servings: 6

INGREDIENTS:

- ✓ 2 tablespoons olive oil
- ✓ 3 zucchinis, cut with a spiralizer
- ✓ 16 ounces mushrooms, sliced
- ✓ ¼ cup sun dried tomatoes, chopped
- ✓ 1 teaspoon garlic, minced
- ✓ ½ cup cherry tomatoes, halved
- ✓ 2 cups tomatoes sauce
- ✓ 2 cups spinach, torn
- ✓ Salt and black pepper to the taste
- ✓ A handful basil, chopped

DIRECTIONS:

- Put zucchini noodles in a bowl, season salt and black pepper and leave them aside for 10 minutes.
- Heat up a pan that fits your air fryer with the oil over medium high heat, add garlic, stir and cook for 1 minute.
- Add mushrooms, sun dried tomatoes, cherry tomatoes, spinach, cayenne, sauce and zucchini noodles, stir, introduce in your air fryer and cook at 320 degrees F for 10 minutes.
- Divide among plates and serve with basil sprinkled on top.
- Enjoy!

Nutrition: calories 120, fat 1, fiber 1, carbs 2, protein 9

Simple Tomatoes and Bell Pepper Sauce

Preparation time: 10 minutes Cooking time: 15 minutes Servings: 4

INGREDIENTS:

- ✓ 2 red bell peppers, chopped
- ✓ 2 garlic cloves, minced
- ✓ 1 pound cherry tomatoes, halved
- ✓ 1 teaspoon rosemary, dried
- ✓ 3 bay leaves
- ✓ 2 tablespoons olive oil

- ✓ 1 tablespoon balsamic vinegar
- ✓ Salt and black pepper to the taste

DIRECTIONS:

- In a bowl mix tomatoes with garlic, salt, black pepper, rosemary, bay leaves, half of the oil and half of the vinegar, toss to coat, introduce in your air fryer and roast them at 320 degrees F for 15 minutes.
- Meanwhile, in your food processor, mix bell peppers with a pinch of sea salt, black pepper, the rest of the oil and the rest of the vinegar and blend very well.
- Divide roasted tomatoes on plates, drizzle the bell peppers sauce over them and serve.
- Enjoy!

Nutrition: calories 123, fat 1, fiber 1, carbs 8, protein 10

Cherry Tomatoes Skewers

Preparation time: 30 minutes Cooking time: 6 minutes Servings: 4

INGREDIENTS:

- ✓ 3 tablespoons balsamic vinegar
- ✓ 24 cherry tomatoes
- ✓ 2 tablespoons olive oil
- ✓ 3 garlic cloves, minced
- ✓ 1 tablespoons thyme, chopped
- ✓ Salt and black pepper to the taste

For the dressing:

- ✓ 2 tablespoons balsamic vinegar
- ✓ Salt and black pepper to the taste
- ✓ 4 tablespoons olive oil

DIRECTIONS:

- In a bowl, mix 2 tablespoons oil with 3 tablespoons vinegar, 3 garlic cloves, thyme, salt and black pepper and whisk well.
- Add tomatoes, toss to coat and leave aside for 30 minutes.
- Arrange 6 tomatoes on one skewer and repeat with the rest of the tomatoes.
- Introduce them in your air fryer and cook at 360 degrees F for 6 minutes.
- In another bowl, mix 2 tablespoons vinegar with salt, pepper and 4 tablespoons oil and whisk well.
- Arrange tomato skewers on plates and serve with the dressing drizzled on top.
- Enjoy

Nutrition: calories 140, fat 1, fiber 1, carbs 2, protein 7

Delicious Portobello Mushrooms

Preparation time: 10 minutes Cooking time: 12 minutes Servings: 4

INGREDIENTS:

- ✓ 10 basil leaves
- ✓ 1 cup baby spinach
- ✓ 3 garlic cloves, chopped
- ✓ 1 cup almonds, roughly chopped
- ✓ 1 tablespoon parsley
- ✓ ¼ cup olive oil
- ✓ 8 cherry tomatoes, halved
- ✓ Salt and black pepper to the taste
- ✓ 4 Portobello mushrooms, stems removed and chopped

DIRECTIONS:

- In your food processor, mix basil with spinach, garlic, almonds, parsley, oil, salt, black pepper to the taste and mushroom stems and blend well.
- Stuff each mushroom with this mix, place them in your air fryer and cook at 350 degrees F for 12 minutes.
- Divide mushrooms on plates and serve.
- Enjoy!

Nutrition: calories 145, fat 3, fiber 2, carbs 6, protein 17

Mexican Peppers

Preparation time: 10 minutes Cooking time: 25 minutes Servings: 4

INGREDIENTS:

- ✓ 4 bell peppers, tops cut off and seeds removed ½ cup tomato juice
- ✓ 2 tablespoons jarred jalapenos, chopped
- ✓ 4 chicken breasts
- ✓ 1 cup tomatoes, chopped
- ✓ ¼ cup yellow onion, chopped
- ✓ ¼ cup green peppers, chopped
- ✓ 2 cups tomato sauce
- ✓ Salt and black pepper to the taste
- ✓ 2 teaspoons onion powder
- ✓ ½ teaspoon red pepper, crushed
- ✓ 1 teaspoon chili powder

- ✓ ½ teaspoons garlic powder
- ✓ 1 teaspoon cumin, ground

DIRECTIONS:

- In a pan that fits your air fryer, mix chicken breasts with tomato juice, jalapenos, tomatoes, onion, green peppers, salt, pepper, onion powder, red pepper, chili powder, garlic powder, oregano and cumin, stir well, introduce in your air fryer and cook at 350 degrees F for 15 minutes,
- Shred meat using 2 forks, stir, stuff bell peppers with this mix, place them in your air fryer and cook at 320 degrees F for 10 minutes more.
- Divide stuffed peppers on plates and serve.
- Enjoy!

Nutrition: calories 180, fat 4, fiber 3, carbs 7, protein 14

Peppers Stuffed With Beef

Preparation time: 10 minutes Cooking time: 55 minutes Servings: 4

INGREDIENTS:

- ✓ 1 pound beef, ground
- ✓ 1 teaspoon coriander, ground
- ✓ 1 onion, chopped
- ✓ 3 garlic cloves, minced
- ✓ 2 tablespoons olive oil
- ✓ 1 tablespoon ginger, grated
- ✓ ½ teaspoon cumin, ground
- ✓ ½ teaspoon turmeric powder
- ✓ 1 tablespoon hot curry powder
- ✓ Salt and black pepper to the taste
- ✓ 1 egg
- ✓ 4 bell peppers, cut into halves and seeds removed

  1/3 cup raisins
- ✓ 1/3 cup walnuts, chopped

DIRECTIONS:

- Heat up a pan with the oil over medium high heat, add onion, stir and cook for 4 minutes.
- Add garlic and beef, stir and cook for 10 minutes.
- Add coriander, ginger, cumin, curry powder, salt, pepper, turmeric, walnuts and raisins, stir take off heat and mix with the egg.
- Stuff pepper halves with this mix, introduce them in your air fryer and cook at 320 degrees F for 20 minutes.
- Divide among plates and serve.

- Enjoy!

Nutrition: calories 170, fat 4, fiber 3, carbs 7, protein 12

Stuffed Poblano Peppers

Preparation time: 10 minutes Cooking time: 15 minutes Servings: 4

INGREDIENTS:

- ✓ 2 teaspoons garlic, minced
- ✓ 1 white onion, chopped
- ✓ 10 poblano peppers, tops cut off and deseeded
- ✓ 1 tablespoon olive oil
- ✓ 8 ounces mushrooms, chopped
- ✓ Salt and black pepper to the taste
- ✓ ½ cup cilantro, chopped

DIRECTIONS:

- Heat up a pan with the oil over medium high heat, add onion and mushrooms, stir and cook for 5 minutes.
- Add garlic, cilantro, salt and black pepper, stir and cook for 2 minutes.
- Divide this mix into poblanos, introduce them in your air fryer and cook at 350 degrees F for 15 minutes.
- Divide among plates and serve.
- Enjoy!

Nutrition: calories 150, fat 3, fiber 2, carbs 7, protein 10

Stuffed Baby Peppers

Preparation time: 10 minutes Cooking time: 6 minutes Servings: 4

INGREDIENTS:

- ✓ 12 baby bell peppers, cut into halves lengthwise ¼ teaspoon red pepper flakes, crushed
- ✓ 1 pound shrimp, cooked, peeled and deveined
- ✓ 6 tablespoons jarred basil pesto
- ✓ Salt and black pepper to the taste
- ✓ 1 tablespoon lemon juice
- ✓ 1 tablespoon olive oil
- ✓ A handful parsley, chopped

DIRECTIONS:

- In a bowl, mix shrimp with pepper flakes, pesto, salt, black pepper, lemon juice, oil and parsley, whisk very well and stuff bell pepper halves with this mix.

- Place them in your air fryer and cook at 320 degrees F for 6 minutes,
- Arrange peppers on plates and serve.
- Enjoy!

Nutrition: calories 130, fat 2, fiber 1, carbs 3, protein 15

Eggplant and Garlic Sauce

Preparation time: 10 minutes Cooking time: 10 minutes Servings: 4

INGREDIENTS:

- ✓ **2 tablespoons olive oil**
- ✓ **2 garlic cloves, minced**
- ✓ **3 eggplants, halved and sliced**
- ✓ **1 red chili pepper, chopped**
- ✓ **1 green onion stalk, chopped**
- ✓ **1 tablespoon ginger, grated**
- ✓ **1 tablespoon soy sauce**
- ✓ **1 tablespoon balsamic vinegar**

DIRECTIONS:

- Heat up a pan that fits your air fryer with the oil over medium high heat, add eggplant slices and cook for 2 minutes.
- Add chili pepper, garlic, green onions, ginger, soy sauce and vinegar, introduce in your air fryer and cook at 320 degrees F for 7 minutes.
- Divide among plates and serve.
- Enjoy!

Nutrition: calories 130, fat 2, fiber 4, carbs 7, protein 9

Eggplant Hash

Preparation time: 20 minutes Cooking time: 10 minutes Servings: 4

INGREDIENTS:

- ✓ **1 eggplant, roughly chopped**
- ✓ **½ cup olive oil**
- ✓ **½ pound cherry tomatoes, halved**
- ✓ **1 teaspoon Tabasco sauce**
- ✓ **¼ cup basil, chopped**
- ✓ **¼ cup mint, chopped**
- ✓ **Salt and black pepper to the taste**

DIRECTIONS:

- Heat up a pan that fits your air fryer with half of the oil over medium high heat, add eggplant pieces, cook for 3 minutes, flip, cook them for 3 minutes more and transfer to a bowl.

- Heat up the same pan with the rest of the oil over medium high heat, add tomatoes, stir and cook for 1-2 minutes.
- Return eggplant pieces to the pan, add salt, black pepper, basil, mint and Tabasco sauce, introduce in your air fryer and cook at 320 degrees F for 6 minutes.
- Divide among plates and serve.
- Enjoy!

Nutrition: calories 120, fat 1, fiber 4, carbs 8, protein 15

Sweet Potato es Mix

Preparation time: 10 minutes Cooking time: 15 minutes Servings: 4

INGREDIENTS:

- ✓ **3 sweet potatoes, cubed**
- ✓ **4 tablespoons olive oil**
- ✓ **4 garlic cloves, minced**
- ✓ **½ pound bacon, chopped**
- ✓ **Juice from 1 lime**
- ✓ **Salt and black pepper to the taste**
- ✓ **2 tablespoons balsamic vinegar**
- ✓ **A handful dill, chopped**
- ✓ **2 green onions, chopped**
- ✓ **A pinch of cinnamon powder**
- ✓ **A pinch of red pepper flakes**

DIRECTIONS:

- Arrange bacon and sweet potatoes in your air fryer's basket, add garlic and half of the oil, toss well and cook at 350 degrees F and bake for 15 minutes.
- Meanwhile, in a bowl, mix vinegar with lime juice, olive oil, green onions, pepper flakes, dill, salt, pepper and cinnamon and whisk.
- Transfer bacon and sweet potatoes to a salad bowl, add salad dressing, toss well and serve right away.
- Enjoy!

Nutrition: calories 170, fat 3, fiber 2, carbs 5, protein 12

Greek Potato Mix

Preparation time: 10 minutes Cooking time: 20 minutes Servings: 2

INGREDIENTS:

- ✓ **2 medium potatoes, cut into wedges**
- ✓ **1 yellow onion, chopped**
- ✓ **2 tablespoons butter**

167

- ✓ **1 small carrot, roughly chopped**
- ✓ **1 and ½ tablespoon flour**
- ✓ **1 bay leaf**
- ✓ **½ cup chicken stock**
- ✓ **2 tablespoons Greek yogurt**
- ✓ **Salt and black pepper to the taste**

DIRECTIONS:

- ⏱ Heat up a pan that fits your air fryer with the butter over medium high heat, add onion and carrot, stir and cook for 3-4 minutes.
- ⏱ Add potatoes, flour, chicken stock, salt, pepper and bay leaf, stir, introduce in your air fryer and cook at 320 degrees F for 16 minutes.
- ⏱ Add Greek yogurt, toss, divide among plates and serve.
- ⏱ Enjoy!

Nutrition: calories 198, fat 3, fiber 2, carbs 6, protein 8

Broccoli Hash

Preparation time: 30 minutes Cooking time: 8 minutes Servings: 2

INGREDIENTS:

- ✓ **10 ounces mushrooms, halved**
- ✓ **1 broccoli head, florets separated**
- ✓ **1 garlic clove, minced**
- ✓ **1 tablespoon balsamic vinegar**
- ✓ **1 yellow onion, chopped**
- ✓ **1 tablespoon olive oil**
- ✓ **Salt and black pepper**
- ✓ **1 teaspoon basil, dried**
- ✓ **1 avocado, peeled and pitted**
- ✓ **A pinch of red pepper flakes**

DIRECTIONS:

- ⏱ In a bowl, mix mushrooms with broccoli, onion, garlic and avocado.
- ⏱ In another bowl, mix vinegar, oil, salt, pepper and basil and whisk well.
- ⏱ Pour this over veggies, toss to coat, leave aside for 30 minutes, transfer to your air fryer's basket and cook at 350 degrees F for 8 minutes,
- ⏱ Divide among plates and serve with pepper flakes on top.
- ⏱ Enjoy!

Nutrition: calories 182, fat 3, fiber 3, carbs 5, protein 8

Air Fried Asparagus

Preparation time: 10 minutes Cooking time: 15 minutes Servings: 4

INGREDIENTS:

- ✓ **2 pounds fresh asparagus, trimmed**
- ✓ **¼ cup olive oil**
- ✓ **Salt and black pepper to the taste**
- ✓ **1 teaspoon lemon zest**
- ✓ **4 garlic cloves, minced**
- ✓ **½ teaspoon oregano, dried**
- ✓ **¼ teaspoon red pepper flakes**
- ✓ **4 ounces feta cheese, crumbled**
- ✓ **2 tablespoons parsley, finely chopped**
- ✓ **Juice from 1 lemon**

DIRECTIONS:

- ⏱ In a bowl, mix oil with lemon zest, garlic, pepper flakes and oregano and whisk.
- ⏱ Add asparagus, cheese, salt and pepper, toss, transfer to your air fryer's basket and cook at 350 degrees F for 8 minutes.
- ⏱ Divide asparagus on plates, drizzle lemon juice and sprinkle parsley on top and serve.
- ⏱ Enjoy!

Nutrition: calories 162, fat 13, fiber 5, carbs 12, protein 8

Stuffed Eggplants

Preparation time: 10 minutes Cooking time: 30 minutes Servings: 4

INGREDIENTS:

- ✓ **4 small eggplants, halved lengthwise**
- ✓ **Salt and black pepper to the taste**
- ✓ **10 tablespoons olive oil**
- ✓ **2 and ½ pounds tomatoes, cut into halves and grated**
- ✓ **1 green bell pepper, chopped**
- ✓ **1 yellow onion, chopped**
- ✓ **1 tablespoon garlic, minced**
- ✓ **½ cup cauliflower, chopped**
- ✓ **1 teaspoon oregano, chopped**
- ✓ **½ cup parsley, chopped**

- ✓ **3 ounces feta cheese, crumbled**

DIRECTIONS:

- Season eggplants with salt, pepper and 4 tablespoons oil, toss, put them in your air fryer and cook at 350 degrees F for 16 minutes.
- Meanwhile, heat up a pan with 3 tablespoons oil over medium high heat, add onion, stir and cook for 5 minutes.
- Add bell pepper, garlic and cauliflower, stir, cook for 5 minutes, take off heat, add parsley, tomato, salt, pepper, oregano and cheese and whisk everything.
- Stuff eggplants with the veggie mix, drizzle the rest of the oil over them, put them in your air fryer and cook at 350 degrees F for 6 minutes more.
- Divide among plates and serve right away.
- Enjoy!

Nutrition: calories 240, fat 4, fiber, 2, carbs 19, protein 2

Green Beans and Parmesan

Preparation time: 10 minutes Cooking time: 8 minutes Servings: 4

INGREDIENTS:

- ✓ **12 ounces green beans**
- ✓ **2 teaspoons garlic, minced**
- ✓ **2 tablespoons olive oil**
- ✓ **Salt and black pepper to the taste**
- ✓ **1 egg, whisked**
- ✓ **1/3 cup parmesan, grated**

DIRECTIONS:

- In a bowl, mix oil with salt, pepper, garlic and egg and whisk well.
- Add green beans to this mix, toss well and sprinkle parmesan all over.
- Transfer green beans to your air fryer and cook them at 390 degrees F for 8 minutes.
- Divide green beans on plates and serve them right away.
- Enjoy!

Nutrition: calories 120, fat 8, fiber 2, carbs 7, protein 4

Delicious Creamy Green Beans

Preparation time: 10 minutes Cooking time: 15 minutes Servings: 4

INGREDIENTS:

- ✓ **½ cup heavy cream**
- ✓ **1 cup mozzarella, shredded**
- ✓ **2/3 cup parmesan, grated**

- ✓ **Salt and black pepper to the taste**
- ✓ **2 pounds green beans**
- ✓ **2 teaspoons lemon zest, grated**
- ✓ **A pinch of red pepper flakes**

DIRECTIONS:

- Put the beans in a dish that fits your air fryer, add heavy cream, salt, pepper, lemon zest, pepper flakes, mozzarella and parmesan, toss, introduce in your air fryer and cook at 350 degrees F for 15 minutes.
- Divide among plates and serve right away.
- Enjoy!

Nutrition: calories 231, fat 6, fiber 7, carbs 8, protein 5

Green Beans and Tomatoes

Preparation time: 10 minutes Cooking time: 15 minutes Servings: 4

INGREDIENTS:

- ✓ **1 pint cherry tomatoes**
- ✓ **1 pound green beans**
- ✓ **2 tablespoons olive oil**
- ✓ **Salt and black pepper to the taste**

DIRECTIONS:

- In a bowl, mix cherry tomatoes with green beans, olive oil, salt and pepper, toss, transfer to your air fryer and cook at 400 degrees F for 15 minutes.
- Divide among plates and serve right away.
- Enjoy!

Nutrition: calories 162, fat 6, fiber 5, carbs 8, protein 9

Easy Green Beans and Potatoes

Preparation time: 10 minutes Cooking time: 15 minutes Servings: 5

INGREDIENTS:

- ✓ **2 pounds green beans**
- ✓ **6 new potatoes, halved**
- ✓ **Salt and black pepper to the taste**
- ✓ **A drizzle of olive oil**
- ✓ **6 bacon slices, cooked and chopped**

DIRECTIONS:

- In a bowl, mix green beans with potatoes, salt, pepper and oil, toss, transfer to your air fryer and cook at 390 degrees F for 15 minutes.

- Divide among plates and serve with bacon sprinkled on top. Enjoy!

Nutrition: calories 374, fat 15, fiber 12, carbs 28, protein 12

Flavored Green Beans

Preparation time: 10 minutes Cooking time: 15 minutes Servings: 4

INGREDIENTS:

- ✓ **1 pound red potatoes, cut into wedges**
- ✓ **1 pound green beans**
- ✓ **2 garlic cloves, minced**
- ✓ **2 tablespoons olive oil**
- ✓ **Salt and black pepper to the taste**
- ✓ **½ teaspoon oregano, dried**

DIRECTIONS:

- In a pan that fits your air fryer, combine potatoes with green beans, garlic, oil, salt, pepper and oregano, toss, introduce in your air fryer and cook at 380 degrees F for 15 minutes.
- Divide among plates and serve.
- Enjoy!

Nutrition: calories 211, fat 6, fiber 7, carbs 8, protein 5

Potatoes and Tomatoes Mix

Preparation time: 10 minutes Cooking time: 16 minutes Servings: 4

INGREDIENTS:

- ✓ **1 and ½ pounds red potatoes, quartered**
- ✓ **2 tablespoons olive oil**
- ✓ **1 pint cherry tomatoes**
- ✓ **1 teaspoon sweet paprika**
- ✓ **1 tablespoons rosemary, chopped**
- ✓ **Salt and black pepper to the taste**
- ✓ **3 garlic cloves, minced**

DIRECTIONS:

- In a bowl, mix potatoes with tomatoes, oil, paprika, rosemary, garlic, salt and pepper, toss, transfer to your air fryer and cook at 380 degrees F for 16 minutes.
- Divide among plates and serve.
- Enjoy!

Nutrition: calories 192, fat 4, fiber 4, carbs 30, protein 3

Balsamic Potatoes

Preparation time: 10 minutes Cooking time: 20 minutes Servings: 4

INGREDIENTS:

- ✓ **1 and ½ pounds baby potatoes, halved**
- ✓ **2 garlic cloves, chopped**
- ✓ **2 red onions, chopped**
- ✓ **9 ounces cherry tomatoes**
- ✓ **3 tablespoons olive oil**
- ✓ **1 and ½ tablespoons balsamic vinegar**
- ✓ **2 thyme springs, chopped**
- ✓ **Salt and black pepper to the taste**

DIRECTIONS:

- In your food processor, mix garlic with onions, oil, vinegar, thyme, salt and pepper and pulse really well.
- In a bowl, mix potatoes with tomatoes and balsamic marinade, toss well, transfer to your air fryer and cook at 380 degrees F for 20 minutes.
- Divide among plates and serve.
- Enjoy!

Nutrition: calories 301, fat 6, fiber 8, carbs 18, protein 6

Potatoes and Special Tomato Sauce

Preparation time: 10 minutes Cooking time: 16 minutes Servings: 4

INGREDIENTS:

- ✓ **2 pounds potatoes, cubed**
- ✓ **4 garlic cloves, minced**
- ✓ **1 yellow onion, chopped**
- ✓ **1 cup tomato sauce**
- ✓ **2 tablespoons basil, chopped**
- ✓ **2 tablespoons olive oil**
- ✓ **½ teaspoon oregano, dried**
- ✓ **½ teaspoon parsley, dried**

DIRECTIONS:

- Heat up a pan that fits your air fryer with the oil over medium heat, add onion, stir and cook for 1-2 minutes.
- Add garlic, potatoes, parsley, tomato sauce and oregano, stir, introduce in your air fryer and cook at 370 degrees F and cook for 16 minutes.

- Add basil, toss everything, divide among plates and serve.
- Enjoy!

Nutrition: calories 211, fat 6, fiber 8, carbs 14, protein 6

Air Fryer Dessert Recipes

Mini Lava Cakes

Preparation time: 10 minutes Cooking time: 20 minutes Servings: 3

INGREDIENTS:

- ✓ **1 egg**
- ✓ **4 tablespoons sugar**
- ✓ **2 tablespoons olive oil**
- ✓ **4 tablespoons milk**
- ✓ **4 tablespoons flour**
- ✓ **1 tablespoon cocoa powder**
- ✓ **½ teaspoon baking powder**
- ✓ **½ teaspoon orange zest**

DIRECTIONS:

- ⏲ In a bowl, mix egg with sugar, oil, milk, flour, salt, cocoa powder, baking powder and orange zest, stir very well and pour this into greased ramekins.
- ⏲ Add ramekins to your air fryer and cook at 320 degrees F for 20 minutes.
- ⏲ Serve lava cakes warm.
- ⏲ Enjoy!

Nutrition: calories 201, fat 7, fiber 8, carbs 23, protein 4

Crispy Apples

Preparation time: 10 minutes Cooking time: 10 minutes Servings: 4

INGREDIENTS:

- ✓ **2 teaspoons cinnamon powder**
- ✓ **5 apples, cored and cut into chunks**
- ✓ **½ teaspoon nutmeg powder**
- ✓ **1 tablespoon maple syrup**
- ✓ **½ cup water**
- ✓ **4 tablespoons butter**
- ✓ **¼ cup flour**
- ✓ **¾ cup old fashioned rolled oats**
- ✓ **¼ cup brown sugar**

DIRECTIONS:

- ⏲ Put the apples in a pan that fits your air fryer, add cinnamon, nutmeg, maple syrup and water.
- ⏲ In a bowl, mix butter with oats, sugar, salt and flour, stir, drop spoonfuls of this mix on top of apples, introduce in your air fryer and cook at 350 degrees F for 10 minutes.
- ⏲ Serve warm.

⏲ Enjoy!
Nutrition: calories 200, fat 6, fiber 8, carbs 29, protein 12

Carrot Cake

Preparation time: 10 minutes Cooking time: 45 minutes Servings: 6

INGREDIENTS:

- ✓ **5 ounces flour**
- ✓ **¾ teaspoon baking powder**
- ✓ **½ teaspoon baking soda**
- ✓ **½ teaspoon cinnamon powder**
- ✓ **¼ teaspoon nutmeg, ground**
- ✓ **½ teaspoon allspice**
- ✓ **1 egg**
- ✓ **3 tablespoons yogurt**
- ✓ **½ cup sugar**
- ✓ **¼ cup pineapple juice**
- ✓ **4 tablespoons sunflower oil**
- ✓ **1/3 cup carrots, grated**
- ✓ **1/3 cup pecans, toasted and chopped**
- ✓ **1/3 cup coconut flakes, shredded**
- ✓ **Cooking spray**

DIRECTIONS:

- ⏲ In a bowl, mix flour with baking soda and powder, salt, allspice, cinnamon and nutmeg and stir.
- ⏲ In another bowl, mix egg with yogurt, sugar, pineapple juice, oil, carrots, pecans and coconut flakes and stir well.
- ⏲ Combine the two mixtures and stir well, pour this into a spring form pan that fits your air fryer which you've greased with some cooking spray, transfer to your air fryer and cook on 320 degrees F for 45 minutes.
- ⏲ Leave cake to cool down, then cut and serve it.
- ⏲ Enjoy!

Nutrition: calories 200, fat 6, fiber 20, carbs 22, protein 4

Ginger Cheesecake

Preparation time: 2 hours and 10 minutes Cooking time: 20 minutes Servings: 6

INGREDIENTS:

- ✓ **2 teaspoons butter, melted**
- ✓ **½ cup ginger cookies, crumbled**

- ✓ **16 ounces cream cheese, soft**
- ✓ **2 eggs**
- ✓ **½ cup sugar**
- ✓ **1 teaspoon rum**
- ✓ **½ teaspoon vanilla extract**
- ✓ **½ teaspoon nutmeg, ground**

DIRECTIONS:

- ⏱ Grease a pan with the butter and spread cookie crumbs on the bottom.
- ⏱ In a bowl, beat cream cheese with nutmeg, vanilla, rum and eggs, whisk well and spread over the cookie crumbs.
- ⏱ Introduce in your air fryer and cook at 340 degrees F for 20 minutes.
- ⏱ Leave cheesecake to cool down and keep in the fridge for 2 hours before slicing and serving it.
- ⏱ Enjoy!

Nutrition: calories 412, fat 12, fiber 6, carbs 20, protein 6

Strawberry Pie

Preparation time: 10 minutes Cooking time: 20 minutes Servings: 12

INGREDIENTS:

For the crust:

- ✓ **1 cup coconut, shredded**
- ✓ **1 cup sunflower seeds**
- ✓ **¼ cup butter**

For the filling:

- ✓ **1 teaspoon gelatin**
- ✓ **8 ounces cream cheese**
- ✓ **4 ounces strawberries**
- ✓ **2 tablespoons water**
- ✓ **½ tablespoon lemon juice**
- ✓ **¼ teaspoon stevia**
- ✓ **½ cup heavy cream**
- ✓ **8 ounces strawberries, chopped for serving**

DIRECTIONS:

- ⏱ In your food processor, mix sunflower seeds with coconut, a pinch of salt and butter, pulse and press this on the bottom of a cake pan that fits your air fryer.

- ⏱ Heat up a pan with the water over medium heat, add gelatin, stir until it dissolves, leave aside to cool down, add this to your food processor, mix with 4 ounces strawberries, cream cheese, lemon juice and stevia and blend well.
- ⏱ Add heavy cream, stir well and spread this over crust.
- ⏱ Top with 8 ounces strawberries, introduce in your air fryer and cook at 330 degrees F for 15 minutes.
- ⏱ Keep in the fridge until you serve it.
- ⏱ Enjoy!

Nutrition: calories 234, fat 23, fiber 2, carbs 6, protein 7

Coffee Cheesecakes

Preparation time: 10 minutes Cooking time: 20 minutes Servings: 6

INGREDIENTS:

For the cheesecakes:

- ✓ **2 tablespoons butter**
- ✓ **8 ounces cream cheese**
- ✓ **3 tablespoons coffee**
- ✓ **3 eggs**
- ✓ **1/3 cup sugar**
- ✓ **1 tablespoon caramel syrup**

For the frosting:

- ✓ **3 tablespoons caramel syrup**
- ✓ **3 tablespoons butter**
- ✓ **8 ounces mascarpone cheese, soft**
- ✓ **2 tablespoons sugar**

DIRECTIONS:

- ⏱ In your blender, mix cream cheese with eggs, 2 tablespoons butter, coffee, 1 tablespoon caramel syrup and 1/3 cup sugar and pulse very well, spoon into a cupcakes pan that fits your air fryer, introduce in the fryer and cook at 320 degrees F and bake for 20 minutes.
- ⏱ Leave aside to cool down and then keep in the freezer for 3 hours.
- ⏱ Meanwhile, in a bowl, mix 3 tablespoons butter with 3 tablespoons caramel syrup, 2 tablespoons sugar and mascarpone, blend well, spoon this over cheesecakes and serve them.
- ⏱ Enjoy!

Nutrition: calories 254, fat 23, fiber 0, carbs 21, protein 5

Cocoa Cookies

Preparation time: 10 minutes Cooking time: 14 minutes Servings: 12

INGREDIENTS:

- ✓ **6 ounces coconut oil, melted**
- ✓ **6 eggs**
- ✓ **3 ounces cocoa powder**
- ✓ **2 teaspoons vanilla**
- ✓ **½ teaspoon baking powder**
- ✓ **4 ounces cream cheese**
- ✓ **5 tablespoons sugar**

DIRECTIONS:

- In a blender, mix eggs with coconut oil, cocoa powder, baking powder, vanilla, cream cheese and swerve and stir using a mixer.
- Pour this into a lined baking dish that fits your air fryer, introduce in the fryer at 320 degrees F and bake for 14 minutes.
- Slice cookie sheet into rectangles and serve.
- Enjoy!

Nutrition: calories 178, fat 14, fiber 2, carbs 3, protein 5

Special Brownies

Preparation time: 10 minutes Cooking time: 17 minutes Servings: 4

INGREDIENTS:

- ✓ **1 egg**
- ✓ **1/3 cup cocoa powder**
- ✓ **1/3 cup sugar**
- ✓ **7 tablespoons butter**
- ✓ **½ teaspoon vanilla extract**
- ✓ **¼ cup white flour**
- ✓ **¼ cup walnuts, chopped**
- ✓ **½ teaspoon baking powder**
- ✓ **1 tablespoon peanut butter**

DIRECTIONS:

- Heat up a pan with 6 tablespoons butter and the sugar over medium heat, stir, cook for 5 minutes, transfer this to a bowl, add salt, vanilla extract, cocoa powder, egg, baking powder, walnuts and flour, stir the whole thing really well and pour into a pan that fits your air fryer.

- In a bowl, mix 1 tablespoon butter with peanut butter, heat up in your microwave for a few seconds, stir well and drizzle this over brownies mix.
- Introduce in your air fryer and bake at 320 degrees F and bake for 17 minutes.
- Leave brownies to cool down, cut and serve.
- Enjoy!

Nutrition: calories 223, fat 32, fiber 1, carbs 3, protein 6

Blueberry Scones

Preparation time: 10 minutes Cooking time: 10 minutes Servings: 10

INGREDIENTS:

- ✓ **1 cup white flour**
- ✓ **1 cup blueberries**
- ✓ **2 eggs**
- ✓ **½ cup heavy cream**
- ✓ **½ cup butter**
- ✓ **5 tablespoons sugar**
- ✓ **2 teaspoons vanilla extract**
- ✓ **2 teaspoons baking powder**

DIRECTIONS:

- In a bowl, mix flour, salt, baking powder and blueberries and stir.
- In another bowl, mix heavy cream with butter, vanilla extract, sugar and eggs and stir well.
- Combine the 2 mixtures, knead until you obtain your dough, shape 10 triangles from this mix, place them on a lined baking sheet that fits your air fryer and cook them at 320 degrees F for 10 minutes.
- Serve them cold.
- Enjoy!

Nutrition: calories 130, fat 2, fiber 2, carbs 4, protein 3

Chocolate Cookies

Preparation time: 10 minutes Cooking time: 25 minutes Servings: 12

INGREDIENTS:

- ✓ **1 teaspoon vanilla extract**
- ✓ **½ cup butter**
- ✓ **1 egg**
- ✓ **4 tablespoons sugar**
- ✓ **2 cups flour**
- ✓ **½ cup unsweetened chocolate chips**

DIRECTIONS:

- Heat up a pan with the butter over medium heat, stir and cook for 1 minute.
- In a bowl, mix egg with vanilla extract and sugar and stir well.
- Add melted butter, flour and half of the chocolate chips and stir everything.
- Transfer this to a pan that fits your air fryer, spread the rest of the chocolate chips on top, introduce in the fryer at 330 degrees F and bake for 25 minutes.
- Slice when it's cold and serve.
- Enjoy!

Nutrition: calories 230, fat 12, fiber 2, carbs 4, protein 5

Tasty Orange Cake

Preparation time: 10 minutes Cooking time: 32 minutes Servings: 12

INGREDIENTS:

- ✓ 6 eggs
- ✓ 1 orange, peeled and cut into quarters
- ✓ 1 teaspoon vanilla extract
- ✓ 1 teaspoon baking powder
- ✓ 9 ounces flour
- ✓ 2 ounces sugar+ 2 tablespoons
- ✓ 2 tablespoons orange zest
- ✓ 4 ounces cream cheese
- ✓ 4 ounces yogurt

DIRECTIONS:

- In your food processor, pulse orange very well.
- Add flour, 2 tablespoons sugar, eggs, baking powder, vanilla extract and pulse well again.
- Transfer this into 2 spring form pans, introduce each in your fryer and cook at 330 degrees F for 16 minutes.
- Meanwhile, in a bowl, mix cream cheese with orange zest, yogurt and the rest of the sugar and stir well.
- Place one cake layer on a plate, add half of the cream cheese mix, add the other cake layer and top with the rest of the cream cheese mix.
- Spread it well, slice and serve.
- Enjoy!

Nutrition: calories 200, fat 13, fiber 2, carbs 9, protein 8

Macaroons

Preparation time: 10 minutes Cooking time: 8 minutes Servings: 20

INGREDIENTS:

- ✓ 2 tablespoons sugar
- ✓ 4 egg whites
- ✓ 2 cup coconut, shredded
- ✓ 1 teaspoon vanilla extract

DIRECTIONS:

- In a bowl, mix egg whites with stevia and beat using your mixer.
- Add coconut and vanilla extract, whisk again, shape small balls out of this mix, introduce them in your air fryer and cook at 340 degrees F for 8 minutes.
- Serve macaroons cold.
- Enjoy!

Nutrition: calories 55, fat 6, fiber 1, carbs 2, protein 1

Lime Cheesecake

Preparation time: 4 hours and 10 minutes Cooking time: 4 minutes Servings: 10

INGREDIENTS:

- ✓ 2 tablespoons butter, melted
- ✓ 2 teaspoons sugar
- ✓ 4 ounces flour
- ✓ ¼ cup coconut, shredded

For the filling:

- ✓ 1 pound cream cheese
- ✓ Zest from 1 lime, grated
- ✓ Juice form 1 lime
- ✓ 2 cups hot water
- ✓ 2 sachets lime jelly

DIRECTIONS:

- In a bowl, mix coconut with flour, butter and sugar, stir well and press this on the bottom of a pan that fits your air fryer.
- Meanwhile, put the hot water in a bowl, add jelly sachets and stir until it dissolves.
- Put cream cheese in a bowl, add jelly, lime juice and zest and whisk really well.
- Add this over the crust, spread, introduce in the air fryer and cook at 300 degrees F for 4 minutes.
- Keep in the fridge for 4 hours before serving.
- Enjoy!

Nutrition: calories 260, fat 23, fiber 2, carbs 5, protein 7

Easy Granola

Preparation time: 10 minutes Cooking time: 35 minutes Servings: 4

INGREDIENTS:

- ✓ **1 cup coconut, shredded**
- ✓ **½ cup almonds**
- ✓ **½ cup pecans, chopped**
- ✓ **2 tablespoons sugar**
- ✓ **½ cup pumpkin seeds**
- ✓ **½ cup sunflower seeds**
- ✓ **2 tablespoons sunflower oil**
- ✓ **1 teaspoon nutmeg, ground**
- ✓ **1 teaspoon apple pie spice mix**

DIRECTIONS:

- ⏱ In a bowl, mix almonds and pecans with pumpkin seeds, sunflower seeds, coconut, nutmeg and apple pie spice mix and stir well.
- ⏱ Heat up a pan with the oil over medium heat, add sugar and stir well.
- ⏱ Pour this over nuts and coconut mix and stir well.
- ⏱ Spread this on a lined baking sheet that fits your air fryer, introduce in your air fryer and cook at 300 degrees F and bake for 25 minutes.
- ⏱ Leave your granola to cool down, cut and serve.
- ⏱ Enjoy!

Nutrition: calories 322, fat 7, fiber 8, carbs 12, protein 7

Strawberry Cobbler

Preparation time: 10 minutes Cooking time: 25 minutes Servings: 6

INGREDIENTS:

- ✓ **¾ cup sugar**
- ✓ **6 cups strawberries, halved**
- ✓ **1/8 teaspoon baking powder**
- ✓ **1 tablespoon lemon juice**
- ✓ **½ cup flour**
- ✓ **A pinch of baking soda**
- ✓ **½ cup water**
- ✓ **3 and ½ tablespoon olive oil**
- ✓ **Cooking spray**

DIRECTIONS:

- ⏱ In a bowl, mix strawberries with half of sugar, sprinkle some flour, add lemon juice, whisk and pour

into the baking dish that fits your air fryer and greased with cooking spray

- ⏱ In another bowl, mix flour with the rest of the sugar, baking powder and soda and stir well.
- ⏱ Add the olive oil and mix until the whole thing with your hands.
- ⏱ Add ½ cup water and spread over strawberries.
- ⏱ Introduce in the fryer at 355 degrees F and bake for 25 minutes.
- ⏱ Leave cobbler aside to cool down, slice and serve.
- ⏱ Enjoy

Nutrition: calories 221, fat 3, fiber 3, carbs 6, protein 9

Black Tea Cake

Preparation time: 10 minutes Cooking time: 35 minutes Servings: 12

INGREDIENTS:

- ✓ **6 tablespoons black tea powder**
- ✓ **2 cups milk**
- ✓ **½ cup butter**
- ✓ **2 cups sugar**
- ✓ **4 eggs**
- ✓ **2 teaspoons vanilla extract**
- ✓ **½ cup olive oil**
- ✓ **3 and ½ cups flour**
- ✓ **1 teaspoon baking soda**
- ✓ **3 teaspoons baking powder**

For the cream:

- ✓ **6 tablespoons honey**
- ✓ **4 cups sugar**
- ✓ **1 cup butter, soft**

DIRECTIONS:

- ⏱ Put the milk in a pot, heat up over medium heat, add tea, stir well, take off heat and leave aside to cool down.
- ⏱ In a bowl, mix ½ cup butter with 2 cups sugar, eggs, vegetable oil, vanilla extract, baking powder, baking soda and 3 and ½ cups flour and stir everything really well.
- ⏱ Pour this into 2 greased round pans, introduce each in the fryer at 330 degrees F and bake for 25 minutes.
- ⏱ In a bowl, mix 1 cup butter with honey and 4 cups sugar and stir really well.

- ⏱ Arrange one cake on a platter, spread the cream all over, top with the other cake and keep in the fridge until you serve it.
- ⏱ Enjoy!

Nutrition: calories 200, fat 4, fiber 4, carbs 6, protein 2

Plum Cake

Preparation time: 1 hour and 20 minutes Cooking time: 36 minutes

Servings: 8

INGREDIENTS:

- ✓ 7 ounces flour
- ✓ 1 package dried yeast
- ✓ 1 ounce butter, soft
- ✓ 1 egg, whisked
- ✓ 5 tablespoons sugar
- ✓ 3 ounces warm milk
- ✓ 1 and ¾ pounds plums, pitted and cut into quarters

  Zest from 1 lemon, grated
- ✓ 1 ounce almond flakes

DIRECTIONS:

- ⏱ In a bowl, mix yeast with butter, flour and 3 tablespoons sugar and stir well.
- ⏱ Add milk and egg and whisk for 4 minutes until your obtain a dough.
- ⏱ Arrange the dough in a spring form pan that fits your air fryer and which you've greased with some butter, cover and leave aside for 1 hour.
- ⏱ Arrange plumps on top of the butter, sprinkle the rest of the sugar, introduce in your air fryer at 350 degrees F, bake for 36 minutes, cool down, sprinkle almond flakes and lemon zest on top, slice and serve.
- ⏱ Enjoy!

Nutrition: calories 192, fat 4, fiber 2, carbs 6, protein 7

Lentils Cookies

Preparation time: 10 minutes Cooking time: 25 minutes Servings:

36

INGREDIENTS:

- ✓ 1 cup water
- ✓ 1 cup canned lentils, drained and mashed
- ✓ 1 cup white flour
- ✓ 1 teaspoon cinnamon powder
- ✓ 1 cup whole wheat flour

- ✓ 1 teaspoon baking powder
- ✓ ½ teaspoon nutmeg, ground
- ✓ 1 cup butter, soft
- ✓ ½ cup brown sugar
- ✓ ½ cup white sugar
- ✓ 1 egg
- ✓ 2 teaspoons almond extract
- ✓ 1 cup raisins
- ✓ 1 cup rolled oats
- ✓ 1 cup coconut, unsweetened and shredded

DIRECTIONS:

- ⏱ In a bowl, mix white and whole wheat flour with salt, cinnamon, baking powder and nutmeg and stir.
- ⏱ In a bowl, mix butter with white and brown sugar and stir using your kitchen mixer for 2 minutes.
- ⏱ Add egg, almond extract, lentils mix, flour mix, oats, raisins and coconut and stir everything well.
- ⏱ Scoop tablespoons of dough on a lined baking sheet that fits your air fryer, introduce them in the fryer and cook at 350 degrees F for 15 minutes.
- ⏱ Arrange cookies on a serving platter and serve
- ⏱ Enjoy!

Nutrition: calories 154, fat 2, fiber 2, carbs 4, protein 7

Lentils and Dates Brownies

Preparation time: 10 minutes Cooking time: 15 minutes Servings: 8

INGREDIENTS:

- ✓ 28 ounces canned lentils, rinsed and drained
- ✓ 12 dates
- ✓ 1 tablespoon honey
- ✓ 1 banana, peeled and chopped
- ✓ ½ teaspoon baking soda
- ✓ 4 tablespoons almond butter
- ✓ 2 tablespoons cocoa powder

DIRECTIONS:

- ⏱ In your food processor, mix lentils with butter, banana, cocoa, baking soda and honey and blend really well.
- ⏱ Add dates, pulse a few more times, pour this into a greased pan that fits your air fryer, spread evenly, introduce in the fryer at 360 degrees F and bake for 15 minutes.
- ⏱ Take brownies mix out of the oven, cut, arrange on a platter and serve. Enjoy!

Maple Cupcakes

Preparation time: 10 minutes Cooking time: 20 minutes Servings: 4

INGREDIENTS:

- ✓ 4 tablespoons butter
- ✓ 4 eggs
- ✓ ½ cup pure applesauce
- ✓ 2 teaspoons cinnamon powder
- ✓ 1 teaspoon vanilla extract
- ✓ ½ apple, cored and chopped
- ✓ 4 teaspoons maple syrup
- ✓ ¾ cup white flour
- ✓ ½ teaspoon baking powder

DIRECTIONS:

- Heat up a pan with the butter over medium heat, add applesauce, vanilla, eggs and maple syrup, stir, take off heat and leave aside to cool down.
- Add flour, cinnamon, baking powder and apples, whisk, pour in a cupcake pan, introduce in your air fryer at 350 degrees F and bake for 20 minutes.
- Leave cupcakes them to cool down, transfer to a platter and serve them. Enjoy!

Nutrition: calories 150, fat 3, fiber 1, carbs 5, protein 4

Coconut Pineapples & Yoghurt Dip

Preparation: 15 minutes Cooking time: 10 minutes Servings: 4

INGREDIENTS:

- ✓ 2 ounces of dried coconut flakes
- ✓ 1 sprig of mint, finely chopped
- ✓ ½ medium size pineapple
- ✓ 8 ounces of vanilla yogurt

DIRECTIONS:

- Heat the Air Fryer to 390°F.
- Slice the pineapple into chips (sticks) and dip them into the diced coconut to allow the coconut stick to them.
- Place the sticks in the fryer basket and cook for about 10 minutes.
- Stir the mint leaves into the vanilla yogurt. Serve with pineapple sticks.

Stuffed Apple Bake

Preparation: 5 minutes Cooking time: 10 minutes Servings: 4

INGREDIENTS:

- ✓ 4 medium sized apples, cored
- ✓ 6 teaspoons of sugar
- ✓ 4 tablespoons of breadcrumbs
- ✓ 2 tablespoons of butter
- ✓ 1 teaspoon of mixed spice
- ✓ 1½ ounce of mixed seeds Zest of
- ✓ 1 lemon

DIRECTIONS:

- Score the skin of the apples with a knife around the circumference to prevent them from dividing during baking.
- Mix the sugar, breadcrumbs, butter, zest, spice and mixed seeds in a bowl and stuff the apples with the mixture.
- Heat the Air Fryer at 356°F and bake the stuffed apples for 10 minutes.

Sesame And Poppy Cheese Cookies

Preparation: 18 minutes Cooking time: 12 minutes Servings: 10

INGREDIENTS:

- ✓ 7 tablespoons of cream
- ✓ ¾ cup of grated Gruyere cheese
- ✓ 3 teaspoons of milk
- ✓ 2 egg yolks, beaten
- ✓ 1 teaspoon of paprika powder
- ✓ 2 ounces of butter
- ✓ 2/3 cup of flour
- ✓ ½ teaspoon of baking powder
- ✓ ½ teaspoon salt Poppy seeds and sesame seeds for garnishing

DIRECTIONS:

- Mix the cheese, butter, salt, cream, and paprika in a bowl until smooth.
- Mix the baking powder and flour together and sieve over a flat surface. Place the cheese-butter mixture on the flour and knead together to form a soft dough. Roll out the dough until thin and then cut into cookie shapes.

- Mix the milk and eggs and use to coat the cookies using a brush. Sprinkle the poppy and sesame seed on top of the cookies.
- Place in the Air Fryer basket and bake at 340°F for 12 minutes.

Banana And Chocolate Muffins

Preparation: 10 minutes Cooking time: 25 minutes Servings: 6-8

INGREDIENTS:

- ✓ 3 medium sized bananas, mashed
- ✓ 4 tablespoons of cocoa
- ✓ ¾ cup of wheat flour
- ✓ ¾ cup of chocolate chips
- ✓ ¾ cup of plain flour
- ✓ ½ cup of sugar
- ✓ ¼ teaspoon of baking powder
- ✓ 1 egg, whisked
- ✓ 1 teaspoon of baking soda
- ✓ 1/3 cup of vegetable oil

DIRECTIONS:

- Mix the bananas, egg and oil together in a bowl. Stir in both flours, cocoa, baking soda, baking flour and sugar using a wooden spatula until thoroughly mixed.
- Put in the chocolate chips and mix slightly.
- Grease your muffin pan with oil and spoon the batter into the holes.
- Heat the Air Fryer to 347°F and bake the muffins in it for 25 minutes. Allow to cool for about 15 minutes then place on a wire rack.

Sweet Cinnamon Bananas Sticks

Preparation: 15 minutes Cooking time: 10 minutes Servings: 6-8

INGREDIENTS:

- ✓ 8 ounces of breadcrumbs
- ✓ 8 ripe bananas, peeled and halved
- ✓ 7 teaspoons of sugar
- ✓ 4 ounces of corn flour
- ✓ 3 tablespoons of coconut oil
- ✓ 2 large eggs, whisked
- ✓ 2 teaspoons of cinnamon

DIRECTIONS:

- Put the coconut oil in a pan over medium heat. Put in the breadcrumbs and stir for 4 minutes until slightly

golden. Remove from heat and transfer to a shallow dish.
- Roll the bananas first in the corn flour, then dip them in the eggs and lastly in the breadcrumbs to coat.
- Place the coated bananas in the cooking basket. Mix the cinnamon and sugar in a bowl thoroughly and sprinkle the mixture on the bananas to cover them.
- Slide the basket into the Air Fryer and cook for 10 minutes at 280°F. When done, shake off excess crumbs, if any.

Berry And Apricot Crumble

Preparation: 10 minutes Cooking time: 20 minutes Servings: 6

INGREDIENTS:

- ✓ 2½ ounces of butter
- ✓ 2¼ cups of apricot
- ✓ ½ pound of flour
- ✓ 8 tablespoons of sugar
- ✓ 6 teaspoons of lemon juice
- ✓ 5½ ounces fresh blackberries Salt to taste

DIRECTIONS:

- Cut the apricots into 2 and take out the stone then cut into cubes.
- Put them in a bowl and add 2 tablespoons of sugar, the blackberries and lemon juice and stir. Pour and spread the mixture evenly in an oven dish.
- Place the flour in a bowl and add 6 tablespoons of sugar, the butter, salt, and a little water and mix thoroughly. Rub the mixture with your fingertips until crumbly.
- Heat your Air Fryer to 390°F.
- Spread the mixture on the fruits and press down lightly.
- Put into the Air Fryer basket and bake for 20 minutes until the crumble appears golden.

Strawberry And Cream Chocolate Cupcake

Preparation: 30 minutes Cooking time: 12 minutes Servings: 4

INGREDIENTS:

- ✓ 1 pound of refined flour
- ✓ 3 eggs
- ✓ 4 tablespoons of strawberry sauce
- ✓ 6 ounces of icing sugar
- ✓ 1 large strawberry, cut into

- ✓ 4½ pound of cream cheese
- ✓ 6 ounces of peanut butter
- ✓ 1 teaspoon of vanilla extract
- ✓ 1 teaspoon of cocoa powder
- ✓ ½ pound of hard butter for frosting
- ✓ 2 teaspoons of beet powder A few crushed colorful chocolate, crushed

DIRECTIONS:

- ⏱ Make a batter by mixing the flour, cocoa, peanut butter, icing sugar, beet powder and eggs together using an electric mixer. Pour the batter into cupcake moulds.
- ⏱ Heat your Air Fryer for 5 minutes at 360°F. Place the cupcakes in the Air Fryer and reduce heat to 340°F. Bake for 12 minutes.
- ⏱ Remove the cakes from the fryer; cool for 10 minutes.
- ⏱ Combine the icing sugar, hard butter and vanilla in an electric mixer and whisk until smooth.
- ⏱ Add the frosting on the cupcakes and sprinkle with strawberry sauce, the crushed chocolates and top with a piece of strawberry.

Strawberry Ring Cake

Preparation: 15 minutes Cooking time: 30 minutes Servings: 4

INGREDIENTS:

- ✓ 1 egg
- ✓ 3½ tablespoons of butter
- ✓ 3 strawberries, mashed
- ✓ ½ teaspoon of cinnamon
- ✓ 6 ounces of sugar
- ✓ 8 ounces of flour
- ✓ 2 tablespoons of maple syrup A pinch of salt

DIRECTIONS:

- ⏱ Heat air fryer to 320°F. Spray a small ring cake pan with oil spray.
- ⏱ Put the sugar and butter into a bowl and mix until creamy. Add the mashed strawberries, eggs and maple syrup and beat the mixture until smooth.
- ⏱ Sieve in the flour, cinnamon and salt and mix to form batter. Pour the batter into the ring cake pan and level with a spoon. Insert the cake pan into the air fryer basket.
- ⏱ Bake for 30 minutes until a knife inserted in the core of the cake comes out clean.

Chocolate Cake Airfry

Preparation: 10 minutes Cooking time: 10 minutes Servings: 4

INGREDIENTS:

- ✓ ½ cup of chopped dark chocolate, melted
- ✓ 8 tablespoons of butter, melted
- ✓ 5 tablespoons of sugar
- ✓ ½ teaspoon of coffee
- ✓ 1 teaspoon of baking powder
- ✓ 2 eggs
- ✓ 1 small lemon, juiced
- ✓ 1/3 cup of flour
- ✓ ¼ teaspoon of salt

DIRECTIONS:

- ⏱ Add the melted chocolate and the butter and lemon together and mix.
- ⏱ Put the egg, coffee and sugar in a mixing bowl and whisk until creamy. Add the chocolate butter mixture and mix. Add and stir the baking powder, flour and salt. Mix the batter gently.
- ⏱ Heat your Air Fryer to 356°F.
- ⏱ Put the batter into a greased baking dish and place in the fryer basket. Air fry for 10 minutes or until firm.

Air Fried Marble Cake

Preparation: 10 minutes Cooking time: 17 minutes Servings: 6

INGREDIENTS:

- ✓ 7 tablespoons of caster sugar
- ✓ ½ cup of flour, sieved
- ✓ 4 eggs, whisked
- ✓ teaspoon of baking powder
- ✓ 5 teaspoons of cocoa powder
- ✓ 2/3 cup of butter, melted
- ✓ ½ teaspoon of lime juice

DIRECTIONS:

- ⏱ Heat your Air Fryer to 356°F.
- ⏱ Mix 3 tablespoons of melted butter with the cocoa powder to form a paste.
- ⏱ Add the sugar to the remaining butter and mix thoroughly. Stir in the eggs, flour and baking powder and mix thoroughly until smooth. Pour in the lime and stir.

- Place a greased baking pan into the Air Fryer and allow to heat for a minute.
- Pour some of the batter into the hot bake then add a layer of the chocolate mixture, then the batter, chocolate and lastly top with the batter. Use a skewer to create a swirl.
- Place in the air fryer and bake for 17 minutes. The cake should be cooled while in the pan before removing.

Rhubarb Pie

Preparation time: 30 minutes Cooking time: 45 minutes Servings: 6

INGREDIENTS:

- ✓ **1 and ¼ cups almond flour**
- ✓ **8 tablespoons butter**
- ✓ **5 tablespoons cold water**
- ✓ **1 teaspoon sugar**

For the filling:

- ✓ **3 cups rhubarb, chopped**
- ✓ **3 tablespoons flour**
- ✓ **1 and ½ cups sugar**
- ✓ **2 eggs**
- ✓ **½ teaspoon nutmeg, ground**
- ✓ **1 tablespoon butter**
- ✓ **2 tablespoons low fat milk**

DIRECTIONS:

- In a bowl, mix 1 and ¼ cups flour with 1 teaspoon sugar, 8 tablespoons butter and cold water, stir and knead until you obtain a dough.
- Transfer dough to a floured working surface, shape a disk, flatten, wrap in plastic, keep in the fridge for about 30 minutes, roll and press on the bottom of a pie pan that fits your air fryer.
- In a bowl, mix rhubarb with 1 and ½ cups sugar, nutmeg, 3 tablespoons flour and whisk.
- In another bowl, whisk eggs with milk, add to rhubarb mix, pour the whole mix into the pie crust, introduce in your air fryer and cook at 390 degrees F for 45 minutes.
- Cut and serve it cold.
- Enjoy!

Nutrition: calories 200, fat 2, fiber 1, carbs 6, protein 3

Lemon Tart

Preparation time: 1 hour Cooking time: 35 minutes Servings: 6

INGREDIENTS:

For the crust:

- ✓ **2 tablespoons sugar**
- ✓ **2 cups white flour**
- ✓ **A pinch of salt**
- ✓ **3 tablespoons ice water**
- ✓ **12 tablespoons cold butter**

For the filling:

- ✓ **2 eggs, whisked**
- ✓ **1 and ¼ cup sugar**
- ✓ **10 tablespoons melted and chilled butter**
- ✓ **Juice from 2 lemons**
- ✓ **Zest from 2 lemons, grated**

DIRECTIONS:

- In a bowl, mix 2 cups flour with a pinch of salt and 2 tablespoons sugar and whisk.
- Add 12 tablespoons butter and the water, knead until you obtain a dough, shape a ball, wrap in foil and keep in the fridge for 1 hour.
- Transfer dough to a floured surface, flatten it, arrange on the bottom of a tart pan, prick with a fork, keep in the fridge for 20 minutes, introduce in your air fryer at 360 degrees F and bake for 15 minutes.
- In a bowl, mix 1 and ¼ cup sugar with eggs, 10 tablespoons butter, lemon juice and lemon zest and whisk very well.
- Pour this into pie crust, spread evenly, introduce in the fryer and cook at 360 degrees F for 20 minutes.
- Cut and serve it.
- Enjoy!

Nutrition: calories 182, fat 4, fiber 1, carbs 2, protein 3

Mandarin Pudding

Preparation time: 20 minutes Cooking time: 40 minutes Servings: 8

INGREDIENTS:

- ✓ **1 mandarin, peeled and sliced**
- ✓ **Juice from 2 mandarins**
- ✓ **2 tablespoons brown sugar**
- ✓ **4 ounces butter, soft**
- ✓ **2 eggs, whisked**
- ✓ **¾ cup sugar**
- ✓ **¾ cup white flour**

- ✓ ¾ cup almonds, ground
- ✓ Honey for serving

DIRECTIONS:

- ① Grease a loaf pan with some butter, sprinkle brown sugar on the bottom and arrange mandarin slices.
- ① In a bowl, mix butter with sugar, eggs, almonds, flour and mandarin juice, stir, spoon this over mandarin slices, place pan in your air fryer and cook at 360 degrees F for 40 minutes.
- ① Transfer pudding to a plate and serve with honey on top.
- ① Enjoy!

Nutrition: calories 162, fat 3, fiber 2, carbs 3, protein 6

Strawberry Shortcakes

Preparation time: 20 minutes Cooking time: 45 minutes Servings: 6

INGREDIENTS:

- ✓ Cooking spray
- ✓ ¼ cup sugar+ 4 tablespoons
- ✓ 1 and ½ cup flour
- ✓ 1 teaspoon baking powder
- ✓ ¼ teaspoon baking soda
- ✓ 1/3 cup butter
- ✓ 1 cup buttermilk
- ✓ 1 egg, whisked
- ✓ 2 cups strawberries, sliced
- ✓ 1 tablespoon rum
- ✓ 1 tablespoon mint, chopped
- ✓ 1 teaspoon lime zest, grated
- ✓ ½ cup whipping cream

DIRECTIONS:

- ① In a bowl, mix flour with ¼ cup sugar, baking powder and baking soda and stir.
- ① In another bowl, mix buttermilk with egg, stir, add to flour mix and whisk.
- ① Spoon this dough into 6 jars greased with cooking spray, cover with tin foil, arrange them in your air fryer cook at 360 degrees F for 45 minutes.
- ① Meanwhile, in a bowl, mix strawberries with 3 tablespoons sugar, rum, mint and lime zest, stir and leave aside in a cold place.
- ① In another bowl, mix whipping cream with 1 tablespoon sugar and stir.
- ① Take jars out, divide strawberry mix and whipped cream on top and serve. Enjoy!

Nutrition: calories 164, fat 2, fiber 3, carbs 5, protein 2

Sponge Cake

Preparation time: 10 minutes Cooking time: 20 minutes Servings: 12

INGREDIENTS:

- ✓ 3 cups flour
- ✓ 3 teaspoons baking powder
- ✓ ½ cup cornstarch
- ✓ 1 teaspoon baking soda
- ✓ 1 cup olive oil
- ✓ 1 and ½ cup milk
- ✓ 1 and 2/3 cup sugar
- ✓ 2 cups water
- ✓ ¼ cup lemon juice
- ✓ 2 teaspoons vanilla extract

DIRECTIONS:

- ① In a bowl, mix flour with cornstarch, baking powder, baking soda and sugar and whisk well.
- ① In another bowl, mix oil with milk, water, vanilla and lemon juice and whisk.
- ① Combine the two mixtures, stir, pour in a greased baking dish that fits your air fryer, introduce in the fryer and cook at 350 degrees F for 20 minutes.
- ① Leave cake to cool down, cut and serve.
- ① Enjoy!

Nutrition: calories 246, fat 3, fiber 1, carbs 6, protein 2

Ricotta and Lemon Cake

Preparation time: 10 minutes Cooking time: 1 hour and 10 minutes Servings: 4

INGREDIENTS:

- ✓ 8 eggs, whisked
- ✓ 3 pounds ricotta cheese
- ✓ ½ pound sugar
- ✓ Zest from 1 lemon, grated
- ✓ Zest from 1 orange, grated
- ✓ Butter for the pan

DIRECTIONS:

- ① In a bowl, mix eggs with sugar, cheese, lemon and orange zest and stir very well.

- Grease a baking pan that fits your air fryer with some batter, spread ricotta mixture, introduce in the fryer at 390 degrees F and bake for 30 minutes.
- Reduce heat at 380 degrees F and bake for 40 more minutes.
- Take out of the oven, leave cake to cool down and serve!
- Enjoy!

Nutrition: calories 110, fat 3, fiber 2, carbs 3, protein 4

Tangerine Cake

Preparation time: 10 minutes Cooking time: 20 minutes Servings: 8

INGREDIENTS:

- ✓ ¾ cup sugar
- ✓ 2 cups flour
- ✓ ¼ cup olive oil
- ✓ ½ cup milk
- ✓ 1 teaspoon cider vinegar
- ✓ ½ teaspoon vanilla extract
- ✓ Juice and zest from 2 lemons
- ✓ Juice and zest from 1 tangerine
- ✓ Tangerine segments, for serving

DIRECTIONS:

- In a bowl, mix flour with sugar and stir.
- In another bowl, mix oil with milk, vinegar, vanilla extract, lemon juice and zest and tangerine zest and whisk very well.
- Add flour, stir well, pour this into a cake pan that fits your air fryer, introduce in the fryer and cook at 360 degrees F for 20 minutes.
- Serve right away with tangerine segments on top.
- Enjoy!

Nutrition: calories 190, fat 1, fiber 1, carbs 4, protein 4

Blueberry Pudding

Preparation time: 10 minutes Cooking time: 25 minutes Servings: 6

INGREDIENTS:

- ✓ 2 cups flour
- ✓ 2 cups rolled oats
- ✓ 8 cups blueberries
- ✓ 1 stick butter, melted

- ✓ 1 cup walnuts, chopped
- ✓ 3 tablespoons maple syrup
- ✓ 2 tablespoons rosemary, chopped

DIRECTIONS:

- Spread blueberries in a greased baking pan and leave aside.
- In your food processor, mix rolled oats with flour, walnuts, butter, maple syrup and rosemary, blend well, layer this over blueberries, introduce everything in your air fryer and cook at 350 degrees for 25 minutes.
- Leave dessert to cool down, cut and serve.
- Enjoy!

Nutrition: calories 150, fat 3, fiber 2, carbs 7, protein 4

Cocoa and Almond Bars

Preparation time: 30 minutes Cooking time: 4 minutes Servings: 6

INGREDIENTS:

- ✓ ¼ cup cocoa nibs
- ✓ 1 cup almonds, soaked and drained
- ✓ 2 tablespoons cocoa powder
- ✓ ¼ cup hemp seeds
- ✓ ¼ cup goji berries
- ✓ ¼ cup coconut, shredded
- ✓ 8 dates, pitted and soaked

DIRECTIONS:

- Put almonds in your food processor, blend, add hemp seeds, cocoa nibs, cocoa powder, goji, coconut and blend very well.
- Add dates, blend well again, spread on a lined baking sheet that fits your air fryer and cook at 320 degrees F for 4 minutes.
- Cut into equal parts and keep in the fridge for 30 minutes before serving.
- Enjoy!

Nutrition: calories 140, fat 6, fiber 3, carbs 7, protein 19

Chocolate and Pomegranate Bars

Preparation time: 2 hours Cooking time: 10 minutes Servings: 6

INGREDIENTS:

- ✓ ½ cup milk
- ✓ 1 teaspoon vanilla extract
- ✓ 1 and ½ cups dark chocolate, chopped
- ✓ ½ cup almonds, chopped

- ✓ ½ cup pomegranate seeds

DIRECTIONS:

- ⏱ Heat up a pan with the milk over medium low heat, add chocolate, stir for 5 minutes, take off heat add vanilla extract, half of the pomegranate seeds and half of the nuts and stir.
- ⏱ Pour this into a lined baking pan, spread, sprinkle a pinch of salt, the rest of the pomegranate arils and nuts, introduce in your air fryer and cook at 300 degrees F for 4 minutes.
- ⏱ Keep in the fridge for 2 hours before serving.
- ⏱ Enjoy!

Nutrition: calories 68, fat 1, fiber 4, carbs 6, protein 1

Tomato Cake

Preparation time: 10 minutes Cooking time: 30 minutes Servings: 4

INGREDIENTS:

- ✓ **1 and ½ cups flour**
- ✓ **1 teaspoon cinnamon powder**
- ✓ **1 teaspoon baking powder**
- ✓ **1 teaspoon baking soda**
- ✓ **¾ cup maple syrup**
- ✓ **1 cup tomatoes chopped**
- ✓ **½ cup olive oil**
- ✓ **2 tablespoon apple cider vinegar**

DIRECTIONS:

- ⏱ In a bowl, mix flour with baking powder, baking soda, cinnamon and maple syrup and stir well.
- ⏱ In another bowl, mix tomatoes with olive oil and vinegar and stir well.
- ⏱ Combine the 2 mixtures, stir well, pour into a greased round pan that fits your air fryer, introduce in the fryer and cook at 360 degrees F for 30 minutes.
- ⏱ Leave cake to cool down, slice and serve.
- ⏱ Enjoy!

Nutrition: calories 153, fat 2, fiber 1, carbs 25, protein 4

Berries Mix

Preparation time: 5 minutes Cooking time: 6 minutes Servings: 4

INGREDIENTS:

- ✓ **2 tablespoons lemon juice**
- ✓ **1 and ½ tablespoons maple syrup**
- ✓ **1 and ½ tablespoons champagne vinegar**

- ✓ **1 tablespoon olive oil**
- ✓ **1 pound strawberries, halved**
- ✓ **1 and ½ cups blueberries**
- ✓ **¼ cup basil leaves, torn**

DIRECTIONS:

- ⏱ In a pan that fits your air fryer, mix lemon juice with maple syrup and vinegar, bring to a boil over medium high heat, add oil, blueberries and strawberries, stir, introduce in your air fryer and cook at 310 degrees F for 6 minutes.
- ⏱ Sprinkle basil on top and serve!
- ⏱ Enjoy!

Nutrition: calories 163, fat 4, fiber 4, carbs 10, protein 2.1

Passion Fruit Pudding

Preparation time: 10 minutes Cooking time: 40 minutes Servings: 6

INGREDIENTS:

- ✓ **1 cup Paleo passion fruit curd**
- ✓ **4 passion fruits, pulp and seeds**
- ✓ **3 and ½ ounces maple syrup**
- ✓ **3 eggs**
- ✓ **2 ounces ghee, melted**
- ✓ **3 and ½ ounces almond milk**
- ✓ **½ cup almond flour**
- ✓ **½ teaspoon baking powder**

DIRECTIONS:

- ⏱ In a bowl, mix the half of the fruit curd with passion fruit seeds and pulp, stir and divide into 6 heat proof ramekins.
- ⏱ In a bowl, whisked eggs with maple syrup, ghee, the rest of the curd, baking powder, milk and flour and stir well.
- ⏱ Divide this into the ramekins as well, introduce in the fryer and cook at 200 degrees F for 40 minutes.
- ⏱ Leave puddings to cool down and serve!
- ⏱ Enjoy!

Nutrition: calories 430, fat 22, fiber 3, carbs 7, protein 8

Air Fried Apples

Preparation time: 10 minutes Cooking time: 17 minutes Servings: 4

INGREDIENTS:

- ✓ **4 big apples, cored**
- ✓ **A handful raisins**

- ✓ **1 tablespoon cinnamon, ground**
- ✓ **Raw honey to the taste**

DIRECTIONS:

- 🕐 Fill each apple with raisins, sprinkle cinnamon, drizzle honey, put them in your air fryer and cook at 367 degrees F for 17 minutes.
- 🕐 Leave them to cool down and serve.
- 🕐 Enjoy!

Nutrition: calories 220, fat 3, fiber 4, carbs 6, protein 10

Pumpkin Cookies

Preparation time: 10 minutes Cooking time: 15 minutes Servings: 24

INGREDIENTS:

- ✓ **2 and ½ cups flour**
- ✓ **½ teaspoon baking soda**
- ✓ **1 tablespoon flax seed, ground**
- ✓ **3 tablespoons water**
- ✓ **½ cup pumpkin flesh, mashed**
- ✓ **¼ cup honey**
- ✓ **2 tablespoons butter**
- ✓ **1 teaspoon vanilla extract**
- ✓ **½ cup dark chocolate chips**

DIRECTIONS:

- 🕐 In a bowl, mix flax seed with water, stir and leave aside for a few minutes.
- 🕐 In another bowl, mix flour with salt and baking soda.
- 🕐 In a third bowl, mix honey with pumpkin puree, butter, vanilla extract and flaxseed.
- 🕐 Combine flour with honey mix and chocolate chips and stir.
- 🕐 Scoop 1 tablespoon of cookie dough on a lined baking sheet that fits your air fryer, repeat with the rest of the dough, introduce them in your air fryer and cook at 350 degrees F for 15 minutes.
- 🕐 Leave cookies to cool down and serve.
- 🕐 Enjoy!

Nutrition: calories 140, fat 2, fiber 2, carbs 7, protein 10

Figs and Coconut Butter Mix

Preparation time: 6 minutes Cooking time: 4 minutes Servings: 3

INGREDIENTS:

- ✓ **2 tablespoons coconut butter**
- ✓ **12 figs, halved**

- ✓ **¼ cup sugar**
- ✓ **1 cup almonds, toasted and chopped**

DIRECTIONS:

- 🕐 Put butter in a pan that fits your air fryer and melt over medium high heat.
- 🕐 Add figs, sugar and almonds, toss, introduce in your air fryer and cook at 300 degrees F for 4 minutes.
- 🕐 Divide into bowls and serve cold.
- 🕐 Enjoy!

Nutrition: calories 170, fat 4, fiber 5, carbs 7, protein 9

Lemon Bars

Preparation time: 10 minutes Cooking time: 25 minutes Servings: 6

INGREDIENTS:

- ✓ **4 eggs**
- ✓ **2 and ¼ cups flour**
- ✓ **Juice from 2 lemons**
- ✓ **1 cup butter, soft**
- ✓ **2 cups sugar**

DIRECTIONS:

- 🕐 In a bowl, mix butter with ½ cup sugar and 2 cups flour, stir well, press on the bottom of a pan that fits your air fryer, introduce in the fryer and cook at 350 degrees F for 10 minutes.
- 🕐 In another bowl, mix the rest of the sugar with the rest of the flour, eggs and lemon juice, whisk well and spread over crust.
- 🕐 Introduce in the fryer at 350 degrees F for 15 minutes more, leave aside to
- 🕐 cool down, cut bars and serve them.
- 🕐 Enjoy!

Nutrition: calories 125, fat 4, fiber 4, carbs 16, protein 2

Pears and Espresso Cream

Preparation time: 10 minutes Cooking time: 30 minutes Servings: 4

INGREDIENTS:

- ✓ **4 pears, halved and cored**
- ✓ **2 tablespoons lemon juice**
- ✓ **1 tablespoon sugar**
- ✓ **2 tablespoons water**
- ✓ **2 tablespoons butter**

For the cream:

- ✓ **1 cup whipping cream**
- ✓ **1 cup mascarpone**
- ✓ **1/3 cup sugar**
- ✓ **2 tablespoons espresso, cold**

DIRECTIONS:

- ⏱ In a bowl, mix pears halves with lemon juice, 1 tablespoons sugar, butter and water, toss well, transfer them to your air fryer and cook at 360 degrees F for 30 minutes.
- ⏱ Meanwhile, in a bowl, mix whipping cream with mascarpone, 1/3 cup sugar and espresso, whisk really well and keep in the fridge until pears are done.
- ⏱ Divide pears on plates, top with espresso cream and serve them.
- ⏱ Enjoy!

Nutrition: calories 211, fat 5, fiber 7, carbs 8, protein 7

Tasty Banana Cake

Preparation time: 10 minutes Cooking time: 30 minutes Servings: 4

INGREDIENTS:

- ✓ **1 tablespoon butter, soft**
- ✓ **1 egg**
- ✓ **1/3 cup brown sugar**
- ✓ **2 tablespoons honey**
- ✓ **1 banana, peeled and mashed**
- ✓ **1 cup white flour**
- ✓ **1 teaspoon baking powder**
- ✓ **½ teaspoon cinnamon powder**
- ✓ **Cooking spray**

DIRECTIONS:

- ⏱ Spray a cake pan with some cooking spray and leave aside.
- ⏱ In a bowl, mix butter with sugar, banana, honey, egg, cinnamon, baking powder and flour and whisk
- ⏱ Pour this into a cake pan greased with cooking spray, introduce in your air fryer and cook at 350 degrees F for 30 minutes.
- ⏱ Leave cake to cool down, slice and serve.
- ⏱ Enjoy!

Nutrition: calories 232, fat 4, fiber 1, carbs 34, protein 4

Simple Cheesecake

Preparation time: 10 minutes Cooking time: 15 minutes Servings: 15

INGREDIENTS:

- ✓ **1 pound cream cheese**
- ✓ **½ teaspoon vanilla extract**
- ✓ **2 eggs**
- ✓ **4 tablespoons sugar**
- ✓ **1 cup graham crackers, crumbled**
- ✓ **2 tablespoons butter**

DIRECTIONS:

- ⏱ In a bowl, mix crackers with butter.
- ⏱ Press crackers mix on the bottom of a lined cake pan, introduce in your air fryer and cook at 350 degrees F for 4 minutes.
- ⏱ Meanwhile, in a bowl, mix sugar with cream cheese, eggs and vanilla and whisk well.
- ⏱ Spread filling over crackers crust and cook your cheesecake in your air fryer at 310 degrees F for 15 minutes.
- ⏱ Leave cake in the fridge for 3 hours, slice and serve.
- ⏱ Enjoy!

Nutrition: calories 245, fat 12, fiber 1, carbs 20, protein 3

Bread Pudding

Preparation time: 10 minutes Cooking time: 1 hour Servings: 4

INGREDIENTS:

- ✓ **6 glazed doughnuts, crumbled**
- ✓ **1 cup cherries**
- ✓ **4 egg yolks**
- ✓ **1 and ½ cups whipping cream**
- ✓ **½ cup raisins**
- ✓ **¼ cup sugar**
- ✓ **½ cup chocolate chips.**

DIRECTIONS:

- ⏱ In a bowl, mix cherries with egg yolks and whipping cream and stir well.
- ⏱ In another bowl, mix raisins with sugar, chocolate chips and doughnuts and stir.
- ⏱ Combine the 2 mixtures, transfer everything to a greased pan that fits your air fryer and cook at 310 degrees F for 1 hour.
- ⏱ Chill pudding before cutting and serving it.

- Enjoy!

Nutrition: calories 302, fat 8, fiber 2, carbs 23, protein 10

Bread Dough and Amaretto Dessert

Preparation time: 10 minutes Cooking time: 12 minutes Servings: 12

INGREDIENTS:

- ✓ **1 pound bread dough**
- ✓ **1 cup sugar**
- ✓ **½ cup butter, melted**
- ✓ **1 cup heavy cream**
- ✓ **12 ounces chocolate chips**
- ✓ **2 tablespoons amaretto liqueur**

DIRECTIONS:

- Roll dough, cut into 20 slices and then cut each slice in halves.
- Brush dough pieces with butter, sprinkle sugar, place them in your air fryer's basket after you've brushed it some butter, cook them at 350 degrees F for 5 minutes, flip them, cook for 3 minutes more and transfer to a platter.
- Heat up a pan with the heavy cream over medium heat, add chocolate chips and stir until they melt.
- Add liqueur, stir again, transfer to a bowl and serve bread dippers with this sauce.
- Enjoy!

Nutrition: calories 200, fat 1, fiber 0, carbs 6, protein 6

Cinnamon Rolls and Cream Cheese Dip

Preparation time: 2 hours Cooking time: 15 minutes Servings: 8

INGREDIENTS:

- ✓ **1 pound bread dough**
- ✓ **¾ cup brown sugar**
- ✓ **1 and ½ tablespoons cinnamon, ground**
- ✓ **¼ cup butter, melted**

For the cream cheese dip:

- ✓ **2 tablespoons butter**
- ✓ **4 ounces cream cheese**
- ✓ **1 and ¼ cups sugar**
- ✓ **½ teaspoon vanilla**

DIRECTIONS:

- Roll dough on a floured working surface, shape a rectangle and brush with ¼ cup butter.
- In a bowl, mix cinnamon with sugar, stir, sprinkle this over dough, roll dough into a log, seal well and cut into 8 pieces.
- Leave rolls to rise for 2 hours, place them in your air fryer's basket, cook at 350 degrees F for 5 minutes, flip them, cook for 4 minutes more and transfer to a platter.
- In a bowl, mix cream cheese with butter, sugar and vanilla and whisk really well.
- Serve your cinnamon rolls with this cream cheese dip.
- Enjoy!

Nutrition: calories 200, fat 1, fiber 0, carbs 5, protein 6

Pumpkin Pie

Preparation time: 10 minutes Cooking time: 15 minutes Servings: 9

INGREDIENTS:

- ✓ **1 tablespoon sugar**
- ✓ **2 tablespoons flour**
- ✓ **1 tablespoon butter**
- ✓ **2 tablespoons water**

For the pumpkin pie filling:

- ✓ **3.5 ounces pumpkin flesh, chopped**
- ✓ **1 teaspoon mixed spice**
- ✓ **1 teaspoon nutmeg**
- ✓ **3 ounces water**
- ✓ **1 egg, whisked**
- ✓ **1 tablespoon sugar**

DIRECTIONS:

- Put 3 ounces water in a pot, bring to a boil over medium high heat, add pumpkin, egg, 1 tablespoon sugar, spice and nutmeg, stir, boil for 20 minutes, take off heat and blend using an immersion blender.
- In a bowl, mix flour with butter, 1 tablespoon sugar and 2 tablespoons water and knead your dough well.
- Grease a pie pan that fits your air fryer with butter, press dough into the pan, fill with pumpkin pie filling, place in your air fryer's basket and cook at 360 degrees F for 15 minutes.
- Slice and serve warm.
- Enjoy!

Nutrition: calories 200, fat 5, fiber 2, carbs 5, protein 6

Wrapped Pears

Preparation time: 10 minutes Cooking time: 15 minutes Servings: 4

INGREDIENTS:

- ✓ **4 puff pastry sheets**
- ✓ **14 ounces vanilla custard**
- ✓ **2 pears, halved**
- ✓ **1 egg, whisked**
- ✓ **½ teaspoon cinnamon powder**
- ✓ **2 tablespoons sugar**

DIRECTIONS:

- Place puff pastry slices on a working surface, add spoonfuls of vanilla custard in the center of each, top with pear halves and wrap.
- Brush pears with egg, sprinkle sugar and cinnamon, place them in your air fryer's basket and cook at 320 degrees F for 15 minutes.
- Divide parcels on plates and serve.
- Enjoy!

Nutrition: calories 200, fat 2, fiber 1, carbs 14, protein 3

Strawberry Donuts

Preparation time: 10 minutes Cooking time: 15 minutes Servings: 4

INGREDIENTS:

- ✓ **8 ounces flour**
- ✓ **1 tablespoon brown sugar**
- ✓ **1 tablespoon white sugar**
- ✓ **1 egg**
- ✓ **2 and ½ tablespoons butter**
- ✓ **4 ounces whole milk**
- ✓ **1 teaspoon baking powder**

For the strawberry icing:

- ✓ **2 tablespoons butter**
- ✓ **3.5 ounces icing sugar**
- ✓ **½ teaspoon pink coloring**
- ✓ **¼ cup strawberries, chopped**
- ✓ **1 tablespoon whipped cream**

DIRECTIONS:

- In a bowl, mix butter, 1 tablespoon brown sugar, 1 tablespoon white sugar and flour and stir.
- In a second bowl, mix egg with 1 and ½ tablespoons butter and milk and stir well.
- Combine the 2 mixtures, stir, shape donuts from this mix, place them in your air fryer's basket and cook at 360 degrees F for 15 minutes.
- Put 1 tablespoon butter, icing sugar, food coloring, whipped cream and strawberry puree and whisk well.
- Arrange donuts on a platter and serve with strawberry icing on top.
- Enjoy!

Nutrition: calories 250, fat 12, fiber 1, carbs 32, protein 4

Air Fried Bananas

Preparation time: 10 minutes Cooking time: 15 minutes Servings: 4

INGREDIENTS:

- ✓ **3 tablespoons butter**
- ✓ **2 eggs**
- ✓ **8 bananas, peeled and halved**
- ✓ **½ cup corn flour**
- ✓ **3 tablespoons cinnamon sugar**
- ✓ **1 cup panko**

DIRECTIONS:

- Heat up a pan with the butter over medium high heat, add panko, stir and cook for 4 minutes and then transfer to a bowl.
- Roll each in flour, eggs and panko mix, arrange them in your air fryer's basket, dust with cinnamon sugar and cook at 280 degrees F for 10 minutes.
- Serve right away.
- Enjoy!

Nutrition: calories 164, fat 1, fiber 4, carbs 32, protein 4

Cocoa Cake

Preparation time: 10 minutes Cooking time: 17 minutes Servings: 6

INGREDIENTS:

- ✓ **3.5 ounces butter, melted**
- ✓ **3 eggs**
- ✓ **3 ounces sugar**
- ✓ **1 teaspoon cocoa powder**
- ✓ **3 ounces flour**
- ✓ **½ teaspoon lemon juice**

DIRECTIONS:

- In a bowl, mix 1 tablespoon butter with cocoa powder and whisk.
- In another bowl, mix the rest of the butter with sugar, eggs, flour and lemon juice, whisk well and pour half into a cake pan that fits your air fryer.
- Add half of the cocoa mix, spread, add the rest of the butter layer and top with the rest of cocoa.
- Introduce in your air fryer and cook at 360 degrees F for 17 minutes.
- Cool cake down before slicing and serving.
- Enjoy!

Nutrition: calories 340, fat 11, fiber 3, carbs 25, protein 5

Chocolate Cake

Preparation time: 10 minutes Cooking time: 30 minutes Servings: 12

INGREDIENTS:

- ¾ cup white flour
- ¾ cup whole wheat flour
- 1 teaspoon baking soda
- ¾ teaspoon pumpkin pie spice
- ¾ cup sugar
- 1 banana, mashed
- ½ teaspoon baking powder
- 2 tablespoons canola oil
- ½ cup Greek yogurt
- 8 ounces canned pumpkin puree
- Cooking spray
- 1 egg
- ½ teaspoon vanilla extract
- 2/3 cup chocolate chips

DIRECTIONS:

- In a bowl, mix white flour with whole wheat flour, salt, baking soda and powder and pumpkin spice and stir.
- In another bowl, mix sugar with oil, banana, yogurt, pumpkin puree, vanilla and egg and stir using a mixer.
- Combine the 2 mixtures, add chocolate chips, stir, pour this into a greased Bundt pan that fits your air fryer.
- Introduce in your air fryer and cook at 330 degrees F for 30 minutes.
- Leave the cake to cool down, before cutting and serving it.

- Enjoy!

Nutrition: calories 232, fat 7, fiber 7, carbs 29, protein 4

Apple Bread

Preparation time: 10 minutes Cooking time: 40 minutes Servings: 6

INGREDIENTS:

- 3 cups apples, cored and cubed
- 1 cup sugar
- 1 tablespoon vanilla
- 2 eggs
- 1 tablespoon apple pie spice
- 2 cups white flour
- 1 tablespoon baking powder
- 1 stick butter
- 1 cup water

DIRECTIONS:

- In a bowl mix egg with 1 butter stick, apple pie spice and sugar and stir using your mixer.
- Add apples and stir again well.
- In another bowl, mix baking powder with flour and stir.
- Combine the 2 mixtures, stir and pour into a spring form pan.
- Put spring form pan in your air fryer and cook at 320 degrees F for 40 minutes
- Slice and serve.
- Enjoy!

Nutrition: calories 192, fat 6, fiber 7, carbs 14, protein 7

Banana Bread

Preparation time: 10 minutes Cooking time: 40 minutes Servings: 6

INGREDIENTS:

- ¾ cup sugar
- 1/3 cup butter
- 1 teaspoon vanilla extract
- 1 egg
- 2 bananas, mashed
- 1 teaspoon baking powder
- 1 and ½ cups flour
- ½ teaspoons baking soda
- 1/3 cup milk
- 1 and ½ teaspoons cream of tartar

- ✓ **Cooking spray**

DIRECTIONS:

- In a bowl, mix milk with cream of tartar, sugar, butter, egg, vanilla and bananas and stir everything.
- In another bowl, mix flour with baking powder and baking soda.
- Combine the 2 mixtures, stir well, pour this into a cake pan greased with some cooking spray, introduce in your air fryer and cook at 320 degrees F for 40 minutes.
- Take bread out, leave aside to cool down, slice and serve it.
- Enjoy!

Nutrition: calories 292, fat 7, fiber 8, carbs 28, protein 4

Poppyseed Cake

Preparation time: 10 minutes Cooking time: 30 minutes Servings: 6

INGREDIENTS:

- ✓ **1 and ¼ cups flour**
- ✓ **1 teaspoon baking powder**
- ✓ **¾ cup sugar**
- ✓ **1 tablespoon orange zest, grated**
- ✓ **2 teaspoons lime zest, grated**
- ✓ **½ cup butter, soft**
- ✓ **2 eggs, whisked**
- ✓ **½ teaspoon vanilla extract**
- ✓ **2 tablespoons poppy seeds**
- ✓ **1 cup milk**

For the cream:

- ✓ **1 cup sugar**
- ✓ **½ cup passion fruit puree**
- ✓ **3 tablespoons butter, melted**
- ✓ **4 egg yolks**

DIRECTIONS:

- In a bowl, mix flour with baking powder, ¾ cup sugar, orange zest and lime zest and stir.
- Add ½ cup butter, eggs, poppy seeds, vanilla and milk, stir using your mixer, pour into a cake pan that fits your air fryer and cook at 350 degrees F for about 30 minutes.
- Meanwhile, heat up a pan with 3 tablespoons butter over medium heat, add sugar and stir until it dissolves.

- Take off heat, add passion fruit puree and egg yolks gradually and whisk really well.
- Take cake out of the fryer, cool it down a bit and cut into halves horizontally.
- Spread ¼ of passion fruit cream over one half, top with the other cake half and spread ¼ of the cream on top.
- Serve cold.
- Enjoy!

Nutrition: calories 211, fat 6, fiber 7, carbs 12, protein 6

Sweet Squares

Preparation time: 10 minutes Cooking time: 30 minutes Servings: 6

INGREDIENTS:

- ✓ **1 cup flour**
- ✓ **½ cup butter, soft**
- ✓ **1 cup sugar**
- ✓ **¼ cup powdered sugar**
- ✓ **2 teaspoons lemon peel, grated**
- ✓ **2 tablespoons lemon juice**
- ✓ **2 eggs, whisked**
- ✓ **½ teaspoon baking powder**

DIRECTIONS:

- In a bowl, mix flour with powdered sugar and butter, stir well, press on the bottom of a pan that fits your air fryer, introduce in the fryer and bake at 350 degrees F for 14 minutes.
- In another bowl, mix sugar with lemon juice, lemon peel, eggs and baking powder, stir using your mixer and spread over baked crust.
- Bake for 15 minutes more, leave aside to cool down, cut into medium squares and serve cold.
- Enjoy!

Nutrition: calories 100, fat 4, fiber 1, carbs 12, protein 1

Plum Bars

Preparation time: 10 minutes Cooking time: 16 minutes Servings: 8

INGREDIENTS:

- ✓ **2 cups dried plums**
- ✓ **6 tablespoons water**
- ✓ **2 cup rolled oats**
- ✓ **1 cup brown sugar**
- ✓ **½ teaspoon baking soda**
- ✓ **1 teaspoon cinnamon powder**

- ✓ **2 tablespoons butter, melted**
- ✓ **1 egg, whisked**
- ✓ **Cooking spray**

DIRECTIONS:

- In your food processor, mix plums with water and blend until you obtain a sticky spread.
- In a bowl, mix oats with cinnamon, baking soda, sugar, egg and butter and whisk really well.
- Press half of the oats mix in a baking pan that fits your air fryer sprayed with cooking oil, spread plums mix and top with the other half of the oats mix.
- Introduce in your air fryer and cook at 350 degrees F for 16 minutes.
- Leave mix aside to cool down, cut into medium bars and serve.
- Enjoy!

Nutrition: calories 111, fat 5, fiber 6, carbs 12, protein 6

Plum and Currant Tart

Preparation time: 30 minutes Cooking time: 35 minutes Servings: 6

INGREDIENTS:

For the crumble:

- ✓ **¼ cup almond flour**
- ✓ **¼ cup millet flour**
- ✓ **1 cup brown rice flour**
- ✓ **½ cup cane sugar**
- ✓ **10 tablespoons butter, soft**
- ✓ **3 tablespoons milk**

For the filling:

- ✓ **1 pound small plums, pitted and halved**
- ✓ **1 cup white currants**
- ✓ **2 tablespoons cornstarch**
- ✓ **3 tablespoons sugar**
- ✓ **½ teaspoon vanilla extract**
- ✓ **½ teaspoon cinnamon powder**
- ✓ **¼ teaspoon ginger powder**
- ✓ **1 teaspoon lime juice**

DIRECTIONS:

- In a bowl, mix brown rice flour with ½ cup sugar, millet flour, almond flour, butter and milk and stir until you obtain a sand like dough.

- Reserve ¼ of the dough, press the rest of the dough into a tart pan that fits your air fryer and keep in the fridge for 30 minutes.
- Meanwhile, in a bowl, mix plums with currants, 3 tablespoons sugar, cornstarch, vanilla extract, cinnamon, ginger and lime juice and stir well.
- Pour this over tart crust, crumble reserved dough on top, introduce in your air fryer and cook at 350 degrees F for 35 minutes.
- Leave tart to cool down, slice and serve.
- Enjoy!

Nutrition: calories 200, fat 5, fiber 4, carbs 8, protein 6

Tasty Orange Cookies

Preparation time: 10 minutes Cooking time: 12 minutes Servings: 8

INGREDIENTS:

- ✓ **2 cups flour**
- ✓ **1 teaspoon baking powder**
- ✓ **½ cup butter, soft**
- ✓ **¾ cup sugar**
- ✓ **1 egg, whisked**
- ✓ **1 teaspoon vanilla extract**
- ✓ **1 tablespoon orange zest, grated**

For the filling:

- ✓ **4 ounces cream cheese, soft**
- ✓ **½ cup butter**
- ✓ **2 cups powdered sugar**

DIRECTIONS:

- In a bowl, mix cream cheese with ½ cup butter and 2 cups powdered sugar, stir well using your mixer and leave aside for now.
- In another bowl, mix flour with baking powder.
- In a third bowl, mix ½ cup butter with ¾ cup sugar, egg, vanilla extract and orange zest and whisk well.
- Combine flour with orange mix, stir well and scoop 1 tablespoon of the mix on a lined baking sheet that fits your air fryer.
- Repeat with the rest of the orange batter, introduce in the fryer and cook at 340 degrees F for 12 minutes.
- Leave cookies to cool down, spread cream filling on half of them top with
- the other cookies and serve.
- Enjoy!

Nutrition: calories 124, fat 5, fiber 6, carbs 8, protein 4

Cashew Bars

Preparation time: 10 minutes Cooking time: 15 minutes Servings: 6

INGREDIENTS:

- ✓ 1/3 cup honey
- ✓ ¼ cup almond meal
- ✓ 1 tablespoon almond butter
- ✓ 1 and ½ cups cashews, chopped
- ✓ 4 dates, chopped
- ✓ ¾ cup coconut, shredded
- ✓ 1 tablespoon chia seeds

DIRECTIONS:

- In a bowl, mix honey with almond meal and almond butter and stir well.
- Add cashews, coconut, dates and chia seeds and stir well again.
- Spread this on a lined baking sheet that fits your air fryer and press well.
- Introduce in the fryer and cook at 300 degrees F for 15 minutes.
- Leave mix to cool down, cut into medium bars and serve.
- Enjoy!

Nutrition: calories 121, fat 4, fiber 7, carbs 5, protein 6

Brown Butter Cookies

Preparation time: 10 minutes Cooking time: 10 minutes Servings: 6

INGREDIENTS:

- ✓ 1 and ½ cups butter
- ✓ 2 cups brown sugar
- ✓ 2 eggs, whisked
- ✓ 3 cups flour
- ✓ 2/3 cup pecans, chopped
- ✓ 2 teaspoons vanilla extract
- ✓ 1 teaspoon baking soda
- ✓ ½ teaspoon baking powder

DIRECTIONS:

- Heat up a pan with the butter over medium heat, stir until it melts, add brown sugar and stir until this dissolves.
- In a bowl, mix flour with pecans, vanilla extract, baking soda, baking powder and eggs and stir well.

- Add brown butter, stir well and arrange spoonfuls of this mix on a lined baking sheet that fits your air fryer.
- Introduce in the fryer and cook at 340 degrees F for 10 minutes.
- Leave cookies to cool down and serve.
- Enjoy!

Nutrition: calories 144, fat 5, fiber 6, carbs 19, protein 2

Sweet Potato Cheesecake

Preparation time: 10 minutes Cooking time: 5 minutes Servings: 4

INGREDIENTS:

- ✓ 4 tablespoons butter, melted
- ✓ 6 ounces mascarpone, soft
- ✓ 8 ounces cream cheese, soft
- ✓ 2/3 cup graham crackers, crumbled
- ✓ ¾ cup milk
- ✓ 1 teaspoon vanilla extract
- ✓ 2/3 cup sweet potato puree
- ✓ ¼ teaspoons cinnamon powder

DIRECTIONS:

- In a bowl, mix butter with crumbled crackers, stir well, press on the bottom of a cake pan that fits your air fryer and keep in the fridge for now.
- In another bowl, mix cream cheese with mascarpone, sweet potato puree, milk, cinnamon and vanilla and whisk really well.
- Spread this over crust, introduce in your air fryer, cook at 300 degrees F for 4 minutes and keep in the fridge for a few hours before serving.
- Enjoy!

Nutrition: calories 172, fat 4, fiber 6, carbs 8, protein 3

Peach Pie

Preparation time: 10 minutes Cooking time: 35 minutes Servings: 4

INGREDIENTS:

- ✓ 1 pie dough
- ✓ 2 and ¼ pounds peaches, pitted and chopped
- ✓ 2 tablespoons cornstarch
- ✓ ½ cup sugar
- ✓ 2 tablespoons flour
- ✓ A pinch of nutmeg, ground
- ✓ 1 tablespoon dark rum

- ✓ **1 tablespoon lemon juice**
- ✓ **2 tablespoons butter, melted**

DIRECTIONS:

- Roll pie dough into a pie pan that fits your air fryer and press well.
- In a bowl, mix peaches with cornstarch, sugar, flour, nutmeg, rum, lemon juice and butter and stir well.
- Pour and spread this into pie pan, introduce in your air fryer and cook at 350 degrees F for 35 minutes.
- Serve warm or cold.
- Enjoy!

Nutrition: calories 231, fat 6, fiber 7, carbs 9, protein 5

Made in the USA
Columbia, SC
27 November 2023

27224756R00107